this is the
siberian
husky

t.f.h.

by joan mcdonald brearley

Cover:
Ch. Monadnock's Misty of Arahaz and Monadnock's Mischa of
Arahaz, owned by Rosemary and Edward Fischer of Canonsburg,
Pennsylvania.

Back cover:
An impressive head study of the equally impressive Ch. Wolfden's
Copper Bullet, bred and owned by Beryl Allen of Jaffrey, New
Hampshire. Photo by Richard K. La Branche of Bristol Connecti-
cut.

Frontispiece:
A beautiful rendition of two Monadnock "greats," a 1961 head
study of Ch. Monadnock's Pando and Ch. Monadnock's King,
owned and bred by Mrs. Lorna B. Demidoff of Fitzwilliam, New
Hampshire.

ISBN 0-87666-392-7

© 1974 by T.F.H. Publications, Inc. Ltd.

Distributed in the U.S.A. by T.F.H. Publications, Inc., 211 West Sylva-
nia Avenue, P.O. Box 27, Neptune City, N.J. 07753; in England by
T.F.H. (Gt. Britain) Ltd., 13 Nutley Lane, Reigate, Surrey; in Canada to
the book store and library trade by Clarke, Irwin & Company, Clarwin
House, 791 St. Clair Avenue West, Toronto 10, Ontario; in Canada to
the pet trade by Rolf C. Hagen Ltd., 3225 Sartelon Street, Montreal
382, Quebec; in Southeast Asia by Y.W. Ong, 9 Lorong 36 Geylang,
Singapore 14; in Australia and the south Pacific by Pet Imports Pty.
Ltd., P.O. Box 149, Brookvale 2100, N.S.W., Australia. Published by
T.F.H. Publications Inc. Ltd., The British Crown Colony of Hong
Kong.

CONTENTS

ACKNOWLEDGEMENTS

The Author wishes to express deep appreciation
to all those who so willingly contributed to this
book. Special gratitude is due to Jean Fournier,
who let me borrow a wealth of material from which
to research, to Judy Rosemarin for marvelous personal photographs, to Joanne Rudnytsky and the
Fred Jacobis for pack dog information, to Short
Seeley for her important recollections, to Carolyn
Windsor for valuable pedigrees, to Little, Brown &
Co., publishers, to the staffs of the Museum of
Natural History, the American Kennel Club and
New York Public Library; to Stephen McDonald
for special information, to Robert R. Shomer,
D.V.M., for expert counsel, and to all of the proud
owners who wished to see their dogs represented
photographically in a book designed to further
glorify this magnificent breed!

JOAN MCDONALD BREARLEY

Joan Brearley has loved animals ever since she was old enough to know what they were. . . .Over the years there has been a constant succession of dogs, cats, birds, fish, rabbits, snakes, turtles, alligators, squirrels, lizards, etc., for her own personal menagerie. Through these same years she has owned over thirty different breeds of pure-bred dogs, as well as countless mixtures, since the door was never closed to a needy or homeless animal.

A graduate of the American Academy of Dramatic Arts, Joan started her career as a writer for movie magazines and as an actress and dancer. She also studied journalism at Columbia University and has been a radio, TV and magazine writer, writing for some of the major New York City agencies. She also was producer-directer for a major network.

Her accomplishments in the dog fancy include becoming an American Kennel Club approved judge, breeder-exhibitor of top show dogs (and cats!), writer for the various dog magazines, author of *This Is the Afghan Hound,* and *The Samoyeds,* and co-author of *This Is the Shih Tzu, This is the Saint Bernard,* and *This is the Bichon Frise.* For five years she was Executive Vice President of the Popular Dogs Publishing Company and editor of *Popular Dogs* magazine, the national prestige publication for the dog fancy at that time.

7

Joan is just as active in the cat fancy, and in almost all the same capacities. She is most interested in animal legislation and is the editor of the Cat Fanciers Association, Inc., *Yearbook*. She speaks at kennel clubs and humane organizations and has received many awards and citations for her work in this field. She is also a contributer on animals to the World Book Encyclopedia.

At present Joan lives in a penthouse apartment overlooking Manhattan in New York City with a Shih Tzu, a Cavalier King Charles Spaniel and a dozen or more cats, many of which are Best in Show winners and have been professional models for television and magazines. Joan has the rare distinction of having bred a Westminster Kennel Club group winner in her first litter of Afghan Hounds, Champion Sahadi (her kennel prefix) Shikari, the top-winning Afghan Hound in the history of the breed.

In addition to her activities in the world of animals Joan Brearley is a movie buff and spends time at the art and auction galleries, the theatre, creating needlepoint (for which she has also won awards,) dancing, the typewriter — and the zoo!

CHAPTER 1
ANCIENT HISTORY

Alaska and Siberia, separated only by 55 miles of Bering Sea —with some of the smaller islands in the straits as close to each other as only 2 miles—have all through the ages shared their ancestry, a way of living and their life-preserving dogs.

Some 35,000 years ago the people of Central Asia migrated farther and farther north to the extreme-most regions of Siberia and the Arctic, and brought with them their jackal-type dogs (*Canis aureus*.) Cross-bred with the Arctic wolves (*Canis lupus*), these animals developed over the centuries into what later came to be referred to as the Northern breeds, including the Malamute, Samoyeds, the Spitz, Keeshonds, Elkhounds, the Nootka dogs of Iceland and the Russian Laikas.

By the Neolithic age, 3500 to 2000 B.C., the Northern dogs had become established with their own type and characteristics which, with periodic breedings to the wolf, managed to endure down through the ages. All of these dogs were referred to as "huskies." The term husky is a corruption of "esky," a slang word for Eskimo; it covered all the sled-pulling breeds that had rough, shaggy coats, pointed faces and plumey tails. Their coats were thick and woolly to protect them from the elements, and they came in almost every color; solids, brindles, white with spots, black with white, white with black patches, reds, yellow, yellow spotted, red spotted, etc.

From the first days of the Eskimos' existence on earth the dogs had been there at their sides, living with them and hunting with them, thousands of years before sleds were thought of or necessary to their existence. As far back as Mesolithic times men travelled on skis, and there are also evidences that they used the travois for ages before they got around to building sleds.

As the Eskimos continued their northward migration across the Arctic Circle, eventually coming then to Greenland, some of the natives moved in behind them and established tribes along the foothills of the Cherski Mountains at the basin of the Kolyma River. One of these tribes was the Chukchi people who were to develop the

Siberian Husky. The early association of dog and tribe led to the dog's being sometimes referred to as the Siberian Chukchi.

All of these tribes consisted of three "divisions": the marine or maritime people, who were largely fishermen and lived along the river where the Huskies were used to pull the umiaks, or large skin boats, along the shore; the sedentary people, who remained in one place and traded to make a living; and the nomadic tribes, which wandered far and wide following the huge herds of reindeer. Travelling by reindeer became less and less satisfactory to the nomads, who became more and more dependent on their dogs not only to help them hunt and herd but also to get them from village to village to trade.

As the wilderness opened up before them, and as their numbers grew, they began to develop a dog bred to meet the requirements of their specific needs. The Husky became the dog with the necessary conformation to provide speed and endurance over great distances with the least expenditure of energy.

While many of the tribes were hostile toward one another, there were times when the tribes depended upon one another and their dog teams for their very survival. When food was scarce, they would join their dogs to one sled when it became necessary to move entire villages and all their belongings from one location to another. At times the women and children would get into harness and pull right along with the dogs to facilitate the move. Their dogs were held in such high esteem that only the babies, the sick or the elderly were allowed to ride.

Drivers led or walked behind the teams guiding their worldly goods to a new less hostile location. In heavy snow or bad weather the drivers would often blaze the trail with their snow shoes ahead of the lead dog, and the teams would follow in his footsteps along the man-made trail. These Northern dogs were seldom fast runners, as it was more important that they maintain the long pull from one village or camp to the next by moderate speed to assure their getting there with their cargo intact. Today as well the Siberian Husky is at his best when he can cover great distances with a comparatively light load at a moderate speed. Under these conditions he has no peer. Pound for pound, the Siberian Husky is the strongest draft dog of them all!

TYPES OF HARNESSING

There were basically three kinds of harnessing in ancient times, as there are today. One type of harnessing was attaching the dogs in

This engraving by Lizars was made from a drawing by H. Smith, circa 1840, and features a Siberian Husky quite different from the breed as we know it today. From the collection of the author.

Another early Eskimo dog, circa 1820, from the collection of the author.

An old drawing by R.H. Moore of Perla, a Lapland sledge dog owned by the Prince of Wales. From the collection of the author.

pairs on both sides of a main line that was attached to the middle of the front of the sled. This was, of course, the ideal method of hauling large, heavy loads.

The second method of harnessing the dogs was with them attached singly, alternately placed on a single tow line to the sled. They used about six or seven dogs on this single team haul. The logic behind the single line was to avoid excessive loss in crevasse accidents and to prevent dogs from going over the precipices during snowstorms.

The third harnessing, method was the fan attachment, where several dogs ran side by side, being attached at a single point and with a single tow line to the sled. This method was satisfactory only on clear wide open terrain.

EARLY SLEDS

The first sleds, or komiatics, were made from whale bone or driftwood gathered from ice floes or from the tundra during the thaws. The runners were usually wooden, preferably hickory, and extended as far as 5 to 30 feet in length with 12 feet being the average. Reindeer antlers tied to the sled with strips of walrus hide were sometimes used as handle bars. The baskets were made of seal or walrus hide; on some sleds, when wood was not available, runners were made from parts of the jawbones of whales. In an emergency sleds could be made from cuttings of ice, frozen together and carved to their individual needs.

HARNESSING THE PUPPIES

Harnessing began when the puppies were a few months old, sometimes as early as two months. It was not uncommon to see entire litters of puppies tied up behind their mother learning to pull in unison even at this early age. These teams often made the best and most efficient workers. Geldings frequently suffered the additional indignity of having their tails cropped, since the Kamchadal and Koryak tribes believed it added to their speed. The Koryaks also put their new-born puppies in underground dugouts and kept them there in total darkness until they were old enough to be harnessed, the result being that the moment the puppies saw daylight for the first time they were so exuberant there was no holding them.

SLED DOG'S CAREER A SHORT ONE

Seven years was about the limit of service for a sled dog, though some of the stronger dogs were used for a dozen or more years. But it was strictly downhill from about seven years on. Others were lost

Arctic Dog and Fox, from the collection of the author.

to frostbite, hunger, accidents on the trail, dog fights, ending up second best in a bout with a bear or other animal, or disease. More still fell victim to their owners' cruelties and neglect.

HARDSHIPS OF EARLY TEAM DOG LIFE

In the wilds of the North the Siberian Husky team dogs were completely different from those we see in more modern times. They were scrappy and vicious, and brutal fights among the dogs were commonplace. All life was a challenge: a defense against the elements or a cruel master, the winning of a female, a fight for its food, its own territory or its status among the rest of the dogs.

If there was a fight for pack leadership between two dogs, it would be a fight to the death. The entire pack would swarm around waiting eagerly to demolish and devour whichever dog turned out to be the loser. No amount of beating on the part of the owner can hold off the pack when the loser in a dog fight goes down. The same applies when for some reason the pack ostracizes a dog in its midst. It may lag behind the rest at first, but sooner or later the pack will gang up on it, close in and finish it off. And what's more — the dog will know it is a goner and will do little to defend itself.

The lead dog realizes this as well. The moment it shows the first sign of weakness or illness or oncoming age it must immediately be replaced or it will meet the same fate as the outcast dog. Life for a working sled dog was a demonstration of the survival of the fittest in its most extreme context.

GELDINGS

The above represent a few reasons why more and more frequently geldings were used on the teams. They ate much less food, did not fight as much among themselves and could be quartered together in small places. The dogs were gelded with an iron knife, and at times only the lead dog on a team was a whole male, making his job of maintaining law and order much easier.

EARLY TEAM TRAINING

On occasion there were dogs which never could "make the team." These dogs were killed, and probably eaten. Quarrelsome dogs had their teeth pulled out or the points broken off. By the time they reached 18 months of age the new young dogs were ready to join the teams in prominent positions, and the older dogs were weeded out.

With this eventual and complete turnover every so often you can readily understand the importance of the lead dog. He leads; the rest follow *him*, not the driver. The team's only as good as the lead dog. And it was perfectly possible for a lead dog to bring that team home when the driver was lost on trail, and against the most unbelievable odds. They may turn up snowblind during a blizzard, but they've kept to the trail and have gotten the team home safely.

Well treated, well fed Huskies take great pleasure in their work, and the closer the relationship between the driver and the lead dog the better the team will function. The winning drivers in the racing events never forget this!

TREATMENT OF THE DOGS

In ancient times, just as today, treatment of dogs varied from person to person, family to family. While all tribes were aware of the importance of the dogs to their very existence, many of the tribes treated their dogs horribly. Dogs which became ill or wouldn't run up to standard were abandoned on the trail and left to die, the rare exception being an extraordinarily good runner, who might be forgiven and put on the sled for the ride home.

Some dogs which were disobedient had their tails cut off on the spot, leaving a trail of blood all along the way. Obedience was taught with a stick, and many severe beatings had to be endured before the dogs came to realize what was expected of them. Sticks used usually were four feet long and thick enough to brake the sled, a usual secondary purpose for them.

Some drivers preferred whips. These were vicious instruments with a lash reaching anywhere from 18 to 24 feet, with a one foot handle. With this, the driver, by cracking it on either side of the lead dog, while shouting and repeating certain guide words, could pretty well hold the team in complete control. These whip handles were frequently used on the heads of the dogs if they didn't shape up.

Other disobedient dogs would have a rope with a knot in it tied around their throats; the rope would be pulled tight until they fell senseless. Dogs that chewed their harness were hung up until they lost consciousness, and then the tips of their rear molars were knocked off so they could no longer chew. While this method was terribly brutal, we must recall that in olden times the teeth of the dogs and the wolves were a great deal larger and sharper. Domestication has reduced the size and sharpness of teeth.

While these Esquimaux dogs were virtually slaves to their owners rather than allies and help-mates, their hard work and bitter treatment did at times make them refuse to move. If there was an especially heavy load and the dogs were badly treated by the drivers, women were frequently called upon to entice the dogs to move. The women, having played with them as puppies, cared for them when they were sick and, in general, just treated them better, could often get them to give their all.

At times a woman would walk ahead of the sled throwing bits of animal skin which she had first placed in her mouth ahead of them in the snow. The dogs would think it was food and move ahead. Certain tribes even harnessed the women and young girls, who helped pull right along with the dogs.

It was only when the explorers began to arrive in the North and demonstrated to the Eskimos that better results could be achieved through training and humane treatment that the Eskimos began to look at their teams in a different light and the brutality and cruelty began to subside. It was the beginning of a man and dog relationship rather than just man's will and dominance over a wild animal.

The tribes that treated their dogs kindly went to other extremes. The children were allowed to play with them, the women played a part in the upbringing of the puppy, and some tribes would build lean-tos or shelter for their dogs outside for protection against the elements.

HOUSING FOR THE HUSKIES

Although the tribesmen built shelters for their dogs, others merely staked them out somewhere near their housing. In the face of violent storms or raging blizzards the dogs were set free to avoid their being buried in the snow drifts or freezing to death for want of exercise. In summer the dogs were set free to fend for themselves. They would dig holes in the ground to keep cool or lie in water to avoid the mosquitos. Some did well for themselves, especially if the seal hunters were successful and threw scraps to them, while others were good at fishing and managed to survive on their own skill. Others had to scrounge for their food, and still others succumbed.

FEEDING IN ANCIENT TIMES

The diets of the Eskimos consisted largely of seal, whale or walrus meat and whatever scraps of meat or blubber were left over would get tossed to the dogs. If they were putrid so much the better. When food was scarce the dogs would devour whatever came in front of them in the way of solid food; they were known to have chewed up their own harness or the thongs that tied the sleds together.

The farther south the dogs were the better they fared. If fishing was good they survived quite nicely on whole dried fish. The dogs got along on very little food, since their owners knew if they got too heavy they could not pull as well or as much. As winter approached the drivers watched to see that the dogs lived off their own fat if they had eaten well over the summer months. During the winter when the dogs were cared for they might be fed a sort of soup made from dried salmon bones, with a piece of blubber thrown in, and slopped in a trough. It is a wonder the dogs survived at all, much less that they were were capable of pulling the great burdens they were expected to haul!

NATURAL INSTINCT

Food was always ravaged by these half-starved dogs, and, of course, more food was required by a dog living and working in a cold climate than those in a temperate zone. Instinctively, however, the Eskimo knew his dogs would be in trouble working on a full stomach or after drinking large quantities of water, so dogs were fed after the day's work was done. Instinctively, the dogs knew that licking snow was a substitute for water. Licking snow caused less contraction of the stomach and avoided cramping and distress; it relieved their hunger pains caused by these contractions. Many of the dogs came back from the long hauls not having been fed for days; they were often weak and hungry and would die of pneumonia or starvation.

WHELPING IN THE WILDS

Unless the women took pity on them, bitches often were pulling sleds up to the moment of delivery. If their puppies were born while they were out on the trail they were usually destined to die. If the puppies were born at home, the wives would frequently care for them as well as take pity on the dam. The Eskimo women have been known to take it upon themselves to nurse the puppies along with their own babies if the dam were to die or be unable to perform this vital function herself.

BITCHES IN SEASON

Since the bitches were smaller and could not pull the weight the dogs could, they were usually not put in a lead position. However, if a male team was reluctant to pull, a bitch in season would be put in the lead to give the males the needed incentive to get up and move. Bitches in season were sometimes tethered out where the male wolves would have access to them when they thought it was necessary to reintroduce wolf blood to their pack to strengthen the stock. Otherwise, the lead dogs were given first opportunity to cover the bitches.

THE SACRIFICIAL DOG

There is not a doubt that vast numbers of Husky dogs were sacrificed to the gods, although there does seem to be some discrepancy as to what was done with the remains once the sacrifice had been offered. We are well aware that the dogs' skins were used for clothing and that in times of famine the flesh was eaten by man and dog alike. There are written records which state that the Koryak did not

Artist Carol Moorland Marshall's lovely model of the Siberian Husky, a treasured piece in the author's collection.

eat dog meat, except when there was famine. There are also reports that the Chukchi kill dogs for food, but do not eat those which are sacrificed. We do know, also, that while the dogs were bred in great numbers, each family seemed to have fewer dogs than they bred. Over the years this could have been a disaster to·the family, as well as the tribe!

The Museum of Natural History in New York City has on file a series of photographs of what was referred to by villagers as the most perfect example and specimen of a Husky dog ever seen until that time. It was to have been sacrificed on the very day it was photographed, but was literally snatched from the arms of death by an explorer who purchased him for a bottle of whiskey! This dog, whelped at the turn of the century, is noticeably more like a brindle Chow Chow than any Siberian Husky, Malamute, Spitz or Samoyed that we have seen in this century.

Not always were the dogs sacrificed to the gods. . .sometimes they were offered to ward off the evil spirits. On the Western Union Telegraph Expedition, on September 24th, 1865, members of the Kamchadals tribe seized one of the dogs from their team; after knifing it to death, they offered its body up to the evil spirits!

MYTHS AND LEGENDS

We have all heard the fantastic stories of the part animals play in various rites and ceremonies, and we have just mentioned the Siberian Husky as a sacrificial dog, as well as a working companion. But beyond this, there were also certain "stories" which the people of the North put great stock in, and were passed down from generation to generation.

Many Eskimos believe that there are dog guards at the gates to paradise. Dog-lover tales are prominent with the Eskimo women who tell of unknown lovers who are dogs by day, men by night. Many Eskimos also tell that Indians and Europeans are descended from a dog. The way the story goes is that at the beginning of the world a woman had ten children by a dog, five of which became inlanders, and the other five she set afloat on a raft to became Europeans!

Lapp women would offer dog sacrifices to the goddesses of childbirth just before they delivered to insure a healthy baby.

STONEHENGE ON THE EXQUIMAUX DOG

One of the most famous writers on the dog in ancient England was a man who used the pen name of Stonehenge. Actually he was the editor of *The Field*, a major dog publication in England in the 19th Century. He wrote books about individual breeds and enormous editions covering all breeds as they were known up to that time.

In the preface to *The Dog In Health and Disease*, dated July 1, 1859, he expounds at great length about his extensive and reliable sources and with this in mind it is fascinating to read the account of The Esquimaux Dog, which states as follows:

"This dog is the only beast of burden in the northern parts of the continent of America and adjacent islands, being sometimes employed to carry materials for hunting or the produce of the chase on his back, and at others he is harnessed to sledges in teams varying from seven to eleven, each being capable of drawing a hundred weight for his share. The team are harnessed to a single yoke-line by a breast-strap, and bing without any guide-reins, they are entirely at liberty to do what they like, being only restrained by the voice of their master and urged forward by his whip. A single dog of tried intelligence and fidelity is placed as leader, and upon him the driver depends for his orders being obeyed.in the summer they are most of them turned off to get their own subsistence by hunting, some few being retained to carry weights on their backs; sledges are then rendered useless by the absence of snow;and as there is a good subsistence for them from the offal of the seal and the walrus which are taken by the men, the dogs become fat at this season of the year.The Siberian and Greenland dogs are nearly similar to those of Kamtschatka, but somewhat larger, and also more manageable, all being used in the same way. The Esquimaux dog is about 22 or 23 inches high, with a pointed, fox-like muzzle, wide head, pricked ears, and wolf-like aspect; the body is low and strong, and clothed with long hair, having an under-coat of thick wool; tail long, gently curved, and hairy; feet and legs strong and well formed; the colour is almost always a dark dun, with slight disposition to brindle, and black muzzle.''

Stonehenge went on to include brief mention of other Northern dogs in a one-sentence paragraph entitled *"Iceland and Lapland Dogs"*:

"These are nearly similar to the Esquimaux, but rather larger, more wolf-like, and far less manageable."

THE SOCIAL HIERARCHY

All descendants of either the wolf or the jackal are dogs which belong to a group which adhere to communal family living. In other words, they lived in packs. And each pack had its leader.

It was the function of the leader not only to protect his position but also to guide, keep order, discipline, and excel in every way over all the rest of the pack. The leader, therefore, was always the strongest, most intelligent, and certainly the bravest and most aggressive of the lot and had to take on all comers at all times, since other males were constantly challenging his position. Since the leaders were first with the females as well, it assured the breeding of the best and strongest specimens within the pack. This "law of the jungle" is as old as time.

While there seems to be little doubt that the ancestors of domestic dogs were the wolves, there is good reason to believe that there was also jackal blood introduced through the centuries. This supposition is based on research in observance of the Asian wolves. The Northern wolf, for instance, blends into the Tibetan wolf, the Tibetan wolf in turn shades into the pale-footed Asian wolf and the Asian wolf shades into the Mesopotamian desert wolf and so on. . . .and all of them most similiar to the jackal.

There is also a supposition among a number of historians that jackals and wolves were actually the same, that jackals were merely wolves which went off in an opposite geographical direction and to a different way of life, developing qualities and characteristics necessary to survive in a particular region. Those which migrated toward the North developed into shaggy, wolf-like creatures able to withstand the colder climates and made conformation adjustments accordingly. When they became domesticated by the Eskimos they were regarded as the Northern breeds of dogs. The wolf-jackal-dog species all can interbreed and produce fertile get, so it was not an impossibility.

Hutchinson's Encyclopedia offers the theory that while the wolf coloration of the Husky may bear out the general impression that Huskies were frequently wolf-crossed, if that were the case most Huskies would be all white, because the Arctic wolf is white. Also, the Arctic wolf is a much larger animal than the Husky, often weighing 150 pounds. They also carry their tails down while the Husky dogs carry them up and over their backs. And strangely enough, the Arctic wolf is the only animal a Husky is afraid to attack.

Additionally, pure-bred wolves have been trained and used to a limited extent as sled animals. They proved most unsatisfactory since they did not have the endurance so necessary for a good sled dog! The only conclusion can be that while the Husky may have originally descended from wolves, there has since been only what could be considered as occasional cross-breedings.

According to Dr. Edward Moffat Weyer, Jr., one of the foremost students of the Eskimo, "It seems altogether likely that the dogs have crossed to some extent with wolves. The skeletal similarity points to a relationship."

Perhaps the most obvious difference seems to be in behavioral pattern of the wolf and of the jackal. While both the wolf and the jackal packs recognize a leader, the wolf packs support a graduated order of superiority from the leader down, in a one, two, three "pecking order." The jackals, on the other hand, are said to recognize a leader, but the rest of the pack share equally in rank, with no dog taking second place to any other dog in importance.

With this comparison in mind, and going beyond the wolf-like physical appearance of today's Siberians, and knowing that they have been interbred with the wolves over the centuries, we must also note that their social behavior resembles that of the jackal. In spite of the virtually complete domestication of the Husky today, they observe the "leader of the pack" social pattern which is one of the reasons they fit in so nicely with our family living. The dog joins the family "pack" and recognizes the dominant member of the family as his "leader." This is the person to whom obedience is paid and to whom his allegence belongs. But it also upholds the jackal social behavior pattern in that he gets along equally well with all other members of the family "pack," a trait attributed to animals descending morphologically from the jackal.

A Siberian Husky grouping from the collection of Carol Moorland Marshall.

EARLY EXPLORERS AND EXPEDITIONS

It was the Northern type dog which the Russians used during the 17th Century when they succeeded in charting the Siberian coastline. All the dogs were described to be merely domesticated wolves and had the same instincts and characteristics as the sled dogs used and described by the members of the Western Union Telegraph Expedition of 1865, 1866 and 1867.

Apperently they did not differ from any of the dogs found along the entire route of the expedition, which extended from its starting point at the lower Kamchatka Peninsula to the top northeastern tip of Siberia. We can be sure that the colonization of the northeastern part of Siberia by Czarist Russia during the last few centuries played a part in improving the lot and expanding the uses of these native dogs, even though breeding between the dogs the Cossacks brought with them and the Northern dogs they encountered along their way disputes the claim that the Chukchi dog was a purebred for over two thousand years!

In actuality there is no different description of the Northern sled dogs in the diaries of Marco Polo written in the thirteenth century while describing their use in relay teams as a means of rapid transportation in the Arctic.

As late as 1900 only slight, very superficial differences could be discerned among the Northern breeds. They were all described by the early explorers as having long, shaggy coats and very definite wolf or fox-like appearance. The very earliest photographs and drawings of these dogs, and writings by explorers such as Olaf Swenson, Vilhjalmur Stefanson, Waldemar Jochelson, Valdemar Borgoras (writing on the Jessup North Pacific Expedition in 1904), George Kenner, Washington B. Vanderlip, Irving Reed and the rest of them seemed to have a single picture in mind of the breed.

CHAPTER 2
THE SIBERIAN HUSKY IN THE TWENTIETH CENTURY

The turn of the century marked the era of the great Alaskan Gold Rush. By 1906 a little village named Nome had burst into a boom town! It was the leading gold mining town in the world but, once winter set in and froze the Bering Sea, it had little more than the telegraph and native dog teams with which to keep in contact with the rest of the world.

The dog teams suddenly became an essential means of transportation for the natives as well as the members of the mining companies. In order to assure the stamina and performance of the vitally necessary dogs, the Nome Kennel Club was organized in 1907. The man responsible was a lawyer named Albert Fink, who was to serve as the first president of the club. The All-Alaska Sweepstakes races were the means devised to create interest in the dogs, and the Club set the first running for 1908.

THE ALL-ALASKA SWEEPSTAKES

A race course between Nome and Candle on the Seward Peninsula was drawn, which would represent a 408-mile trail round trip with a $10,000 first prize! It was to be run each April, the exact date depending on the weather conditions. The course was to follow as closely as possible the Nome to Candle telephone line, and presented every possible kind of terrain.

In 1908 a man named Goosak, a Russian fur trader, imported a team of small dogs from Siberia; driven by a man named Louis Thustrup, this team won third place in this running of the Sweeps, in spite of 100 to 1 odds against them! There was great speculation that Thustrup might have done better if he had not become snowblind before reaching the finish line.

At this time a young Scotsman named Fox Maule Ramsey, in Alaska to supervise, with his two uncles, Colonel Charles Ramsay and Colonel Weatherly Stuart, his family's investments in the gold fields, showed up on the scene. The second son to the Earl of Dalhousie, he was fascinated by the excitement of the races and chartered a schooner for $2500. to cross the Bering Sea. He brought back 70 dogs of mixed breeding (several of which he claimed swam out to the ship to meet him) in the Siberian settlement named Markova, 300 miles up the Anadyr River.

He had driven his own team of dogs in the 1909 event and had not placed, so on the advice of his friend Ivor Olsen, he trained his new mixed breeds and entered three teams in the 1910 event. He drove one team himself and placed second. One of the two other teams, entered in the names of his uncles, placed first. He hired John "Iron Man" Johnson to drive one of the teams, and Johnson won in the record time of 74 hours, 14 minutes, and 37 seconds. Third place went to the mixed breed Malamute team entered by Allen and Darling.

After the race he turned the dogs over to the drivers, never to compete again; he eventually returned to Scotland, where he succeeded to the Earldom of Dalhousie upon the death of his older brother.

1911 saw the entry of two Siberian dog teams, one by Johnson and Madsen and driven by Charles Johnson. Scotty Allen won the race with his mixed-Malamute team entered by Allen and Darling; second position went to another mixed Malamute team driven by Coke Hill, who later became U.S. District judge for the 4th Judicial Division. Charles Johnson and his team of Siberian Huskies were third. Iron Man Johnson with his team of Huskies did not place in the top three this year, and there was much talk and rumor that he had thrown the race, since there was so much money bet on the outcome of this one, based on his remarkable record the year before.

The enthusiasm waned the next year. . . .only four teams entered the 1912 All-Alaska Sweepstake Race. Scotty Allen won with the Allen Darling mixed-Malamute team, and Alec Holmsen, also with a mixed-breed team, placed second. Charles Johnson and his Siberians placed third.

The sixth running of the Sweepstakes in 1913 was won by the mixed-breed entry of Bowen and Delzene, driven by Fay Delzene. Iron Man Johnson and his Siberians took 2nd place and Scotty Allen was third with the Allen-Darling team. 1914 was Iron Man Johnson's year once again; the Allen-Darling team was second, and third spot went to Fred Ayer with an entry of half-Malamute and half-Foxhound team. This was also the year a stalwart young man named Leonhard Seppala arrived on the scene with his mixed-breed team, although after several misfortunes he was obliged to drop out of the competition.

The 1915 All-Alaska Sweepstakes was a different story, however. Leonhard Seppala entered and won with his Siberians. Second to Seppala was a mixed-breed entry of Bowen and Delzene, driven by Fay Delzene, and third was the Fred Ayer Malamute-Foxhound team.

This triumphant and satisfying win by Seppala in 1915 was one which

Siberians of the Ricker-Seppala Kennels, the winning team at the finish of a three-day race in Laconia, New Hampshire, many years ago. . .

he repeated in 1916 and 1917. Probably he would have repeated in 1918 but the World War had hit Nome hard, and the greatest dog team races ever run at this annual Alaskan event came to an end.

RACING WITH THE BLACK DEATH IN ALASKA: THE GREAT SERUM RUN IN 1925

One of the greatest tales of heroism ever to come out of the frozen North is the story of the great Serum Run of 1925, when a group of drivers and their stalwart sled dogs fought their way through fifty below zero weather and an 80 mile an hour blizzard to get serum to the inhabitants of Nome to halt the march of diphtheria.

In spite of the waist-high drifts and the mountainous crags of the pack ice, they covered the distance of 655 miles in five and a half days under the most excruciating circumstances, safely delivering the 20-pound package containing the precious three hundred thousand units of antitoxin serum. At 5:30 A.M., on the morning of February 2, 1925, Gunnar Kasson and his half-frozen team of dogs with bloody, torn feet pulled into Nome and handed over the serum to Curtis Welch of the

United States Public Health Service. Welch was Nome's only doctor, and together with a handful of nurses in an area containing 11,000 inhabitants, stretching one thousand miles to the east and as far north as the Arctic Ocean, they got busy putting the serum to work. The epidemic *had* to be halted, since diphtheria is certain death to Eskimos. . . .

Prayers of thanks were echoed throughout the area and all over the world, for this crisis was big news everywhere. Newspapers had carried the progress reports of the relay teams of Eskimo Pete Olsen, Leonhard Seppala, Gunnar Kasson and the rest of those involved in the run, and everyone seemed to realize instinctively the icy terror in the black Alaskan night these brave men were facing. The names of Titus Nicolai, John Folger, Jim Kalland, Tom Green and Bill Shannon became household words as the journey proceeded to Nome by the Bering Sea.

Not only did the names of the drivers remain foremost in the minds of the people, but so did the names of the dogs which led and pulled on the teams. There were the names of Togo and Scotty, Seppala's two lead dogs, and the most famous of all, Balto, the dog which pulled into Nome with Kasson. The moment the team halted at the end of their 60-mile run, Kasson fell into the snow beside his dog and began pulling the ice splinters from Balto's torn and bloody paws. Exhausted, Kasson still paid tribute to his lead dog. Newspapers all over the world carried his words of praise for Balto: "Damn fine dog! I've been mushing in Alaska since 1903. This was the toughest I've ever had on the trails. But Balto, he brought us through."

Kasson was referring to Balto's scenting the trail when Kasson got lost on the bare ice and had run into an overflow while crossing the Topkok River. Balto had proved his worth before on more than one occasion. He had led Kasson's team in 1915 when they won the Moose race, and two years before had led the team which carried explorer Roald Amundsen north from Nome when he planned an airplane flight over the North Pole. He well earned and deserved his title of the best lead dog in Alaska.

Seppala's dogs had come through for him on many occasions also. Togo and Scotty were the leads on his teams and were known throughout Alaska as the very fastest dogs. At the start of the run Seppala had been warned by officials not to cut across Norton Sound, since weather officials had reported the ice was breaking up and drifting out to sea. There was a storm raging over the area at the time as well. He was urged to take the longer distance around which circled Norton Bay, but Seppala preferred to throw caution to the winds to gain speed. He felt his dogs were in good condition to make it although they had already mushed 80 miles.

The crossing of Norton Bay was hazardous and stormy, but once they reached the other side they headed for Isaac's Point. Seppala pulled the sled into a cabin and by a roaring fire, undid the wrappings around the package containing the serum and warmed it as best he could. His instructions were that the serum had to be warmed up at intervals and the wrapping could be removed down to a certain seal which could not be broken. Once the heat had penetrated the last wrapping which he was authorized to remove, Seppala once again rewrapped the package in its canvas coverings, several thicknesses of reindeer skin, and a final wrapping of a full fur sleeping bag. Then, once again, he started on his way.

Seppala delivered the precious cargo into the hands of Charlie Olson at Golofnin. Olson then with his team of seven Huskies ran the twenty-five miles from Golofnin to Bluff, where he turned over the package to Kasson. Every one of Olson's dogs pulled into Bluff frozen in the groin. They could not have gone on much farther, but true grit made them run on until their mission was completed, even though they all pulled up stiff and sore.

Olson lived in Bluff. He owned a quartz mine and stamp mill there and when he and Kasson met they took the package into a cabin and warmed it before Kasson struck out in the 28 degree below zero temperature and a raging wind. They had waited two hours for the storm to abate, but Kasson finally decided to buck the snow rather than lose the trail or have it become impassable. He was advised not to attempt it, but he was adamant. The ice was in constant motion from the ground-swell, and it was at this point that he soon ran into trouble crossing the Topkok River. They hit an overflow, and the winds and snow had become so severe he could not see even as far as the wheel dogs. His right cheek became frozen and he lost the trail completely. But Balto came to the rescue. He kept to the trail and ploughed on through snow and over ice, allowing nothing to alter his direction. Kasson recalls that he himself did not even know when they passed right by Solomon, where they were to have picked up a message from Nome which would advise him not to go on until the weather improved.

When Kasson finally pulled into Port Safety, Ed Rohn was waiting to take off as relay, but Kasson felt his dogs were doing so well that he decided not to awaken Rohn and drove right on the final 21 miles from Port Safety to Nome. The trail ran along the beach of the Bering Sea, and it was at this point that two of the dogs which had been frozen on another trip began to stiffen up. Kasson had rabbit-skin coverings for them, but the cold was so severe that it still penetrated.

Three volunteer flyers were standing by with their airplanes at Fairbanks for the shipment of serum when the dog-teams went through. They knew, however, that weather conditions being what they were, the planes could never get through. Governor Scott C. Bone of Alaska, in a special dispatch to the *New York Times*, stated that any attempt to fly would have been a hazardous undertaking because their flying equipment was inadeqate and only unskilled flyers were available.

Once again, the mushers and their legendary sled dogs came through. Man and animal had fought a bitter battle against the elements—and had won! Another epic tale has become part of the history of the vast Yukon country in the far North.

THE TRIBUTE TO BALTO

In New York City's Central Park there is a magnificent bronze statue of Balto with a trace hanging over his back; it bears the following inscription:

"Dedicated to the indomitable spirit of the sled dogs that relayed anti-toxin six hundred miles over rough ice, across treacherous waters, through arctic blizzards from Nenana to the relief of a stricken Nome in the winter of 1925. Endurance—fidelity—intelligence."

WHO GOT TO THE NORTH POLE FIRST?: THE PEARY-COOK CONTROVERSY

Hutchinson's Encyclopedia pays tribute to the Husky as helping to make the remarkable strides in exploration at both the North and South Pole regions, declaring that it was indespensable to its owner as no other breed. The same holds true with the explorer. Every expedition had to depend largely on the use of the sled dogs, and therefore it is very probable that no other breed has had such a wide natural distribution.

The year was 1909 when two creditable, adventurous men claimed to have reached the North Pole. . .Navy Commander Robert E. Peary and Dr. Frederick A. Cook each put in his claim to fame. Comm. Peary was steadfastly backed by the Peary Arctic Club, composed of 21 millionaire sportsmen who all secretly yearned to have accomplished the feat themselves. Dr. Cook, backed by a notorious gambler, John R. Bradley, lost the honor in a raging controversy which ensued.

Dr. Cook was discredited, ridiculed and on the verge of a breakdown as all his previous accomplishments were placed in doubt and he was dubbed the "prince of losers." The campaign waged against him by Peary's wealthy backers led him to desperation and despair to the end of his days.

Cook returned to civilization first to announce his achievement. Cook was a "loner" and made the journey with 2 Greenlanders, doing all the charting and navigating himself. Peary had 25 men go along to support his claim. It worked. Years of trying to clear his name of the Peary accusations, and a prison sentence for stock fraud, all took their toll on Dr. Cook. The sentence was commuted by President Franklin D. Roosevelt on Cook's deathbed. He rallied upon hearing this news, but it was mild consolation to this dedicated explorer.

The paths of Peary and Cook had crossed before. In 1892 Cook had been signed on as medic on one of Peary's expeditions to Greenland. During the journey Peary sent Cook and another man back, while Peary and a few of the others went on with three sledges and 14 dogs until 34 days later they reached 82 degrees north latitude. Peary believed he had proved that Greenland is an island, and when he and his party reached a great body of water he proclaimed it Peary Channel. In 97 days Peary had travelled 1130 miles. In 1915, however, Peary Channel was removed from the maps, as Danish explorers proved that Greenland went a great deal beyond Peary's calculations. His first expedition thus discredited, his second was also a failure. In 1893-1895 they tried again, but were forced to return, having to eat some of the dogs on the return journey. In 1898 he made another unsuccessful attempt to reach the Pole and met the famous Norwegian explorer Otto Sverdrup when their ships both became frozen in the ice about 700 miles south of the Pole. This was 3½ months before Peary sailed from New York.

Before sailing, on July 6, 1908, Peary said goodbye to President Theodore Roosevelt, who said to him, "I believe in you, Peary, and believe in your success—if it is within the possibility of man." At this time news of Dr. Cook's departure reached him. Dr. Cook had come up with a new way to reach the Pole and had written "There will be game to the 82 degree point and there are natives and dogs for the task, so here is for the Pole." On March 18, 1908, he reduced his party to two 20-year-old Eskimos, two sleds and 26 dogs and started for the North Pole.

When Peary arrived at Etah, the starting-off point in the North, he claimed it was difficult to get Eskimos and dogs because Cook had gotten there first. This simply was not true, since Peary left Etah with 49 Eskimos and 246 dogs. A pair of dogs could be had in a trade for a tin cup and saucer.

The cold was excrutiating for Cook and his group. The dogs' tails, ears and noses drooped and perspiration froze and coated their bodies with ice. A hundred miles from the Pole, Etukishook and Ahwelah, the Eskimos, decided they did not want to go on. The knife and gun each was to receive as payment no longer seemed enough. But they trusted Cook, who convinced them to go on.

On April 21, 1908 Cook and his two Eskimos reached the Pole. Cook later said, "I strode forward with undaunted glory in my soul. . .The desolation was such that it was almost palpable. . .What a cheerless spot this was, to have aroused the ambition of man for so many years."

He buried a short note, mentioning the good health of the men and dogs, and part of a flag in a metal tube. He later admitted that he felt a. . ."sense of the utter uselessness of this thing, of the empty reward of my endurance," which had followed his exhilaration at his accomplishment.

Peary on his last assault had with him four Eskimos and his Negro servant Matthew Henson, along with 5 sledges and 40 dogs. Peary also expressed almost the same disappointment in the face of his success. He recorded in his diary, "The Pole at last. The prize of three centuries. Mine at last! I cannot bring myself to realize it. It all seems so simple and commonplace."

Peary also buried a jar with a piece of the flag in it and took possession of the territory in the name of the President of the United States. Their route back was aided somewhat by following the urine stains left by the forty dogs which accompanied him to the North Pole. . . .

MACMILLAN ON THE HUSKIES

Lieutenant-Commander Donald B. MacMillan, an Arctic explorer whom Peary referred to as an excellent dog man, made several trips to the North Pole. In 1908-1909 he went with 250 dogs, during 1913-1917 with 400 dogs, 1923-1924 with 60 dogs. His 1927-1928 journey to Northern Labrador gives us considerably more information regarding the part the dogs played in these expeditions. He definitely claimed the dogs from Labrador were better looking and the best of all the Northern dogs he had seen. MacMillan, who is accredited with running an authentic trip of 100 miles in less than 18 hours, had nothing but good to say about the ability and endurance of the dogs.

He noted that for fast travelling they limited the load to approximately the combined weight of all dogs in the team. For ordinary hauls they limited it to 1½ times the team's total weight, and for heavy hauling the limit was double the weight. When the going was good, and with a light load, the team made six to eight miles an hour.

He further stated: "The usual gait is a fast steady trot, which they keep up hour after hour. Some dogs will frequently shift from this trot to a pace, evidently as a measure of rest. Occasionally too, they will gallop, probably for the same reason." He also made the same observation that most of us have; that once a lead dog is trained, he never forgets. Photographs of all expeditions show pie-balds, solid blacks and all

Rear Admiral Richard E. Byrd, the explorer who headed up so many of the polar expeditions using Siberian Huskies.

variations of colors and color combinations. The Husky type dog is evident, they are Husky dogs! Their value is further evidenced by a paragraph contained in *Hutchinson's Encyclopedia* which reads: "As poor Captain Scott and his brave companions were struggling to their death after reaching the South Pole (in 1911) Amundsen was riding back in comparative comfort with his team of 11 Greenland Eskimo dogs."

ADMIRAL BYRD AND THE HUSKIES

Rear Admiral Richard E. Byrd, USN, was the first man to fly over the North Pole and the South Pole and the only man to fly over both. He gazed upon more square miles of unknown, uncharted territory than any other human being in all history. During his wartime duties he was decorated four times, receiving the Congressional Medal of Honor, the Congressional Lifesaving Medal, three specially voted Congressional medals, and many others.

In an article in *National Geographic* magazine in October, 1947, Rear Admiral Byrd wrote extensively about his 1946-1947 return to the Antarctic. Entitled "Our Navy Explores Antarctica," the article refers only briefly, but no less signifigantly, to the role of the Husky dog in that exploration.

Over 4,000 men and 13 ships played a part in this particular expedition, Operation Highjump, which was the largest polar expedition Admiral Byrd had undertaken up to that time; it even was accompanied by an aircraft carrier, the *Philippine Sea*. The objective was to sail as far as possible around the 16,000-mile coast of the continent, since most of the coastline up until that time was mostly conjectural. Expedition leaders proposed to send seaplanes from sea plane tenders to explore the coast and make flights inland and to have their ships establish a base for ski-equipped land planes which would make photo-reconnaissance flights across the unmapped interior of the continent.

On this trip all the aircraft were equipped with the latest inventions which World War II had provided: new weapons and photo-reconnaissance tools and aerial cameras which could photograph about 100,000 square miles of territory in one shot. All this equipment, plus the wide use of snow tractors, produced remarkable information. But there was still a "dog town" in Little America! The marvelous Husky dogs were still useful and very necessary on the rough, crevassed terrain, where no mechanical equipment could function to full advantage.

Large dogs were usually chosen, because it was thought they could better withstand the ardors of the Antarctic climate. But for Byrd's latest expedition Milton Seeley chose fifty dogs of the smaller, faster type

Admiral Richard E. Byrd, center, accepts one of two Husky puppies as mascots for his ship *East Wind* (pictured in background)
as the expedition departs for the Antarctic from Boston on Operation Deepfreeze. Mrs. Seeley provided thirty sled dogs for the expedition from her Chinook Kennels, in Wonalancet, New Hampshire, where many of the dogs for the Byrd expeditions were trained and conditioned.

represented by the Siberian Husky. Upon their return the explorers reported that the smaller dogs got them farther per pound of dog
food and that their speed and smaller appetites more than made up for
their lower pulling power. While the Husky at that time had an average
weight of about fifty pounds to the Malamute's eighty-five, the Husky
could still travel at about thirteen miles an hour under regular conditions,
whereas the heavier dogs could manage only nine or ten.

Subsequently the Siberian Husky became the favorite racing dog of the
Northern varieties by offering both speed and endurance.

ED MOODY AND ADMIRAL BYRD

Ed Moody, prominent racer and sled-maker, had accompanied Admiral Bryd on his earlier 1933 expedition during which the sled dogs

played an important part. They took along nine dog sled teams, as well as fifty tons of Purina Dog Chow to feed them. Admiral Byrd later referred to the dog teams as the backbone of the expedition. At that time they could not have done without the dogs. Here again, mechanical equipment broke down while the dogs did not.

Weather, claimed Moody, was even for the dogs the biggest problem they had to overcome on the trip. Blizzards, crevasses, ice breaks. . .all played havoc with their progress, but the crucial point in the journey

A photograph of an exhibit by the Siberian Husky Club of America commemorating 50 years of service from Pole to Pole. This exhibit, co-chaired by Mr. and Mrs. Paul J. Koehler, displayed items from various members of the club and featured in the center a photograph of Admiral Richard E. Byrd and Mrs. Milton Seeley taken just prior to the jump-off of "Operation Deepfreeze." Mrs. Seeley is the owner of the famous Chinook Kennels in Wonalancent, New Hampshire, where most of the dogs used by Byrd and other expeditions were trained. The exhibition was held in conjunction with the Westchester Kennel Club dog show.

came in the Bay of Whales. The dog teams were hauling 1,000 pounds a load and finally even they could not work when the temperature dropped to sixty degrees below zero. Below that their lips and foot pads froze. But there is, there was and there always will be a place for dog teams among the inhabitants of the extreme frozen lands of the Arctic and Antarctic!'

OUTSTANDING KENNELS OF THE FIRST HALF OF THE TWENTIETH CENTURY

The Siberian Husky during the first decade of the twentieth century rested in the hands of some very important and dynamic people. They obviously had no idea of it then, but they were establishing this breed for future generations of dog lovers and racing enthusiasts who would carry the breed to unbelievable heights of popularity that would spread all over the world.

It was in the years before 1910 when Goosak brought the first dogs to Alaska for the races, and which caught the keen interest of Leonhard Seppala, John Johnson, Fox Maule Ramsey and Olaf Swenson. Leonhard Seppala maintained his kennels in Nome, Alaska, from 1909 until 1926, racing and winning with his dogs all along the way. Shortly after the Serum Run he took off for Canada and New England, where his friend Elizabeth Ricker had a kennel of Siberian Huskies at her Poland Springs, Maine, Kennels which included the last brought out of Siberia by Olaf Swenson, the American fur trader, in 1929.

Swenson had spent over 40 years trading and hunting in northern Siberia. He had nothing but good things to say for the great shaggy dogs of the desolate northern wastelands. He felt it was impossible to name a price for a good one, comparing it to buying a person with whom you would undertake a perilous journey, and to whom you would entrust your life. In those days the Eskimo tribesmen would trade one dog for another, but never their lead dogs.

While in New England Leonhard Seppala entered just about every race that was run, breaking records and continuing to make a name for himself as the world's top racing driver. Elizabeth Ricker, by the way, did much to get the breed recognized by the American Kennel Club. Today she is Mrs. Nansen and still resides in Poland Springs.

Around this same period in time Frank Dufresne, formerly head of the Alaska Game Commission and an avid racing enthusiast, had a magnificent team of all-white Siberian Huskies. It was from these white Alaskan dogs that Julian Hurley purchased his first dogs from a breeding of Dufresne's Jack Frost and Snow White. Hurley, a Fairbanks, Alaska, lawyer and judge, sold many dogs to New England and Michigan, but unfortunately the line stopped there, though the second bench show champion in the breed in the United States was Northern Light Kobuk, sold by Hurley to Oliver Shattuck in New England. The year of the championship was 1932. Hurley's kennel Northern Light was in operation from approximately 1926 to 1947. It was Hurley who registered some of the first Siberian Huskies, over a dozen, as a matter of fact, and most of them were white.

The undisputed matriarch of the breed, "Short" Seeley, photographed by Judith Rosemarin to commemorate her 80th birthday.

In the late 1920's we see the appearance of Arthur Walden with his still famous Chinook Kennels in Wonalancet, New Hampshire. It was Walden who was directly responsible for bringing Eva (also known as "Short") and Milton Seeley into the breed. They purchased the Chinook Kennels from Walden and kept the name Chinook in addition to their own Alyeska and Wonalancet names on their dogs. Still active in the breeding and judging of the Huskies, Short Seeley maintains this most extraordinary kennel today. The Chinook stock came originally from Seppala and direct Alaskan imports.

Homey scene in the family room at Eva Seeley's Chinook Kennels. Pictured in the background is a photo of the famous Ch. Alyeska Suggen of Chinook, one of the early great stud dogs, and in the foreground Suggen's daughter, Alyeska Cheenah of Chinook, at eleven years of age.

This same period saw the start of a major kennel which is also active today, the Monadnock Kennels of Mrs. Lorna Demidoff in Fitzwilliam, New Hampshire, among the most successful and well known. Mrs. Demidoff is a leading breeder and judge; her original stock also came from some of the Seppala dogs and a few Alaskan imports.

Doctors Alex and Charles Belford appeared on the scene in 1928, and both members of this prominent father and son team have been racing for years. Their Belford's kennel is in Laconia, New Hampshire, and while less active it is still remembered in the breed.

Roland Bowles' Calivali Kennels were also in New Hampshire, and formed in the late twenties. It is still active today, based on stock which came from White Water Lake, Foxstand and Gatineau lines.

THE 1930'S

Harry Wheeler also bought some of the original Seppala dogs in 1932 and established his Gatineau Kennels in St. Jovite, Quebec, Canada. The kennel remained in operation until 1948. Shortly thereafter he sold out.

From the early 1930's until 1963 Don McFaul of Maniwaki, Quebec, Canada, was active in Siberian Huskies. He bought up some of the original Seppala stock which Seppala had been racing in New England in the late 1920's, and used Seppala as his kennel name. In the winter of 1963 he sold out the kennel; the dogs returned to Alaska with Earl and Natalie Norris, who bought them from him.

Some of the Seppala dogs were the basis for William Shearer's Foxstand Kennels in New Hampshire, and he was active in the breed from 1936 through 1956.

In 1938 Earl and Natalie Norris established their Anadyr Kennels in Anchorage, Alaska, and are still very active today. They also used the Alaskan kennel name on some of their dogs which go back to the Milton and Short Seeley lines. The Norrises transferred to Alaska from Lake Placid, New York, taking with them two registered Siberian Huskies from Chinook. Chinooks Alladin of Alyeska became the top stud dog in Alaska. Red dogs were first bred by the Norrises in 1948, and the red dog that went to Austin Moorecroft they believe is the red coloration behind so many of the red dogs in the eastern United States. Natalie Norris is

Eva B. Seeley's team of all AKC-registered dogs including five champions and the foundation stock of many of our present-day kennels. This rare old photograph was taken at the Chinook Kennels training trail at Wonalancet, New Hampshire. All the dogs pictured were house pets, brood bitches and studs as well as top show and racing dogs, with many bearing the Alyeska name, the oldest established foundation stock in the breed.

Lorna B. Demidoff and one of her pleasure teams at the grounds of the Monadnock Kennels in Fitzwilliam, New Hampshire.

active in club work in Alaska, and in March, 1973 she was invited to judge the breed at the Bronx County Kennel Club show in New York.

Charles and Kit McInnes and their Tyndrum Kennels in Alaska began in the 1930's and were active intil 1961. Their stock is behind the S-K-Mo lines.

From the 1930's to the 1950's the names of Major John Rodman and Lowell Fields sprang up in Montana. They did not have an official kennel name, but their stock was founded on Monadnock breeding and the McFaul dogs. Their breeding is behind many Siberian Huskies found in the mid-west.

It was during the 1930's also when Dr. Roland Lombard and his Igloo-Pak dogs, based on Chinook Kennel bloodlines, began making a name for themselves. We give a more complete accounting of Dr. Lombard's remarkable success in the fancy from the 1930's right on up to the present day in another chapter. His dogs are still breaking records and setting the pace along the racing trail.

THE 1940'S

Malamak Kennels arrived on the scene in the 1940's. Based on McFaul and Seppala breeding, J. Malcolm McDougall's kennel was located at Ste. Agathe, Quebec, Canada. The kennel is in existence today.

In the late 1940's Harold Frendt and his Little Alaska Kennels appeared. They were active in New York and Pennsylvania dog circles. His stock was based on the Gatineau and Bow Lake lines and was active until 1967.

Earl Snodie and Leonhard Seppala had the Bow Lake Kennels in Seattle, Washington, from the late 1940's until 1960. Their kennel contained some of Frendt's breeding plus representatives of Monadnock, Lombard and Little Alaska.

The Nagles' Kabkol Kennels in Washington, D. C. started in the 1940's and continued until the late 1950's. Their lines were established on Monadnock stock.

Frank Brayton started his Dichoda Kennels in Escalon, California in 1947, and he is still producing winning dogs today. Founded originally on the Kabkol line, the Dichoda record in the show ring is to be envied.

During the 1940's Bunty Dunlop Goodreau, Elizabeth Ricker Nansen's daughter, established her Snow Ridge Kennels in Chelmsford, Ontario, Canada. Based on the early Seppala stock from three of his original kennels, this kennel is still active.

Jean Bryar, formerly Jean Lane, got her start in New Hampshire in the late 1940's and was active until 1968 with her Mulpus, Bryar's and Norvik lines which stemmed from the early McFaul, Seppala, Gatineau and Monadnock bloodlines.

Mrs. Earle R. Nagle's Kabloona.

Tony Landru began in the late 1940's with the White Water Lake kennel in Ontario, and continued in the breed until 1968. This kennel line was formed on the McFaul, Seppala and Gatineau bloodlines. .

Other names from this era come to mind in reviewing early kennels. The Sylvan Dell Kennels of Doris Cassady in New Hampshire is one. Her kennel was built on stock from several of the northeastern kennel lines. Another is Eva Havlicek, Shady Lane Kennels, Ontario, Canada. There were a few active kennels in Alaska in the late 1940's belonging to Donald and Virginia Clark and Jack and Sid Worbass. Also in Alaska were the Koiri Koti Kennels of Orville and Doris Lake, the Nikohna Kennels of Roger and Reta Gidney, Lakota Kennels of Joe and Gladys Traversie, Hank Buege's, and Darrell and Angie Reynolds' Kossa Kennels.

Ch. Noho of Anadyr with his owner and handler, Phyllis Brayton, Dichoda Kennels, Escalon, California.

CHAPTER THREE
IMPORTANT KENNELS IN
THE 1970'S

By 1970, just a little more than half a century after the first Siberian Husky reached Alaska, the breed had flourished and had reached the very heights of popularity. The great sport of sled dog racing has by now mushroomed all over the United States, and entries at the dog shows and obedience trials are increasing at an amazing rate.

1963 was a record-breaking year for Siberian Husky registration with the American Kennel Club. For the first time they went over the one thousand mark. By 1969 registrations were just under five thousand.

Entries at the dog shows show equal interest in the breed. An early 1970 Specialty Show drew over 150 entries, and many of the larger dog shows pull entries in the three figure category each year. The future of this magnificent breed is in the hands of many, many newcomers recently attracted to this exotic dog. Some of them are one-dog owners, but a large number of them are kennel owners, breeding to show and to race their dogs.

To present a comprehensive picture of what the kennels are breeding and who the breeders are, we present here an alphabetical series of kennel histories, all of which are active in the breed today.

ADJANAK

Robert and Brenda Wallace's kennel came into being in 1969 when they bought their first Siberian Husky. Brenda Wallace says that once you have one Husky you just have to get more. . .and they did. Their interest in showing and racing increased with their admiration for their dogs, and in 1973 they started racing in earnest. Bob Wallace now races a five-dog team; their lead dog's name is Adja.

The Wallaces have two Junior Teams also, son Bobby, age 9, and son Gary, age 6. They both raced in 1972 and won five trophies. Wins repeated the following year and probably for many more years to come, since all four of the Wallaces are sold on this wonderful outdoor family sport.

The Wallaces race in the winter and show their dogs in the summer and admit quite frankly they could not give up either one! This was admitted when their lead dog Adja won her first 4-point major from the puppy classes at just over six months of age and went on to Best of Opposite Sex at the same show.

AKALAN

Dean and Dolores Warner established their Akalan Kennels in the mid-1960's in Livermore, California. They based their breeding on the Dichoda bloodline and have been active in both showing and the obedience ring.

Ch. Dichoda's Arora Nikki, C.D.X., is pictured winning third in the Working Group under judge Heywood Hartley at the San Mateo Kennel Club show in November, 1969. Nikki was also seventh ranking Siberian Husky in the July, 1970 Phillips System rating, and fourth ranking Husky in the 1970 *Kennel Review* Awards. Owned by the Akalan Kennels, Livermore, California.

Their kennel includes many obedience titled dogs, several of which have their C.D. titles and many of which have gone on to acquire their C.D.X. Prominent C.D.X. winners are Ch. Dichoda's Arora Nikki, and Ch. Akalans Yuri. Ch. Dichoda's Arora Chena, C.D., and Ch. Akalan's Sonia, C.D. are also prominent members of the kennel.

ALAKAZAN

Paul J. and Margaret A. Koehler's Alakazan Kennels in Gill, Massachusetts was original called Kazan. Since 1954 they have been active in the breed and feel their greatest satisfaction is having had the opportunity to work in various ways for the Siberian Husky Club of America, the parent club for the breed they love so much.

Paul served for three years as club president and Peggy has been on the board of directors since 1967. They published the club's newsletter for several years, and Peggy was editor from 1968 to 1971. She has also written the Siberian Husky breed columns for the *American Kennel Gazette* and *Popular Dogs* magazine on and off for several years.

One of their outstanding show and sled dogs is Ch. Kira of Kazan. Kira was Best of Opposite Sex at the National Specialty Show in Chicago in 1962. Ch. Kronprinz of Kazan was Best of Breed at the National Specialty Show in Detroit in 1965 and also Best of Breed at Westminster in 1966. Ch. Monadnock's Volcana was Best of Opposite Sex at the National Specialty Show in Cleveland in 1971. All were bred and are owned by the Alakazan Kennels.

The Koehlers have finished 10 champions themselves and have bred many, many more which have been finished or are finishing with other owners.

Ch. Monadnock's Konyak of Kazan has sired 10 champions plus a Best in Show winner in Finland. Kameo of Kazanis is the dam of five champions and two others which live abroad. Ch. Alakazan's Nikolai is the sire of six champions, including Ch. Dudley's Tavar of Innisfree, which won Best In Show in 1972 at the Ramapo Kennel Club event and was bred by Kathleen Kanzler and Margaret Koehler.

The Koehlers keep active in racing, and their Ch. Monadnock's Serge, Ch. Kronprinz of Kazan, Ch. Monadnock's Konyak of Kazan and Ch. Kandia of Kazan comprise their top team, which won the Siberian Husky Club of America Racing Trophy in 1964.

ARAHAZ

Edward and Rosemary Fischer first got into the Siberian Husky breed in the early 1960's; and in the years that followed they have finished 10 champions, with many more pointed. They have sold puppies throughout the U.S.A. and to Canada, Alaska, the Virgin Islands and Puerto Rico. Their stud, Ch. Toki of Rockrimmon, has sired six Arahaz-bred champions to date (1973), with many others about to finish.

While the Fischers claim to be "a bit past the sled working age," they have sold puppies to friends who are working the dogs with sleds, and they are enjoying the sport through their friends. They maintain a kennel of about 30 dogs and are active in two all-breed kennel clubs and a Siberian Husky Club they helped to get started in 1970.

Ch. Monadnock's Volcana, pictured winning Best of Opposite Sex at the Siberian Husky Club of America National Specialty Show in Cleveland, Ohio in December, 1971 under judge Mrs. Milton "Short" Seeley. Owners and breeders of Volcana are the Alakazan Kennels, Gill, Massachusetts. Handling for the owners is Carl Lacchia.

Ch. Toki of Rockrimmon, one of the foundation bitches at the Arahaz Kennels in Canonsburg, Pennsylvania.

Mrs. Fischer is very interested in judging, and at the time of this writing she has had her name published in the *American Kennel Gazette* as having applied for her judging status.

ARCTIC

1954 saw the establishment of Charlotte and Earl Reynolds' Arctic Kennels in Dryden, Michigan. Since the beginning their goal has been to breed good Siberians which excelled in both the show ring and in harness.

While they have had all colors of Siberians at their kennel, they have for many years specialized in the silver Siberian, and it is for this color they are best known. Perhaps their best known individual dog was American and Canadian Ch. Arctics Storm Frost, who distinguished himself in the show rings of both countries and helped to bring the breed to the attention of the fancy.

All of the Reynolds dogs both show and race.

ARCTURA

Thomas and Sylvia Palmer got started in the breed in 1967 with their purchase of a Dichoda puppy, and their Arctura Kennels have now grown to an establishment of 13 Siberian Huskies. Tom and Sylvia and their two sons enjoy both showing and racing the dogs, and each member of the family has its own team.

The Palmers recently purchased a Greyhound bus which they have converted into a mobile home for themselves; the back 10-foot section has been converted to kenneling for when they travel with the dogs to the shows and races.

American and Canadian Ch. Arctic's Storm Frost, beautiful male lead dog at Charlotte and Earl Reynolds' Arctic Kennels in Dryden, Michigan.

Ch. Dichoda's Gjoa Grey Cloud, Best of Breed and fourth in the Working Group at the Sacramento Kennel Club Show in California in October, 1969. Gjoa is owned by Thomas and Sylvia Palmer, owners of the Arctura Kennels, Napa, California.

Ch. Dichoda's Gjoa Grey Cloud was ranked #10 in the national *Kennel Review* system in 1970 and has a Group Placement to his credit. Arctura's Taurus of Sundana won Best Puppy in Match at 10 weeks of age over an entry of 714 dogs, and their Arctura's Aries of Mokelumne at the Sister, Oregon, race in January, 1973 won the under 65-pound weight pull by pulling 2,727 pounds.

BIG TRAIL

Herbert and Barbara Hitchcock, owners of the Big Trail Kennels in Holly, Michigan, started in Siberians in 1966. They loved the breed so much they moved from the city to the country where they could better accommodate their dogs.

They are members of the Dog Breeders Registry of Michigan and exhibit their dogs as a team several times a year at various civic functions in their area. Their team was selected by the Ford Motor Company to be featured in their brochures for the 1972 Ford pick-up trucks.

The Hitchcocks are members of the Greater Siberian Husky Club of Detroit, and Mrs. Hitchcock has served as its treasurer since its beginning. They are also charter members of the Livingston Kennel Club and have served on the board for several years.

Two of their dogs, Lostland's Toshya My Lady and Satan of Big Trail, are both Canadian and American Champions, and Toshy received an award from the International Siberian Husky Club for winning Best of Breed or Best of Opposite Sex ten times for major point competition in bitches.

BLACKWATCH

MacKnight Black, owner of the Blackwatch Kennels, which he established in 1965, considers his kennel a relatively small operation since they never have more than three to six adult dogs at one time. They concentrate on the black and white Huskies and hope to gain recognition as top breeders in the nation with them.

Ch. Lostland's Toshya My Lady, owned by Herbert and Barbara Hitchcock of the Big Trail Kennels in Holly, Michigan, pictured winning at a recent show. E.H. Frank photo.

St. Nicholas of Blackwatch has a Group Second placement, and he and Norka of Blackwatch are being shown to their championships at the time of this writing. Their other dogs are Sabrina, Mata Hari and Nasha, all of Blackwatch. The Blackwatch Kennels are located in Arlington, Virginia.

CHERSKIY

Thom and Claudia Ainsworth are the owners of the Cherskiy Kennels in Novato, California, which has been in existence since 1968. Thom has been proud to serve as founding president of the Northern California Siberian Husky Club, which has held its first Match Show with an entry of 92.

While they intend to expand their kennel in the future and do a great deal more showing and racing, they are justifiably proud of their two present owner-handled champions, Ch. Cherskiy's Royal Bandit and Ch. Sandyhill's Chukchi Red.

Three Cherwenlo's Siberian Huskies. . . Cherwenlo's Silver Tina, Ch. Karnovanda's Miss Vodka, and Arahaz' Snow Tar, CD. Owners Mr. and Mrs. Richard Dauer of Glenshaw, Pennsylvania.

In his first year of race competition in C Class, five times he placed in the top five and once in 9th place with 22 entered. They both show and race each dog, and in 1973 Claudia entered into racing competition. Their son has raced only twice in the Pee Wee Competition and placed second both times.

In the near future they expect to finish their other dogs which are now pointed and get into racing for the sheer fun of it.

Thom's occupation is licensed instructor at Guide Dogs for the Blind in San Rafael, California. He trains dogs for six months, then trains blind students in their use of the dogs, a most worthy profession in which he has been engaged for several years.

CHERWENLO

In addition to Ch. Karnovanda Miss Vodka and Arahaz Snow Tar, C.D., the pride and joy of the Cherwenlo Kennels of Richard and Joanne Dauer is their daughter Lori, who was top junior handler for two years in 1969 and 1970. Not only did Lori finish Snow Tar to her obedience title in three straight shows, but showing Miss Vodka managed to win a coveted junior handling award. Lori did all the training herself as well.

Their kennel began in 1968 with Lori's interest in showing and training their dogs.

Ch. Cherskiys Royal Bandit on the left and his pal Ch. Sandyhill's Chukchi Red, owned by Thom and Claudia Ainsworth of the Cherskiy Kennels, Novato, California.

Best Brace in the Working Group judged by the late Alva Rosenberg and owned by Bob Page, handling Ch. Chotovotka's Napachee and Ch. Chotovotka's Kaytee. C. Wescott Gallup presents the trophy. Bob and Dorothy Page's kennels are in Chatham, Illinois. Photo by Ritter.

CHOTOVOTKA

The Chotovotka Kennels of Bob and Dorothy Page in Chatham, Illinois were established in 1963. The Pages puchased their first dog from the Frosty Aire Kennels in Mishawaka, Indiana; the dog's name was Frosty Aire's Masked Bandit, and he finished in 11 shows at the age of 11 months.

The Pages limit their kennel to six dogs and have bred only seven litters in nine years of breeding. Since its beginning the Pages have owner-handled seven dogs to their championship. As Bob Page says, "Breeder-owner-handled is the name of the game for us!"

The Pages are particularly proud of their Ch. Chotovotka's Nota Yankidrink, which won a Best of Breed under Lorna Demidoff at a Steel City Kennel Club Show and then went on to win the Working Group under Mrs. Demidoff, and all wins were from the classes. They also are pleased with the Group First win with their black and white brace, Ch. Chotovotka's Napachee and Ch. Chotovotka's Kaytee, won under the late Alva Rosenberg at the International Kennel Club of Chicago show when the dogs were just six months and 11 days old. Later they went on to win several Groups and a Best Brace in Show.

Dorothy was a past president of the Decatur Obedience Training Club, and Bob is a judge of Siberian Huskies and a second vice president of the Siberian Husky Club of America; he also is chairman of the membership committee. He has also served a second term as president of the all-breed Illinois Capitol Kennel Club and has been their show chairman on two occasions.

And in case you hadn't noticed. . .Chotovotka is pronounced 'Shot of Vodka!'

CHU-NIK

A 1961 trip to Anchorage, Alaska where Harry and Velma Wade of Amboy, Washington, first saw a team of Siberian Huskies and fell in love with the breed was the beginning of the Chu-Nik Kennels. They purchased their first bitch, Nikki of Anadyr, from Earl and Natalie Norris and within two months purchased a lovely male, later Ch. Chuchi of Anadyr.

The Wades contend that almost 80% of the Siberian Huskies in the area boast Chuchi in their backgrounds, and they are proud of it. Their dog was the first Siberian Husky in the Pacific Northwest to win a Group First. This he did in 1966 under judge Ted Wurmser.

The Wades kept one entire litter and made them their first team. Tammi of Chu-Nik has been their lead dog for many years. The Wades also point out that their kennel name is a combination of the names of their first two Huskies which were responsible for their getting into the breed and bringing them so much pleasure.

Ch. Nikoluk of Chu-Nik, one of the magnificent Huskies at Harry and Velma Wades' Kennels in Amboy, Washington, which excels in the show ring and at the races.

CINNAMINSON

Sy and Ann Goldberg own the Cinnaminson Kennels in Cream Ridge, New Jersey, which they started in 1967. Sy Goldberg states that his is at present the only sled team in America running an all-champion dog team. To his knowledge this has been done only twice before. . .once in Alaska and once in New Hampshire. So enthusiastic is he about the sport of racing that he managed to win the coveted Siberian Husky Club of America's Racing Trophy for 1971, and he was first runner-up for the same trophy in 1970.

The Goldbergs have done very well in the show and obedience ring also. Some of their outstanding show dogs are Ch. Tokco of Bolshoi, who needs but one point to finish for a Canadian championship and is presently (1973) working for a C.D. degree; Ch. Mischa of Chaya, C.D.; American and Canadian Ch. Tanya of Cinnaminson; Ch. Koryaks Black Charger, Ch. Chachka of Cinnaminson and Ch. Cinnaminson's Soaya Fournier.

American and Canadian Ch. Tanya of Cinnaminson winning Best of Breed under judge William Kendrick at the Fayetteville Kennel Club show in March, 1970, with George Heitzman handling for owners Sy and Ann Goldberg of Cream Ridge, New Jersey. Graham photograph.

Ch. Tanya of Cinnaminson is their lead dog and has helped them to at least always place in the running because of her ability.

Tokco has produced the top-winning obedience Husky for 1971, Ch. Kuno of Cinnaminson, C.D.X., owned by Larry and Lynn Frambes of Ventnor, New Jersey.

DICHODA

The kennel prefix Dichoda combines letters from the first three Huskies owned by Frank and Phyllis Brayton, who established their kennel in 1946. (Di)ngo, E(cho) and Gou(da) were the first Siberian Huskies shown in California and among the first west of the Mississippi. They had their first litter in 1948, when only 105 Siberian Huskies were registered with the American Kennel Club. They observe with concern that today registrations are numbered at over 10,000.

Dichoda is located in Escalon, California, in the San Joaquin valley, but the 25°F. temperature in winter and up to 108°F. temperature in the summer is of little concern to their dogs. All dogs and all litters have done nicely in their location. The Braytons show their dogs and use them for pleasure driving with a three-wheel training rig as a "sled." Siberian Huskies of their breeding can be found in teams from Alaska to New England.

In 1948 Ch. Dichoda's Aurelia, C.D., from their first litter also became the third Husky in the U.S. to earn both her championship and her Companion Dog title. And she did it in three shows with all scores above 190. Their Ch. Noho of Anadyr was never defeated in breed competition in the five years he was shown. The second copper champion was Ch. Dichoda's Roja, a championship which did not come easy, for it was accomplished at a time when "reds" were rare.

Ch. Monadnock's Rurik of Nanook was added to their kennel in 1961 and was owner-handled. He won Best of Breed at the Siberian Husky Club of America Specialty Show in Long Beach, California in 1964. It was at this same show that his daughter, Dichoda's Rurik Tika, was Best of Opposite Sex and his son, Czar Nicholas, was Winners Dog to complete his championship. Judge Lorna Demidoff also awarded him first in the stud dog class when eight of his get appeared in the ring with him.

Ch. Dichoda's Yukon Red was the number five highest-winning Siberian Husky in the USA for 1971 in the *Popular Dogs* Phillips System ratings, and number one on the West Coast. Although not heavily campaigned, he is a consistent winner; handled by Thomas Witcher, he is owned and bred by Frank and Phyllis Brayton, Dichoda Kennels in Escalon, California.

Ch. Czar Nicholas won Best of Breed at the 1966 Siberian Husky Club of America Specialty at Santa Barbara under judge Alice Seekins and was the first Siberian Husky owner-handled at Dichoda to place in the Working Group.

The greatest achievement of all was attained by the copper-coated, blue-eyed Ch. Dichoda's Yukon Red. Shown to his championship by Frank Brayton, he was turned over to handler Tom Witcher, and after being show just 14 times he was rated top-winning Siberian Husky in the United States according the Phillips System in 1967. Competition in California is now very keen, and this record was a fine achievement.

For the next five years after his 1967 rating he remained on the list of Top Ten Huskies although never heavily campaigned. Yukon was also the third Dichoda Siberian to win Best of Breed at a parent club Specialty Show. This win was under judge Lorna Demidoff in 1969 at Beverly Hills, California, where he went on to Group Second under judge Maxwell Riddle.

DOMEYKO

The Domeyko Kennels are owned by Peggy and Ed Samerson of Woodland Park, Colorado, and have been in existence for ten years. Since their beginning in the early 1960's the Samersons finished numerous champions and also work their dogs in harness. While they like to think of their dogs as pets first, they are also show dogs and sled dogs as well.

One of their outstanding show and stud dogs is Ch. Darbo Domeyko of Long's Peak. Darbo has taken a Best in Show and picked up ten Group Placings during his ring career. In 1967, 1968 and 1969 he ranked in the top ten list of Siberian Huskies according to the Phillips System ratings which appear in *Popular Dogs* magazine. Darbo's son, Ch. Domeyko's Zadar, has had three Group Placings and also ranked in the Top Ten Siberian Huskies in the 1971 Phillips System.

Ed Samerson is a licensed handler for several of the working breeds but takes a special joy in showing his own dogs in the show ring.

DONJU

In 1969 Martin and Judy Rosemarin established their Donju Kennels in Roslyn, New York. They keep two Siberians which they show, Ch. Donju's Devil of Yukon Red and Ch. Chilka's Treska of Weldon.

While they do not breed extensively, the Rosemarins are active in the breed and are members of the Siberian Husky Club of America. Mrs. Rosemarin headed the Committee for the Short Seeley Testimonial Dinner in the fall of 1971 which was such a tremendous success and great tribute to the matriarch of the breed.

Ch. Domeyko Zadar. Zadar has
had three group placings in his
show career and ranking in the
Phillips System during 1971. He
is owned by Peggy and Ed
Samerson, Domeyko Kennels,
Woodland Park, Colorado.

Nine-year-old Donna Rosemarin of Roslyn, New York, wins Best of Opposite Sex at the Monmouth County Kennel Club show in 1972 under judge Vincent Buoniello, Jr. with her Ch. Chilka's Treska of Weldon. A William P. Gilbert photograph.

The members of the committee for the testimonial dinner for Short
Seeley's 80th Birthday banquet were, left to right: Joseph Ens-
minger, Bob Shirone, Phyllis Buoneillo, Violet Schirone, Debby
Ensminger, Sy Goldberg, Judy Rosemarin, Martin Rosemarin,
Jean Fournier, Peggy Grant, Beryl Allen, Vincent Buoneillo. Photo
by F. Dysart.

Judy is also known for her photographic efforts where the Siberian
Husky is concerned. Some of her photographs are remarkably
beautiful, and many are featured in this book.

DUD'S

Clarence and Gladys Dudley, of North Syracuse, New York, while
only getting into the breed in 1970, have found almost phenomenal
success! Their American and Canadian Ch. Dudley's Tavar of Innisfree
was winner of Best in Show at the Ramapo Kennel Club in New Jersey in
November of 1972. Clipper's show ring successes have been impressive.
He finished his American Championship from the puppy classes at just 11
months of age, and under all different judges, and finished his Canadian
championship at 19 months.

Best of Breed and Group First on the way to Best in Show at Ramapo Kennel Club in November 1972 is the fabulous American and Canadian Ch. Dudley's Tavar of Innisfree. Breed and Group judge is Donald M. Booxbaum. Clipper is handled here by Mrs. Jane Huber for owners Clarence and Gladys Dudley of North Syracuse, New York. Clipper was whelped in November, 1969, sired by Ch. Alakazan's Nikolai *ex* Ch. Innisfree's Oomachuk.

By the time he was three years of age he had won 35 Bests of Breed, two Group Fourths, one Group Third, four Group Seconds, one Group First, and one all-breed Best in Show. Clipper was sired by Ch. Alakazan's Nikolai *ex* Ch. Innisfree's Oomachuk and was whelped November 3, 1969. He also has 19 Bests of Breed in Canada and was rated second-ranking Siberian Husky in Canada for 1971.

The Dudleys also own Canadian Ch. Dudley's Tava of Innisfree. Bred by Kathleen Kanzler and Ernest E. Schenk, Star finished her Canadian championship at 13 months of age and at the time of this writing is finishing her American championship.

EU MOR

Eunice Moreno established Eu Mor Kennels in 1962. After years of interest in Northern breeds she purchased her first Siberian from Fra Mar Kennels in Ohio. Fra Mar's Nao Diavol, C. D. was to be used in obedience and was to be the start of her dog team. During the next few

Ch. Eu Mor's Zhulek of Siber and litter sister, Eu Mor's Milaska, photographed in January, 1973. Eu Mor Kennels are owned by Eunice Moreno and Lynne Witkin, Long Island, New York.

years she purchased two bitches, and one, Gypsy Queen, produced 4 champions, all of which finished with majors, and her very own Ch. Eu Mor's Taiga.

In 1968 Eunice met her associate Lynne Witkin, and later they entered their ''pleasure'' team in some of the local races. When they began to win in 3-,5-, and 7-dog events they were hooked! Their kennel is situated on Long Island, New York, where snowfalls are undependable, so extensive racing was out of the question, but their interest continues; they are currently involved in operating the Smithtown Progressive School for Dogs, which offers obedience and breed handling classes.

The have also bred six champions, have finished four others, and have had two of their Huskies, Ch. Eu Mor's Zhulek of Siber and Ch. Eu Mor's Taiga, place in the Groups. They have completed three obedience titles, two C.D.'s and a C.D.X. Eunice has served on the board of the Owner-Handler Association and as a vice president on the board of the Siberian Husky Club of Greater New York. She is now a professional handler. Lynne was president of the Siberian Husky Club of Greater New York in 1972 and as past racing chairman she started the club's racing program.

For many years Nao and Eunice performed on an obedience drill team, and they have participated in public obedience demonstrations and in sled dog demonstrations. . .they've even made a TV commercial with a sea lion! Nao also at one point in her public performances chased an elephant around Roosevelt Raceway. Eunice explains that it is said that a Siberian will chase anything!

Their Ch. Eu Mor's Misty Morn and Ch. Eu Mor's Kiev are both C.D.X. title holders, and their kennel has many champions as well as C.D. dogs for them to be proud of.

FIRESIDE

Mr.and Mrs. Andrew Rossetto established their kennel in 1963 when they purchased a Siberian Husky for their daughter Diane as a 4-H Club project in dog husbandry. Diane trained, showed and finished American and Canadian Ch. Lostland's Leading Lady and also their American and Canadian Ch. Lostland's Trademark.

Not only did Diane Rossetto take top awards in her 4-H endeavors but with Leading Lady also won a 5-point major over 50 Huskies at the Detroit Kennel Club show as Best of Opposite Sex from the puppy classes, and she followed this with a Reserve win at the Chicago International show with an entry of 73.

Trademark, their stud dog, is the sire of three champions at the time of this writing, with several others pointed. Leading Lady is the dam of two champions to date, with other offspring pointed.

Fireside Kennels is situated at Walled Lake, Michigan.

American and Canadian Ch. Lostland's Trademark pictured winning Best of Breed under judge Connie Bosold at the Pontiac Kennel Club show in January, 1970. Here he is owner-handled by Mrs. Andrew Rossetto, Fireside Kennels, Walled Lake, Michigan. Norton of Kent photograph.

FORTSALONG

1963 saw the beginnings of Vincent and Phyllis Buoniello's Fortsalong Kennels in Northport, New York. They bought their first Husky from the Baltic Kennels of Mr. and Mrs. John Cline in Commerce City, Colorado. Since that time they have seen six Huskies of their own breeding finish for their championships, with several more pointed and

Ch. Fort Salong's Kemo of Baltic, owned by Mr. and Mrs. Vincent Buoniello, Jr. Photo by Judy Rosemarin.

well on the way. Vincent Buoniello became an American Kennel Club judge for Siberians in 1971 and has been very active in the show and racing circles.

The Buoniellos point with pride to their dog Ch. Chateauguay's Charlie and the great human interest story behind him. Charlie was given to the Buoniellos when he was seven years old. They felt the dog had something to offer the breed and began showing him. In less than one year Charlie had become champion and had sired his first litter! Before joining the Buoniellos the dog had done nothing but work. . .he raced on some of the better racing teams in New England; he is still enjoying the racing scene, running wheel position on a 5-dog team in the New England races for the Buoniellos and is sharing a family life as well!

The Buoniellos are active in the Mid-Atlantic Sled Dog Club races in New York, New Jersey, Pennsylvania and Virginia. Charlie's zest for running still continues to delight them, as does his devotion to his family. They are also particularly pleased that Charlie's get are pointed and have majors while working toward their show ring championships!

FOURNIER

Atlantic Highlands, New Jersey is the site of Jean and Rift Fournier's kennel with the distinguished name of Fournier's Siberian Estates. The Fourniers established their kennels in the late 1960's and have been winning since their inception, with outstanding Siberian Husky dogs and a real dedication to the breed. Their bitch, Ch. Dovercrest Alehta Pesna, C.D. was their very first Siberian Husky and she was top-winning Husky for the state of New Jersey in 1970 and 1971. She has had but one litter at the time of this writing, and two of the puppies became champions. She is shown with her litter sister as a brace; they were the top-winning brace in New Jersey with two Working Group Firsts and winner of one National Specialty brace win. She also ran lead dog on a 5-dog sled team for two years.

She is the second Siberian Husky in New Jersey to obtain dual titles of Champion and Companion Dog, which she attained in 1971. She is also a charter member of the Garden State Siberian Husky Club Obedience Team. All of the Fournier Siberian Estates dogs have distinguished themselves, as have their owners. Jean was winner of the Top Driver Award in New Jersey for 1970-1971. She accumulated the most points in the racing program and is also the only regular lady driver now competing in all Mid-Atlantic Sled Dog Racing Association events in the 5-dog class. She is editor of the Garden State Siberian Husky Club newsletter since 1969, Secretary of the Garden State Siberian Husky Club since 1971, and Secretary of the Mid-Atlantic Sled Dog Racing Association.

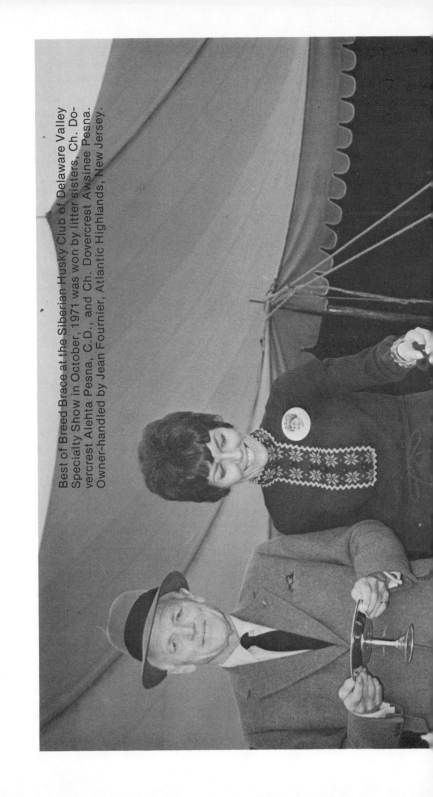

Best of Breed Brace at the Siberian Husky Club of Delaware Valley Specialty Show in October, 1971 was won by litter sisters, Ch. Dovercrest Alehta Pesna, C.D., and Ch. Dovercrest Awsinee Pesna. Owner-handled by Jean Fournier, Atlantic Highlands, New Jersey.

Ch. Fournier's Zachariah of Toko going Best of Winners on the way to his championship in August, 1952, at Newton Kennel Club under judge Short Seeley. Owner-breeder-handler is Jean Fournier of Atlantic Highlands, New Jersey.

Jean has also been Production Manager of the Siberian Husky Club of America newsletter since 1971, Secretary of the New Jersey Dog Federation in 1971 and 1972, and Trophy Chairman for the Monmouth County Kennel Club for 1971, 1972, and 1973. She was the originator and coordinator of the Garden State Siberian Husky Club's 1973 calendar. This was the first time that anything of this type has ever been printed in the breed.

Jean Fournier is a member of or delegate to the New England Sled Dog Club, Siberian Husky Club of Delaware Valley, Pennsylvania Sled Dog Club, Siberian Husky Club of America, Garden State Siberian Husky Club, Dog Owners Association, Mid-Atlantic Sled Dog Racing Association, International Sled Dog Racing Association, New Jersey Dog Federation, Monmouth County Kennel Club, Dog Fanciers Club (New York) and the Bayshore Companion Dog Club.

Some of the Fourniers' other top dogs are Ch. Fournier's Tiffany of Toko, who attained her championship from Bred by Exhibitor class at 1½ years of age and was top winning bitch in New Jersey for 1972; Ch. Fournier's Zachariah of Toko, shown to his championship from Bred by Exhibitor class and wheel dog on Jean's 5-dog team; and Ch. Dovercrest Awsinee Pesna and Ch. Cinnaminson's Soaya Fournier, co-owned with Sy and Ann Goldberg.

Jean's proudest "claims to fame" are being the only breeder to ever finish two dogs in one year from the Bred-by-Exhibitor class and winning the parent club's Racing-Working Trophy for 1973!'

FRA-MAR

Marie Wamser's Fra-Mar Kennels in Cleveland, Ohio, has produced two Best in Show dogs since its beginning in the late 1950's. American, Canadian, and Bermudian Champion Fra-Mar's Soan Diavol is perhaps her best known dog, and is the son of her other illustrious Best in Show winner, Ch.Frosty Aire's Alcan King.

Ch. Fra-Mar's Soan Diavol with owner Marie Wamser handling her dog to a win under judge William Kendrick. The Fra-Mar Kennels are in Cleveland, Ohio.

King was top stud dog in 1968, and Ch. Fra-Mar's Misarah was top brood bitch. This same year Soan was top Siberian Husky. His record is one Best in Show, 37 Group Placings in the U.S.A., five in Bermuda, and six in Canada. King finished his championship undefeated and was the second Husky to win Best in Show in America, which he did in 1964. He is the sire of 11 champions, 5 of which placed in the Groups and, of course, his Best in Show son Soan.

Soan was handled and finished by his owner within 29 days at just 14 months of age. He was #1 Siberian Husky in 1966, 1968, and 1969 according to the Phillips System Ratings, and was Top Siberian Husky in Canada in 1970.

While Marie is actively engaged in business with her husband, is an avid gardener, and plays several musical instuments she hastens to add she is now judging the breed!

THE HULEN KENNELS

While the Hulens do not have an official kennel name, they have been associated with the breed since Mr. Hulen bought his first Siberian Husky in 1944. It was one of only fourteen registered with the American Kennel Club in 1943.

Mrs. Hulen became involved with breed activities through her love and admiration for their first dog, and for eight years she wrote the Siberian Husky Club of America newsletter and was Husky columnist for the *American Kennel Gazette* for ten years.

The Hulens currently own Ch. Monadnock's Echo, a bitch which lived as a staked-out team dog until she was four years old and then became their house pet! She was "crash campaigned" in the show ring, where she completed her championship with all major wins, and was handled for the Hulens by Damara Bolte. The Hulens reside in Washington, D.C.

KAMAR

Martin J. Carlson got his first Husky in 1966 and has been running teams since 1967. Carlson, who stables about a dozen Siberians behind his trailer home near the Allegheny River in Warren, Pennsylvania, is sold on the Northern breeds and took naturally to the Husky after deciding his first love—the wolf—would not be practical to keep.

Carlson, a teacher by profession, enjoys both showing and racing his dogs, and is active in the races scheduled by the Jackson Valley Country Club. Some of Carlson's top show dogs in addition to those bearing the Kamar prefix are Kuno of Koryak and Fra-Mar's Ember Diavol.

KANTUA

Frank and Marie King's Kantua Kennels in Coalinga, California,

BEST OF
OPPOSITE SEX

Ch. Monadnock's Echo, pictured here completing her championship by going Best of Opposite Sex under judge Robert Waters at the Lancaster Kennel Club in May, 1969. Echo lived as a stakedout team dog until she was four years old and then went on to attain her championship with all majors. She is handled by Damara Bolte for her owner, Katherine (Mrs. Bertram D.) Hulen of Washington, D.C.

consists of 11 Siberian Huskies and was established in the late 1960's. They finished Ch. Kiska of Kantua, but their main interest is in racing and they take great pride in the fact that Frank makes his own sleds.

Through Kiska the Kantua Kennels stock was founded on the Dichoda lines; at the age of nine Kiska was shown as a veteran and won the Best of Opposite Sex Trophy at a Kern County Kennel Club show, and she went on to win five more Best Opposite Sex awards the same year. From time to time she still practice runs with the Kings' wheel cart and sled, but her daughter Koya Czarina of Kantua has beaten her out of her lead position.

In every other way, however, the Kings will tell you, of 11 of their dogs, Kiska is the boss!

KARNOVANDA

Karnovanda began in 1959 with a puppy bitch which later became Ch. Eska's Nonie, U.D. While Judith Russell and her husband were graduate students in California, Nonie was bred to Ch. Monadnock's Pando, and the foundation stock for the Russells' Karnovanda Kennels was established. Puppies from this breeding were to become Ch. Baron of Karnovanda, C.D., and Ch. Karnovanda's Zenda, C.D. After moving to Minnesota the Russells obtained a seven-month-old red male puppy from the Frosty Aires Kennels. He was to become Ch. Frosty Aire's Jolly Red Giant, another of their foundation dogs. Zenda produced ten champions to date.

Three of the Karnovanda males have rated in the Top Ten Siberian Husky listings for a number of years. Owner-breeder handled Ch. Karnovanda's Wolfgang won Best in Show at the Macomb Kennel Club Show in July, 1972. Wolfy has also won at three Specialty Shows and has 51 Bests of Breed, 21 Group Placings, and the aforementioned Best in Show.

Karnovanda usually keeps from 20 to 30 adult Huskies and some young stock, and litters are whelped and raised in the house with the house dogs. Present location for Karnovanda Kennels is in Davisburg, Michigan. The Russells have three children and Mrs. Russell teaches junior high school mathematics full time as well as maintaining the kennel.

KAYLEE

Carolyn McDonough Windsor started her Kaylee Kennels in 1968 in Baltimore, Maryland, though the name Kaylee was adopted only after she had been in the breed for three years. She had always been impressed with the stories of the Great Serum Run in Alaska. She bought her first Siberian sight unseen from the Fischers in Canonsburg, Pennsylvania in March, 1968. This dog was her Ch. Arahaz' Tengri Khan. He was just eight months old at the time, and her joy at owning Tengri has never ceased. Several other Huskies were purchased shortly thereafter from the Arahaz Kennels.

Carolyn Windsor is founder and President Emeritus of the Chesapeake Siberian Husky Club and also a member of the Siberian Husky Club of America, the Siberian Husky Club of Delaware Valley, the all-breed

Catonsville Kennel Club and the Dog Owners Training Club of Maryland. She also researched the AKC stud book through 1956 and presented the results of her work to the parent club.

All seven of the Kaylee Huskies run free in a large fenced-in area. Tengri has sired 80 offspring, though the Windsors themselves have bred but one litter—and kept them all! Carolyn's daughter Sue is also active showing and helping care for the dogs.

Ch. Karnovanda's Wolfgang, pictured winning the breed under judge Joseph Faigel. Owner-handled by Judith M. Russell, Karnovanda Kennels, Davisburg, Michigan.

KEACHI

Karl and Patricia Hahn, Jr., established their Keachi Kennels in Anchorage, Alaska, in 1966. Keachi Kennels is a small kennel, as Pat Hahn explains it, out of necessity, so the Hahns are exceptionally selective about their stock. While there are but four Huskies in residence, they are all American Kennel Club champions. There is Ch. Baranof Koyukuk, Ch. Joli Badga, Ch. Keachi's Eltigre Torvo and Ch. Monadnock's Kiana of Keachi.

Best Working Dog at the Alaska Kennel Club show in 1968 under judge Theodore Wurmser was Ch. Keachi's Eltigre Torvo, owned by Karl and Patricia Hahn, Jr., Keachi Kennels, Anchorage, Alaska. Pat Hahn handling.

Ch. Keachi's Eltigre Torvo has two Bests of Breed and a Group First and Third to his credit, and has defeated more dogs in Alaska than any other Siberian Husky in history, making him Alaska's top-winning Siberian. His sire, Ch. Baranof Koyukuk, is undefeated from the time of his first win in 1967, having four consecutive Bests of Breed and a Group Second and Group Third. He is number two top-winning Siberian Husky. The newest member of the kennels is Ch. Monadnock's Kiana of Keachi, who distinguished herself by finishing her championship with three 5-point major wins, two of them in Alaska and one in Oregon.

In addition to her kennel, Pat Hahn is chairman of the Bibliography Committee for the International Siberian Husky Club.

LAMARK

Elsa and Alfred Marchesano of Levittown, New York, are the owners of the Lamark Kennels. The kennel was established in 1963, and by 1970 their Ch. Savdajaure's Eska Lamarchese, C.D. was Winners Bitch and Best of Opposite Sex at the Westminster Kennel Club Show in New York City. In Eska's first litter of four, three went on to finish for their championship within one year.

The Marchesanos are active in the breed, with Mrs. Marchesano serving as president of the Siberian Husky Club of Greater New York in 1973, and are active in showing, breeding and racing.

MARLYTUK

The Marlytuk Kennels of Mr. and Mrs. Lyle Grant go back to 1958. The original Marlytuk stock came from the Cold River Kennel, whose dogs had been purchased from Harry Wheeler in Ste. Jovite, Quebec, who had purchased his dogs from Leonhard Seppala when Seppala came east in the 1920's.

Peggy Grant has always felt it was important to have a sled team, and the Grants have raced with the New England Sled Dog Club and have done well. Their Ch. Loonah's Red Kiska became a champion at just nine months of age and is the dam of Ch. Marlytuk's Red Sun of Kiska, with over 60 Bests of Breed awards and several Group Placings to his credit. She is part of a brace with her son, and they have won 5 Best Brace in Show awards.

Best Team in Show at the Western Pennsylvania event in 1973 was Carolyn Windsor's four look-alikes, handled by her daughter Sue. The BIS judge was Mrs. Helen Walsh, and the Group judge was Mrs. Maynard K. Drury. Dogs are Ch. Arahaz' Tengri Khan, his grandson, Kaylee Kitkit Kaykikay, his brother Kaylee Kitkit Kulik and Tengri's son Arahaz' Kaylee Konkon. Mrs. Windsor's Kaylee Kennels are in Baltimore, Maryland. William Gilbert photograph.

Ch. Savdajaure's Eska Lamarchese, C.D., pictured on the way to finishing for her championship. Eska, handled by Alan Levine, is owned by Elsa Marchesano of Levittown, New York. Evelyn Shafer photograph.

Best Brace in the Working Group at the Eastern Dog Club show in December, 1962 went to the Marlytuk Kennels entry, Ch. Koonah's Red Kiska and Ch. Marlytuk's Red Sun of Kiska. Owners Mr. and Mrs. Lyle L. Grant of Carlisle, Massachusetts. Evelyn Shafer photograph.

Red Sun for two years was the #2 Siberian Husky, and he is winner of two Specialty Shows,at the Philadelphia event in1970 and in 1971 when the show was held in Cleveland. The Grants have finished 10 champions since 1956.

NOMAD

Robert Dickson Crane of Vienna, Virginia established his kennel in 1935 with the purchase of his first Siberian Husky. She was a handsome bitch from the first Foxstand stock, with litters going back to the 1930's and 1940's. After a hiatus during the 1950's, Bob Crane reactivated his kennel in 1963 under the Nomad prefix. His major achievement has been to highlight the importance of breeding for the natural qualities of the original Siberian Chukchi sled dog.

Mr. Crane believes that, as he puts it, "The breed's strongest point is the still outstanding uniformity of the natural or "primitive" behavioral characteristics in the gene pool which evolved during 3000 years of ecological adaptation in the Siberian Arctic."

One of Robert Crane's outstanding show dogs was Ch. Nomad's Chuchanka, a bitch whelped in October, 1965 and shot as a suspected wolf in October of 1967. His Ch. Nomad's Shane is a lead dog on Lynne Witkin's team in New York.

Robert Crane has done an enormous amount of research on the breed over the past years and considers the breed's important qualities today are AKC conformation, the inherited desire to run long distances, and the ability to build rapidly from endurance training.

NORSTARR

David and Alice Marie Angel are owners of the Norstarr Kennels in Rockford, Illinois. The kennel began about 1965 with a pet quality Husky, but the Angels loved the breed so much they began to look around for some top quality dogs to breed.

A dog they bred, Norstarr's Baanchi, was exported to Finland and won a Best in Show in that country. He is owned by the Siren family there and is also used for sled work. Baanchi's sire was Ch. Frosty Aire's Banner Boy, C.D., *ex* Ch. Koryak's Cherda of Norstarr, C.D.

Another of their Siberians, Ch. Alakazan's Saanki, finished for his title with four major wins in seven shows at the age of 13 months. Monadnock's Elsa is another of their top brood bitches.

PANUCK-DENALI

Laconia, New Hampshire is the location of the Panuck-Denali Kennels, owned by Charlotte B. Anderson and her daughter Judith.

Their kennel was established in 1963 with a male Husky from the Savdajaure Kennels in Ashland, Massachusetts. In 1966 they purchased Doonauk's Gidget, and when these two were bred, the puppies established the Panuck-Denali Kennels.

For a long time the Andersons have been interested in the white

Ch. Koryak's Cherda of North Star, C.D., owned by Dave and Alice Angel. Cherda was sired by Ch. Kineki of Koryak *ex* Monadnock's Kira of Koryak. Norstarr is located in Rockford, Illinois.

Husky and now have three, Prince of Calivali, their team leader and stud dog, and Alaakon's Attu and Snowbear of Denali. The latter two are brother and sister and hold great promise.

The Andersons have finished champions, and Judi drives their five-dog team in the New England Sled Dog Club races, placing well in the top half of Class B, five-dog professionals.

Ever since 1971 the Andersons have been invited to represent the New England Sled Dog Club and give an exhibition of racing Huskies at the Hartford, Connecticut Winter Sports Show each October. This four-day show has resulted in a great deal of good publicity for the breed due largely to the beauty and training of the Panuck-Denali dogs.

Ch. Savdajaure's Panuck, founding stud at the Panuck-Denali Kennels owned by the Andersons of Laconia, New Hampshire. Panuck was from the Forsberg Kennels and is a grandson of Ch. Monadnock's Pando and a full brother to the Forsbergs' Ch. Savdajaure's Cognac.

POLAR STAR

Susan E. Gumb and her husband Bob are the owners of the Polar Star Kennels in Bedford, Massachusetts, which dates back to 1965. They did not originally plan to show or race, but bought their first puppy for their daughter, who was in 9th grade at the time and ran a Junior Team for five years.

Daughter Susan, who is now a grown young lady, was also an assistant timer for the New England Sled Dog Club for three years. Bob Gumb has been a senior race manager for several years. Susan is a member of the parent club, and Mrs. Gumb is active in the Yankee Siberian Husky Club. She was chairman for the 1972 spring match, and trains their sled dogs.

The Gumbs have two cats and a Welsh Corgi (Pembroke) as other pets, but the real "star" at Polar Star is Admiral's Panda of Polar Star. He was lead dog on their three-dog team and has also run one-dog. He also runs on a five-dog team.

ROWANS

Bob and Nancy Trundle have been active in Siberian Huskies since 1964, in North Lancaster, Massachusetts. The year after their marriage they got their first Husky and soon started a family of two children—a boy and a girl—and 23 dogs.

Racing is their chief occupation with the dogs, and by the time Robin Trundle was eight years old she had won nine trophies in two years of racing in Class A. Nancy goes in for pleasure racing, but both children race in competition, as does Bob, and he has managed to come up with an upper class B team from the dogs which they have raised themselves.

The Trundles admit that their entire lives are centered around the dogs and building a fine racing team, and somehow all the hours of cleaning, feeding, watering and grooming are forgotten when the dogs do well!

RUNAWAY FARM

Runaway Farm Kennels is owned by Dr. and Mrs. Daniel Rice III in Shrewsbury, Massachusetts. The Rices bought their first Husky, Mulpus Brooks The Reno, in 1955, and started breeding nine years later with their original bitch, Monadnock's Czarya.

Active in racing, all the Rice team dogs are descendants of this bitch, Czarya, and all are bred for sled use and pleasure and racing teams. Mrs. Rice believes she is the only competitor who breeds, raises, trains and races her own dogs. All the dogs are matched black and white and wear bright red padding and pompons on their harness.

Her lead dogs have been Czarya's Kier, Czarya's Valeska and Gilena's Lara leading with her son Lara's Vodka.

Along with New England Sled Dog class trophies her team has won the following special trophies: 1970, Siberian Husky Club of America Racing Trophy; 1971 and 1972, Monadnock Racing Trophy; 1972 Gaines Racing Trophy, and in 1971 the Douglas Fairbanks Racing Trophy.

SETTING SUN

Clyde and Catherine Halcomb's interest in Siberian Huskies began in 1961 when while visiting friends the heat went off and the friends had their two Huskies sleep with them for warmth! They bought their first Siberian in 1962 and over the years have tried to sell to show homes and to breed sound dogs which would be a credit to the breed.

They are members of the Siberian Husky Club of America and the Northern California Siberian Husky Club. They are also working toward obedience degrees for each of their dogs and race more for pleasure than for "speed." The Halcomb children are now taking up sledding, and it was an exciting moment for the family when

Anezeka of the Setting Sun took Best of Breed at the Sierra Nevada Dog Drivers Match Show in 1971.

Clyde Halcomb also enjoys dressing up as Santa Claus at Christmas time and having a team of Huskies deliver Santa Claus and his season's greetings to the neighborhood children!

The youngest Best in Show Brace in the history of the Siberian Husky—or perhaps any breed! Just six months and three days old, Setting Sun's Sunny Vnoochka and Setting Sun's Miss Vnoochka win under judge Maxwell Riddle. The same day the Vnoochka Kennels took Winners Bitch and Best of Opposite Sex, and Sunny was Reserve Winners. These beautifully matched Huskies were bred, owned and handled by Kay Halcomb, Setting Sun Kennel, Portola, California. This remarkable pair also took Best Brace in show at the Golden Gate Kennel Club show in San Francisco.

SNOANA

Arthur and Mary Ann Piunti of Hobart, Indiana started their kennel in 1960. Ch. Frosty Aire's Banner Boy, C.D. brought fame to their kennel and has sired 29 champions up to the time of this writing. Banner Boy finished his championship at the age of 10 months, and while he never won higher than Group Second, he placed in the Working Group 18 times, always handled by his owners. His daughter, Ch. Sno-Ana's Kenai Suzee, was Best of Winners at the 1965 Specialty Show.

The Piuntis' Frosty Aire's Norvik is a C.D.X. dog and races as well, as does Banner Boy. The Piuntis have finished more than half a dozen champions and are more than proud of Banner Boy's record which is as follows: Top Producer for three consecutive years, 1970 through 1972; was one of the Top Ten Siberian Huskies in the Phillips System Ratings several times, and was Best of Breed winner at the International Kennel Club show in 1964 and 1968.

Arthur Piunti is both an obedience judge and approved to judge both Siberian Huskies and Alaskan Malamutes in the conformation classes.

SNO-DAK

Lillian Peitzman of Mapleton, North Dakota boasts that her first Siberian Husky was a great one! It was all white and brown-eyed and became American and Canadian Ch. Little Sepp's Story of Sno-Dak, C.D.X. Whelped in September, 1955 this beautiful bitch was one of the few Huskies to attain a C.D.X. title; she died August 10, 1968.

SNOMOUND

J. Jack Bean, owner of the SnoMound Kennels in Minnetonka, Minnesota, began in 1958 with a brood bitch named Marina of Mulpus Brook Farms and a stud dog, Ch. Inuk. Over the years he has sold puppies to most of the states in the U.S.A and to Canada.

Ch. Frosty Aire's Inuk of SnoMound was the second highest-winning Husky in 1963 according to Phillips System listings, and many of his offspring are Group and Group Placement winners. Also many are lead and team dogs in the Colorado, Oregon and Illinois areas, and he is the sire of American and Canadian champions.

One of the SnoMound dogs became the mascot for Northern Illinois University.

SO HUCK

Bill and Emily Kirkman, owners of the So Huck Kennels in Warrens-

Ch. Frosty Aires Inuk of Snomound, owned and shown by J. Jack Bean of Minnetonka, Minnesota. Inuk and his owner were photographed in May, 1964.

burg, Illinois, have been in the kennel business on a small scale since 1966. They started with a small puppy, Frosty Aire's So Cold. She gained her championship with 11 of her 15 points from the puppy class and finished at the age 1 year and 10 days.

Their kennel now consists of eight black and white Siberians; two are champions, two have obedience titles, and four have points toward their championships. The Kirkmans also have a German Shepherd, which was with them before the Huskies and has helped then raise and herd the eight Siberians. At times he has even been known to allow himself to be hooked up to the sled with them! This at times seems to be beneath his dignity, since Baron Von Huck is a C.D.X. dog and knows the requirements for U.D. only when the mood strikes him!

Ch. Aniko of So Huck, stud dog from Bill and Emily Kirkman's So Huck Kennel in Warrensburg, Illinois. A Dorothy Bender photo.

The Kirkmans and the Huskies participate in community activities a great deal by appearing in parades, with Santa Claus, for United Fund, etc., in addition to their show and obidience work. Their Ch. Aniko of So Huck finished for his title in eight shows and has two Group Placings to his credit.

SUBAHKA

The Subahka Kennels (Subahka is the Siberian word for dog) are owned by Roger and June Reitano of Tok, Alaska and were established in 1966. In the subsequent years nine dogs were finished from their kennel. Not only are the Subahka dogs bench show champions, but all are raced in open competition in Alaska as well as five other states. Roger Reitano emphasizes, ''All our dogs are show caliber which are bred from proven working stock *only*.'' The Reitanos have won many races and broken many records in Alaska. Roger is also a licensed handler for 15 breeds, judges match shows, and teaches obedience.

Top Subahka dogs are Ch. Tucker of Chilkat, a Best in Show winner, Ch. Subahkas Red Cedar, a Group winner, Ch. Subahka's Shoom, also a Group winner, and Subahka's Shang, Roger's pure white lead dog. With these dogs the kennel has won the Siberian Husky Club of America's Racing Trophy two years in a row and is the winner of four Siberian Husky Club of America Dual Achievement Awards (given to dogs which excel in both racing and show ring); Tucker was awarded the bronze medallion for the Outstanding Siberian Husky in 1971 offered by Raymond Dworsky (they broke two Alaska trail records in Tok and

Fairbanks) and Tucker was also his lead dog when Roger raced in the Anchorage Fur Rendezvous in Fairbanks, plus the Tok Race of Champions.

Tucker won a Best in Show in May, 1972 in Canada, where he is a champion and has other Group wins, even though he is ten years of age and is still racing. Roger estimates he must have over 1,000 miles of racing on him.

The Reitanos' Red Cedar dog was the 1972 winner of the Alaska State Junior Championship one-dog race, defeating teams from Anchorage, Fairbanks and Tok, and he is also ten years old!

In October, 1973 the movie *The Mad Trapper of the Yukon*, starring many of the Subahka sled dogs, including both Tucker and Red in leading roles, was released. Roger plays the part of Eli Zane in the movie, and he drives a dog sled throughout the picture. This movie is based on a true story taken from the records of the Royal Canadian Mounted Police. While the Reitanos lived in California Roger also appeared in two television specials covering the breed, the Reitano kennel and dogs and their training and racing operation.

The Reitano kennel harbors thirty to forty dogs, and the Reitanos exhibit in all the Alaskan shows along with keeping up with their racing schedule. Roger was also a director in the International Sled Dog and Racing Association for three years, while Dr. Lombard was president. His greatest claim to fame is the fact he has much of Dr. Lombard's running Siberian Husky bloodlines in his kennel, and Roger is confident that he will win the Big Alaska Races in the future!

Roger Reitano also enjoys building his racing sleds, and also builds them for other team drivers. He has also been a columnist for dog magazines and has written for the Siberian Husky Club of America newsletter, and for the International Siberian Husky Club of America.

SYNORDIK

The Synordik Kennels of Richard T. Nist, M.D., and Cynthia R. Nist, Ph.D., had its beginnings in 1970 in a one-bedroom apartment in the graduate students' residence at the Rockefeller University in New York City. The Nists raised three puppy bitches and went to shows, and as they put it, "sat at the feet of the masters" for three years while they studied dogs.

In June, 1972 they moved to California, where they now have eight dogs selected from Monadnock, Marlytuk and Savdajaure breeding.

Their Tara's Rhory has had several Bests of Breed over Specials while finishing, and their first litter, sired by Rhory ex Ch. Koritea of Kettle Moraine, was productive.

Tara's Rhory, pictured winning under judge Len Carey at a recent California show. Rhory is owned by Dr. Richard and Dr. Cynthia Nist of the Synordik Kennels, Snohomish, Washington.

Cynthia Nist is a cell biologist and molecular geneticist by profession; Richard Nist is in pediatrics and now a resident in obstetrics and gynecology at the University of Washington in Seattle.

TANDARA

Mrs. M. W. Patterson, Jr. enjoys obedience work with her dogs, and most of them have at least one title. During the seven years Tandara has been in existence in Gig Harbor, Washington, Lynne Patterson has finished her Çh. Juneau of Tandara and Ch. Kayak of Martha Lake, C.D., and has also put C.D. titles on Lyn's Kotzebue; and Tandara's Zarevna Tatiana C.D.X. is currently working on her Utility Dog title.

While wanting to maintain a small kennel, Lynne Patterson is concentrating on obedience and runs her dogs in teams, but she actually has no intention of getting into racing, since time does not permit. But she is proud of the fact that her Ch. Juneau of Tandara was #7 in the *Kennel Review* ratings and #10 in the Phillips System for 1970.

A pretty pair of puppies from True C. Giffen's Verite Kennels in Moorestown, New Jersey.

TASKAN

Tom and Randy Hacker got started with their kennel in January, 1967 and have been showing ever since. One of their outstanding show dogs is Ch. Tvarski of the Midnight Sun, and he is also their stud dog. They are a small kennel and maintain the one champion stud and have two pointed bitches which will be the basis of their kennel, located in Milwaukee, Wisconsin.

They are members of the Siberian Husky Club of America and the International Siberian Husky Club.

TOKOL

John and Martha Hankowsky of Poway, California, have been interested in Siberian Huskies since the early 1960's. Their Ch. Dichoda's Tokusak, C.D., was owner-handled in both the show ring and obedience. Olivet, a beautiful white with black pigmentation, was their second Husky, and the combination of the two dogs' names was the basis for their Tokol Kennel name.

Mr. Hankowsky states that when Tok was first shown it was unusual for a Siberian Husky to win Group placings in the show ring, but Tok did! It is also mentioned that Tok was the only red and white Siberian shown in northern California at that time. His color was unusual, and he brought much attention to the breed.

TUN-DRA

Deane and Roma Cheadle's Tun-Dra Kennels are located in Nunica, Michigan, where there is plenty of snow. And it is a good thing, since the Cheadles are most active in many phases of the dog fancy—particularly Siberian Huskies. Not only do they breed, show and work their dogs pulling sleds, but have sold puppies to owners in thirty of the United States.

Deane also carries a complete line of supplies and equipment for sled

Ch. Juneau of Tandara is pictured winning a group Fourth for owner Lynne Patterson of the Tandara Kennels, Gig Harbor, Washington. Juneau was whelped in 1864. Lila Weir, handler.

Ch. Tvarski of the Midnight Sun, stud dog for the Taskan Kennels, owned by Mr. and Mrs. Tom Hacker of Milwaukee, Wisconsin.

Ch. Dichoda's Tokusak, C.D., owned and shown to bench and obedience titles by his owners, John and Martha Hankowsky of the Tokol Kennels in Poway, California. Tok was finished ten years ago, and at that time was the only red and white Siberian shown in northern California. He also managed to capture a couple of group placings during his show career, which was also most unusual in the breed ten years ago.

dog racing and harnesses which has been sold in the United States, Canada and some foreign countries as well. Tun-Dra Kennels began in 1960.

USSURI

Kenneth W. Fowler became interested in Siberian Huskies in 1963 while he was in the Air Force in Tacoma, Wasington, and helped a friend run his Husky. Three years later, he bought his first Siberian as a pet. Then his interest in the breed grew still further, and as more and more Siberians began to appear Ussuri came into being.

Kenneth Fowler has helped found and served on the board of directors of a Missouri sled dog club and is a member of the Siberian Husky Club of America and the International Siberian Husky Club. His top show dogs are Ch. Cossack of the Midnight Sun, Ch. Natashia's Tatany of Ussuri, and coming up is Ussuri's Russian Nomad. One of his show dogs has a Group Placement, and his pedigrees bear the names of some of the breed's top Best in Show winners.

VALESKAMO

Florissant, Missouri is the location of the Valeskamo Kennels of Mr. and Mrs. Kenneth Grahn. Started in 1964, the Grahns consider their kennel small but have shown their Ch. Alakazan's Valeska to her C.D. title. They were the first in their area to both show and breed and personally handled their foundation bitch to her championship and obedience title. She finished her obedience work in three trials, and is also a lead dog on what Mrs. Grahn describes as a "just for fun team."

The pedigrees of their dogs are basically founded on the Alyeska and Monadnock lines, and they pride themselves on having a few top quality bitches which they breed to top quality studs.

To the best of their knowledge they were the first members of the Siberian Husky Club of America in the state of Missouri, and their Valeska was the first Husky champion and obedience title holder in the St. Louis area. Eleanor Grahn states further that the only other champion to date in their area is a daughter of Valeska, so they share the glory.

WINSUM

The Huskies at the Winsum Kennels of Warren and Winnie Keefer in Rocky Ridge, Maryland are a family project, with Mom, Dad and the kids all actively engaged in the sport of dogs. Started in 1963, the Keefers only began showing around 1967 and are enthusiastic racing fans.

Daughter Schelly is tremendously involved with the dogs and whelps

Two Valeskamo bitches owned by Eleanor Grahn . . . Annuschka and Kelly, important parts of the kennel operation at her Valeskamo Kennels in Florissant, Missouri.

Ch. Miss Frosty Aire of Tun-Dra, lovely Siberian Husky owned by Deane and Roma Chaedle of the Tun-Dra Kennels, Nunica, Michigan. The Chaedles both race and show their dogs.

puppies—something she has been doing since she was eight—and is in charge of their feeding and training. She has hopes of becoming a veterinarian. Son Warren is in charge of the runs, Mother takes care of correspondence and Dad trains.

While their first dog was not top quality, it did lead them into the breed, and when the time came to get into actually breeding and establishing a kennel they bought the best breeding stock they could find. Since then they have been showing and racing all their dogs and always give them unusual Russian names. For instance, their stud dog is Ch. Winsum's Salacious Sergei and their top brood bitch is Ch. Karnovanda's Kinetic Katya. The Keefers show along the Eastern seaboard and race as well. With daughter Schelly and son Warren they travel around in a van with

Winning at the show! Warren and Winnie Keefer are pictured in this Ashbey photograph with Ch. Winsum's Salacious Sergei on the left and Ch. Winsum's Sagazcious Stepan on the right. Winsum Kennels features both show and racing Siberian Huskies.

Canadian Ch. Petya of Monadnock, pictured finishing for his championship and on to Group Fourth. Owned by Raymond and Paula Miner of the Woody Glen Kennels in Penacook, New Hampshire.

Ch. Kaptain Kijes Kommand, Siberian Husky show dog owned by Barbara and Kenneth Kauffman of the Yakutska Kennels in Burnsville, Minnesota.

the dogs to enjoy the sport racing. At Winsum the dogs are definitely a "family affair"!

WOLFDEN

The late 1950's saw the establishment of Beryl Allen's Wolfden Kennels in Jaffrey, New Hampshire. Ch. Tosca of Monadnock and Ch. Wolfden's Copper Bullet are two of the outstanding show dogs which have brought fame to Wolfden. While they have been breeding and showing only since the late 1960's, their success has been great with Ch. Wolfden's Copper Bullet winning the 1972 Siberian Husky Club of America Specialty Show over 42 Specials and an entry of 240. . . .the largest to date at that time. He was #5 Siberian Husky in the *Kennel Review* System and has several Group Placings to his credit, after finishing for his championship at 18 months of age.

WOODY GLEN

1963 saw the establishment of the Woody Glen Kennels of Raymond and Paula Miner of Penacook, New Hampshire. It began with one bitch and four puppies. The Miners believed then, as they believe now, that a Siberian Husky must be a good racing dog as well as have good breed conformation, and they have been active in the racing of their dogs since the beginning of their operation.

Through these efforts they have won the Millie C. Remick Trophy, Milton Seeley Trophy and the Memorial Trophy, all awarded by the New England Sled Dog Club and awarded for excellence in different phases of racing.

Their kennel boasts about twenty Siberians, and the Miners claim the record for the largest litter in the breed: twelve puppies, and all survived and the dam took care of them all. Their current team consists of the mother and ten of her puppies! Their Canadian Ch. Inatuk of Woody Glen is half way to her American championship at the time of this writing.

Like so many other breeders, Ray and Paula are concerned about over-exploitation of the breed, so keep their breeding program within reason with the purpose of breeding good quality racing and show Siberian Huskies.

YAKUTSKA

Barbara and Kenneth Kauffman have been operating their Yakutska Kennel in Burnsville, Minnesota since 1961, though their experience with dogs and breeding goes back to 1940.

Selective breeding for quality has produced Ch. Alexoff Ot Yakutsk, C.D. and Ch. Kaptain Kije's Kommand. Like so many other breeders and lovers of the Siberian Husky breed, the Kauffmans admire most the temperament of the dogs which have kept them in the fancy since they discovered the breed.

Two of Vivienne Lundquist's Siberians peek out a porthole aboard the Lundquist yacht they live on in Marina Del Rey, California.

CHAPTER 4
THE BREED IN OTHER PARTS
OF THE WORLD

THE BREED TODAY IN CANADA

Mrs. J. W. Anderson established her Racecrest Kennels in Ontario, Canada, in 1958. Her Ch. Racecrest's Bandit is her top stud dog and has been active at the Canadian Kennel Club shows. Mrs. Anderson also enjoys showing her dogs in Obedience; her bitch Shady Lane's Kolyma Princess has earned her Companion Dog title.

Mrs. Anderson believes the temperament of the Siberian Husky is of prime importance when considering a breeding program, and she breeds for quality, not quantity, at Racecrest.

Whelped in March, 1961, Bandit finished for his Canadian Championship at 15 months of age, undefeated in the classes. He has three Group Placings as well. He was also Breed Leader in all-breed competition in Canada in 1962, and was handled for his owner by Lorna Jackson.

Judge James Trullinger declares a win for Mrs. J.W. Anderson's Ch. Racecrest's Marika's Katrina.

OTHER CANADIAN KENNELS

Other Canadian Siberian Husky owners in Canada include the Jeffrey Braggs, Mr. Ian McDonald, Mrs. Robert Auslitz, Mr. J. M. McDougall, Mr. Robert Murray and Mrs. Clare A. Vipond. All of these people are members of the Siberian Husky Club of America, thereby helping to keep their interest in the breed alive in both their country and the United States.

THE BREED IN ENGLAND

Through the combined efforts of Lt. Commander William Cracknell and Mr. Derrick C. Iverton, the Registrar of the Kennel Club in England, the Siberian Husky is now recognized as a breed in Great Britain. Early in 1969, when Lt. Col. Cracknell was assigned as a naval liaison officer with the Ministry of Defense in England, his Siberian Husky, Yeso Pack's Tasha, won great admiration. She survived a lengthy quarantine, lengthy because of the then-present rabies scare in Britain, but was released in July, 1968. The Kennel Club was initially going to register Tasha in the Husky category, but Cracknell and Mr. Iverton managed to establish the Siberian Husky as an individual breed, and Tasha became the first Siberian Husky registered in England.

Upon her release from quarantine, the Cracknells imported a mate for her. They imported Savdajaure's Samovar from the Forsbergs' kennels in the United States. While they showed only sparingly while in England,

Across the seas . . . Lisbeth Leich in Kent, England, sends this lovely picture of two of the Leichs' Siberians.

Sally Leich and a litter
of puppies in Kent,
England.

they entered many times and won many prizes. They returned to the United States in the early 1970's with their original pair, but left in England the puppies from two litters from the above mentioned dogs.

When the rabies scare abated in England and the quarantine was reduced to the usual six months, additional Siberian Huskies were imported into England. Peter Proffitt of Lancashire purchased two from Helge and Benedict Ingstad's kennels in Norway. They were named Togli and Killik of Brattali.

Don and Liz Leich returned to England from America in 1971 with their Doushka of Northwood and Ilya of Northwood. That same year they established their Forstal Kennels in Kent. The Leichs were the first English people to register a Siberian Husky kennel in the United Kingdom, and consider themselves "pioneers" in the breed over there. They have won numerous awards and Best of Breed with Ilya in a rare breed class as well as awards in variety classes. Their puppy,Nanuska, is the only red and white Siberian Husky in England.

The Leichs attend obedience classes also, but in England "the retrieve" is included even in the beginners' classes, and so far they have gotten only one of their dogs to do this consistently. The Leichs also have a training cart for the dogs; like all other Siberian Husky enthusiasts in England, they are hoping that the law that now exists forbidding the working of a dog in harness will be repealed.

Part of the great and growing interest in the breed in England is due to the efforts of Mrs. Stella-Colling Mudge, president of the Husky Club of Great Britain,who has championed the breed for many years.

Mrs. Leich informs us that as of the beginning of 1973 there are approximately 30 Siberian Huskies in England. They've come a long way since the first import in 1969 and the first registered litter of seven (three males, four females) born on May 30, 1971.

103

The bitch with blue eyes is Lumimaan Alasuq, owned by Mrs. Benedicte Ingstad-Sandberg of Norway. Photo by Kerttu Alm.

THE BREED IN NORWAY

In 1958 Molinka of Bowlake made her appearance in Norway and was bred to a Siberian Husky which had been exported to that country some time before. The Siberians caught on in Norway, much to the credit of Benedicte Ingstad, who established the breed and is still said to be active today.

Other exports to Norway followed Molinka, and about the time of her appearance in Norway, three other Bowlake Siberian Huskies were exported to France.

THE BREED IN FRANCE

A French airline pilot imported three Bowlake Siberian Huskies, but in France (as in Switzerland) the cross breeding with France's recognized Greenland dog destroyed the purebred Siberian Husky lines, and the breed did not flourish or even establish itself to any degree.

A young male, Lumimaan Tojon, owned by Mrs. Kerttu Alm, Ulvila, Finland. Tojon is the son of Mrs. Alm's Ch. Anya-Alaska and Finnish Champion Ahtojaan Tanoo. Tojon has one certificate. . . he needs three to be a champion in Finland. Photo by Kerttu Alm.

SIBERIAN HUSKIES IN FINLAND

The Siberian Husky first appeared in Finland in 1965, where Mrs. Kerttu Alm imported a puppy from Switzerland. Mrs. Alm's Lumimaan Kennel was established this same year with her Finnish Ch. Anya-Alaska, a bitch she imported from Switzerland. Anya was the first Siberian Husky in Finland and has whelped five litters to date. Her sire was the International Ch. Savdajaure's Paavo, imported to Switzerland from the United States, and her dam was Maya v. Nordpol.

Another of Mrs. Alm's outstanding Huskies is a son of Anya, Lumimaan Tojon. Mrs. Alm has also exported four Siberian Huskies, Nor-

The first Siberian Husky in Finland, the bitch Ch. Anya-Alaska owned by Mrs. Kerttu Alm, Ulvila, Finland. The picture was taken in the summer of 1972, when Anya was seven years old. Mrs. Alm took this photograph herself.

wegian Champion Lumimaan Alasuq and Lumimaan Salka, both bitches, and two males, Lumimaan Talvi to Switzerland and Lumimaan Ukko-Pekka to Norway. Mrs. Alm is pleased to say they are all used for sledding.

As a dedicated breeder Mr. Alm is somewhat concerned about the appearance of monorchidism in the breed, along with faulty bites, dogs which are too heavy, faulty coats and too much curve to the tails.

Lumimaan Panuck and Anya-Alaska take off across the snow in this beautiful Finnish snow scene. Photo by Kerttu Alm.

Stina Blomquist of Nickby, Finland and her three-dog team. Green Berets Snowy Angara is in the lead, with Finnish Ch. Ahtojaan Pikoo and the white Husky Green Berets Snowy Anusjka behind.

Northern dog breeds, especially Siberian Huskies, have been commemorated on stamps issued by a number of different countries. Shown here, for example, are (left) Finnish semi-postal stamps portraying the Siberian Husky in a snowy woodland setting; a United States issue (center) commemorating Arctic explorations; and (right) a recent Greenland issue showing a sled-dog team and its driver.

A picture of Anya-Alaska as a young bitch which makes her owner state that "I think she has a drop of wolfblood. . ." Photo by J. Wirmavirta for Anya's owner, Kerttu Alm, Finland.

Finnish Champion Ahtojaan Pikoo, sired by Ch. Monadnock's Konyak of Kazan out of Kanakanaks Kishka, and owned and imported to Finland by Stina Blomquist of Nickby, Finland.

International Champion Norstarr's Baanchi, owned by Mr. Sakan and Mrs. Elsa Siren of Luhalann, Finland. Baanchi has sired about 70 puppies, and his show record is most impressive, including Best in Show wins. He was bred at Mrs. David Angel's Norstarr Kennel in Rockford, Illinois by Ch. Frosty Aire's Banner Boy, C.D., ex Ch. Koryak's Cherda of North Star, C.D.

A young puppy and his thrilled young owner photographed in Switzerland by photographer Rita Trainin.

We are most grateful to Mrs. Alm for the magnificent photographs she sent us which appear in this book and were taken by her as well.

Also in Finland, and active since 1966, is Stina Blomquist of Nickby. All of her dogs are shown in conformation rings and are used as sled dogs and are raced. Stina Blomquist was winner of the Ladies Championship Race in 1971, 1972 and 1973. The few litters Stina Blomquist plans will be bred for both showing and racing quality.

Her kennel features Finnish Ch. Ahtojaan Pikoo (Ch. Monadnock's Konyak of Kaza ex Kanakanaks Kishka), Green Berets Snowy Angara and Green Berets Snowy Anusjka. Pikoo is an American import, and Angara and Anusjka she imported from Holland. Their ancestry goes back to the Alaskan Kennels in the USA. Pikoo was also the winner in 1968 of the Ladies Championship Race with his mistress and was rated one of the "Top Ten" in Finland.

THE BREED IN HOLLAND

In 1965 a puppy exchange was made between the United States and the Netherlands, where a Miss Elizabeth M. R. Urlus had been promoting the breed for several years. She imported Kayak's Thunder Taku and Vaskresenya's Tanana Taku, the first Siberian Huskies to appear in Holland.

Other Dutch Siberian Husky enthusiasts are Mrs. L.J. H. Van Leeuwen, Mr. Bareld Van Der Meer, Ernst Muller-Tuoff and Mr. Josef Felder.

110

Dingo-Alaska was the male lead dog when Mr. Joseph Felder won the Best Swiss Musher in 1971. This happened in a Swiss sled dog camp in the Swiss Alps. Mr. Felder is the breeder and owner of this dog. Dingo-Alaska is pictured at 16 months of age. Photo by Mrs. Kerttu Alm.

SIBERIANS IN SWITZERLAND

The Siberian Husky more than likely appeared first on the European continent in the early 1950's, and the first of record were exported to Switzerland in 1955 from America. They were named Grey Cloud of Little Tanana and Winemuca of Little Tanana. They were followed by Manitoba of Little Tanana. Grey Cloud was the first Siberian Husky to become an International Champion, and, unfortunately, died in 1959.

It was only after 1963, when the Swiss Club for Northern Dogs was established, that cross-breeds were frowned upon and Siberian Husky owners began once again to have interest in promoting the purebred Siberian Husky.

More importing from the United States began at this time when Winnie of Whalom arrived in Switzerland; she was followed in 1964 by Savdajaure's Paavo, and Arctica of Baltic, which went to Switzerland with Mr. Thomas Althaus, who fell in love with the breed while he was an exchange student at Colorado College. Today's Swiss Siberian Huskies are of such quality that they are being exported to establish and improve bloodlines in Italy, Holland, Germany and Finland.

Before this breakthrough in 1963 the Alaskan Malamute, the Samoyed, the Greenland Dog, the Norwegian Elkhound, the Karelian Bear Hound and the Akita Inu, as well as our Siberian Husky, came under the protection of the Swiss Club for Northern Dogs. This organization maintained a firm hold on the breed, much more so even than any breed club in this country.

Annually, or semi-annually, the official breed clubs hold a meeting for a selection of dogs worthy of breeding. No dog receives papers unless his parents have also passed this breeding selection and abilities test.

First of all they maintained that the dog must be one year of age or older, must be X-rayed and declared by a veterinarian to be free of hip dysplasia. The dog is weighed and measured and examined thoroughly by a judge and the president of the breeding committee for any and all breed disorders or major faults. Even character defects are duly noted on the record for their registry.

The club has a record of every dog and bitch in the country to record which are and which are not eligible to be bred, thereby giving them complete control of any breeding programs. They further declare that no dog under 18 months of age is eligible to be bred and only six or fewer puppies per litter are allowed. Furthermore, breeders must put their dogs through this judging every three years, and even non-members of the Swiss Club for Northern Dogs must have the club approval of their dogs if they wish to breed.

In Denmark the first breeder of Siberian Huskies was Mrs. Grethe Westring, and here we picture her first bitch, Allerlies Candy, with her three-week-old puppies.

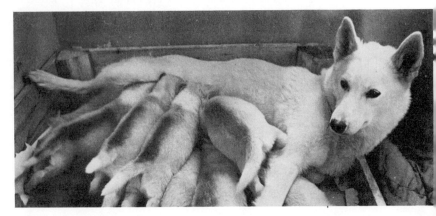

These are rather stringent methods of control, to be sure, but they have held quality high in Europe and eliminated further cross-breeding of the Northern breeds, and establishing beyond doubt quality in the individual breeds, which is, after all, what we are striving for all over the world.

THE FEDERATION CYNOLOGIQUE INTER-NATIONALE

The Standard for the Siberian Husky was officially recognized by the Federation Cynologique Internationale (FCI) in June, 1966. The FCI is the top European organization in the world of dogs and was formed in the early 1930's. It is the central governing body and is composed of a few selected representatives and delegates of each of the national kennel clubs whose purpose it is to standardize breeds and shows. They establish the rules for the shows, select the recognized breeds and put them in their groupings and settle all disagreements which might arise within the establishing of International Championship titles. Their group consists of 21 member countries and 13 associate member countries. They issue points toward the titled called the Certificate of Beauty and Aptitude.

The International Champion title is the highest award a dog can achieve. Before a dog can be called an International Champion, he must have received the CACIB certificate four times, at four different shows in three different countries (including his home country) and under three different judges. The CACIB certificate stands for Certificate of Ability to Compete for the Title of National Champion and can be compared to the United States Winners Dog or Winners Bitch wins in that they are receiving points toward their titles. CACIB wins are earned from the Open Classes.

While there is a Youth Class for dogs from 10 to 15 months, the minimum age for Open Class is 15 months, so most European dogs are entered in the Open Class starting with their very first show at exactly 15 months of age. They are working toward their championship from their very first ring appearance. There are at times classes for braces or groups of the same breed, but there are no Specials Classes as we know them in this country. Champions also compete from Open Class, and there is no Best of Breed, Best of Winners, or Group judging, nor is there any Best in Show award in Europe.

In Switzerland, the title is awarded for one year's duration only! If a dog competes and wins again he is said to be a Plural Swiss champion.

Other countries give CAC's as well. Three of these certificates give the right for the dog to be called Champion of France, or Champion of Italy, etc., for a lifetime. These hard-won multiple titles and championships keep the Europeans entering dog shows on a fairly regular basis.

The Siberian Husky is judged in Europe by those judges qualified to judge all the Northern dog breeds, or by an all-breed judge.

CHAPTER 5
PINNACLES IN THE BREED

In the world of sports there are always heroes who stand head and shoulders above the crowd and go down in history as great leaders in their field. While everyone who has owned a Siberian Husky can claim, to some degree, a part in bringing the breed to the attention of the public, special praise is due to a certain few exceptional people who pioneered in the breed and were instrumental in the Siberian Husky's taking its rightful place in the world of dogs.

Here, then, are the success stories of some of the pinnacles in the breed, people who with their devoted dogs went all the way to fame and greatness in making their memorable contributions to our breed.

LEONHARD SEPPALA

Leonhard Seppala, born in Skyjaervoy, Norway, lived a long, full life and had the great pleasure of becoming a legend in his own time. He, perhaps more than any other single person, established the Siberian Husky breed in the minds of dog lovers and sled dog racing enthusiasts. Today, almost a half century later, one of his heroic feats, his part in the Great Serum Run, lives on as a historic highlight in the history of the breed.

In 1914 Seppala emigrated to Alaska and got involved in sled dog racing. A ski champion in his native country, he had some experience driving freight teams in the gold fields of Alaska and transporting supplies to and from the railroads from Nome. His first Siberian Huskies, which he had acquired less than a year before he came to Alaska, presesented a challenge to him. Seppala decided to race the dogs and pit his skill against the racing heroes of the day.

These dogs were given to Seppala by his friend Jafet Lindeberg. Lindeberg had intended to hand them over to Roald Amundsen for his expedition to Alaska, and Seppala was training them for the trip. World War I cancelled plans for the expedition, and Seppala used the dogs to enter the 1914 Sweepstakes.

This first exposure was a complete disappointment to Seppala. He had to withdraw from the race after a series of mishaps which included sore feet on several of the dogs, frostbite, blizzard conditions and an almost fatal accident along the trail. But in actuality this bad start only served to fire his determination to return and to succeed. . .and the following year he did! Victory was doubly sweet. . .his future wife, Constance, was Queen of the All-Alaska Sweepstakes. They were married and later had one child, a daughter, Sigrid.

Seppala went on to win the race again in 1916 and 1917, and he claimed that his chief reward was his pride in proving the stamina of the Siberian Huskies when he brought them across the finish line in such magnificent condition.

The All-Alaska Sweepstake victories were followed by the Borden Handicap, Borden Marathon, Ruby Derby, and the Yukon Dog Derby, to name a few. Breeding his own team dogs while he was winning was also a source of great pride to him. During this period of intensive breeding came Seppala's most famous dog, and one of the most famous dogs in the breed, Togo. With Togo in the lead Seppala and his team of Huskies won races and did rescue work in the mine fields and logging camps, making a wonderful reputation for themselves.

But Seppala's chief service to his fellow man came about in 1925, during what has since been referred to as the Great Serum Run. A diphtheria epidemic broke out in Alaska and wiped out whites and Eskimos alike along its path. Many drivers participated in that 655-mile relay run between Nenana and Nome, but it was Leonhard Seppala who had the longest and most arduous stretch of it, proving his strength and stamina and driving ability.

Seppala was honored for this contribution by Washington's Senator Dill, who introduced the account of the Serum Run into the Congressional Record. Sportsman Lowell Thomas paid additional tribute to Seppala at the Alaskan Press Club Banquet in Anchorage in 1961 by saying, ". . .but justice was never done as the eyes of the world were focused on Alaska and the man who made the final dash into Nome and had driven his dogs only a few miles when as all the drivers who actually took part in the Serum Run none but Seppala mushed more than 55 miles."

A certificate was awarded by Governor Bone to Seppala for his heroic service in the Nome Diphtheria Crisis. It read: "In the Name of The Territory of Alaska Grateful Recognition and Appreciative Acknowledgment are Hereby Given to the Self-sacrificing Service Rendered by Leonhard Seppala in response to humanity's call in speeding relief by dog team to the diphtheria sufferers at Nome during the epidemic in January-February, 1925. His prompt performance of duty under severe climatic conditions and hardships stamped him as a true Alaskan and will ever be remembered by his fellow-countrymen. Given under my hand and the Seal of the Territory of Alaska, in Juneau, the Captial, this 4th day of

March, in the year of Our Lord one thousand nine hundred twenty five. Scott C. Bone, Governor.''

In 1927 Seppala was invited to compete in the sled dog races in New Hampshire. He not only competed but broke all records in the New Hampshire events and Canada while doing it! Seppala did much in those early days to endear the Siberian Husky breed to all, and he helped Huskies gain future recogntion with the American Kennel Club. Important pedigrees today still bear traces of the names of the dogs brought to the New England scene in the late 1920's.

Seppala retired to Seattle, Washington, in 1948, and lived there until his death from a cerebral hemmorhage on January 28, 1967. The true character of this great man can best be captured in his own words. When asked what he considered to be his greatest achievement, he did not recall the prize money he won or the speed records he had set or even the deeds he had done: he replied simply that his greatest satisfaction was in the good influence he had had toward the better treatment of sled dogs in Alaska!

Small wonder his name has become synomynous with greatness, strength and with the breed!

TOGO, ONE OF THE BREED'S MOST REMARKABLE DOGS

There are many memorable and remarkable stories to be told about man's uncanny relationships with dogs. If you are interested in the Northern breeds, and Siberian Huskies in particular, the story of Togo is one that must be told, the story of Togo and the remarkable Leonhard Seppala.

Togo's parents came to Seppala's kennel from Siberia. His dam, Dolly, though gentle, was an independent bitch which took a special delight in Suggen, the lead dog on Seppala's team. Both dogs had come from the Kolyma River region of Siberia. It was Suggen who saved Seppala's life on the 400-mile grueling trail in the 1914 All-Alaska Sweepstakes race. There was a raging blizzard and they strayed off the path and came within twenty feet of dropping over a precipice which dropped down 200 feet. Seppala just managed to stop the team in time, and it was Suggen who, sensing the danger, obeyed his commands and successfully pivoted the team around to a reverse position and headed back up the mountain once again.

From this skilled, intelligent sire and gentle dam came Togo. Born in Little Creek, Alaska, he was originally the property of Victor Anderson, though bred and raised by Seppala and his wife. An Englishman named Fox Ramsey had first imported Siberians to Alaska, and these dogs represented the early beginnings of the breed there. Togo was an "only child" and was spoiled because of it. He was small and not very attractive; only Constance Seppala could handle him. When he was six months old Anderson gave him to Mrs. Seppala for her trouble. Like other arbitrary adolescents, Togo ran away from home a few times only to be brought back again by the Seppalas before he finally made up his mind to stay with them. He teased the other dogs by snapping at their heels and biting their ears and in general was a nuisance to Seppala.

But the day was to come when it was more important to Togo to impress than to distress Leonhard Seppala. It happened one November day when Leonhard headed off with a friend and a team for Dime Creek. Togo wanted to go along and had to jump a seven-foot fence to do it. His foot was badly injured when it caught in the fence; a kennel man had to cut him free, but he took out across the snow to follow Seppala in spite of it.

After running all night to catch up with Seppala and his group, he spotted them the next morning. At first the two men thought it was a fox bearing down on them, but as Togo came up to the team and bit the ear of the lead dog, Seppala knew it was Togo! Seppala was impressed with the fortitude of the dog from that moment on, and a close relationship which was to last a lifetime was spawned. Togo ran free with the team for a while before Seppala took out an extra harness and started him out close to the wheel.

Togo's spirit made for a quick promotion; he was soon up near the lead dog, and when they reached their destination at the end of the day's run he was in the lead with old Russky. Seppala realized that Togo, like his father before him, was a born lead dog. From then on he was Seppala's favorite. How could he be denied, an eight month old puppy running 75 miles his first day in harness and pulling in ahead of the team! Togo's respect for his master earned him the reputation of being a "one man dog."

In the years that followed Seppala had Togo out on the trails training. All during the winter of 1919 they crossed the peninsula a total of six times. Togo was stubborn at times, with a mind of his own, but always Seppala realized he possessed all the attributes of the perfect lead dog—a lead dog he had been trying to breed for a long time.

Seppala was out on the trail when the scheduled April Borden Race was to be run, and he had very much wanted to run against Fred Ayer's team. He thought they would miss competing, but the people of Nome demanded that the Kennel Club invite Seppala to run once he returned. Seppala accepted with great pleasure, and over Fred Ayer's objections.

The race was run in May, when it was warm, which put Seppala's dogs at a disadvantage. But they ploughed ahead and even passed Fort Davis, where they were missed by the people, and who therefore thought they had lost the race. But they crossed the finish line in Nome, breaking the speed record by 55 seconds. Seppala's time was 26 miles in 1 hour, 50 minutes, 25 seconds, a record which stood for many years in Alaska, Canada and the United States. It also proved Seppala's firm belief that Siberian Huskies could run equally as fast as any other dog. Siberians at that time were mostly believed to be at their best only on long, steady hauls.

Seppala and Togo were to share many exciting times together, both racing and with their miraculous rescue work against amazing odds. In 1921 Major John Gotwals, Chief Engineer of the Alaska Road Commission, hired Seppala to proceed from Nome to Nenana. Many exciting experiences occurred during this 400-mile adventure, including Togo's participation in a relay race to save the life of a banker. By the end of that year Seppala and Togo had logged nearly 8,000 miles. This feat helped Togo earn another of his many deserved titles. . .this one, the most traveled dog in the world!

In 1923 Togo and Seppala won the Borden Race again, beating the nearest competitor by 12 minutes, and made several trips over the Seward Peninsula with Seppala's friend Roald Amundsen. In 1924 they traveled to Nenana once again, which kept them in good training condition for the most important event in their lifetime. . .the 1925 Great Serum Run.

Seppala was chosen to carry the serum for the terrible epidemic in the area. He got off with a rousing send-off with his lead dogs, Togo and Scotty, and 18 other Siberian Huskies, on one of the most heroic and difficult missions in Alaskan history. Along the trail he would leave some of the dogs behind to be cared for by the villagers and readied for the return trip.

Originally Seppala had been asked to run the whole distance with the serum, but the epidemic was spreading so rapidly that it called for a relay race, and when Seppala reached Golofnin he learned his job was done. They had covered about 96 miles all told, more distance than any other team, and returned home tired but with the satisfaction of a job well done.

This event marked Togo's last long run. He was used only sparingly thereafter, and in 1927 he was presented to Elizabeth Ricker (Nansen) to spend his last years at her home in Poland Springs, Maine. In a letter to Mrs. Ricker dated February 15, 1927, from Frank Dupresne of Fairbanks, Alaska, this event is commemorated as follows:

". . .I wonder if you realize what a beautiful gift you have received. Up here in Alaska where sentiment gives way to cold reality we think superlatively of Seppala and his wonder dog. They have been unseparably linked for the past ten years, and one does not speak of one without mention of the other."

"We in Alaska envy you the gift of this dog, 'Togo,' but find consolation in knowing the appreciation he will receive in your hands, and of the very high esteem in which Leonhard must have held you to part with his gritty little pal of the trails. I congratulate you on your wonderful gift of the greatest little racing leader in the history of Alaskan Sweepstakes."

This is just a brief revelation of the wonderful life of Togo and his feats of bravery. More about him appears in a delightful book titled *Togo's Fireside Reflections*, by Elizabeth M. Ricker, published in 1928. But most of Togo's life is recorded on the pages of the history books on the great state of Alaska!

ARTHUR TREADWELL WALDEN AND CHINOOK

Arthur Treadwell Walden left his home in New Hampshire and headed for the Alaskan gold fields in 1896. He was not as caught up in the idea of striking it rich as he was with the idea of what could be accomplished by using the native dogs and sleds for freighting purposes. His endeavors along these lines won him renown of one of Alaska's best-known dog-punchers.

In later years he was to gain additional fame with a book he wrote entitled *A Dog Puncher on the Yukon*, the story of the freight dogs and their uses in Alaska. Later still he handled the training and the conditioning of the dogs for Admiral Byrd's expeditions; the training was carried on at his Chinook Kennels in Wonalancet, New Hampshire. It was at his Chinook Kennels that Milton and Short Seeley got to know the breed and eventually purchased and took over Walden's kennels, still operated by Short Seeley today. The Seeleys also became involved here in the training and conditioning of the Byrd expedition dogs. Walden firmly believed that a dog team could go farther "on its own food" than any other team in the world and did much to prove his belief.

Walden's most famous dog was Chinook, after whom he named his famous kennel; it still carries that name today. Walden said of his dog, "One of the best dogs I ever owned was Chinook, a large, half-bred MacKenzie River Husky. I got him in Dawson in 1898. The man who owned him had used him as a one-man's dog. He wouldn't sell him for money, but I traded him for three sacks of flour, worth sixty dollars a sack, and two sacks of rolled oats, making two hundred dollars in all. He claimed that Chinook could start a heavier load than any other dog in the Yukon. He cried when he left, carrying his food." Walden rejoiced at his good fortune!

MILTON AND EVA "SHORT" SEELEY

Short Seeley deserves her title of Matriarch of the Breed. In 1971 she celebrated her 80th birthday and almost a half century of devotion to the breed at Wonalancet, New Hampshire, at her world-famous Chinook Kennels. The name Chinook came from Arthur Treadwell Walden's lead dog which won the dog sled race of the first International competition between Canada and the United States in Berlin, New Hampshire, in 1922. The Seeleys eventually purchased the Chinook Kennels from Walden and established the great interest in sled dogs and sled dog racing which thrives today. For this Siberian Husky devotees shall be eternally grateful.

Eva Brunell Seeley, known today as Short Seeley, was born and brought up in Worcester, Massachusetts, and prepared herself for a teaching career. In 1922 she was Director of Sports at the Bancroft School in Worcester. At Bancroft she met Milton Seeley, also on the school staff and a brilliant chemist, and they were married in May, 1924. It was while on their honeymoon mountain climbing in New England that they first met Arthur Walden and his dog team. They ordered a son of Chinook before their visit had ended and they knew they were "hooked" on the breed.

For reasons relating to Mr. Seeley's health, in 1928 they moved to Wonalancet, where there was great activity going on at the Chinook Kennels. Intensive training was underway for dogs which were to accompany Admiral Byrd's expedition.

Milton Seeley instantly saw the need for a substantial diet for dogs which would be expected to endure the hardships of the frozen North, and he brought all his knowledge of chemistry to bear in order to perfect just such a diet for them. While his formula was never patented, it was undeniably the basis for some of our best commercial dog foods today.

Arthur Walden went along with Byrd on one of the expeditions and took Chinook with him. Unfortunately, Chinook did not return. Short and Milton went into partnership with Walden before he left and kept the inn and the kennel running while he was in Antarctica. It was during their first winter at the Chinook Kennels that Short learned to drive a team, and her interest in racing and sled dogs became firmly established in her heart.

When the Seeleys first arrived at Chinook, a Siberian Husky bitch named Toto caught their attention. They leased Toto, a daughter of Leonhard Seppala's lead dog, Togo, which had been left with Walter Channing, and they bred her to Moseley Taylor's blue-eyed black and white lead dog, Tuck. Toto had one lone female puppy which the Seeleys named Tanta of Alyeska. They also managed to get her accepted as a trial bitch by the American Kennel Club. At her first dog show in Manchester, New Hampshire, she won Best of Breed over the nine males competing!

Receiving the awards presented to her for her outstanding contributions to dogs, especially Siberian Huskies and Alaskan Malamutes, Short Seeley reflects on her years of activities in the dog world. Judy Rosemarin and Sy Goldberg deliver two more plaques to commemorate her achievements.

When Arthur Walden returned from the Byrd expedition, he sold his share of the kennel to the Seeleys. They built new kennels on the present site and in 1932 moved into what was intended to be the museum and trophy building when their house burned down.

Tanta was bred to a male named Duke which had come from Seppala's bloodlines in Alaska; one of the litter, Togo of Alyeska, was purchased along with six others by Moseley Taylor to be driven as a team by his wife, Lorna. Lorna Demidoff, as she is now known, is another of the great people in the breed, and she is still driving her pleasure teams today. Her successes and contributions to the breed are recorded in this chapter also.

At least three more expeditions were made by Admiral Byrd, with the dogs all being trained at Chinook Kennels, and it was during this time that the friendship between Admiral Bryd and the Seeleys developed. Also during this time the Seeleys' interest broadened to include the Alaskan Malamute, and it was largely through their efforts that this breed became recognized and registered by the American Kennel Club. In 1932 Short drove a team of Malamutes in the Olympics at Lake Placid, New York and brought additional fame to the breed. A second Chinook team was driven by Norman Vaughan and included their Tanta of Alyeska as a member of that top team.

With World War II raging in 1942, Army dogs were being assembled at the kennel. Dogs for search and rescue units used in the war were trained at Chinook. Many dogs were offered by members of the New England Sled Dog Club drivers, and several went off to Camp Rimini in Montana for training.

Milton and Short were very active with the New England Sled Dog Club; Short served the club as secretary for many years, while Milton served as president and as a member of the executive committee. Eventually both were made life-long honorary members. All during their time as active officers and racing participants with the group, their interest extended to include the children of the members of the club. They were successful in establishing a Junior Sled Dog Club. This juvenile extension of the parent Club is still most active today, with as many as 60 teams competing at their events.

In 1937 Short started to organize a breed club and to set the Standard for the breed. She asked Dean Jackson to help her set up an organizational meeting to be held on April 19, 1938, in Cambridge, Massachusetts, to do just that. At this meeting, where a constitution and by-laws were laid down, and a Standard, the list of those present included Lorna Demidoff, Richard Moulton, Millie Remick, Dean Jackson (officiating), and, of course, Short Seeley. Short served the club in just about every capacity and in 1963 was given a life membership.

Milton Seeley died in 1944, but Short never had any doubt in her mind about maintaining the kennel herself; she continues to do so with help from the young people in the area who have helped Short make the Chinook Kennels a popular tourist atraction for dog lovers from all over the world.

Short Seeley's interests extend beyond the dog world. For many years she was an active worker for the Republican Party on all levels, and she includes congressmen, senators, governors and presidents among her personal friends. We include in this chapter a letter sent to Short on the occasion of her 80th birthday by President Richard M. Nixon.

On October, 1971, in the city of Philadelphia, a testimonial dinner was given in Short Seeley's honor to commemorate her 80th birthday and to pay tribute to her many accomplishments in the fancy. Some of the accomplishments mentioned in a "This Is Your Life, Short Seeley" pageant were her initiating the Siberian Husky and Alaskan Malamute Clubs, her formation of the New England Sled Dog Club, being a breeder-owner of the first Siberian Husky bitch to become a champion, being the only woman to be given a military award by President Eisenhower, and receiving the award from Admiral Richard Byrd as Chief Consultant for the Sledge Dog Division of Operation Deep Freeze.

An acknowledgment of this testimonial dinner and a list of these accomplishments was read into the Congressional Record on October 29, 1972, by the Hon. Norris Cotton of New Hampshire.

THE WHITE HOUSE
WASHINGTON

October 5, 1971

Dear Mrs. Seeley:

On your eightieth birthday I am delighted for the opportunity to join your many friends in wishing you every happiness and all the satisfaction that a full, active life such as yours has earned.

As you look back on a half a century of dedication to showing and raising sleddogs you have much to be proud of. Your special work in helping to perpetuate the Alaskan Malamute and Siberian Chukchi Sleddog is to be applauded as an important contribution to the preservation of the heritage of the native peoples in the American and Asian Arctic.

I know that I am joined by countless fellow citizens who value and appreciate your efforts in wishing you all the best on this milestone and in the years ahead.

Sincerely,
Richard Nixon

LORNA B. DEMIDOFF

Training all her dogs to harness and driving her team is now, and for many years has been, Lorna Demidoff's greatest pleasure. Lorna was just 16 when her parents moved to Fitzwilliam, New Hampshire, and it was there that she had her first ride behind a team; she decided then and there that someday she would have her very own team.

Lorna married Moseley Taylor, publisher of the *Boston Globe*, and a sportsman in his own right who had imported several racing Siberian Huskies from Alaska. Early in their marriage they lived in Massachusetts while the dogs were kept in Fitzwilliam. Lorna's kennel was established in 1931, and she took its name from the Monadnock Mountains. It was primarily a racing kennel for about 25 years, with Lorna racing in top competition. Roger Haines became their kennel manager and helped train the teams for racing; he drove the team in the 1932 Olympics Exhibition Race.

Ch. Monadnock's King going Best in Show at the Mohawk Valley Kennel Club show in November, 1961, under judge Mrs. Edward P. Renner. Arnold E. Houck, show chairman and Miss Suzanne V. Bellinger, president of the Club, present the trophies. Breeder, owner and handler Mrs. Lorna B. Demidoff of the Monadnock Kennels, Fitzwilliam, New Hampshire. Evelyn Shafer photograph.

Ch. Monadnock Akela, top stud dog at Mrs. Lorna Demidoff's Kennels in the early 1970's. Bernice Perry photograph.

Lorna began showing in the conformation classes in the 1930's to have something to do with the dogs during the summer months, and she finished her first champion, Togo of Alyeska, in 1939. Togo was purchased from the Chinook Kennels and was a fine lead dog in the racing competition and racked up many victories at several of the New England Sled Dog Club races. Lorna's first homebred champion was Panda of Monadnock, finished in 1941. Other top racing and show dogs were Ch. Belka of Monadnock, Ch. Otchki of Monadnock, C.D., all racing leaders, and Ch. Monadnock Norina, Ch. Monadnock Penelope and Ch. Monadnocks Zita, leaders of her pleasure teams.

In 1941 Lorna married Prince Nikolai Alexandrovitch Lopouchine-Demidoff, a Russian nobleman who emigrated to the United States during the revolution in his country. Many champions and racing greats followed, since Lorna wanted them to excel in both fields, but just how many champions with the Monadnock name there are Lorna does not know, since she does not keep score. But it is safe to say she has won all the big important shows a couple of times over and has the silverware and the ribbons to prove it!

While Lorna still derives a tremendous amount of pleasure from driving her pleasure teams in the Monadnock Mountains, she is also active as a judge of Siberian Huskies and several other breeds.

DR. ROLAND LOMBARD

The highly respected Dr. Roland Lombard is a veterinarian in his mid-sixties from Wayland, Massachusetts; he is also the world's leading sled dog driver of all time. He is a past founder of the Siberian Husky Club of America and his kennel name is Igloo-Pak, which means ''House of the White Man'' in Eskimo language.

Dr. Lombard was 14 years old when his interest in sled dog racing manifested itself. It was in Poland Springs, Maine, and the 1927 race featuring winning teams and drivers like Leonhard Seppala and Arthur Walden from New Hampshire who did so much to spur interest in the sport with teams from his famous Chinook Kennels.

It was his tremendous interest in the sport that led Seppala and Mrs. Ricker to give him his first Siberian Huskies, named Paddy, Frosty and Arctic. This led to a five-dog team. His winning of a handicap race in Laconia, New Hampshire in the early 1930's produced a $1,000.00 prize which started his education in veterinary medicine.

Since then Dr. Lombard has won every major title race, with the exception of the Laconia Open, since he is away from home (competing in other major races) at the time this race is run. He has trophies representing wins at Quebec City, Maniwaki, Ste. Agathe, Ottawa, La Pas, Manitoba, to name a few, and he has raced in competition with other great racing drivers, including Emile St. Goddard, Emile Martel, Charles Belford, Earle Brydges, Keith Bryar, the aforementioned Seppala, and others.

Dr. Lombard is an eight-time winner of the Rondy Races, having won this event in 1963, 1964, 1965, 1967, 1969, 1970, 1971 and 1974. . .he hasn't finished competing!

There is no denying that Dr. Lombard is the idol in the racing circles and sets the pace for the sport. He is the ''one to beat,'' the driver to watch, to emulate, to admire for both his driving skill and demeanor and for his remarkable workmanship on his sleds, which he makes himself. Those who follow the races know that he is a perfectionist, that his powers of concentration on the day of a race are remarkable and that every last detail is personally handled by the doctor himself. His wife Louise might be his only helper, and there is no time for talk.

This concentration, the checking of every minute detail and the great affection and expert training of the dogs all are contributing factors to the fantastic winning record tallied by this man and his team. The mutual devotion really pays off when there is a race to be won!

Dr. Lombard shares his interest in the junior races as well as the adult events and frequently sponsors the junior competitions, realizing that the future of the sport lies in the hands of the young folks coming up in the ranks. The Lombards have been married for over a quarter of a century, and Louise Lombard is also greatly admired by the fancy for her quiet support and devotion to both the good doctor and the dogs. In 1973 she distinguished herself by winning second in the Women's Championship race, missing first place position by only 15 seconds. For many years she has been active in the Alaskan Malamute Club.

The Igloo-Pak kennel name applies to the registered Siberian Huskies, and Dr. Lombard uses the name Sweepstakes for his racing dogs. He holds the Number 1 number with the New England Sled Dog Club, where the members retain their numbers for as long as they maintain their membership. However, the Number ''ONE'' seems particularly appropriate and well-deserved in the case of Dr. Roland Lombard, the Number One racing driver of all times!

The Story of Nellie

Nellie was Dr. Roland Lombard's remarkable lead dog, and she well deserves her place of honor in the Sled Dog Hall of Fame in Alaska.

Dr. Lombard purchased Nellie from George Attla several years ago in Alaska. The price was a record-breaker for the time: one thousand dollars! But as time was to prove, Nellie was worth every penny of it both on and off the racing trail. So highly did the Lombards value Nellie that the phrase ''her gift is devotion'' was often quoted when speaking of this dog.

Nellie lived over a dozen years, every one in devotion to her equally devoted owners. Her admirers extend far and wide, and when at the 1969 Anchorage races Nellie caught the flu and was pulled, ''get well'' cards found their way to the Lombards' lodgings at Orville Lakes, Alaska, addressed simply to''Nellie'' at that address. At the last race at Tok that year, Dr. Lombard's lead dog tired and quit. She sat down at the starting line and refused to move. After valuable minutes of the race were lost, Dr. Lombard immediately substituted the recovered Nellie at the lead. Although nearly twelve years old at the time, Nellie knew what the doctor wanted and they took off down the trail!

CHAPTER 6
THE SIBERIAN HUSKY
IN THE SHOW RING

SIBERIAN DOGS AT THE FIRST
WESTMINSTER SHOW

The first annual Westminster Kennel Club show was held at Gilmore's Garden (Hippodrome), on Tuesday, Wednesday and Thursday, May 8, 9, and 10, in 1877. Charles Lincoln was the superintendent, and the bench show committee for the first event listed the names of the famous pioneers of the dog fancy in this country. On the list was Wm. M. Tileston, C. Du Bois Wagstaff, H. Walter Webb, Dr. W. S. Webb, Louis B. Wright and E. H. Dixon.

The catalogue, consisting of 49 pages of entries, featured Siberian or Ulm Dogs as listings #704 through #711. It is interesting to note that every entry but one, apparently a recent import, was listed as for sale. The catalogue read as follows:

704 J. Fortune, Marion, Jersey City Heights, N.J.
    ROMAN, ash and wh., 2 years and 8 mons. $100.
705 E. Bolenius, 229 Bowery, N.Y.
    GUIDO, yellow and wh., 2 years. From the State of Wurtem-
    burg, $200.
706 Lewis Lintz, West Winfield, Herk. Co. N.Y.
    DARLING, mouse, 4 years; impt. $500.
707 Lewis Lintz, West Winfield, Herk. Co. N.Y.
    CENTENNIAL, mouse, 8 mos; by Darling. $75.
708 Max Borchardt, 54 Garden St., Hoboken, N.J.
    RALPH, bl. and wh., 2 years. $25.
709 F. Bencing. 27½ Christy st., N.Y.
    CAESAR, bl. and wh., 2½ years. $150.
710 J. W. Jones, Plainfield, N.J.
    BRUNO, grey and gl., 6 years. $150.
711 J. B. Miller, Box 170, Newburg, N.Y.
    FRANK, wh. and brown, 2 years. Imported.

FIRST SIBERIAN HUSKY IN
THE AKC STUD BOOK

The first appearance of a Siberian Husky in the American Kennel Club Stud Book was in the December, 1930 issue, Vol. 47: Fairbanks Princess Chena, a bitch which was number 758,529 and owned by Mrs. Elsie K. Reeser. The breeder was Julian A. Hurley of Fairbanks, Alaska. The bitch was whelped September 16, 1927. The lineage was recorded as follows: "Ch. By Bingo II out of Alaska Princess by Jack Frost out of Snowflake. Jack Frost by Scotty out of Vasta. Bingo II out of Topsy."

The very next issue of the Stud Book, January 1931, Vol. 48, was quite another story. There were 21 entries, every one bearing the Northern Light kennel prefix; eight of the 21 were bitches. Until 1952 the count went as follows:

Year	Number of Entries
1930	1
1931	69
1932	11
1933	4
1934	2
1935	17
1936	25
1937	10
1938	2
1939	38
1940	49
1941	55
1942	15
1943	16
1944	12
1945	14
1946	21
1947	72
1948	105
1949	84
1950	124
1951	80

After June, 1952 the stud book was not published again until December, 1952. With that December issue, the stud book listed only dogs which had been bred.

SIBERIAN HUSKY BEST IN SHOW WINNERS

CH. MONADNOCK'S KING

>(Ch. Monadnock's Pando *ex* Monadnock's Czarina)
>Bred and owned by Lorna Demidoff
>Show: Mohawk Valley Kennel Club
>Date: November 11, 1961

Ch. Monadnock's DMITRI

>(Ch. Monadnock's Pando *ex* Monadnock's Ekatrina)
>Bred by Lorna Demidoff
>Owner: Dr. James Brillhart
>Show: Kokomo Kennel Club
>Date: October 18, 1964
>Show: Danville Kennel Club   Date: December, 1965

American and Canadian Ch. Dudley's Tavar of Innisfree, pictured going Best in Show at the Ramapo Kennel Club event in November, 1972 under judge Joseph Feigel. "Clipper" was handled by Jane Forsyth for owners Clarence and Gladys Dudley of North Syracuse, New York. William P. Gilbert photograph.

Ch. Frosty Aire's Alcan King, top stud dog at Marie Wamser's Fra-Mar Kennels in Cleveland, Ohio. King finished his championship undefeated and was the second Siberian Husky to go Best in Show in 1964 at Springfield, Ohio. He has sired 11 champions to date; five have placed in the Group, and one went all the way to Best in Show. His name is American, Bermudian and Canadian Ch. Fra-Mar's Soan Diavol. King was the top stud dog in the breed in 1968.

CH. FROSTY AIRES ALCAN KING

(Ch. Monadnock's Pando *ex* Kura
Bred by Frosty Aire's Kennels
Owner: Marie Wamser
Show: Gambier, Ohio, show
Date: October, 1964

CH. FRA-MAR'S SOAN DIAVOL (Bermudian, Canadian and American)

(Ch. Frosty Aire's Alcan King *ex* Ch. Fra-Mar's Misarah)
Bred by Nina Fisher
Owned by Marie Wamser
Show: Dan Emmett Kennel Club
Date: August 10, 1968

CH. DARBO DOMEYKO OF LONG'S PEAK

(Ch. Reginald of Baltic *ex* Misti of Longs Peak)
Bred by Beth Murphy and John Brown
Owned by Edward Samberson
Show: Greeley (Colorado) Kennel Club
Date: August 24, 1969

CH. DUDLEY'S TAVAR OF INNISFREE (American & Canadian)

(Ch. Alakazan's Nikolai *ex* Ch. Innisfree's Domachuk)
Bred by Margaret Koehler and Kathleen Kanzler
Owned by Clarence and Gladys Dudley
Show: Ramapo Kennel Club
Date: November, 1972
Show: South Shore Kennel Club
Date: April 14, 1973

CH. INNISFREE'S O'MURTAGH

(Ch. Baron of Karnovanda, C.D. *ex* Ch. Weldon's Enuch Balto
Bred by Nancy Perkins
Owned by Major and Mrs. Milton Dohn
Show: Rapid City Kennel Club
Date: October 22, 1972

CH. BONZO OF ANADYR, C.D.

Owned by Earl and Natalie Norris, Bonzo was the first All-Breed
Best in Show winner in Alaska, and the first C.D. title winner there
also.

Ch. Wonalancet's Baldy of Chinook, the first Siberian Husky to win first place in a Working Group, later became with his brother a member of the first Siberian Husky brace to win a Best in Show. This popular stud and Group winner owned by Eva Seeley of the Chinook Kennels, Wonalancet, New Hampshire.

A COMPLETE LIST OF
UNITED STATES CHAMPION
SIBERIAN HUSKIES

1931
Pola
1932
Northern Light Kobuk
1936
Shankhassock Lobo
1938
Cheenah of Alyeska
1939
Togo of Alyeska
1940
Kazon of Waldeck
Laddy of Wonalancet
Tosca Kreevanka of Kolyma
Vanka of Seppala II
1941
Komatik Chico
Panda of Monadnock
Wonalancet's Baldy of Alyeska
1945
Kolya of Monadnock
Sitka's Wona of Alyeska
Turu of Alyeska
1946
Vanya of Monadnock III
1947
Agra of Kabkol
Belka of Monadnock II
Chornyi of Kabkol
1948
Kira of Monadnock
1949 ,
Igloo Pac's Anvic
Wonalancet's Disko of Alyeska
Otchki of Monadnock, CD
1950
Holya of Kabkol
Helen of Cold River

1952
Aleka's Czarina
Dichoda's Aurelia, CD
1953
Khiva II of Monadnock
1954
U-Chee Of Anadyr
Monadnock's Nina
Aleka of Monadnock
1955
Taku
Wanja
Prin-Sar's Gay Tanya
Kiev of Gap Mountain

1956
Ivanka of Kabkol
Kara
Taglook
Stony River's Rinda
Klutuk's Carrie
Geah of Terraria
Stony River's Frosty Boy
1957
Dichoda's Czar
Stony River's Karluk
Kara's Idyl
Stony River's Gay Panda
Dichoda's Chiota
Bonzo of Anadyr
Monadnock's Pando
Alyeska's Suggen of Chinook
Kenai Kittee of Beauchein
Monadnock's Belka
Murex's Snow King
Murex's Rowdy Gus
Nokoma Chief of Eagle Mountain

A famous first: this photo shows the first time in the history of the breed that a Siberian Husky won a Group! The 8th Annual dog show of the North Shore Kennel Club held at Hamilton, Massachusetts on August 23, 1941, saw Working Group award go to Wonalancet's Baldy of Alyeska, pictured here with his owner-handler, Mrs. Milton J. Seeley of the Chinook Kennels, Wonalancet, New Hampshire.

1958
Brandy's Star
Kyge of Terraria
Sieksuh's Korrol
Kara's Aral
Kenai Kristyee of Kakota
Monadnock's Red Tango of Murex
Noho of Anadyr
Prin-Sar's Kari
Tyndrum's Oslo
Monadnock's Aleska
Nootka of Nanook
Sieksuh's Cissie
Stony River's Ootah
Klitina Tarina
Tamerlane of Heathcrest
Tyndrum's Chynik
1959
Stony River's Shutka
Stony River's Valuiki
Akela of Alasug
Dichoda's Elan
Shutnik
Grey Shadow of the North
Skog's Nakatla of High Country
Kara's Umlak
Markay's Stardust
Monadnock's King
Sieksuh's Kono
Dichoda's Jenu Kenu
Nauten of A-Baska
Sassara's Ozera
Sieksuh's Chesny
1960
Sintaluta
Chuchi of Tinker Mountain
Monadnock's Savda Bakko
Cheechako's Madam Easha
Tottam II of Cheenah
Dichoda's Gjoa
Snow King
Koyuk of Nakohna, CD
Donette Kasha, CD

Kira of Kazan
Monadnock's Prince Igor, CD
Nome
Markay's Bonfire
Monadnock's Rurik of Nanook
Keni of Triple Dee
Markay's Aral's Bourbon
1961
Atu of Glacier Valley
Chickaloon
Frosty Aire's Susitna, CD
Ziok of Foxhaunt
Kola of Anadyr
Monadnock's Serge
Frosty Aire's Beauchein
Markay's The Panda Prince
Baltic Chilla's Gay Charmer
Wiard's Conyak Tanya
Frosty Aire's Peter
Mulpus Brook's The Pepper
Nordholm's Jonas
Babbet of Lakota
Frosty Aire's Akiak
Harmul's Tulik
Marlytuk's Ahkee
Cold Creek's Sable
Sylvan Dell Sarnia
Frosty Aire's Alcan King
Nome Joker
Checkers of Yeso-Pac
Frosty Aire's Beau Tuk Balto
S-K-Mo's Obras Sova
Yeso-Pac's Aurora
1962
Stony River's Miss Aurora
Skog's Nalakatuk
Beau-Tuk Evil One
Koga
Frosty Aire's Beau Tuk Belka
Beau-Tuk Katrina
Frosty Aire's Tofty
Frosty Aire's Inuk

The National Capital show in Washington, D.C., in March, 1960 saw judge Anna Katherine Nicholas award Best Team in Show to Lorna Demidoff's Siberian Huskies. Brown photograph.

Winner of the Best Team in Show at the 1960 International Kennel Club show in Chicago was Mrs. Lorna Demidoff's beautifully matched Siberian Huskies. Frasie photograph. Dogs are (left to right): Ch. Monadnock Savda Bakko, Ch. Monadnock Serge, Ch. Monadnock King, and Ch. Monadnock Pando. The judge was the late Walter Reeves.

Monadnock's Molinka
Dichoda Monadnock's Lorna
Monadnock's Liska
Monadnock's Dmitri
Sieksuh's Preentessa of Adak
Beautuk's Beauvallon
Kenick of Colfax
Schpielkas of Colfax
Yeso-Pac's Reynard
Kazel of Colfax
Little Sepp's Stormy of Sno-Dak
Monadnock's Norina
S-K-Mo's Charney Sooka
Ty-Cheko of Baltic
Kalooch Katella of Greenview
Dichoda's Nukeerah Amur
Savdajaure's Cognac
Stony River's Frosty Aurelia
Bennet's Digger
Foxhaunt's Tovarisch
Frosty Aire's Chena
Togo
Monadnock's Konyak of Kazan
Stony River's Jet Siobhan
Stony River's Tikki Tue
Canem's Tuski
Chickaloon of Sihu

1963
Frosty Aire's Kenai Kittee
Snow Ridge Czar
Bel Ami of Yeso Pac
Kanuti of Triple Dee
Jura's Sanya
Snow Ridge Rina
Czarina Toschia of Chucki
Fra-Mar's Misrah
Shadow from Monadnock
Susitna's Aarik
Columbia's Smokey
Eska's Nonie
Frosty Aire's Eric
Loki Easter of Baltic

Dichoda's Manitou Taku
Dichoda's Susitka
Marlytuk's Noonah
S-K-Mo's Charney Sambo
Stony River's Taiki-O
Chamois of Stowe Crest
Yeso-Pac's Tamara
Kheta's Tanya
Kim of Martha Lake
Sihu's Bal Tam Panda
Suggen of Susitna

1964
Frosty Aire's Banner Boy
Frosty Aire's Starfire
Igor's Princess
Kim's Karen CDX
Monadnock's Pavlick
Savdajaure's Li'l Teeka
Kronprinz of Kazan
S-K-Mo's Matushka Katrina
The Muscovite Maiden, CD
Dichoda's Torik
Duchska of Martha Lake
Flahive's Glacier Wonder
Frosty Aire's Sno-Ana Kaltag
Savdajaure Keemah's Tova
Kodiikuska de Sforza, CD
Yeso-Pac's Rasputin
Checo of Marly
Frosty Aire's Masked Bandit
Mikhail of Koryak
Tocka of Monadnock
Dichoda's Tokusak, CD
Sherry Sue
Alapha Oonik of Baltic
Czar Nicholas
S-K-Mo's Charney Koshka
Tyoek Alyeska of Pine View
Innisfree's Beau-Tuk
Koonah's Red Kiska
Sir Echo of Timberland
Susitna's Dirka

Ch. Frosty Aire's Banner Boy, C. D., one of the top-producing Siberian Huskies for 1970, 1971 and 1972. Banner was also among the Top Ten Siberians in the Phillips System ratings several times during his show career. He is owned by Arthur and Mary Ann Piunti, Snoana Kennels, Hobart, Indiana.

Ch. Monadnock Pando winning the Working Group at the Philadelphia Kennel Club in 1958 under the late judge Alva Rosenberg. Owner, breeder and handler was Lorna B. Demidoff, Monadnock Kennels, Fitzwilliam, New Hampshire.

Czar Petronis
Joli Tchike of Martha Lake
Kandia of Kazan
Mike of Martha Lake
Noonok of Marly
Dichoda's Rurik's Tika
Sihu's Bal-Tam Kiki
S-K-Mo's Tazie
Teko's Mushka of Baltic
Umiak of Martha Lake
Kingo Solomon
Susitna's Khan
1965
Monadnock's Lisa
Susitna's Mit-Sah Konya, CD
S-K-Mo's Charney Korsar
Susitna's Mit-Sah Tanya
Skog's Nicki Kazan
Innisfree's El Ferro
Innisfree's Lobo
Yogi of Yankeeczar
Czar of Kolima II, CD
Reginald of Baltic
Rob-Ida's Princess Natasha
Susitna's Laika
Colorado's State Badge
Darbo Domeyko of Long's Peak
Dichoda's Yukon Red
Frosty Aire's Beauchiena
Yukonamute, CD
Badger of Kolyma
Doonauk Keema's Che-Co
Doonauk's Keemah
Double O's Morgan
Frosty Aire's Starbrite
Staschis Gonya of Baltic
Amur's Chena Kimara
Arctic's Chertuk
Fra-Mar's Karo Mia Diavol
Fra-Mar's Mr. Nimo
Frosty Aire's Kenai Baltiko
Thor of Snoridge

Tuk of Natomah
Alexoff Ot Yakutsk
Arctic's Storm Frost
Frosty Aire's Black Panda
Kimo's Troika
Zucane's Dieva of Nakhodka
Bluebelle's Panda Bear, CD
Ishim of Snoridge
Khane of Sirius
Marvel Black Mask
Mikiuk Tuktu Tornyak
Monadnock's Penelope
Susitna's Grisha
Frosty Aire's Persimmon
Mishka of Nor-Pak
Pendah Lickoyee
S-K-Mo's Charney Shek
Bandit of Wind Willow
Baron of Karnovanda
Jo-L's Leea
Misty Story
Sihu's Bal-Tam Tiger
Sno-Ana's Kenai Suzee
1966
Monadnock's Boris Goudonoff
Monadnock's Tasco Del Norte
Yeso Pac's Vodka
Alaskan's Kiska of Anadyr
Dean's Snow Czar
Fra-Mar's Czarina
Huf-Nik of Amchitka
Snow Ridge Oolik II
Frosty Aire's Anvic
Knappko of Klutuk
Susitna's Konya
Blue Glacier of Martha Lake
Kursk of Sakhalin
Nor-Dic of Natomah
Rob-Ida's Prince Cuatro
Robida's Timiska Rey Del Cerro
Sampson's Toluck
Tenana of Toluck

Ch. Dichoda's Arora Chena, C.D., pictured winning Best of Winners at the Santa Barbara Kennel Club, which hosted the Siberian Husky Club of America Specialty Show in July, 1966. Chena finished for her championship at 18 months of age. Owned by Dean and Dolores Warner, Akalan Kennels, Livermore, California.

Doonauk Doonah's Tambov
Fra-Mar's Soan Diavol
Heather of Tundra
Kineki of Koryak
Koryak's Pandy
Monadnock's Midnight Musya
Tenana of Chilkat
Amur's Zar Kola
Kache Dash De Distance
Keefer Feeley of Bolshoi
Nanook's Kari
Nanook's Tchootke
Rob-Ida's Tanya
Savdajaure's Harlequin
Simba of Nor-Pak
Tchumi's Tishka of Tajo
Tonkova of the Midnight Sun
Hubbs Three-Alkolette
Kelen's Reba Star
Romka Koryak of Bolshoi
Susitna's Chort
The Paragon Panther
Frosty Aire's Nyak of Sihu
Karen's Token of Karnovanda, CD
Karnovanda's Zenda, CD
Kiscko
Koryak's Scarlet Scandal
Monadnock's Misty of Arahaz
S-K-Mo's Kolyema Snova
Fra-Mar's Kyak
Innisfree's Chilka
Kimo's Nikka
Kimo's Smo-Ki-Luk
Klutuk's Kno-Kno of Sno-Ana
Monadnock's Sir Grayling
Nakhodka's Samara
Savdajaure of Oakwood
Sendu's Katrina
Snoshu's Noatuk
Ahshan Blackie
Alyeska Li'l Suggen of Chinook
Dichoda's Arora-Chena

Innisfree's Banshee Tu
Kanangnark Aleka
Keluk of Martha Lake
Lostlands Frosted Sunbeam
Monadnock's Zita
Tok Niklo of Martha Lake
Yeso-Pac's Cindy
Chuchi's Dusty Bandit
Fort Salonga's Kemo of Baltic
Frosty Aire's So Cold
Kitza of Timberland
Kodiak's Geeda of Long's Peak
Natasha's Byk-Byk
Natasha's Sasha
Savdajaure's Mekki
Sham-Rock of White River
Susitna's Mit-Sah Sonya
Yeso Pac's Minx
1967
Balh-Shoy Volk of Tajo
George's Yukon King
Kanaktuk Zapodna of Ivy-K
Lo-Jack's Nikolaevsk
Amur's Teigari Shondi
Innisfree's Krimbo
Snoridge's Tristan
Capatain Zorro of Nor-Pac
Double O's Dammerung
Dyea of Toluck
Frosty Aire's Jolly Red Giant
Kiska Tytiki of Alpine-Glenn
Marlytuk's Dom
Sikkim of Sakhalin
Doonauk's Kazak of Kazan
Koryak's Domino-A-Go-Go, CD
Nakhodka's Hallene
Frosty's Blaze
Karnovanda's Zenzarya
Monadnock's Coronation Sasha
Subahkas Shoom of Tchumi
Weldon's Quicksilver
Chebco's Copper Prestige

Ch. Dichoda's Yukon Red, pictured going Best of Breed at the Siberian Husky Club of America national specialty show held in conjunction with the Beverly Hills Kennel Club show in June of 1969. Tom Witcher handled for owners Frank and Phyllis Brayton, Dichoda Kennels, in Escalon, California. The judge is Lorna Demidoff; Anna Mae Forsberg, then president of the Siberian Husky Club of America, presents the trophy. Joan Ludwig photograph.

Cinnaminson Kiyak cooling his feet in a stream. Kiyak (Monadnocks Aleka Ch. Mischa of Chaza, C.D.) is owned by Sy and Ann Goldberg, Cream Ridge, New Jersey.

Toyon of Tun-Dra being campaigned to championship by her owners, Mr. and Mrs. Deane Cheadle of the Tun-Dra Kennels, Nunica, Michigan.

Crown Fire of Al-Co
Kozan Fleet Foot
Rob-Ida's Princess Chica
Innisfree's Barbarrosa
Arahaz' Ebony Beauty
Berik's Big Mac
Chebco's Copper Nooya
Chifa of the Midnight Sun
Karnovanda's Ivan Groznyi
Nakhodka's Sakima
Tova II of Koryak
Hawk of Little Alaska
Innisfree's King Karl
Kanaiok's Chhota Karki
Tucker of Chilkat
Chotovotka's Mischa
Doonauk Keemah's Chuchi
Foxhuant's Cozak of Kesam
Frosty Aire's Red Devil Beau
Frosty Aire's Sno-Ana Christee
Galya of Koryak
Innisfree's Oomachuk
Joli Rakuun
Nikos of Karnovanda
S-K-Mo's Charney Sobaka
Alakazan's Moroznaya Zvezda
Andrew of Talkeetna
Ketchikan of Husky Acres
Klutuk's Mummy
Koyanna of Wilderness Trace
Lostlands Leading Lady
Monadnock's Illya
Monadnock's Taika
Savdajaure's Panuck
Sno-Cap's Arluk of Artiksong,
Suntrana's Siberian Sundown
Susitna's Kahndirka
Tonya My Lady
Tookany's Copper Penny
1968
Amur Kiska of Dougmarland
Beau Banner Blue

Dichoda's Roho Totem of Nanuk
Dovercrest's Yana of Arahza
Frosty Aire's Bittersweet
Klik of Koryak
Kodiak of Leawood
Tonnia Tokeen
Baronof Koyukuk
Jo-L's Stormy*
Kanaktuk Kuska of Ivy-K, CDX
Marlytuk's Cognac
Nanook of Koryak
Nomad's Chuchanka
Razin of Bolshoi
Keneu
Lostland's Yukon Queen, CD
Mikiluk's Zakhar of Oakwood
Yak Ka Lot
Amur's Natascha of Newbury
Arctic's Timber
Chotovotka's Mapachee
Del's Artic Star
Dichoda's Arora Nikki
Kimnik's Stormy
Kira of Wilderness Trace
Rob-Ida's Le Voyaguer
Alakazan's Kio Kam of Snoana
Colo Silver King of Baltic
Eu-Mor's Misty Morn
Fra-Mar's Troisk Diavol
Innisfree's Kitka
Karnovanda's Kinetic Katya
Kayak of Martha Lake, CD
Kodiak's Komiak
Princess Pika of Ty-O-Baltic
Arctic's Nyte
Bolshoi's Molyinka
Boom Boom's Shanghai
Natomah's Kee Na
Alakazan's Nikki
Eu-Mor's Taiga
Foxhaunt's Zorina
Kainino's Miss Muffet Od Sirius

Kanaktuk Tunguska of Ivy-K
Kanangnark's Kief
Karnovanda's Koytikuk King
King Togo of Husky Acres
Kodiak of Martha Lake
Koritza of Kettle Moraine
Koryak's Naughty Ninotchka
Koryak's Scandal's Cheechako
Subahka's Red Cedar of Zanyuk
Weldon's Enuk Balto
Tonka Chu's Yuri
Alakazan's Yishra
Loyka of Lustigleben
Marlytuk's Red Sun of Kiska
Savdajaure's Vackra Docka
Tookany's Copper Prince
Diablo Snow
Dichoda's Chiota of Berik
Fort Salonga's Nada of Yeso Pac
Joli Bandito
Karnovanda's Koyikuk
Koryak's Cherda of North Star
Ot-Key-Luk Miss-U-Tu
Togolaska Ande of Martha Lake
Tokusak's Koyanna of Sunshine
Zhulik of SnoMound
Alaskazan's Satan Sitka, CD
Dichoda's Bingo Silver Arrow
Doonauk's Tomgass of Ahkee
Jamar's Ginger Snap
Koryak's Red Ragamunchkin
Koryak's The Red Baron
Yoho Taiga
Ebony Tuff of Lion Point, CD
Morrison's Miss Kris
Savdajaure's Sampo
Souhegan's Thunder Head
Suntrana's Pandi of Ken Tuk
Tamara's Nema
Wikdaire Kira
Amur's Volk Ko Angliya
Fra-Mar's Omar Kyan

Kler's Rosie
Monadnock's Snow Prince Kazan
Racecrest Amarok-Keno
Snoridge's Lorelei
Val-Soc's Hanki-Panki
1969
Alakazan's Kossak
Colorado Silver Nuggat
Koryak's Tanya
Snow Scout Kam
Arahaz Kelieti
Babbitts Princess Tanya
Egor Easter
Frosty Aire's Red Baron
Honey Bear of Paradise Found
Kodiak Of Alpine-Glenn, CD
Lostland's Viking
Monadnock's Midnight Sun
Nonook's Marka
Shadow of the Yukon
Wausor's Yurii
Fra-Mar's Rising Sun Dancer
Akalan's Aurora of Rim-Ski
Eu-Mor's Oka
Wintersett Bo Gentry
Altasierra Shaver of Syek
Baltic Kitekee
Copper Penny of Lustigleben
Coronation Northern Flyer
Fra-Mar's Shiva Diavol
Juneau of Tondara
Klutuk's Funny Girl
Starlite's Shelli Tantoo
Toki of Rockrimmon
Alakazan's Saanki
Arahaz's Astrakhan
Dichoda's Gjoa Gray Cloud
Fra-Mar's Challa Diavol
Kiska of Mueller Lane
Monadnock's Dimitri C Bernlee
Rob-Ida's Kayak
Scandia's Frosty Mist

Ch. Fournier's Zachariah of Toko with Joene Fournier, daughter of owner Jean Fournier, Atlantic Highlands, New Jersey. Photograph by Judy Rosemarin.

Weldon's Tar Baby
Arahaz' Nahshon
Arctic's Blizzard
Dichoda's Fantastik Amorok
Frosty Aire's Beau Deuxieme
Jet Spray
Joli Badga
Oomik's Ouista
Savdajaure's Miuk
Tosac of Monadnock
Baltic Ty-Chan's Charmer
Dichoda's Udacha of S-K-Mo
Doonauk's Keemah of Holly
Foxhaunt's Patu
Frebka's Kiki
Frosty Aire's Miss Cinders
Karnovanda's Juneau
Karnovanda's Stormmy Bear
Monadnock's Akela
Nikoda Fleet Foot
Racecrest Mirakusa
Sandyhill's Heidiska of Nebo
Takoka of Wabash Valley
Acorn Hill's Niok
Amur's Pandora of Matanuska
Arctic's Pretti
Doonauk's Ivanovas
Harms Chanuk Pandy
Kipnuk of Leawood
Knega's Tschenka
Knyki of Timberland
Koywyŋ's Sannurai
Lostland's Trademark
Monadnock's Echo
Rob-Ida's Bewitching Samantha
Susitna's Dirka of Tomahawk
Doonauks Doonah
Kiska of Kantua
Sandyhill's Red Czar
Twilight's Frosty Aire
Wind Willows Gray Mystery
Chotovotka's Kaytee

Karnovanda's Anitra Kodira
Kognac Of The Midnight Sun
Lostlands Nanuck
Nome Of Ty-O-Baltic
Schneiders Angel
Alakazan's Valeska
Cossack Of The Midnight Sun
Eu-Mor's Lara
Karnovanda's Yuri Baronovitch
Tokco of Bolshoi
Tookany's Mitka
Wildaires Misha
1970
Arizona State Germo V. Toluck, C.D.
Doonauks Czar of Siberia
Karden's Nova Polara
K-C's Val Rurik
Marlytuk Sandyhill's Red Czar
Susitna's Blink
Butterfields Chevak Taku
Dane Viking Of The Midnite Sun
Joli Chison
Karnovanda's Lara Baronova
Nomad's Shane
Riley's Rokitri Of Koryak
Rob-Ida's Volcan
Steven's Klondike Mengo
Winsum's Salacious Sergei
Amur's Nikita of Newbury
Arctic Flame of Longs Peak
Baron's Mishka
Myown Lura
Sno-Blitz's De-O-Ge Of Domeyko
Stone Front's Black Bandit
Thib's Sir Oliver Hardy
Tonya of Snow Valley
Akalan's Sonia
Alakazan's Nikolai
Arctics Colorado Sleet
Koryak's Erika of Northland
Larisa of Weldon
Savdajaures Eska La Marchese, C.D.

Sy and Ann Goldberg's Ch. Chachka of Cinnaminson wins Best of Breed under judge Connie Bosold at the 1970 Charleston, South Carolina, Kennel Club show. Handler George Heitzman. Graham photo.

Benton-Mar's Aurora's Echo
Dovercrest Aletha Pesna
Karmet Of The Lost Alaskan
Karnovanda's Macho
Lobo of Fort Salonga
Nikkina Of Colorado's Badge
Blue Smoke of Ka-Mia-Kin
Czar of Georgia
Dracula of Lustigleben
Jamar's Red Devil
Overlook's Nanook
Subahka's Red Devil Wow
Bowlsam's Happy Warlock
Cossock Of Moon Valley
Dichoda's Icon Cinnamon
Karluk Of Baltic, C.D.
Karnovanda's Kara Bogaz
Sabowu Of Wind Willow
Tangara Of Whispering Pines
Tonka Chu's Chekov
Almaring's Alai
Eu-Mor's Zhulek Of Silver
Fra-Mar's Aja-Tu Diavol
Klutuk's Bang-Go Bang-Go
Lord Kim
Narda Of Krushsada
Sunnybrook's Ilya Tambovich
Tanya Of Cinnaminson
Alakazan's Cayuga's Frosty
Diomede's Midnight Cissie
Kaptain Kije's Kommand
Kroshka Of The Midnight Sun
Mikhail Nootka Of Rolyat
Nikandre's Tanya of Siberia
Savdajaure's Kam
Sno-Fame Koona's Chuka
Tartarian's Sierra Smoke
Doremic's Kemo Sabe
Jamar's Paprika
Karnovanda's Tamara
Koryak's Black Charger
Marcia's My Nook

Mar-Lynn's Tyee Tanglefoot, C.D.
Misty Ah-Kee
Rob-Ida's Rey Timiska Tambien
Karnovanda's Miss Vodka
Monadnock's Volcana
Sandyhill's Chukchi Red
Tanga Of Greenwell
Valhalla's Azure Talisman
Karnovanda's Banner Bright
Kopak's Tomanco of Snoridge
Natahnni's Desbah of Domeyko
Ogadai of Karakorum
Savdajaure's Kunuk
Savdajaure's Tanni
Steven's Mighty Nor-Ell Kodiak
Weldon's Beau-Buck

1971
Edric Of Arahaz
Hilltop's Midnite Bandit
Linder's Princess Tanya
Mischa Of Chaya
Pasha IV
Silver Nugget's Nuka
Togolaska Blizzard
Alaskan's Bonzana of Anadyr
Binkie's Ou 'Zoo Nook Nook
Diomede's Koritza of Leawood
Dranoel's Banshee of Tandara
Dudley's Tavar of Innisfree
Kamchatka's Bandit, C.D.
Nateya of the Midnight Sun
Princess Bushka of Hanjpange
Sepp's Boy of Martha Lake
Tsar Nikki Av Balkan
Yankee Trader's Baron Nikolai
Aniko of So Huck
Arahaz Vania
Baron Sasha
Chiri of Blazeridge
Doonauks Gidget
Innisfree's Severnyj Niki
Joli Stilyagi

Ch. Wanser's Cara Mia finishing for her championship under Mrs. Milton Seeley. Bred by the Alakazan Kennels, she is owned by the Weydigs and handled for them by Carl Lacchia. Mia's sire is Ch. Frosty Aire's Banner Boy, C.D., *ex* Alakazan's Kristi. Photo by Ashbey.

Judge Mrs. Maynard K. Drury gives Best Brace in Show at the Western Pennsylvania Kennel Club show to Carolyn Windsor's pair of Huskies, handled by her daughter Sue. Mrs. Windsor's Kaylee Kennels are in Baltimore, Maryland.

Power Tan of Tsar
Rega of the Midnight Sun
Savdajaure's Bushka
Tajo's Li'l D of Hatu
Carmalin's Fresca of Snoridge
Chateaugay's Charlie
Eu-Mor's Kiev, C.D.
Eu-Mor's Tania
Fireside's Ladies Man
Jeb's Shangri La
Karnovanda's Wolfgang
Nena's Bolshoi Sheena Too
Tajo's Kazacheof Tallac
Tobuck Atu Nicci
Wildaire Tasha of Idol Acres
Winsum's Rakish Romanov, C.D.
Innisfree's Royal Purple
Karnovanda's Taska II
Lostland's Miss Siberia
Natomah's Zhivago
Pandy's Brandy of Lost Alaskan
Sabrina Sibidawg Maxima
Sobaka of Kistefjall
Taggarik of Stapleton Park
Wolfden's Copper Bullet
Arctic's Isar Tygre
Bernlee's Kometa
Brookbend's Gedaloadadis
Colorado's Little Medallion
Gre-To-Da's Antiquem Of Kadosa
Kipnuks
Lightning Gigolo Van Ellen
Lostlands' Midnight Sun
Miss Frosty Aire of Tun-Dra
Monadnock's King Of The Tundra
Muskoka Sandyhill's Red Flash
Yeso Pac's Red Sceptre
Arahaz' Tengri Khan
Behling's Snow Princess
Bernlee's Copper Ottehok
Chimakuan
Domeyko's Zadar

Klutuk's B'Nai Solomon
Lamark's Yana
Orseno's Ivan The Terrific
Satan of Big Trail
Sundana's Kvac of Kavan
Tahpu of Ki-Mia-Kin
Totem's Echo Nikko of Nebo
Yana's Erik The Red Viking
Yankeeczar's Anya
Arctic's Starfire
Frosted Valentine's Thunder
Highwayman Of Amchitka
Lamark's Chaku
Monadnock's Rogue Bandit
Nitchka Lieojoem
Wansor's Cara Mia
Cherski's Royal Bandit
Chotovotka's Set'um Up Joe
Diomede's Midnight Orsha
Fra-Mar's Arctic Challenger
Karnovanda's Khan Of Kiev
Lady-Bird Of Mt. View
Leonard's Tokla Of Tamara
Monadnock's Cossack Of Akela
Prince Mikita Of Echoinuk
Tawny Hill Larna Of Monadnock
Alakazan's Banner Blue
Chachka Of Cinnaminson
Domeyko's Zarka
Klutuk's Subo Of Black Frost
Kosha Of Devil Creek
S-K-Mo's Single Sapphire
Tawny Hill Baikal O'Monadnock
Cinnaminson's Soaya Fournier
Doonauk's Jeuahnee Of Keemah
Karnovanda's Brunhilda
Keachi's Eltigre Torvo
Monadnock's Lara Of Irlocon
Amur's Chatka Of Julewood
Bentonmar's Mr. George
Chanuque Of Seldom Seen
Chebco's Tashinka

Dovercrest Awsinee Pesna
Kistefjall Yuri
Koonah's Red Gold
Lady Na-Nook Of Tun-Dra
Marlytuk's Koonuk Of Koonah
Rob-Ida's Tilichiki
Scandia's Bobby Dazzler
Snow Storm's Laika
Tassha Ot Yakutska

1972
Akalan's Yuri, C.D.X.
Baltic Kitwanga
Eu-Mor's Milaska
Honey Bee of Iliamna Lake
Innisfree's O'Murtagh
Lobo of Suntrana
Maximo of Maxima
Natashia's Tatanya of Ussuri
Nika Alexoff
Snoridge's Smokey
Wildaire's Seri Sobaka
Yana's Tochka
Fortsalong's Banner Brown
Knega's Blaze of Glory
Knega's Crimson Tide
Mokelumne's Red Sonda
Savdajaure's King
Snow-Bound Niki of Amarok
Wind Country's Eskimo Boy
Winsum's Dogmatic Darya
Alyta Of Anadyr
Baltic Pacesetter
Baltic Teko Zema's Mikiluk
Binnie's Silver Saska, C.D.
Chebco's Terrible Ivan
Gro-Mee-Ko Of Kiyak
King Magic
Koryak's Oric
Lobo-Rey
Marlytuk's Elektra
Nagelah Of Wilderness Trace
Princess Pika's Kei-Ie

S-K-Mo's Jezebel Tu
Tawny Hill's Gaibryel
Valhalla's Nisensky
Welch's Tonya Sno-Queen
Windiana's Prancer
Winnether Of Seldom Seen
Winsum's Loquacious Lida
Winsum's Sagacious Stepan
S-K-Mo's J. P. McMorgan
Tsar's Sundance Kid
Wolfden's Ricochet of Hilltop
Karnovanda's Jascha Mir-Ro
Koryak's Dina
Monadnock's Ekatrina
Payne's Pasha Mikhail
Princess Sequoia Of Koryak
Sir Suggen The Great
S-K-Mo's Smudge Pot
Domeyko's Akiachak
Donju's Devil of Yukon Red
Fra-Mar's Cherry Puff Diavol
Irlocon's Encore
Koyukuk's Kopper Kahda
Lamark's Bullet
Mr. Smokee of Big Trail
Niki Yermak
Savdajaure's Tikkiluck
Snoana's Winter Wind
Tunguska's Pyuwacket
Fra-Mar's Bronze Star
Fra-Mar's Konets Diavol
Kodiak Rorchack
Kunu of Cinnaminson, C.D.X.
Lenotchka Of Bolshoi
Sierra's Highland Copper Mist
Timber Hills Artic Wolf
Wintersett Instant Replay
Chilka's Treska of Weldon
Harm's Bad News J.J.
Karnovanda's El Bandito
Ken-Tuk's Silver Mist
Nikmute's Kenia of Tsar

Ch. Monadnock's Rurik of Nanook, Best of Breed at the Siberian Husky Club of America specialty show held in conjunction with the Harbor Cities Kennel Club show in 1964. Mrs. Nicholas Demidoff was the judge. Rurik was handled by his owner, Frank Brayton, Dichoda Kennels, Escalon, California.

Silver Fawn of Tun-Dra
Snomound's Midnight Sun
Snow Storm's Sasha
Tasha of Maxima
Tawny Hill Tanya of Monadnock
Tvarski of The Midnight Sun
Valeska's Nicola Chukchi
Doonauks Bakku Of Nootka
Knega's Total Eclipse
Mount Holly's Noble Nikki
Sochi Of Koryaska
Arahaz' Red Rocket
Domino's Tinker Toy
Fournier's Tiffany Of Toko
Frebka's Lightning
Irlocon's Eric
Mary-Sue's Siberian Tiger
Sandyhill's Icy Blue Shyak
Sno-Tips Igor The Terror
Snowmass Copper Kaylee

Tankoo Of Spring Pond
Tawny Hills Malachi
Tawny Hills Molina
Tovarin's Merry Anarchist
Tsar's Enchantress
Winter's Run Little Bear
Alakazan's Pashaga
Dohenic's Nukenak
Rob-Ida's Kazan Tambien
Aslaular's Ice Blue
Fournier's Zachariah Of Toko
Kaia-Blu
Karnovanda's Wotan
Marlytuk Georgie Girl
Monadnock's Kiana Of Keachi
Monte Alban San Saba
S-K-Mo's Firebrand Of Silver-Sno
Snoridge's Pandi
Zarkita Of The Midnight Sun

1972 Champions Are Listed Through the December 1972 Issue Of the *American Kennel Gazette*

CHAPTER 7
THE SIBERIAN HUSKY IN OBEDIENCE

The intelligence of the Siberian Husky is beyond doubt. Its willingness to want to work in the obedience ring is something else again! A Siberian knows what he is supposed to do once he has been taught, but he doesn't always want to do it, and if he doesn't want to, he seldom will!

Just how much your Siberian Husky learns is up to you or the trainer and your ability to communicate with the dog, plus the degree of patience and time you or the trainer is willing to spend toward the ultimate achievement of that C.D., C.D.X., or any other title.

Each and every year there are more and more obedience Siberian Husky title holders in all classes in both the United States and Canada, and an impressive number of C.D.X., U.D. and even U.D.T. dogs. So it can be done. Those who know the breed realize that the great innate desire to run straight out ahead of a sled is the complete opposite behavior to the constrained discipline which must be displayed in the obedience ring. But as we said before, it can be done, and it *is* being done. And once that degree has been won the victory is twice as sweet, since the challenge has been twice as great!

COMPANION DOG DEGREE

To achieve the Companion Dog degree, your Siberian Husky must compete and earn a total of 170 or more points out of a possible 200 under three different judges at three different trials. The novice obedience degree is based on the performance given in six exercises as follows: The Heel on Leash, 35 points; Stand for Examination, 30 points; Heel Free, 45 points; Recall, 30 points; Long Sit, 30 points and the Long Down, 30 points.

The first Siberian Husky to earn a Companion Dog, or C.D., title was named King, and the year was 1941. Since 1941 there have been many others who have worked willingly and well to earn their titles, and we list them here (list compiled from the *American Kennel Gazette*).

Companion Dog Siberian Huskies
Title Holders

1941
King
1946
Ivan Alyeska Kolymski
Chornyi of Kabkol
1947
Ted
1948
Boris of Kabkol
Otchki of Monadnock
1949
Foxstand's Sparkle
Pavlik of Monadnock
Dichoda's Aurelia
Kurt's Kazan of Long's Peak
1955
Alaskan Twilite of Long's Peak
Che'Mo
1956
Dichoda's Foyukuk Oolinka
Huskie
1957
Heidi Ho Of Long's Peak
1958
Grey Shadow of the North
Kenai Kristyee of Lakota
Little Sepp's Stormy of Sno-Dak
Ch. Bonzo of Anadyr
Ch. Kenai Kittee of Beauchien
Ch. Murex's Snow King
Dichoda's Husky
Ch. Tyndrum's Oslo
Oso Del Norte
1959
General Nuisance
Sno-Dak's Blizzard of Anadyr
1960
Ice Chip of Murex
Kingmik's Terek
Dichoda's Idona
Donette Kasha
Monadnock's Prince Igor
Frosty Aire's Noorvik
Tonyek's Kanaiok

Russo of Kulik
Sadiq of Kanaiok
Ch. Brandy's Star
Ch. Chuchi of Tinker Mountain
Cinder of Cold Creek
Frosty Aire's Susitna
1961
Harmul's Taku
Togo
1962
Foxhaunt's Tovarisch
Ch. Harmul's Tulik
Hubb's Three-Kutie
Savage of Erebus
Kinem Ikerra
Ffoff's Tabagfac
Ch. Frosty Aire's Peter
Ch. Tyndrum's Oslo
Panda
1963
Suggen of Susitna
The Muscovite Maiden
Ch. Ty Cheko of Baltic
Kodilkuska De Sforsa
Schatze of Greenview
Shady Lane's Tanina del Norte
Kim's Karen
Susitna's Mit-Sah Konya
Ch. Beau Tuk Evil One
Ch. Eska's Nonie
Mazul of Miksham
Abaska's Nanook
Koko Nor of Kuskokwim
Laska
Tanana of Kolima
Queen Troika of Lion Point
1964
Lyn's Kotzebue
Ch. Dichoda's Tokusak
Sitka Snow Queen
Yukonamute
Zucane's Masou of Nakhodka
Ch. Frosty Aire's Sno-Ana Kaltag
Storm's Ice-Chip of Sno-Dak

Ch. Dichoda's Aurelia, C.D., the third Siberian Husky to earn a championship and Companion Dog degree! Phyllis Brayton and her son Bill are pictured in 1949 with Aurelia, from the very first litter bred at the famous Dichoda Kennels.

Taku of Alyeska
Bluebelle's Panda Bear
Czar of Kolima II
Fra-Mar's Kaia-Diavol
J-Bet's Alaskan Honey
Kanaiok's Ferlin Husky
Kanaiok's Konshik
Ch. Kheta's Tanya
Nonie's Clover
Berg's Grey Wolf
Fra-Mar's Nao Diavol
1965
Ch. Frosty Aire's Beauchien
Storm's Little Sleet of Sno-Dak
Ch. Susitna's Khan
Juno's Lad
Yukon Yogi
Lady Vikhr
Tovarish of Erebus
Ch. Tyoek Alyeska of Pine View
Taneskatou
Cody
Katrina of Kent
Ch. Karnovanda's Zenda
Ron's Shasta of Lion Point
Vicki of Kolima
1966
A-Baska's Lisitsa Cheechako
Ch. Baron of Karnovanda
Tinot Vohlk
Crown Jewel's Tanya
Frosty Aire's Gray Heather
Tungortok Iyes
Ch. Zucane's Dieva of Nakhodka
Sno-Caps Arluk of Artiksong
Savdajaure Kak-Tovik
Caribou's Keki of Nanook
Ch. Frosty Aire's Banner Boy
Ch. Karen's Token of Karnovanda
King Jobi of Cibby
Lady Puschenka
Kheta's Snowbird of Paumanok

Nomei of Baronoff
Velika's Gay Sasha
Baltic Chilla's Hao-Chi-La
Nietchievo of Natomah
Nikolayev of Booran
Storm's Winter Girl of Sno-Dak
Tuktoyaktuk
Yusun Bulak of Laptev
Ch. Czar Petronia
Storm's Polar of Sno-Dak
Keld's Tip of the Wind
1967
Kris Quitoxe
Pataud of Taku
Alakazan's Tocan of Christmas
Karnovanda's Nina
Kayak of Martha Lake
Ch. Rob-Ida's Tanya
Ch. Tonkova of the Midnight Sun
Ch. Frosty Aire's Anvic
Ch. Kursk of Sakhalin
Martin's King Tiki
Ch. Nakhodka's Samara
Polaris' Petya Pandovitch
Tiki Devitsa
Koryak's Domino-A-Go-Go
Nina's Stormey Fox
Ch. Bandit of Wind Willow
Bluebell's Brave Buckaroo
Eu-Mor's Misty Morn
Kanaktuk's Kuska of Ivy
Egay's Freckled Valentine
Ki's Kim Nunivak
Lostland's Yukon Queen
Ch. Frosty's Blaze
Mar-Lynn's Sitka
Dichoda's Arora Nikki
Nonie's Misty
Sinsi Ky
Teklok of North Star
Tuck of Chinook
Ty-Sun of Baltic

Ch. Alakazan's
Valeska, C.D.,
Siberian Husky
obedience titlist
owned by Eleanor
Grahn of Valeskamo
Kennels, Florissant,
Missouri.

Ch. Alexoff of
Yakutska, C.D., one
of the Siberian
Huskies at the Yakut-
ska Kennels of Bar-
bara and Kenneth
Kauffman, Burnsville,
Minnesota. The
Kauffmans have been
in the breed since
1961, in dogs since
1940.

Ch. Kayak of Martha
Lake, C.D., is owned
by Maurice and Lynne
Patterson of Gig
Harbor, Washington.
Yaki was whelped in
August, 1963 and is
one of the outstand-
ing show and
obedience dogs at the
Pattersons' Tandara
Kennels.

Warpath
Candy's Spitfire of Lion Point
Katmai's Nuee Ardente
Kodiak of Alpine Glenn
Koryak's Co-Ma-Tek of Lion Point
Snoridge's Niko
Storm's North Wind of Sno-Dak
1968
Kamchatka's Bandit
Arizona State Germo V Toluck
Kelso's Cloudy Sno-Job
Nisha Northern Star
Norther Echo's Kivi
Reeder's Nicole Ron
Koryak's Rashka Demi
Ch. Beau Tuk Katrina
Czarina Jara Harlequinoma
Ch. Del's Artic Star
Jester's White River Queen
Karnovanda's Cheeka
Ch. Ebony Tuff of Lion Point
Kamchatka's Clear Cadance
Laika La Marchese
Ch. Alakazan's Satan Sitka
Alakazan's Valeska
Chuchi's Princess Snowflake
Doonauk King Husky
Teko's Kelsak of Baltic
Ch. Dichoda's Arora-Chena
Dichoda's Echo of the Yukon
Frosty Aire's Black Baron
Gay Karamia
Kim of Chu-Nik
Ch. King Togo of Husky Acres
Natomah's Mikilak
Ch. Alexoff Of Yakutsk
Ch. Kimmiks Stormy
Storm of Green Mountain
Kodiak King of the North
Miowak of the Bastion
Ch. Natomah's Kee Na
Ot-Key-Luk
Bandit of Chuchi

Ch. Frosty Aire's So Cold
Karluk of Baltic
Nataha VI
1969
Mar-Lynn's Tyee Tanglefoot
Rimski of Lion Point
Sampo's Wolf
Arahaz Czar Nalchik
Arctic's Tishka
Doonauk King Kol-Tov Kiak
Grand Dutchess Victoria
Kolyma's Kalak
Maxell's Princess Frosty
Tawnya's Frost Bite
Chajeba's Nijinsky
Kashga of Niviasar
Boom Boom's Pudibuk of Yeso Pac
Colorado's Silver Dushka
Savdajaure's Eska La Marchese
Sitka's Sahuaro
Ch. Tuk of Natomah
Frosty Tark
Niviasar Niketia of Koryak
Sun Ray Suki
Zero's Kepa of Oomik
Maxell's Eskimo Prince
Ivan the Terrible
Nicholas Sebastian of Pouder
Ch. Scandia's Frosty Mist
Volpino of the Midnight Sun
Czar Niki of Rehnoll
Sno-Ana's Sukhama Kem
Snogold's Misty North Land
Ch. Diablo Snow
Dichoda's Echo Lobo
Ch. The Pargon Panther
Dichoda's Echo Chiota
Jocamkas Taku
Kodiak's Tundra Blue
Lamberdoon Tzalzkele Tiara
Tashnik's King Nikki
Trinka II

A lovely characteristic head study of Ch. Dichoda's Arora Chena, C.D. owned by the Akalan Kennels, Livermore, California.

A magnificent headstudy of Ch. Baron of Karnovanda, C.D., taken by E.H. Frank. Lillian M. Russell is the owner of the famous Karnovanda Kennels in Davisburg, Michigan.

Ch. Karnovanda's Zenda, C.D., show and obedience winner owned by Lillian M. Russell, Karnovanda Kennels, Davisburg, Michigan.

Ch. Arctic's Donette Kasha, C.D., one of the outstanding show, sled and obedience dogs at Charlotte and Earl Reynolds Arctic Kennels in Dryden, Michigan.

1970
Forsythe's Lara
Kineki's Tonka
Nadia Crushenka
Nanook's Wild Wind of Sno-Dak
Amur's Apache
Arahaz' Snow Tar
Benton-Mar's Demetrius
Chinook of Spring Hill
Enfield's Czar Nicholas
Karnovanda's Raki Von Ref
Mintaku's Theda
Silver Sergeant
Tandara's Zarevna Totiana
Doncar's Snow Valley Flicka
Cheeching Panda Bear
Colo's Silver Wind of Gonya
Chotovotka's Papreeka
Ethel's Tatiana of Arahaz
Kilmalcolm's Akela
Ch. Nakhodka's Hallene
Yuri Mal-Luk
Akalan's Yuri
Azul Diablo
Ma Pal's Lady Charrakassy
Nikandre's Sasha
S-K-Mo's Bright Star
Czar of Northfield
Kossack's Neewa
Onachee Gay of Husky Acres
Berik's Shagilluk
Blizzard's Mynnyk of Norpak
Igor's Noko
Klondike of Eistmark
Prince Nikolai of Altai
Shelta's Yutan Czarvich
Tasha's Our Girl
Kiva of Kolima
Mt. Sanitas Kobuk
Phillips Kamchatka
1971
Alyeska Kiev of Chinook

Baika of Tovarin
Natasha of Misty Mountain
Willowa's Frosty Niska
Winsum's Rakish Romanov
Zambeck's Khan of Kamchatka
Amur's Keiko Of Si Wes
Binnie's Silver Saska
Honeymist's Blue Bandit
Keena Keeta's Mebsa
Manitou's Umilik
Mysovaya Of Dreamalot
Bruno's Ivan Grovonovich
Fra-Mar's Ko-No
Ch. Mischa of Chaya
Princess Nikki
Toluck's Sun King Nikita
Igloo Cooyan Le Count
Princess Kiska
Robann's Heidi Ho
Savdajaure's Kunuk
Koyuk From The North
Paitot's Polara of Sno-Dak
Ta Taneesha of Cherski
Eu-Mor's Kiev
Goosaks Amaroq of Nanook
Kunu of Cinnaminson
Sibra of Frosty Hills
Big Mac's Loki
Kimo XIV
Klik's Lady Misha
Meriken's Natasha Keeferovna
Nikolai Of Noorvik
Prince Toyon Of Blue Hill
Reddings Princess Kachina
Robann's Lady Sheba
Ch. Tanga Of Greenwell
Troika Sobaka Of Blazeridge
Ch. Dovercrest Alehta Pesna
Erdman's Little Tasha
Freckle Foot
Sergay Of Gray Ghost
Shilka's Black Natasha

Jean and Rift Fournier's Ch. Dovercrest Alehta Pesna, CD. The Fourniers are from Atlantic Highlands, New Jersey. Photo by Judy Rosemarin.

Blue Smoke of Tandara
Duchess Katya of Rehnoll
Duke Ronka of Karnovanda
Fluffy II
1972
Klutuk's Rudolph Czar
Nicholas of Northland
Pandanouk of Quantas
Eu-Mor's Cinnamic
Kochikha Of Copper Creek
Naviska's Keeya
Cherni Meshka
Karnovanda's Baronina Kukla
Kee's Norvik Blaza
Kopak's Kayak
Koyukuk's Nakomek
Oden of Keni
Prince Rurik of Novgorod
Siberias Dusty Demon
Snoridge's Keemah
Togiak of Wabash Valley
Cherski's Sandor
Domino Of Yankee Czar
Fra-Mar's Kahn
Gay-Don's Nikolai
Kara Khaya
Peri's Kingmikai
Robco's Lady Natasha
S-K-Mo's Sierra Echo
Ch. Kosha Of Devil Creek
Nanuk's Husky
Princess Natasha Of Altai
Tokis
Vihuco's Pinegrove Mikhail
Wissahickon Beowulf
Arcticdawn's Troko
Cheechako Black Party Punch
Nina Of Bolta
Snoridge's Larah Of Varykino
Frosty's Bandit Chief
Janterrs Ludmilla

Karnovanda Kiev of Chuchi
Kochevoey's Dushenka Of Akela
Nikmute's Tanka
White Fox's Kayakin Of Anadyr
Alakazan's Zipa
Koywyn's Applejack
Mir-Amu's Tava
Ch Akalan's Sonia
Beowulf Telcontar
Cheechako III
Dichoda's Myuk Karahleva
Kiska Of Sowasco
Mi-Ko Tashya
Northland's Gay Sara
Northland's Kris Kringle
Yoch's Arctic Kushka
Amorak's Miss Sasha
Cindyred's Lublu
Cinnaminson's Sasha II
Gusbadan Of Anadyr
Ch. Koryak's Cherda Of North Star
Marushka Of The Midnight Sun
Monarch's Krasna
Naviska's Little Miss Grummit
Ch. Savdajaure's Mink
Silver Bay's Quiet Red
Suki's Frosty Tannya
Tanana's Sun Shadow
Tini's Shooting Star O'Halidom
Bentonmar's Natasha
Ga-Ril's Naku
Margaret's Komaberg of Akron
Maun Eka's Zarina Katrina
Niki's Dream Anouk
Sashelik Leorah
Ch. Scandia's Bobby Dazzler
Shrader's Cactus Saxa
Dichoda's Oma Turakh
Jubo's Shannon of Snoshu
Mandak's Itchcon Paka
Noovik's Tania Acziak

C.D. dogs recorded through December 1972 issue of AK Gazette

Ch. Akalan's Sonia, C.D., whelped in 1968 and became an outstanding brood bitch at the Akalan Kennels in Livermore, California. The lovely Sonia was sired by Ch. Stony River's Taiki-O *ex* Ch. Dichoda's Arora Chena, C.D. also owned by the Akalan Kennels of Dean and Dolores Warner.

THE COMPANION DOG EXCELLENT DEGREE

There are seven exercises which must be executed to achieve the C.D.X. degree, and the percentages for achieving these are the same as for the U.D. degree. Candidates must qualify in three different obedience trials and under three different judges and must have received scores of more than 50% of the available points in each exercise, with a total of 170 points or more out of the possible 200. At that time they may add the letter C.D.X. after their name.

C.D.X. titles have been granted to the following dogs since the first one was awarded to Ch. Chornyi of Kabkol in 1947: their names have been published in the *American Kennel Gazette:*

1947
Ch. Chornyi of Kabkol
1952
Foxstand's Sparkle
1959
Little Sepp's Stormy of Sno-Dak
1961
Ch. Chuchi of Tinker Mountain
1962
Ch. Kenai Kittee of Beauchein
Frosty Aire's Noorvik
Ch. Tyndrum's Oslo
1963
Snow-Dak's Blizzard of Anadyr
Ch. Eska's Nonie
Kim's Karen
Savag of Erebus
Ffoff's Tabagfac
1964
Ch. Kodii Kuska de Sforza
Koko-Nor of Kuskokwin
1965
Sadiq of Kanaiok
Tovarish of Erebus
Abaska's Nanook
Sitka Snow Queen
1966
J-Bet's Alaskan Honey
Ch. Foxhaunt's Tovarisch

1967
Kanaiok's Ferlin Husky
Tinot Vohlk
1968
Niva's Stormey Fox
Velika's Gay Sasha
1969
Ch. Dichoda's Arora Nikki
Warpath
Ch. Kanaktuk's Kuska of Ivy-K
Mat-Lynn's Sitka
Kodiak King of the North
Ch. Scandia's Frosty Mist
Kolyma's Kolak
1970
Ch. Eu-Mor's Misty Morn
Frosty Tark
Doncar's Snow Valley Flicka
1971
Colo's Silver Wind of Gonya
Nadia Grushenka
Silver Sergeant
Klondike of Eistmark
Forsythe's Lara
Kunu of Cinnaminson
1972
Akalan's Yuri
Amur's Keikoe of Siwes
Robann's Heidi Ho

Impressive head study of Ch. Akalan's Yuri, C.D.X., and owned by the Akalan Kennels in Livermore, California. Sired by Ch. Czar Nicholas *ex* Ch. Dichoda's Arora Chena, C.D., Yuri was whelped in 1967.

Ch. Kodii Kuska De Sforza, C.D.X., owned by Antonio J. Zarlenga, earned both his C.D., and C.D.X. degrees in his first three trials and received an award for saving his owner's life when gas escaped in their home, and has frequently entertained with his owner at various local civic affairs.

Ch. Dichoda's Arora Nikki, C.D.X., owned by Dean and Dolores Warner, Akalan Kennels, Livermore, California. Whelped January 18, 1965 she was sired by Ch. Monadnock's Rurik of Nanook *ex* Dichoda's Beauty of S-K-Mo.

Klutuk's Rudolf Czar
Tandara's Zarevna Tatiana
Ch. Eu-Mor's Kiev
Naviska's Keeya
Nikolai of Noorvik

1973
Princess Kiska
Ch. Savdajaure's Kunuk
Volpino of the Midnight Sun
Mir-Amu's Tara
Phillips Kamchatka
Ch. Winsum's Rakish Romanov

Names listed as of the June, 1973, issue of the *American Kennel Gazette*.

Over the top! Ch. Kunu of Cinnaminson, C.D.X., goes through his paces for photographer and Husky owner Judy Rosemarin of Roslyn, New York. Kunu is owned by Sy and Ann Goldberg.

Right on! John A. Holad's Ch. Savdajaure's Kunuk, C.D.X. of Revere, Massachusetts, clears the hurdle in good order.

THE UTILITY DOG DEGREE

The Utility Dog degree is awarded to dogs which have qualified by successfully completing six exercises under three different judges at three different obedience trials, with a score of more than 50% of available points in each exercise, and with a score of 170 or more out of a possible 200 points.

These six exercises consist of Scent Discrimination, with two different articles for which they receive thirty points each if successfully completed; Direct Retrieving, for 30 points; Signal Exercise for 35 points; Directed Jumping for 40 points and a Group Examination for 35 points.

The following Siberian Huskies have completed the requirements for the Utility Dog title and have had their names published in the American Kennel Gazette:

1948
Ch. Chornyi of Kabkol
1963
Ch. Chuchi of Tinker Mountain
1964
Ch. Kim's Karen
1965
Ch. Eska's Nonie
Ffoff's Tabagfac
1967
Tovarish of Erebus
Ch. Kodii Kuska de Sforza
1969
J-Bet's Alaskan Honey
1971
Tinot Vohlk
Ch. Scandia's Frosty Mist
1972
Doncar's Snow Valley Flicka
Frosty Tark
Klondike of Eistmark
1973
Silver Sergeant
Names listed as of the June, 1973 issue of the American Kennel Gazette

Ch. Kim's Karen, U.D. Karen is one of two Utility Dog titlists owned by Judith M. Russell of Karnovanda Kennels in Michigan.

Ch. Scandia's Frosty Mist, U.D., takes off for a romp in the snow. Owned by Vivienne Lundquist of California.

THE TRACKING DOG DEGREE

The Tracking Dog trials are not held, as the others are, with the dog shows, and need be passed only once.

The dog must work continuously on a strange track at least 440 yards long and with two right angle turns. There is no time limit, and the dog must retrieve an article laid at the other end of the trail. There is no score given; the dog either earns the degree or fails. The dog is worked by his trainer on a long leash, usually in harness.

There are comparatively few dogs in any breed which attain this degree, so the Siberian Huskies which have earned it are to be especially commended. The three which have met the requirements and have had their names published in the *American Kennel Gazette* as having done so are:

1949
Ch. Chornyi of Kabkol
1966
Ch. Chuchi of Tinker Mountain
1969
Juno's Lad CD

Chornyi and Chuchi are entitled to use the letters U.D.T. after their names which includes their U.D. title. Lad uses T.D. for Tracking Dog only.

THE STORY OF CHORNYI OF KABKOL, U.D.T.

We live in an age of great progress and achievement, and we all know that records are made to be broken. But there is a great deal to be said for those who set the records that we must live up to and strive to break in the name of progress. Such is the story of Ch. Chornyi of Kabkol, the first U.D.T. (Utility Dog Tracking) Siberian Husky in the history of the breed. Others may follow, but Chornyi will always remain first!

The H. Richard Garretts of Washington, D.C. obtained Chornyi in April, 1946, and he earned his C.D. degree by December of that same year. With Mr. Garrett handling the dog exclusively he had earned his C.D.X. title less than one year later, by September, 1947. By December of 1947 he had won his championship in the show ring and within four months of championship won his Utility Dog degree (in April, 1948). A year later he was the first U.D.T. dog in our breed's history.

Ch. Chornyi of Kabkol, U.D.T., the first champion U.D.T. dog in the Siberian Husky breed. Chornyi's record was as follows: C.D. title December, 1946; C.D.X. title in September, 1947; Championship December, 1947; U.D. Degree, April, 1948; and U.D.T. Degree in April, 1949. Chornyi (1945-1959) was owner-handled all the way by H. Richard Garrett, Washington, D.C.

During this time Chornyi was winning friends for the breed and setting records at the same time. In earning his C.D. title he finished in three consecutive shows, the second C.D. Husky on record. He was the first Siberian to finish for a C.D.X. degree, and on April 8, 1948 he finished first in his class, earning his U.D. title. The tracking test was granted on the first try.

Through the years Chornyi got to putting his training to good purpose. He has not only performed at hospitals and schools and before church groups but also has used his remarkable tracking ability to help the police on two occasions. The first time he located a boy's body wedged between rocks and out of sight of the rescue team, and on the second occasion he was instrumental in saving an old woman lost in the woods.

Chornyi, whelped in 1945, died in 1959, after having lived a full and useful life with his devoted family.

Ch. Chuchi of Tinker Mt., U.D.T. was the second champion U.D.T. in the Siberian Husky breed and the first bitch to complete the title. While a champion when Richard and Virginia Garrett of Washington, D.C., obtained her, she earned all her obedience titles with her new owner, H. Richard Garrett. Chuchi (1956-1970) and Chornyi are still the only two U.D.T. dogs in the breed. Chuchi's record was as follows: Championship in December, 1959; C.D. in October, 1960; C.D.X. Degree October 1961; U.D. Degree September, 1963 and U.D.T. Degree in October, 1965.

THE STORY OF CHUCHI
OF TINKER MOUNTAIN, U.D.T.

Chuchi came to live with the H. Richard Garretts as a champion and at the age of four. So sorely did they miss their beloved Chornyi that they decided they must have another Siberian Husky to obedience train and love and bring attention to the breed the way Chornyi had. They obtained Chuchi from Louise Foley and Jimmy Whitfield, and they made her the second Siberian Husky and first Siberian Husky bitch to become a dual champion in breed and obedience.

Chuchi acquired her C.D. in October, 1960, her C.D.X. by October, 1961, her U.D. by September, 1963, and the record of being the second Siberian to earn the Utility Dog title. In 1965 she acquired her Tracking

Dog title and the honor of being the second U.D.T. Siberian Husky in the history of the breed. Her good long life was from 1956 to 1970.

The Garretts are most pleased and proud of their achievements with their two Siberian Huskies. They teach obedience in the Washington, D.C. Rock Creek Park, and obedience is their prime pleasure. We can be justly proud that these two accomplished and dedicated people chose our breed to set records that reflect glory on all of us.

THE STORY OF DONCAR'S SNOW VALLEY FLICKA, U.D.

One of the most outstanding all-around Siberian Huskies in the breed is Don Carlough's Doncar's Snow Valley Flicka, U.D. Bred by C. B. Hitchins, Flicka was sired by Cognac's Snow Lad of Koryak out of Vyesna Pulchrissimo Kindera. A true working dog in every sense of the word, Flicka now lives with her owner at the Doncar Kennels in Suffern, New York.

Flicka got off to a remarkable start in the obedience field. She received her C.D. title as a nine-month-old puppy in her first three trials. By the time she reached a year and a half, she had won her C.D.X. title, also in three consecutive shows. At 2½ she was a Utility Dog title holder and was being used in obedience demonstrations in the area. She was also a member of an all-breed obedience team which used lighted lanterns in their routine.

Flicka is also a member of the Garden State Obedience Demonstration Team which performed at the National Specialty Show in 1972. Flicka is also active in competition in obedience brace class and is a member of a Scent Hurdle Relay Race Team which is active in Northern New Jersey. She is trained in tracking, and was cited by *Chips,* the national dog obedience magazine, as the top-ranking Siberian Husky in obedience in the United States for the year 1970.

Flicka has been shown in the conformation classes and holds points toward championship; she also runs on Don Carlough's sled dog team and is used for ski-joring. She is also trained for mountain and trail pack hiking. . . a true all-around dog for the Husky Hall of Fame!

THE STORY OF CH. SAVDAJAURE'S KUNUK, C.D.X.

John A. Holad wanted to prove something with his Siberian Husky. He wanted to dispel the idea that obedience training spoils a dog for the show ring! He wanted to prove that a dog can excel in both fields. And he did.

One of the most remarkable Siberian Huskies in the breed. . . Doncar's Snow Valley Flicka, U.D. Flicka received her C.D. title in three trials at the age of nine months, her C.D.X. title in three trials also. Her U.D. title was won when she was only 2½. Flicka has been shown in obedience competition in the Obedience Brace class and is a member of a scent hurdle relay race team in New Jersey. She is trained in tracking and has championship points. She is also pack-, sled-, mountain- and trail-hiking-trained and is used by her owner, Don Carlough of Suffern, New York, for ski-jourring.

A beautiful headstudy of Ch. Savdajaure's Kunuk, C.D.X., owned by John A. Holad of Revere, Massachusetts.

As a puppy Kunuk was shown at match shows, and at his first two matches he won over entries of 400 dogs as Best in Match. At the 1970 Ladies Dog Club show he won his first five-point major, and ten weeks later he finished for his championship under Short Seeley with his fifth five-point major. By this time he was doing some serious obedience training as well with Margaret Ambrose, who is largely responsible for seeing him through to his C.D.X. title.

To finish for his C.D. title, he scored 193, 197 (and was fourth highest scoring dog in a class of 54) and 194 in three consecutive shows. His C.D.X. title was also earned in three consecutive shows with scores of 183, 192 (and tied for 1st in open class) and 187, on November 11, 1972.

Kunuk is a proven stud and is hard at work training for his Utility Dog Title. And while he is working toward that U.D., he is also being shown as a Special, which certainly proves what John A. Holad set out to prove: a good dog can win in both the show and obedience rings. . .and love every minute of it!

THE THREE MUSKETEERS

Vivienne P. Lundquist of Marina del Rey, California is, by her own admission, completely dedicated to her three Siberian Huskies. There would be more than three, but the fact that she lives in an apartment at a West Coast marina forbids the kind of kennel breeding program Vivienne would really like to delve into. Until the situation changes she keeps very busy with what she refers to as her "Three Musketeers." They are Ch. Scandia's Frosty Mist, U.D., Ch. Scandia's Bobby Dazzler, C.D. and Ch. Scandia's Turukham Tyger, C.D.

Finishing the dogs to their championships wasn't enough for Vivienne; she wanted the dogs to prove their great intelligence in the obedience ring as well. She knew that the dogs could go as far as she would take them, so they went to work to earn their titles. The dogs and Vivienne do their thing in the parking lot in front of their apartment house, with all the sail and power boats moored at the dock at the marina. They always draw a big crowd whenever they practice their obedience commands or go through their paces while pulling their cart. Vivienne says the local residents got used to it after awhile; they've even helped set up the jumps, and then sat around cheering the dogs on no matter *what* they did!

Frosty Mist, Vivienne's first Husky, had one litter. Vivienne kept the two males, Dazzler and Tyger, and they earned their C.D. degrees within six months of each other, each earning the Dog World of Distinction Award for consecutive scores over 195. They are both working toward their C.D.X. degrees. Frosty Mist got her Utility Degree with all scores over 190, and Vivienne's next goal is for her to earn a Tracking

Lying down on the job! Vivienne Lundquist and her team of obedi-
ence-racing dogs take time out.

Degree. Misty spent her early life and got her obedience training aboard a
private yacht on an Alaskan cruise. Her championship was won in six
straight shows with four majors in 30 days!

But for the great change of pace Vivienne gets out the go-cart, and she
and the dogs break the stillness of the cool marina morning air by racing
up and around the paths and along the boat docks, ending up on their
beach, where the rest of the morning is spent chasing ducks in and out of
the water. Obedience training notwithstanding, the dogs suddenly behave like retrievers! Vivienne hastens to add, however, that the story
has a happy ending. The ducks have gotten used to them, and when
the dogs get within three feet of them, they take off and land about
three feet *behind* them.

Quite obviously these dogs are in no way underprivileged; they have
their own snow sled also, and this they put to good use on winter
vacations up north. Vivienne reports that their manners are excellent,
even though they live in an apartment and are the pride of the building
because of their perfect behavior. Vivienne states that the neighbors
always stop by their balcony to visit when the dogs are out there, and
everyone loves to see them do their "chores." Each dog has his own mail
to carry back from the mailroom, and Vivienne says that Bobby Dazzler
usually wins because he runs the fastest AND remembers to hold onto the

Ch. Scandia's Turukhan Tyger takes top honors in the Obedience Trial at a recent Imperial Valley Kennel Club dog show. Presenting the award to owner Vivienne Lundquist of Marina Del Rey, California, is club president Ronald R. Smith and the current Miss Cattle Call Queen, Vickie York. Photo by Henry.

mail. They also are kept busy carrying the bags of laundry down the hall to the laundry room.

Vivienne had a special pen built into the back of her motor home and they frequently take off with enough supplies for a month's trek through the desert or on a dog show circuit. The motor home is appropriately named Igloo.

CHAPTER 8
THE SIBERIAN HUSKY AS A RACING DOG

Relatively few Siberian Huskies become outstanding racing dogs. If they are good, it is usually because top quality racing dogs are in their background and show in their pedigree. Just as a good "nose" is almost always hereditary with a Beagle, so is the desire to run inherent in the Husky.

If they are good racers they are usually under 60 pounds, well angulated, with longer legs and lighter bones, with large and strong feet, a long and deep chest and an independence that sets them apart from others in the kennel.

If these qualifications are wrapped up in your dog, you are still only half way there! You must remember that the dog still has to be properly trained and be able to run with all the other dogs on the team, and *then,* if you don't have a top notch lead dog you probably won't win anyway, especially if the dog doesn't have the most essential ingredient of all—the innate desire to run! The most worrisome thing about the breed today is that so many of the Huskies being bred just do not have that desire to run above all else. Without it, you can never have better than a good team; you will never have a top-winning team!

STARTING THE PUPPY

There is probably no better breed for racing or pulling than the Siberian Husky, because of his stamina and sustained power over long distances. Whether your dog will just race, or race and pull weight, training should start around two or three months of age. Start with a soft harness and let him drag a small log or board around. Judge the weight of the log by the weight of the dog. Don't let it be so heavy that the puppy could not possibly move it without a struggle; if you do that, he'll lose interest or get discouraged. By the same token, don't let it be so light that it will catch up with him on the down grade, or he'll never learn the meaning of what it is to "pull." Try what you think is just right, and then observe the puppy's behavior with it for a while; make any necessary adjustments at this time and, of course, as the puppy continues to grow.

At this time, while the puppy is learning to pull, he should be encouraged to pull along a given path, so that the idea of a trail can be established in his mind should you wish to enter competition in the future.

EARLY TRAINING FOR THE RACING DOG

We have just stressed how important it is that each Husky destined to race have the innate desire to run and to win. This eagerness to compete will enable the trainer to start his harness training at an earlier age and thereby give a head start to the dog on the training as well as conditioning him to his purpose of running and pulling.

If you are fortunate enough to live in snow country, your sled, harness and towline will be your initial equipment for training. If you

Tanya, Black Charger and Tokco rest up after the big race. . . Sy and Ann Goldberg's Siberian Huskies love a good race. The Goldbergs' Cinnaminson Kennels are in Cream Ridge, New Jersey.

Vincent Buoniello, Jr. and his team gathering up steam for a race.

live in a comparatively snowless area you will need a three-wheeled balanced substitute for training. Training should be a serious matter and in no way the same as or comparable to playtime. Start with each dog individually pulling some weight. This individual training will help you determine which of the puppies has the strongest desire to pull ahead in spite of the weight. You will find that invariably the dog with the strongest desire to pull will make the best lead dog by the time your training nears completion.

Mrs. Jean Fournier with her five-dog team competing in a gig race at MASDRA Race in Lebanon State Forest, New Jersey. Gigs for training dogs and the gig races in areas where there is no snow are becoming very popular all over the United States. Mrs. Fournier's team includes three champions. Left lead is Ch. Dovercrest Awsinee Pesna; Right lead is Ch. Fournier's Zachariah of Toko; right point is the peebald Marlytuk's Casper the Ghost; left wheel is Ch. Fournier's Tiffany of Toko; and right wheel is Yeso Pac's Southern Belle (13 points at this writing). Jean and Rift Fournier's kennels are in Atlantic Highlands, New Jersey.

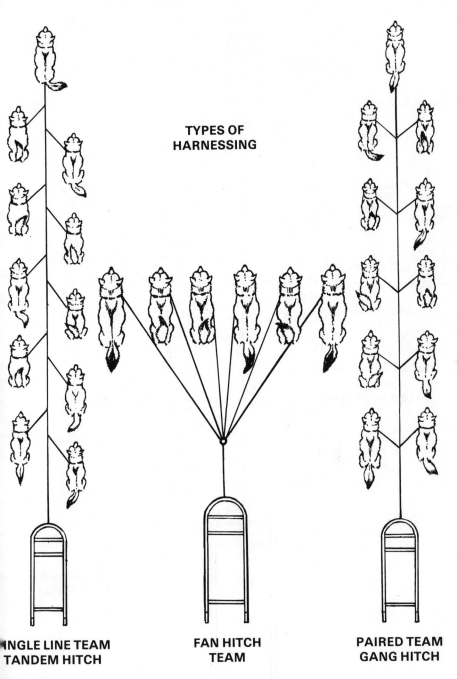

TYPES OF HARNESSING

SINGLE LINE TEAM TANDEM HITCH

FAN HITCH TEAM

PAIRED TEAM GANG HITCH

Types of harnessing. Drawings by Ernest H. Hart.

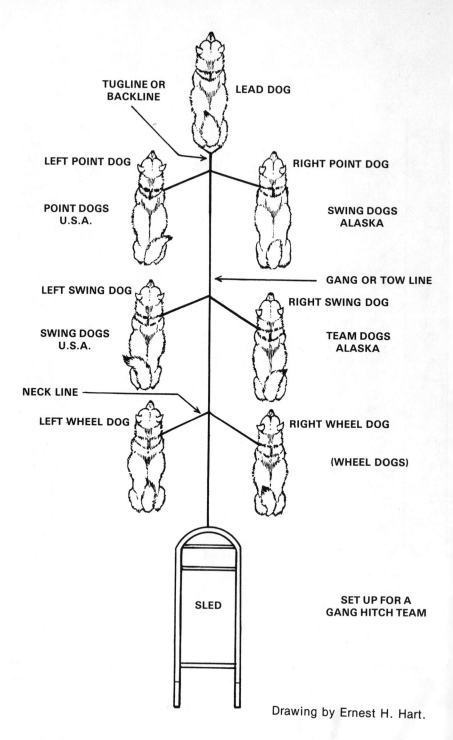

TUGLINE OR
BACKLINE

LEAD DOG

LEFT POINT DOG

RIGHT POINT DOG

POINT DOGS
U.S.A.

SWING DOGS
ALASKA

GANG OR TOW LINE

LEFT SWING DOG

RIGHT SWING DOG

SWING DOGS
U.S.A.

TEAM DOGS
ALASKA

NECK LINE

LEFT WHEEL DOG

RIGHT WHEEL DOG

(WHEEL DOGS)

SLED

SET UP FOR A
GANG HITCH TEAM

Drawing by Ernest H. Hart.

American, Bermudian and Canadian Ch. Fra-Mar's Soan Diavol pictured winning a Working Group at the Dan Emmett Kennel Club Show with his handler George Heitzman. Judge was Nelson Groh. Photo by Norton of Kent. Owner Marie Wamser of Cleveland, Ohio. Soan was handled and finished to his championship in 29 days at 14 months of age by his owner and was top Husky in the Phillips System in 1966, 1968 and 1969. He was top Siberian Husky in Canada in 1970. Soan and his father, Ch. Frosty Aire's Alcan King, are the first father and son combination to each win a Best in Show award. His record is one Best in Show, 37 Group placings in the U.S.A., five Group placings in Bermuda, and six Group placings in Canada.

THE TRAINING GROUND

One of the most difficult aspects of training will be finding the proper place to train the puppies. If you do not live in the country it will be necessary to locate a park or wooded area, or better still, a local race track where the dogs can run a distance with minimum danger of interruption by uncertain terrain. Too many distractions in populated areas will throw puppies or young dogs off until they are used to what is expected of them. With too many spectators around there is always the danger of having the team bowl them over if they get in the way. Therefore, until the puppies get used to running and keeping on the trail, bridle paths, fields and or farm lands are the best places to work out. Remember the safety of others when tearing down a path with a team of Huskies! Under no circumstances train your dogs on the street or a concrete surface. The irritation to the pads of the feet somehow prevents the dogs from reaching out to their full stride, so they never become good distance runners in a race. Ideal conditions are snow or sand, but if such surfaces are not available, train on dirt surfaces to prevent the hackneyed gait of the dogs

Marie Wamser, owner of the Fra-Mar Kennels, drives her team with Ch. Fra-Mar's Karo Mia Diavol in the lead.

A six-mile Pennsylvania Sled Dog Club race in 1971 finds driver Jean Fournier coming around the bend with her five-dog team. The Fournier Siberian Husky Kennels are in Atlantic Highlands, New Jersey, and the dogs compete in both the show ring and the races.

The male Lumimaan Talvi pictured with "musher" Walter Schmidt by a Swiss sled dog camp in 1971. Owner is Toni Schmidt, Switzerland. Photo by Kerttu Alm.

Ch. Chotovotka's Nota Yankidrink wins Best of Breed and Group First under judge Lorna Demidoff at the Steel City Kennel Club Show in Indiana in February, 1973. Nota is owned by Bob and Dorothy Page, Chotovotkas' Kennels. Robert Holiday photograph.

which are trying to preserve their own feet, or which will pull up with bloody pads if forced to run on pavement.

As the puppies grow and begin their working together, you will undoubtedly have joined a club in your area where members are equally interested in racing. You will learn a great deal from your association with other members, and it is advisable to take full advantage of their advice, knowledge and experience. But there still are going to be many hours of training on your own where a few essential rules will apply.

Important to remember in your training is this: do not teach too many commands. Young puppies can not retain too many words, and expecting too much of them too soon will only confuse them and perhaps make them lose interest entirely. Remember to praise them lavishly for their good work and efforts. Remember to keep your puppies and dogs in top racing condition so that they will be able to give what is expected of them without draining every last bit of energy. Remember common sense rules which apply to racing as well as obedience or show training; namely, do not feed or water immediately before training, and exercise the puppies before starting the training so there will be no interruption. And perhaps most important of all, do not go on to another command or lesson until the dog has already learned the last one!

You will find that your puppy can cover a mile comfortably by the time he is eight months old, which should increase to 15 or 16 miles at the peak of his training and performance at two years of age.

DISPOSITION AND ATTITUDE

One of the determining factors in selecting your team will be each dog's disposition. The training may have gone along very well, but if the dog is a "scrapper" and will be undependable when harnessed with other dogs in a team, you will eventually run into trouble. While it is allowable to remove a dog from a team during a race, it would make more sense to have all members of your team able to finish if you really want to win and need that full team to do it!

When we talk about Huskies' being smart in their own special way, we must explain that at times there is an almost obvious "holding back" or lack of complete communication between you and the dog, which manifests itself noticeably in their training for racing competition. When a Husky is being trained to race he will usually pace himself to fit the distance he must cover on his own. Therefore, it is wise when training the dog for the race to steadily increase the distance each day, rather than varying the ground mileage to be cov-

Ch. Sandyhill's Chukchi Red, better known as "Red," lead dog for owners Thom and Claudia Ainsworth of Novato, California. Red seems to be saying, "You mean we lost the race?" Photograph by Thom Ainsworth.

An informal at-home photo of the magnificent blue-eyed dark red Best in Show winner Ch. Wolfden's Copper Bullet. Bullet is owned by Beryl Allen of the Wolfden Kennels in Jaffrey, New Hampshire. The Wolfden Siberians both race and show.

Two teams race for the finish line at the 1972 Tamworth Race. Finish photographed by Judy Rosemarin.

Four puppies. . . four weeks old! These Siberian Husky puppies are enjoying their first outing and their first session before the camera with photographer Judy Rosemarin.

Vivienne Lundquist of Marina Del Rey, California, on holiday in the snow country with three friends. . . Bobby, Frosty and Tyger.

The Panuck-Denali Kennel Team, Judi Anderson driving the five-dog team (their Prince in the lead, Natasha and Melinki on point, Shoshanna and Attu on wheel. Start of the 1973 Ridge Race on the NESDC Circuit. The Panuck-Denali Kennels are owned by Charlotte and Judith Anderson in Laconia, New Hampshire.

ered from one day to the next. Increasing distance each day will increase his desire to always "go further," and to the end of the race.

FORMING YOUR TEAMS

A tenet in animal behavior studies acknowledges that there is a leader in every pack. So it is with a racing team. Your lead dog must be the most respected member of your kennel or the other dogs simply will not give their all and "follow the leader." Whatever the sex of the lead dog, put your next two fastest dogs behind the lead dog and your biggest, or strongest, two at the wheel positions.

While your lead dog will assert himself to keep order in the pack, to maintain a good team you must have harmony among all members of the team. Drivers will find that on occasion if they buy dogs from other teams to add to their own, the new dog is apt not to pull and will be dragged by the rest unless he feels he has been accepted by the other dogs as a member of the pack. Puppies from the same litter, trained together, often make the best teams for this reason. They "grow into the saddle."

Practice makes perfect, as the saying goes, and hours of practice and training are necessary to get all your dogs working together as a team. There is no easy way to accomplish this other than hard work. It is a magnificent challenge.

SLED DOG RACING EVENTS
Sled Dog Racing in Idaho

1917 was the first year of the American Dog Derby in Ashtown, Idaho. This event is still held for racing enthusiasts. Today, however, the club holds several racing events in several different towns each year. They feature ten mile courses each day for two days. This is quite a different schedule from the 1917 event, when a half dozen teams of mixed breeds raced from West Yellowstone, Montana to Ashtown, Idaho—a distance of 75 miles!

Don Hanson of the Windwillow Kennels, in Leavenworth, Washington, driving his team at the Priest Lake races in 1971. Lead dog is Unyuk of Igluk, Dwikar's Kuger, an Alaskan dog, Windwillow's Foxrun, and Windwillow's Dark Secret.

Mrs. Lorna B. Demidoff and her team, led by the famous Ch. Monadnock Pando, pictured on the grounds of the Monadnock Kennels in Fitzwilliam, New Hampshire.

Sy Goldberg and his five-dog team coming in from a race. The team of all champion dogs finds Am. and Can Ch. Tanya of Cinnaminson in the lead position; right point, Ch. Koryak's Black Charger; left point, Ch. Mischa of Chaya, C.D., right wheel, Ch. Tokco of Bolshoi and left wheel Ch. Chachka of Cinnaminson. Sy and Ann Goldberg's Cinnaminson Kennels are in Cream Ridge, New Jersey.

Number 3 team with driver Tom Palmer approaches finish line at Priest Lake, Idaho competition. Tom Palmer is owner of Arctura Kennels, Napa, California.

Sled Dog Racing in Minnesota

The St. Paul, Minnesota, Winter Carnival in 1962 was the site of the first sled dog racing in the state, in conjunction with the special events at the State Fair.

In 1965 the North Star Sled Dog Club, Inc, was started as a racing club, and by 1969, the club decided to sponsor a major national racing event at the Winter Carnival, they called it "East Meets West". A total of 55 teams competed that year in St. Paul, representing 11 states and Canada. The event was a major breakthrough for racing enthusiasts and has been growing in popularity and competition ever since. The purses get larger each year and the spectators increase notably as well.

While a reasonably new group, the club membership keeps increasing and participating in other racing events, and plans for the future are bright.

Mutt Races

Each year the All American Championship Sled Dog Races are held in Ely, Minnesota, and feature mutt races as part of the special events program. These mutt races are usually held following a torchlight parade, and are run for boys and girls from six to eight years of age, eight to ten years of age, and children from ten to twelve years of age. Each child runs a single hitch, and the one dog may be of any type or breed. The only differential is that they separate the experienced and trained sled dogs from the amateur dogs and run them in separate categories.

There is no entry fee and, of course, trophies are provided for the winners. This is always a popular event with racing enthusiasts of all ages.

Ch. Frosty Aire's Alcan King in full harness. King's sire was Ch. Monadnock's Pando *ex* Kura. He was whelped in January, 1959 and died in August, 1972. Owned by Marie Wamser, Fra-Mar Kennels, Cleveland, Ohio.

Ch. Latarians Sierra Smoke, C.D., owned by Michael E. Burnside of Saugus, California.

Ch. Arahaz' Kaylee Konkon is pictured winning in the show ring with handler Sue Windsor. The Kaylee Siberians are show, obedience and sled dogs and are owned by Mrs. Carolyn McDonough Windsor of Baltimore, Maryland. Photography by US.

Beauty Queens

The Ely event also has been known to feature a beauty queen to appear in the torchlight parade. In 1971, and a repeat performance in 1972, it was Britt-Inger Johannsen, a former Miss Scandinavia and former Miss Sweden, invited by the Sled Dog Committee to head up the parade and to judge such events as a "beard contest" where she rubbed cheeks with those racing participants who sported "beavers."

Special Events

The sled dog gathering usually opens with a community center show which features the latest in sleds, equipment, accessories and demonstrations of anything and everything pertaining to racing, including items which can be purchased.

This is followed on the Firday night by a torchlight parade, with the aforementioned beauty queen, sleds, snowmobiles, floats, and the like. The parade is followed by the special events program, which features weight pulling contests, celebrity races, ski-jorring, a scramble race, a beard contest and the kids' mutt races. Entertainment of the indoor variety follows the activities in these categories.

Warren Keefer, owner of the Winsum Kennels, poised and ready to go. . . at the Winter Festival in February, 1972.

The second day at the 1971 Cle Elum race, B Class, Don Hanson driver on a muddy track. Hilands photo. Don Hanson is owner with wife Anne of the Windwillow Kennels in Leavenworth, Washington.

Ed Dayton of Wilton, California, running a Class B race in Bear Valley, California, in March, 1972. Photograph submitted by the Akalan Kennels in Livermore, California.

Photographed in Lapland, 600 miles from the North Pole, at 40 degrees below zero, this scene shows a Siberian Husky puppy in the arms of the lady in the sled. It was taken as part of an advertising campaign for Glenoit Mills, Inc., subsidiary of Botany Industries. Glenoit Fashion Coordinator Violet Porte characterized Siberians as. . . "the sweetest little dogs you would ever want to know."

Ch. Sierra's Highland Copper Mist, owned by Michael E. Burnside of Saugus, California.

All-champion racing team belonging to the Karnovanda Kennels in Davisburg, Michigan. The lead dog is Ch. Baron of Karnovanda, C.D. Baron is the perfect example of the versatility of the Siberian . . . he excels in both the show and obedience ring and is a spirited racing dog as well.

Saturday sees the first heats of the All American Championship Sled Dog Race. Usually over 100 teams compete. Saturday night there is a banquet and entertainment, and on Sunday the second heats are run; prizes are awarded at the completion of the day's events.

There is over $5000 in prize money awarded to the racers as well as hundreds of dollars worth of trophies to the winners who manage to triumph on one of the finest racing trails in the world. The best known racers from all over the United States (including Alaska, of course) and Canada manage to show up to compete.

Because of the great beauty of the dogs, and the excitement of the chase, there is always a great deal of spectator enthusiasm as well as newspaper, radio and television coverage and stories in major magazines all over the world. Over 20,000 fans show up to cheer on their favorite dog teams. The Chamber of Commerce of Ely, Minnesota, can be proud of their Expo-Mini Sports Show and Sled Dog Races which are the biggest winter sports event in northern Minnesota.

First Race at Bear Valley, Ebbetts Pass, California, in 1971 pictures driver-owner Frank L. King, with Koya Czarina of Kantua and Khan of Kantua (double lead dogs) and King of Kantua at the wheel. This exciting photograph was taken by Joe and Virginia Parrott of Redwood City, California.

Harry Wade and a team of his Siberian Huskies, with Tammi of Chu-Nik in lead position. Harry and Velma Wades' Chu-Nik Kennels are in Amboy, Washington.

Vincent Buoniello's team ready to race at Gardner, Maine in 1972 in Open C Class. The Buoniellos, Phyllis and Vincent, of Northport, New York, own the Fortsalong Kennels and have been in Huskies since 1963. Mr. Buoniello is also a judge of Siberian Huskies at the bench shows.

Group Fourth well as Best of Breed under judge Mrs. Jean Fletcher at the Kitchener-Waterloo Kennel Club show in Ontario, Canada in November, 1971 is American and Canadian Ch. Dudley's Tavar of Innisfree. Clipper, a Best in Show Siberian, is shown by Clarence Dudley of North Syracuse, New York. A Hodges photograph.

Ray Miner about to take off in a Tamworth, New Hampshire race in 1968 with his 9-dog team. Ray and Paula Miner are owners of the Woody Glen Kennels in Penacook, New Hampshire. Ray is president of the New England Sled Dog Club, and Paula is its publicity director. Their record includes many trophies for racing even though the kennel has only been in existence for about ten years.

WORLD CHAMPIONSHIP SLED DOG DERBY

On the eastern seaboard the sledding event takes over the main street of Laconia, New Hampshire, when the racing enthusiasts participate in this major event. Snow-making machines cover the main street with snow if none has fallen from the sky. Laconia also presents a Musher's Ball and crowns a Musher's Queen amid much fanfare.

JUNIOR RACERS

While discussing mutt racing and the wide range of ages which can be found competing, we cannot fail to mention the former junior who made such a name for herself in racing circles. I refer to Darlene Huckins of Tilton, New Hampshire.

Darlene began racing at the age of ten with a three-dog team which she raised and trained herself. By the time she was 15 she had won just about every prize a junior could win with her splendid dogs. Later she became the youngest woman ever to enter the World's Championship Sled Dog Derby in Laconia, New Hampshire. On the first day she placed ninth, and after three days of racing was in 19th place, having won a higher position than many other older and more experienced drivers. In 1968 she finished 16th in the placings and won a trophy for having the best conditioned team in the

Getting ready for the Tamworth Race. . . one dog, one mile distance. Donna Rosendris gets ready for the start of this junior event. Photo by Judy Rosemarin.

This handsome trio of Siberian Huskies belongs to Mrs. Carolyn McDonough Windsor of Baltimore, Maryland and consists of Kaylee Kitkit Kulik, Kaylee Kittee Katek, and Kaylee Kitkit Kayikay at just ten months of age. The litter was sired by Savdajaure's Cognac *ex* Arahaz' Kaylee Keenu. Photography by US.

Judy Rosemarin of Roslyn, New York, takes Winners ribbons at the Long Island show in May, 1972 under Judge Jones with her Chilka's Treska of Weldon.
Photograph by William P. Gilbert.

event. In 1970 she received the Jonathan Allen Memorial Trophy as the top scoring former junior racer.

Darlene's success set a marvelous example for other juniors who loved to race and win with their own teams.

SOME RULES FOR ENTRY

Some of the rules of the Siberian Husky Club of America Sled Sled Dog Class are as follows:

1. Entry must be an American Kennel Club registered Siberian Husky.
2. Dogs and bitches are combined in this class.
3. If entered in one of the regular classes or in Best of Breed Competition, no additional entry fee is required.
4. Entry must have completed two races during the previous racing season, each race having been ten or more miles on consecutive days.

Children's competition at Tahoe Vista, California, sees Richard Palmer come in as number four with his two-dog team. Richard's parents are owners of the Arctura Kennels in Napa, California.

Adorable Jane Anne Houston, of Peterborough, New Hampshire, with Wolfden's Teuqui, owned by Beryl Allen of the Wolfden Kennels in Jaffrey, N.H. The local children race the Siberians, and this handsome pair are winners in the New England Sled Dog Club races.

A barrel of beauties! A litter of four of Elsa Marchesano's puppies, three of which finished for their championships within one year. Mrs. Marchesano is active in the Siberian Husky Club of Greater New York and resides in Levittown, New York.

Ch. Fournier's Tiffany of Toko, pictured winning Best of Breed at the Boardwalk Kennel Club show in December, 1972 under judge Arnold Woolf over an entry of 114 Siberian Huskies. Owner, breeder, and handler is Jean Fournier of Atlantic Highlands, New Jersey.

5. Races must have been held under the direction of a recognized sled dog racing club.
6. Proof of competition must be made available at ringside if challenged. Evidence such as a letter from the race manager or published results, giving dates, finishing positions, times and lengths of races will be sufficient.

VARIATIONS ON THE RULES

Racing rules can sometimes vary according to local conditions, and geographical conditions also enter into it. Some races feature three classes: Class A, teams having a minimum limit of five dogs, with the trail usually 15 to 20 miles, and run in two or three heats on successive days. Total elapsed time determines the winner; Class B, runs from four to seven dogs over an approximate 7- to 10-mile run. This class is also run in heats, with the fastest total elapsed time determining the winner; Class C, or what is referred to as the Novice Class, has a two or three dog limit on a 2- to 3-mile mile course. This class usually awards trophies rather than money prizes. One of the most important things for the beginner to remember is to enter his team in the proper class.

SECURING RACING INFORMATION

If you have decided that you wish to enter a team in a race, you must write to the race-giving club well in advance asking for all pertinent information along with an entry blank. Ask the race marshall for specific information regarding not only the race, but information on joining the club, which you will want to do eventually, if you haven't already. State the size of your team, and ascertain at this time if it is necessary to be a member of the club in order to enter the race. With some clubs this is a requirement.

While waiting for this information to reach you, consider once again whether or not you are *really ready* to enter your first race. Ask yourself whether your dogs are sufficiently trained, run well together, fight in harness, stick to the trail, tangle with other teams, can be distracted by people or other animals on the sidelines? And perhaps most important of all, are all the dogs equal in strength and endurance, and do they all really want to run more than anything else?!?

THE DAY OF THE RACE

You've entered your first race and have received your notification and rules regarding the race, time, place and requirements. Needless

Nine-dog team owned by the Marlytuk Kennels of Mr. and Mrs. Lyle Grant of Carlisle, Massachusetts.

Arahaz' Kaylee Koenu, owned by Carolyn and Sue Windsor of the Kaylee Kennels in Baltimore.

One of the all-time top-winning Siberian Huskies, Ch. Fra-Mars Soan Diavol, pictured here winning a Best In Show award under judge Virgil Johnson. Norton of Kent photo.

Three-dog race at Kingston, New Hampshire, in January, 1973, shows David Wentzell, 16 years old, racing. Photo provided by the Polar Star Kennels, owned by Susan E. Gumb of Bedford, Massachusetts.

to say, the beginner should arrive early to observe the procedures others follow and have plenty of time to ask questions. Be sure you park in the correct area, stake your dogs out in the proper area, exercise them, and determine within plenty of time when the drivers' meeting will be held so that you can attend it.

While you are waiting for the meeting to begin, take the time to reread the rules of the race. As a beginner you may forget. . .and knowing what to do when and where can make a difference! Also check out your equipment.

Always include a complete substitute for your harness and tow lines, collars, leashes, etc., in your tack box. Accidents do happen, and it would be a shame to miss your first experience because a break left you without complete equipment. Don't be afraid to ask questions or to ask for help. Remember that everyone else was a beginner once also, and most of them remember how much it meant to them to have a helping hand or a genuine good word of advice.

Remember good manners during the race. Don't spoil someone else's chances because of your mistake or mistakes. They will be watching out for you if they know you are new at the game, but it is your responsibility not to spoil the race for others. You are expected to know the passing rules, re-passing rules, etc., and you will gain more respect for your sportsmanship and knowledge than you will for trying to stick it out when you should get out of the race. No one expects you to win your first race anyway! But whether you win or lose, once you've gotten into the competition you will become addicted to the sport and sooner or later you will win if your dogs are good and properly trained.

RACING MANNERS

Need we say that bad language, complaining and excuses, rough handling of your dogs (for any reason whatsoever!) drinking, or

Winnie Keefer heads for the finish line so fast the dogs are a blur. Winsum's Yermak is the wheel dog. The Keefers own the Winsum Kennels in Rocky Ridge, Maryland.

Gilena's Lara, right lead on racing team of owner Carol Rice of Shrewsbury, Massachusetts, pictured here with hew New England Sled Dog Racing Trophies, plus the Monadnock Racing Trophy for 1971 and 1972, Siberian Husky club of America Racing Trophy for 1970 and the Douglas Fairbanks Racing Trophy for 1971.

Another fascinating head study from the Windsors' Kaylee
Kennels.

Carol W. Rice driving her racing team at a New England Sled Dog Race at Temple, New Hampshire in 1970. The dogs, all bearing the Czarya's prefix, are Valeska, Kiev, Aleka, Etkatrina, Dakko, Rasputin, and Tovar. Dr. and Mrs. Daniel Rice III own the Runaway Farm Kennels in Shrewsbury Mass.

pushing your dogs beyond their endurance are strictly taboo? How you conduct yourself under any and all conditions will determine how much help and respect you win from your fellow drivers, and if you want to continue in the racing field you had better stick to the rules or you will find yourself strictly an outsider. And that isn't the name of the game!

PROFESSIONAL RACING TEAMS

You must realize that racing for fun and pleasure or in local club meets or contests is entirely different from the professional racing meets where the stakes and purses are high and the owners and drivers are out to win. Professional racing teams are serious business, and it is a completely different world for the professional racing dog!

The trainers and drivers of the professional teams are usually those dedicated to doing nothing else but training and racing the dogs. It is their profession; the lives of the dogs are dedicated to racing and winning.

Laconia, New Hampshire races in 1970 featured Raymond Miner and a thirteen-dog team striking out across the snow. Ray and Paula Miner, owners of the Woody Glen Kennels, are racing enthusiasts and have many trophies to their credit.

American and Canadian Ch. Lostland's Trademark, pictured winning in the show ring and handled by Diane Rossetto, whose parents, Mr. and Mrs. Andrew Rossetto of Walled Lake, Michigan, own the Fireside Kennels. Diane finished Trademark to his championship. Photo by Earl Graham.

So beautiful—can it be real?!? This magnificent photograph was the Christmas card for Sy and Ann Goldberg in 1972. The picture of Ch. Kuno of Cinnaminson, CDX, in a sylvan glen shows the Husky in all its beauty. Kuno was bred by the Goldbergs and is owned by the Franks.

Ch. Eu Mor's Kiev, C.D.X., going through his paces in the back yard of his home in Central Islip, New York. Kiev, owned by Lynne Witkin, is a member of a kennel established in 1962 and famous for obedience-titled Huskies as well as bench show champions.

This intent and purpose begins with the picking of the dogs which show—above all else—the natural desire to run and to win. The training is more rigorous, the culling more ruthless, and the proper rearing and selection of the dogs even more essential. Professional team owners will spare no expense and will travel the globe to acquire just the right dog to enhance their team. The studying of pedigrees becomes almost a science, and the health, care and feeding of their teams is of major concern.

While the purses for the winners of the big races are large, so are the costs of maintaining a professional team. The costs far exceed the winnings, and before one considers getting into the professional aspect of this sport, financial considerations must be taken into account.

With the professional racing teams there is also a more strict, concentrated training schedule. The dogs must be kept in top racing condition all the time, not just before racing seasons, which means they must not become overweight. Bad dispositions are weeded out

Sy Goldberg, who with his wife Ann owns the Cinnaminson Kennels in Cream Ridge, New Jersey, poses proudly with the Siberian Husky Club of America sled dog trophy. Ed Samerson of Colorado, Chairman of the Racing Committee, presents the trophy.

Eight-year-old sled driver Gerri Lynn Goldberg and her Husky named Tokco coming in to win first place at a race! Photo by Sam Psoras of the *Philadelphia Daily News*.

at the first moment of discovery, grooming and training are on a regular schedule and more frequent, and the serious racing training begins in earnest at six or seven months of age.

Most racing dogs are staked out at about three to four months old, and the confined conditions seem to heighten their desire to run.

PROFESSIONAL RACING HUSKIES

While there are more Siberian Huskies on professional racing teams now than ever before, there are not as many as one would expect. There are reasons for this. . .the owners of the professional teams are interested to a great extent in the money prizes and will use any dog—purebred or otherwise—if the dog will run to win. Expenses are high to maintain and breed purebred Huskies exclusively while waiting for the top ones to come along. Mixed breeds offer more opportunities to buy up the fastest dogs in spite of their ancestry, giving the owners a "faster team faster!" So unless money is no

The beautiful male dog Lumimaan Talvi, photographed in
Switzerland and showing the Swiss ski dog harness.

Carolyn Windsor's team winning the Working Group at the Western Pennsylvania Kennel Club show in 1973, with daughter Sue handling under judge Mrs. Maynard K. Drury. Gilbert photograph.

object, more of the pros will not stick to one breed, but will shop around. Though price may be no object, there is a time limit involved. It is only the dedicated Siberian Husky lover who also races and can afford to support a team of purebreds who brings out a matched team that has a good chance of winning!

RACING IN ALASKA

The first All Alaska Sweepstakes race was run in 1908, as reported in detail in Chapter 2, with the Nome Kennel Club providing pennants and each team choosing its racing colors to gain instant recognition to win glory. Training began in the late fall for the spring races, and many hours were spent over the long winter months training the dogs for this big event.

The only communication with the outside world was by radio and with the dog teams which brought the mail. In those days the teams left at two-hour intervals, but this wide difference was later reduced to the point where the teams left within minutes—or even seconds—of each other.

In extremely cold weather the dogs were rubbed down with alcohol; they sometimes even wore blankets and flannel moccasins for their feet or eye covers for their eyes. So important was the winning of the races that the drivers fed and bedded down their dogs before they considered their own comforts, so that the dogs would be in good condition to run again the next day.

Even today Alaska considers sled dog racing as its very own sport and features two of the world's most famous races, North American Championship Race, held in Fairbanks, and the Fur Rendezvous, or the Rondy, in Anchorage. The Fur Rendezvous began in 1936, and by the following year fur trappers in the area were selling their furs *and* racing their dogs. The rendezvous became a virtual festival for everyone, with a fur auction, parties, dances, and exhibitions all being held at the one gathering place. But even from the beginning the dog racing was the main event, and today the 75-mile race still is!

There was a brief halt in the festivities from 1924 to 1936 when only the races were held with the carnival atmosphere, and again during World War II (1942 through 1945) but the annual event was eagerly resumed in 1946 and is gaining in popularity with each year! The schools close on the Friday of the Rendezvous, and the city turns out *en masse* to watch the four-dog team demonstrations which became the regular feature in 1946.

The North American race is 70 miles in length and both events are run in three heats which divide the distance in three parts, over three

Roger Reitano of Tok, Alaska with Shang, his·lovely pure white dog having the desirable black points.

Ch. Scandia's Bobby Dazzler pictured going Best of Breed under the late judge Alva Rosenberg at the Beverly Hills Kennel Club show on January 9, 1972. The Dazzler was handled by Walt Shellenbarger for owner-breeder Vivienne Lundquist of Marina Del Rey, California.

A lovely head study of Ch. Cinnaminson's Soaya Fournier, owned by Sy and Ann Goldberg, Cream Ridge, New Jersey.

days. After the third day the winner is announced and the celebrating begins anew!

There are also state championship races held in Kenai and Soldotna, and also one in Tok. In 1967 the Iditarod Trail Race was also held; it was referred to as an "endurance" event and used part of the trail used years ago to bring gold from Iditorod to Knik at the turn of the century. There are attempts being made to open up this rugged trail once again as an 800-mile endurance race. Plans are to restore the shelter cabins to house food for the dogs every fifty miles. Participants will use sleeping bags and carry survival equipment and the committee looks toward $2000 in gold as the reward for the winner!

Racing in Alaska, which had diminished during World War II, picked up again with new enthusiasm in the late 1940's, when the Alaska Dog Musher's Association was formed in Fairbanks. There were few members, however, who bred pure Siberian Huskies; the dogs were mostly mixtures. But the Earl Norrises, Hortense Landru, Jack and Sid Worbass, and Don and Virginia Clark were dedicated breeders for several years though are no longer active.

In 1949, in Anchorage, the Alaska Sled Dog and Racing Association was organized. This club had several members who bred Siberian Huskies and they formed the Alaska Siberian Husky Club from within the ranks of members of ASDRA. They joined the parent club and held several American Kennel Club-recognized dog shows. This club worked diligently to advertise the Husky as a race and show dog, and the Siberian Husky was a top dog during the 1950's.

Ch. Bonzo of Anadyr, C.D., was the first Siberian Husky to win Best in Show in the Alaska All-Breed show and was Best in Match at their first sanctioned obedience trial; he was the first Siberian Husky to earn his C.D. in Alaska. Ch. Tyndrum's Oslo, C.D.X., was the first and, to date, the only winner of this title. Both of these dogs were famous racing lead dogs as well.

THE RONDY RACES

As racing became more and more popular in the late 1940's, the Rondy Races came into being officially in 1946. It is still popular today, and the winning of the Rondy Race is considered of major importance. We list here the annual winners since the event's inception:

1946 - Jake Butler	1949 - Jake Butler
1947 - Earl Norris	1950 - Gareth Wright
1948 - Earl Norris	1951 - Raymond Paul

1952 - Gareth Wright	1964 - Dr. Roland Lombard
1953 - Clem Tellman	1965 - Dr. Roland Lombard
1954 - Raymond Paul	1966 - Joe Redington
1955 - Raymond Paul	1967 - Dr. Roland Lombard
1956 - Jim Hunington	1968 - George Attla
1957 - Gareth Wright	1969 - Dr. Roland Lombard
1958 - George Attla	1970 - Dr. Roland Lombard
1959 - Jimmy Malemute	1971 - Dr. Roland Lombard
1960 - Cue Bifelt	1972 - George Attla
1961 - Leo Kriska	1973 - Carl Huntington
1962 - George Attla	1974 - Dr. Roland Lombard
1963 - Dr. Roland Lombard	

A 1972 5-mile gig race in New Jersey with driver Jean Fournier and four champions on a five-dog team. The Fourniers' kennels are in Atlantic Highlands, New Jersey.

Mrs. Carolyn Windsor's daughter Sue wins Best Brace in Show at the Siberian Husky Club of America's Specialty Show in 1972 with Ch. Arahaz' Tengri Khan (outisde dog) and his son Arahaz' Kayler Konkon.

The remarkable Doncar's Snow Valley Flicka, U.D., and her owner and trainer Don Carlough, owner of the Doncar Kennels in Suffern, New York on a packing trip in Maine.

THE HUSLIA HERITAGE AND THE HUSLIA HUSTLERS

The Athabascan Indian village named Huslia, which has given to the racing world in Alaska so many of its top dogs and top drivers, is situated 260 miles northwest of Fairbanks on a river about one mile from the Koyukuk. The village remains very remote, still steeped in its Indian culture, but with modern ways and communications now gradually creeping up on it.

Jimmy Hunington was a trapper originally but gained fame for Huslia when in 1939 he entered the dog derbies in Nome. Jimmy borrowed dogs, got a team together and by mushing and getting a ride on a mail plane (along with his 14 dogs!) arrived in Fairbanks to race in the North American Race intent on winning enough money to open his own trading post in Huslia. He placed fourth but went home broke because he was unable to collect his prize money.

The desire to race stayed with him, and in 1956 the villagers urged him to try again and loaned him their best dogs; he emerged the winner of the North American Race in Fairbanks and the Fur Rendezvous in Anchorage. He thereby became known as The Huslia Hustler, until 1958, when George Attla, Jr., also from Huslia, appeared on the scene; George now carries the title as well! Looking at the line-up of any big Alaskan race today, you'll probably find either a winning team of dogs and/or drivers from Huslia!

In 1958 George Attla, Jr. appeared in his first Rondy Race and won handily with a 12-dog team. He owned only one of them, his lead dog named Tennessee. The rest of the dogs belonged to members of his family. Today, after having won the Rondy again in 1962, 1968 and 1972, George is the Huslia Hustler—the greatest hustler of them all!

George Attla was born in 1933, one of eight children born to George and Eliza Attla. A form of tuberculosis caused the fusing of the bones in George's knee, but the defect in no way stopped him from sled racing; in addition to the four Rondy wins, he has captured the number one spot in just about every other major race in Alaska.

George is also known as a great dog trainer. In addition to training his own dogs, he sometimes trains dogs for his competition! He excels in training lead dogs which have made winning teams for many of his competitors in the major races. . .some of which have beaten his team!

George has recently authored a book entitled *Everything I Know About Training and Racing Sled Dogs,* in collaboration with Bella Levorsen, a racing enthusiast in her own right, which reveals

George's secrets of success as a World Champion Racer four times to date! His 1972 racing records at Bemidji, Minnesota, Ely, Minnesota, Kalkaska, Michigan, Anchorage, Nenana, Fairbanks, Tok and Tanana, Alaska, earned George Attla the Gold Medal from the International Sled Dog Racing Association's first annual competition for a Point Champion.

WOMEN MUSHERS

It seems women have always shared their husbands' interest in driving dog teams and racing. We are all familiar with the successes of Short Seeley, Lorna Demidoff, and Louise Lombard, who in 1949 was the only woman entered in the 90-mile Ottawa, Canada, Dog Sled Derby, competing right along with her husband.

Mrs. E. P. Ricker, now Mrs. Nansen, was driving dog teams in 1928 and placed second at the Lake Placid fourth annual Sled Dog Derby in 1931. Bunty Dunlap, Mrs. Ricker's daughter, went on to follow in her mother's footsteps and became a top sled dog driver. And don't let us forget Jean Bryar, winner of the North American Women's Championship in Alaska, the first woman from the States to do it. She also gave a good account of herself in many of the gruelling Canadian races, not to mention New Hampshire events. Millie Turner was active at the New England events in the 1930's and 1940's, and Natalie Norris and Joyce Wells have been active at the Rondy races.

Today's representatives are Kit Macinnes, Rosie Losonsky, Vera Wright, Barbara Parker, Shari Wright, Shirley Gavin, Anne Wing, Carol Lundgren and Carol Sheppard. In addition, let's stand by to see what Darlene Huckins will do!

No doubt about it, the women are active in the sport and play by the men's rules. A strong case for sled dog racing as a family sport!

THE WOMEN'S WORLD CHAMPIONSHIP

1953 was the first year of the Women's World Championship Sled Dog Races in Alaska, an event that has been run every year since except for 1956. The same rules apply to the women's races as apply to the regular races, and the women train their own dogs.

In the beginning the purses were small, but by 1972 the winner walked away with $1000 prize. But then again, the race was not always as long. The early days featured a two-day race of 20 miles, but by 1972 the winner is determined after three days of racing twelve miles each day for a total run of 36 miles. The total time is tallied to determine the winner.

Ch. Monadnock's Misty of Arahaz and Monadnock's Mischa of Arahaz, owned by Rosemary and Edward Fischer of Canonsburg, Pennsylvania.

An impressive head study of the equally impressive Ch. Wolfden's Copper Bullet, bred and owned by Beryl Allen of Jaffrey, New Hampshire. Photo by Richard K. La Branche of Bristol, Connecticut.

The teams usually average 9 or 11 dogs, and there are on an average of ten to fifteen teams competing for the purse and the title of top female musher in Alaska—and the world!

The Women's World Championship Race Winners
1953 - Joyce Wells
1954 - Natalie Norris
1955 - Kit Macinnes
1957 - Rosie Losonsky
1958 - Vera Wright
1959 - Kit Macinnes
1960 - Kit Macinnes
1961 - Kit Macinnes
1962 - Barbara Parker
1963 - Barbara Parker
1964 - Barbara Parker
1965 - Sheri Wright
1966 - Shirley Gavin
1967 - Shari Wright
1968 - Anne Wing
1969 - Shirley Gavin
1970 - Shirley Gavin
1971 - Carol Lundgren
1972 - Carol Sheppard

CHILDREN AND RACING IN ALASKA
At the end of December each year in Anchorage, Alaska, the Junior Alaskan Sled Dog and Racing Association opens its season. The club holds a meeting each Friday night to discuss weather and trail conditions and to draw for starting positions for the race at the Anchorage Tudor Track. Races are held each week throughout the month of January.

These juniors must adhere to all the rules and regulations followed by the adults, which are held on the same trails as the adults run and are often eight to twelve miles long. To be a junior musher, the child must be from six to eighteen years of age. There are five classes of junior races consisting of one-, two-, three-, five- and seven-dog teams. The one-doggers race for a quarter of a mile on a straight track, while the two-dog class and most of the three-dog classes run three miles. The five- and seven-dog classes increase the mileage still farther, running a six-mile trail for the opening race with a vote determining the length of future races.

Schelly Keefer and Winsum's Yermak at the races, where Yermak and his young mistress celebrate their victory! Winsum Kennels are in Rocky Ridge, Maryland.

255

"Watch it back there!" seems to be the plea as Ch. Fournier's Zachariah of Toko gets groomed for the show ring by owner Jean Fournier's daughter. This intimate moment filmed by Judy Rosemarin of Roslyn, New York.

RACING IN CANADA

In Canada the major race is the PAS held in Manitoba. This race is not widely known but is acknowledged to be the longest and the toughest in the world. The dogs travel a distance of anywhere from 100 to 150 miles during the three-day race.

The Quebec race, while not as long, covers a 100-mile distance. The purses for these races are large and the drivers take the winning of these two events very seriously.

SIBERIAN HUSKY RACING IN FINLAND

The year 1969 saw the beginnings of sled dog racing in Finland. The first race, organized by Mr. P. Uimonen, was held in January, with four teams participating. The club uses the American ISDRA rules, but they limit the number of dogs to five even in the A class. Four teams took part in the Class A event of 16 miles, and six teams participated in the Class C event of about three miles with three dogs.

Anya-Alaska as a young bitch, photographed and owned by Kerttu Alm, Finland.

The Siberian Husky Club of Finland, as it is called, held its fifth race of the season in February on the Kuurila estate, with trails made by ski-doo machines and over a course running through forests, fields and ice-covered lakes. Most of the dogs are Siberian Huskies; each year the numbers increase so that there are usually over a hundred dogs competing.

Finland has strict quarantine laws, but borders are open between Norway, Sweden and Finland and the drivers and their teams travel quite freely between those countries.

Interest is keen, and the number of races seems to depend largely on the weather conditions.

A GLOSSARY OF RACING TERMS

ALASKAN HUSKY   A name applied to any Arctic-type cross-bred dog, usually a Husky, Malamute, Samoyed or Eskimo cross.

ALASKAN MALAMUTE   Used more for hauling than racing because of its great size and endurance.

ATTITUDE RUN   A short "fun" race.

BABICHE   Strips of rawhide used to join the parts of a sled.

BACKLINE   A line from the harness to the towline. Sometimes referred to as a tugline.

BASKET   The section of the sled which carries either passenger or cargo.

BRAKE   The metal fork stepped on by the driver to bring the sled to a halt. A fork on the underside of the sled which hits the ground and stops the sled.

BRIDLE   The collection of ropes gathered with a ring to which the towline is attached.

CART TRAINING   When there is no snow, training dogs with a three- or four-wheel cart is undertaken. Also carts are used in racing in warm climates.

CHAIN   Lengths of chain are used to stake a dog outdoors; usually about six feet in length and attached with snaps at the dog's collar and to the stake.

CHIEF STEWARD   Chief steward takes the other stewards out to their posts. He remains at start and finish lines.

CHUTE   The first several feet beyond the starting line is referred to as the chute.

DNF   Letters standing for Did Not Finish, which means a racer did not finish the race.

DOG BOX   The compartment mounted on a truck in which the dogs are transported to and from the racing site.

DRAGGING   When a dog is dragged along by his neckline, either after he falters, or if he is merely lagging behind.

GANGLINE   Center line fastened to the sled and to which the dogs are hitched. Also known as towline.

GEE   A term used with the dog to indicate a right turn.

GO   Same as start, begin, etc. Response to this word can mean the difference between getting off to a head start or merely starting along with the others.

HANDLE BAR   Topmost portion at the rear of the sled to which the driver holds on.

HARNESS   The canvas of mylong webbing which covers the dog and is attached to the lines.

HAW   Term used to indicate a left turn.

HEAT   A heat is one race.

HOLDING AREA   A section near the racing site where dogs are staked until race time.

HOOK, SNOW HOOK   A metal hook attached to the bridle of the sled by a line to hold the team in place. It can be driven into the ground or attached to a stationary object.

HOOK-UP AREA   Same as holding area—a place where the dogs are held until race time.

INDIAN DOG   A dog bred and owned by an Indian in an Indian village

JINGLER   A collection of bells or noisy trinkets used to get the attention of the dogs and spur them on.

LEAD DOG   The dog at the head of the team, usually the fastest, most experienced and best trained.

LEADER   Same as a lead dog.

LOWER 48 OR LOWER 49   Term used when referring to racing in any of the United States other than Alaska.

MARSHALL   A term used when referring to the racing official in charge at the race.

MUSH   Originally a French term meaning to walk or to march. While mush can be a term used for starting a team, more often "Let's Go!" or "Take Off!" work just as well. Usually only in the movies do the drivers yell Mush!

MUSHER   The term applied to the driver of a team.

NECKLINE   A light line that hooks the dog's collar to the towline.

NO   Word used to keep the dogs on the trail should they start to veer off, or to stop them from chewing on the line, to ward off a scrap, etc.

The Panuck-Denali Kennels team driven by Judi Anderson, who runs the kennels with her mother in Laconia, New Hampshire.

The nicely matched team of Felix A. Lison.

Ch. Baranof Koyukuk as an eight month-old puppy pulling his young mistress on a sled. Earl and Patricia Hahn, Jr., Keachi Kennels, Anchorage, Alaska.

Edward Clark and a team of Eskimo dogs alert but waiting patiently and obediently for word to "go!".

Ed Samerson and the dogs take off across the snow. The Domey-ko Kennel team try out in harness.

PEDALING   When the driver keeps one foot on the runner of the sled and pedals or pushes with the other.

PUMPING   A term used meaning the same as pedaling.

PUNCHING THROUGH   When the dog's feet break through the crust of ice on top of the snow they are said to punch through. The term punchy is the word used for the snow.

RACE MARSHALL   Man in charge of the races.

RIGGING   All the lines collectively to which dogs are hooked.

RUNNERS   Two bottom strips of wood on which the sled runs and are covered with steel or plastic strips called runner shoes.

SIBERIAN HUSKY   Purebred dog used extensively in sled racing.

SKI-JORRING   A short race with the driver on ski's rather than with a sled. Line is attached around his waist with a slip knot.

SLED BAG   The canvas bag which holds items necessary to the race and usually carried in the basket.

SNOW BERM   The ridges of snow made along the side of the roads by the snow plows.

SNOW FENCE   Fencing made of wooden upright slats fastened together with wire used to mark off areas or to prevent heavy drifting of snow.

SNOW HOOK   A hook used to stake a team temporarily.

STANCHIONS   Vertical parts of a sled.

STARTER   The man who starts the race.

STAY   Same as Whoa, or stop or halt. Used to stop the dogs at end of race or any other reason. Choose one and stick with it.

STEWARD   One of the officials placed along the trail to avoid trouble at traffic spots, sharp curves, etc. They must stay on the trail until the last team has passed.

STOVE UP   When a dog pulls up lame, or stiff.

SWING DOGS   Dog that runs directly behind the leader either on the right side of the tow line (right swing) or on the left side (left swing dog).

TEAM DOGS   Dogs hitched into the team between the swing dogs and the wheel dogs.

TO MUSH DOGS   To drive a team.

TOWLINE, OR GANGLINE   The center line fastened to the sled and to which the dogs are hitched.

TRAIL!   Term shouted by mushers to ask another driver for the right away.

TUGLINE OR TUG   Line from harness to the towline, same as backline.

Getting ready for racing: owner Sy Goldberg with his Tokco, Mischa and Tanya. Sy and Ann Goldberg own the Cinnaminson Kennels in Cream Ridge, New Jersey.

A team runs along the trail in an Alaskan dog race depicted in this photograph by Mal Lockwood.

VET CHECK   Before each race a veterinarian checks over each dog to see that it has not been drugged, if it is in good health and running condition, etc.

WHEEL DOGS   The two dogs directly in front of the sled which determine the direction of the sled.

WHIP   Usually whips are not permitted, but if they are, they must be under three feet in length so that they cannot touch the dogs.

WHOA!   With dogs, as with horses, this means one thing—STOP!

CHAPTER 9
THE SIBERIAN HUSKY AS A PACK DOG

Strong and sure-footed, and steady in all kinds of weather, it is only natural that the Siberian Husky could be counted on as a first rate pack dog. In the far north Siberian Huskies pack dogs are used when there is not adequate snow for sleds, and are used also by fur trappers and hunters to bring pelts back in their packs rather than on the sleds, when snow is scarce. Pack trips are becoming very popular in this country, as more and more Husky owners learn to enjoy mountain hiking with their dogs.

EARLY TRAINING

Training a dog to pack is relatively simple, with the main concern being the addition of the pack and the weight it carries. Start your early training with an empty pack, of course, and once the dog is used to the feel of it on his body, fill it with something to get the dog used to the sensation of weight. Many packers suggest a light but bulky load right from the beginning to get the dog used to the feel and the "swing" of the pack. Naturally, you will not overload your dog, and especially not at the beginning of the training.

Ten pounds is an ideal weight for the average size Husky, though there are those who will pack almost one half the dog's weight, if properly packed, and the dog properly conditioned. You will find the dog will take to the pack quite easily and will eventually get rather protective of it, guarding it when you make camp and take the packs off!

In temperate climates, just as in the frozen north, during the very cold weather, if you are hiking it may become necessary to have moccasins for the dogs. At any rate, in cold weather and on very rough terrain, check out the dogs' feet for cut pads or ice balls between the toes. After you've made a few hikes their feet may toughen, but it is always best to be careful. It's a long way to carry them back home!

Since Siberian Huskies are such natural outdoor dogs, you will find they love to charge ahead of you along the trail. At a very early age you must train your Huskies to return promptly when called when they are off lead. Some packers use whistles, but in any case, make sure you and your dogs understand each other completely on this point to avoid unfortunate disappearances. The reward system will really pay off on this point.

Siberian Huskies show a great deal of good sense when it comes to identifying trails and summits, and Joanne Rudnytsky, whose Wissahickon Beowulf, C.D., is a member of the Appalachian Mountain Club's Four Thousand Footer Club, is a veteran at backpacking with her over the years. Mrs. Rudnytsky claims that they never go too far away on circular hikes, but now and then on hikes which are just "up and back" may tend to run off. She tells of just such a happening on a climb when the day was particularly warm and one of her dogs, Tala, took off. She returned to the car after the trip down the mountain and found Tala lying in its shade. . . .all of which proves you must keep a close eye on your dogs and be sure to have them wear their identification tags on their collars.

FEEDING THE PACK DOG

It is not a good idea to feed the dog before starting on a trip. Feed at night before bedding down and when the dog can relax and properly rest while digesting his food. Water is essential for the pack dog and you will find they require much more water than they usually consume, and generally twice as much as a thirsty person. Since they do not drink out of canteens, remember to take along Sierra Club cups or aluminum dishes for them!

Dry foods, or semi-moist foods, carried in plastic bags are best and should be of the concentrated varieties which are high in protein for extra energy. Make sure everything is wrapped tightly in double plastic with wire twists so no water gets into the food in case you cross streams along the trail. You especially do not want water to get into the first aid kit! The first aid kit is something else that hikers are sure to want to take along.

Two of the chief worries when back-packing with the dogs are encounters with skunks and porcupines. Again, a voice of experience in the person of Joanne Rudnytsky states that you are wise to carry alligator-nose pliers along to remove porcupine quills if necessary. Tweezers are equally essential for the removal of ticks, and alcohol and swabs go hand in hand with both afflictions!

A past issue of *Field and Stream* magazine advocated the use of a solution of two teaspoonsful of common ordinary baking soda mixed with one cup of vinegar, patted on all exposed portions of each quill and then after a ten-minute wait, repeat the procedure. In another ten

Happy trailers! Dick Brumbaugh, Beverly Brumbaugh, Marker, Barbara Jacobi, Cowboy Blue, Robert Brumbaugh, and Amanda Brumbaugh with Totyana and pack in July, 1972 on Big Creek Trail in the Bitterroot Mountains of Montana.

minutes you should be able to remove the quills painlessly, since the combined action of the soda and vinegar softens the quill to the point where it shrinks and can be removed. It is surely worth a try—but we sincerely hope the occasion will not arise! Death has been known to occur as a result of a dog's tangling with a porcupine, so do your best to steer clear of them.

Confrontations with skunks are less dangerous but certainly no more pleasant. A bath with strong soap and several rinses with tomato juice when you get home are about the only remedy for this.

AGE TO START PACK TRAINING

Training can start at about four months of age and should consist of the simple initial obedience training work for heel, sit, sit-stay, down, down stay, and the extremely important recall! The recall can be either vocal or whistle, and as Joanne Rudnytsky has advocated, two different whistles, one whistle to mean return immediately and another whistle to mean for the dog merely to show itself on the trail to establish visual contact. A reward for a return is in order. Vocal commands can be taught in the backyard, whistle training on walks in the woods near home before starting on the longer hikes in the mountains.

It is best to take the puppies along with older dogs, which set an example and will help teach the puppies what trailing is all about.

Make sure these first trips are not difficult or dangerous ones and *not too long*, which will tire the puppies and perhaps discourage them from future enjoyment. Start them off on the trail with empty packs on the home ground or on long walks. Then begin stuffing the packs with crumpled newspaper of magazines in increasing amounts until their capacity load has been attained. Then they will be ready for the longer, rougher trails in the mountains.

A rest period during a pack trip along the Kootenai Creek Trail to Kootenai Lake in the Bitterroot Mountains of Montana. Wolfden's Cowboy Blue and Totyana of Ravalli are owned by Barbara and Fred Jacobi of Missoula, Montana.

THE PACK ITSELF

The pack is made of heavy canvas, leather and ripstop nylon. It is in several parts. There is a heavy canvas saddle with a leather cinch. Sewn to the saddle are two ripstop nylon bags. The bags have a breast strap and a belly strap, and are usually bright red in color to help hikers identify and spot their dogs at a distance.

The bag is placed on the dog as far forward as possible so that it rides over the withers. The cinch is secured firmly as far forward on the brisket as possible but not so tight that it in any way restricts the breathing or will be a discomfort to the dog. The breast and belly straps are loosely secured and help keep the bag in place, so that it does not shift too much when the dog is going up or down steep inclines.

There are eight D-rings sewn on the bag, one on top, one forward, one rear and one low on each bag. A wrap-around strap is passed through the D-rings to further hold the pack in place. The wrap-around is long, with an O-ring on one end. This passes over, under, in front of, and under the belly and back to the O-ring, where it is secured by a squaw hitch.

These packs come in three different sizes and styles and at the time of this writing can be obtained from Wenaha Dog Packs, 14421 Cascadian Way, Lynnwood, Washington, 98036. There are other sources of supply. Since one of the rules of backpacking is to try not to go alone, we assume you can ask the other party you will be hiking with for other places from which you can obtain any supplies.

PACKING THE PACK

Veteran packers Fred and Barbara Jacobi, who hike in the Montana mountains with their Huskies, emphasize their extreme consideration in the packing of the pack. They load sweaters and soft smooth items on the side of the pack that rests against the dog, and when packing their fishing shoes, for instance, pack one shoe each side to balance the weight. With wise packing they also reveal they can take along "extras" they would normally leave behind. The point is that even balance on either side of the dog is essential.

We enjoy Fred Jacobis' story about the sense in not packing perishable items on the dogs. Since they run and frolick along the way as they revel in their freedom, often the pack gets knocked against trees, or logs, or rocks, as they trot down the trail. When allowed to carry the Jacobis' lunch, consisting of a sandwich and an apple, the Jacobis found merely a mashed sandwich and applesauce!

At times it might be necessary to unpack the dogs when hiking through rough streams to assure their safety. It is important that you plan ahead and not allow the dogs to plunge into a swift current with full pack if the current is too swift for them to handle.

BEDDING DOWN

When it comes time to bed down for the night it is common sense to let the dogs play for a bit without their packs and before feeding and watering. Make sure the dogs have their collars on and for added safety tie them to your sleeping bags so if an interesting sound or creature ambles by in the night the dogs aren't tempted into wandering off into the hills. Night running is dangerous for them, since they are even more likely to encounter deer, elk, bear, or the aforementioned porcupines and skunks!

If you are trailing in the mountains near streams you are likely to find the dogs treating themselves to trout! The Jacobis supplement their dogs' diet with cutthroat trout. Fred Jacobi states he prefers to feed them fresh fish that is uncleaned. He feels there is less danger from fish bones in uncleaned fish, since they are consumed in large chunks with the bones encased in flesh. The dogs instinctively start eating the fish from the head end, which also protects them from bones. He further states he does not feed trout to puppies without permanent teeth, since he does not feel anything but permanent teeth are adequate for masticating the fish.

CLIMBING CLUBS

Joanne Rudnytsky of Philadelphia is a member of the Appalachian Mountain Club's Four Thousand Footer Club, which requires climb-

Owner Joanne Rudnytsky of Philadelphia is pictured after a day's hike up the Flume Slide Trail in the White Mountains of New Hampshire with her two dogs. The gray dog is Wissahickon Beowolf, C.D. and the red is Wissahickon Zephyr Fournier, some get of Ch. Savdajaure's Miuk, C.D., and of Ch. Dovercrest's Alehta Pesna, C.D. Beo has his 4,000-Footer badge which he wears proudly on his pack.

6,288 feet above sea level, on top of Mount Washington in the White Mountains of New Hampshire, is Wissahickon Beowolf, C.D. Beo is a member of the 4,000-Footer Club of the White Mountains, the Appalachain Mountain Club located in Boston, and is pictured with his 4,000-Footer Club badge on his pack. Summit House and the weather observatory are in the background. Beo is owned by Joanne Rudnystky of Philadelphia, Pennsylvania; he was sired by Ch. Huf-nik Amchitka *ex* Tiksi of Longhail.

ing the 46 mountains over 4,000 feet in the White Mountains of New England. Any climber is eligible for membership in this club if he or she has hiked to the summit of all of the listed peaks selected as official by the 4,000 Footer Committee and the Council of the Appalachian Mountain Club. The actual ascent of any of these peaks can be made at any time during his or her lifetime. They are provided with a form which lists the name of the mountain, its height, and the date which the climber enters upon his ascent; the form also includes a record of his trip companions. Mrs. Rudnytsky's three Siberian Huskies, Wissahickon Beowulf, C.D., Wissahickon Natala, and Wissahickon Zephyr Fournier, are all members! Beo has climbed all 46 peaks, Tala and/or Zeph have also climbed them with Beo.

DON CARLOUGH'S FAMOUS FRIEND FLICKA

Perhaps one of the most famous of the pack-trained dogs is the Siberian Husky bitch belonging to Don Carlough of Suffern, New York. Doncar's Snow Valley Flicka, U.D., is her name, and she is not only pack trained for mountain and trail hiking, but is trained in ski-joring as well. For her complete record of accomplishments in the obedience rings, we recommend you read about Flicka in greater detail in the obedience chapter of this book, where we pay additional tribute to her as one of the best trained all-around dogs in the breed.

CHAPTER 10
THE SIBERIAN HUSKY CLUBS

While the Siberian Husky was recognized in 1930 by the American Kennel Club, it was not until 1938 that the Siberian Husky Club of America was founded. The purposes of the club are to support specialty shows, promote the use of this working dog in racing competition and. . .what is even more important. . .to encourage members and breeders to breed true to the Standard approved by the American Kennel Club toward a Standard of excellence which brings out the true qualities for which the breed originated.

The increased popularity of the breed—which is almost alarming in numbers of registrations—has made the role of the parent club even more important than ever before in working toward control and strict breeding principles within the membership and the education of those who are not members. In accordance with this, the club recommends and actively promotes the purchase of purebred Siberian Huskies from amongst their membership and the education of the public to the importance of buying good stock from reputable breeders.

The Club also counsels and advises, and distributes a newsletter which contains the latest information pertinent to the breed.

REGIONAL CLUBS

All this increased popularity in the breed and activity in conformation, obedience, racing, etc., has brought about rapid growth within the parent club and has led to the establishment of several regional clubs throughout the United States. To name a few, there is the Golden State Siberian Husky Club, the Siberian Husky Club of New England, the Siberian Husky Club of Greater Pittsburgh, The Siberian Husky Club of Central Ohio, and the clubs of Greater New York, Delaware Valley, Garden State, Rocky Mountain and others which might have formed since this book went to press.

Since corresponding secretaries for clubs change almost yearly, it would be advisable to write to the parent club for the name and address of the current officer for the club in your area at the time you wish to join. The parent club secretary and corresponding secretary can be reached through the American Kennel Club, 51 Madison Avenue, New York, N.Y. 10010.

It is most advisable to join a club. Do so by all means. It is the best way to keep up on the latest happenings in the breed, and you will make new friends who can help you enjoy and learn about your breed, and you will certainly profit from their experience.

You will find that the club also has available a comprehensive list of publications on the Siberian Husky including books and bulletins and their newsletter which will help you get better acquainted with the breed; it can also inform you of where to buy sleds, racing gear, harness, etc, if you intend to get into the other working talents of the Husky. You will find your association with a breed club to be most beneficial for both you and your dog.

Memberships in all-breed clubs can also be advantageous if you intend to show your dog in conformation classes for championship or obedience. Familiarity with shows and dog show people will help you learn rules and regulations and will broaden your world of dogs in general.

THE SIBERIAN HUSKY CLUB OF AMERICA NEWSLETTER

If you have any questions or problems with your dog and you are not able to belong to a club or be active in a club because you live too far away from the nearest one, we still advise that you become a member of the parent club, if only to receive the club's *Newsletter*. The *Newsletter* for the parent club is so well done and so informative that the Dog Writers Association of America awarded it a Certificate of Merit at their 1973 Awards Dinner.

SPECIAL PRIZES AND TROPHIES

Based on an idea proposed by Lorna Demidoff in 1959, each year since 1960 the Siberian Husky Club of America has awarded a special trophy to the team of Siberians whose performance in both the show ring and on the trail best exemplifies the valued dual capabilities of the breed. The trophy is a reproduction of an antique English Georgian sterling silver punch bowl and is a most cherished prize. We present here a list of all the winners to date:

1960 - Mrs. Peggy Grant	1967 - Mrs. Peggy Grant
1961 - Natalie Norris	1968 - Roger Reitano
1962 - Thomas O'Neil	1969 - Roger Reitano
1963 - Thomas O'Neil	1970 - Carol Rice
1964 - Paul Koehler	1971 - Mrs. Peggy Grant
1965 - Malcolm McDougall	1972 - Sy Goldberg
1966 - Mrs. Peggy Grant	1973 - Jean Fournier.

Mrs. Jean Fournier, winner of the 1973 Siberian Husky Club of America showing-working trophy receives the silver bowl from Sy Goldberg, 1972 winner. Club President L. Stewart Cochrane looks on.

In 1973 the name was changed to the Showing—Working Trophy, with the idea that the "all around" Siberian Husky should be honored. The point system will be based on wins in the show ring, wins in sled dog racing, and obedience degrees, and no more than 2/3 of the applicant's total points can come from either racing or showing.

FIRST INDEPENDENT SPECIALTY

The first national specialty show to be held independently by the Siberian Husky Club of America was staged on June 2, 1972 in Wel-

Ch. Wolfden's Copper Bullet pictured going Best in Show at the first independent specialty show of the Siberian Husky Club of America, Inc., in June, 1972. The judge was Mrs. Augustus Riggs. Siberian Husky Club of America President L. Stewart Cochrane presents the trophy. Bruce Crabb handles for owner Beryl Allen of the Wolfden Kennels, Jaffrey, New Hampshire.

lesley, Massachusetts. The judges for this event were Mrs. Norbert Kanzler, dogs, and Mrs. Lou Richardson, bitches; Mrs. Augustus Riggs, III, offieiated in the Inter-Sex and Non-Regular Classes.

THE INTERNATIONAL SIBERIAN HUSKY CLUB

In the spring of 1961 the Seppala Siberian Husky Club was formed, in honor of the man whose name it bore. Charter members were Mr. and Mrs. Leonhard Seppala, Mrs. Louis Foley, Mr. and Mrs. Raymond Thompson, and Mrs. Virginia Emrich. However, in 1964 the name was changed to the International Siberian Husky Club. Its membership has grown to include over 500 members in 40

Alakazan's Napako, seven-month-old puppy class winner at the 1972 National Specialty Show of the Siberian Husky Club of America. Owners: Robert and Brenda Wallace of Nattick, Massachusetts.

states, 5 provinces of Canada and 5 other countries by the end of the decade.

By 1964 for the information of its members, the club published a bi-monthly newsletter edited by Mrs. Beth Murphy and Miss Jane Smith. In 1965 editor Arnie Hed was in charge and changed the publication to a quarterly. By 1966 it was a monthly publication and the editorship had passed to Miss Doris Lovrine.

In 1961 committees formed to serve their membership in specific categories. Among the noteworthy committees was the Research and Records Committee headed by Mrs. Louis Foley. Mrs. Foley researched the breed and presented the club with a great deal of information on the early history of the Siberian Husky in Siberia. This committee was discontinued in 1965. In 1967 the ISHC Pedigree Directory was published under the guidance of Mrs. Peggy Hazlett; the directory presented a listing of various dogs, their pedigrees and characteristics.

Also in 1967 the club held its first booster show in Toronto, Canada. An entry of 42 appeared which was a record entry for the breed in Canada up to that time. Gunnar Allerellie and Mrs. Carol Sutliff were largely responsible for this initial effort.

The Award Committee was started in 1967 offering a number of achievement awards. Every dog which attained a championship or obedience title received a certificate of recognition. The racing award is presented to the Siberian which has raced on a team that has completed 20 single races or 10 two-heat races of not less than ten miles. The team must have finished in the upper half of the total entries as well. An obedience award for C.D.X. was given and a special award to C.D. dogs which won with scores of 190 or better on all three legs.

The Championship award was given to the Siberian Husky which earned the title and has 10 Bests of or Bests of Opposite Sex in shows where three or more points were awarded. A special Outstanding Achievement Award is given to the dog which completed the championship requirements and raced in 20 heats of 10 miles or more and finished in the upper half of the total number of entries. The award is given to the racing dog which meets these requirements and also meets the obedience requirements.

There is also a Combination Achievement Award with slightly different requirements and members are advised to write the club for detailed requirements on all rules.

CHAPTER 11
STANDARD FOR THE BREED

The Board of Directors of the American Kennel Club approved a revised Standard for the Siberian Husky, submitted by the Siberian Husky Club of America, and which was published in the December, 1971, issue of their *American Kennel Gazette*. The Standard for the breed is as follows:

GENERAL APPEARANCE: The Siberian Husky is a medium-sized working dog, quick and light on his feet and free and graceful in action. His moderately compact and well-furred body, erect ears and brush tail suggest his Northern heritage. His characteristic gait is smooth and seemingly effortless. He performs his original function in harness most capably, carrying a light load at moderate speed over great distances. His body proportions and form reflect this basic balance of power, speed and endurance. The males of the Siberian Husky breed are masculine but never coarse; the bitches are feminine but without weakness of structure. In proper condition, with muscle firm and well-developed, the Siberian Husky does not carry excess weight.

HEAD: *Skull*—Of medium size and in proportion to the body; slightly rounded on top and tapering gradually from the widest point to the eyes. *Faults*—Head clumsy or heavy; head too finely chiseled. *Muzzle*—Of medium length; that is, the distance from the tip of the nose to the stop is equal to the distance from the stop to the occiput. The stop is well-defined and the bridge of the nose is straight from the stop to the tip. The muzzle is of medium width, tapering gradually to the nose, with the tip neither pointed nor square. The lips are well-pigmented and close fitting; teeth closing in a scissors bite. *Faults*—Muzzle either too snipy or too coarse; muzzle too short or too long; insufficient stop; any bite other than scissors. *Ears*—Of medium size, triangular in shape, close fitting and set high on the head. They are thick, well-furred, slightly arched at the back, and strongly erect, with slightly rounded tips pointing straight up. *Faults*—Ears too large in proportion to the head; too wide-set; not strongly erect. *Eyes*—Almond shaped, moderately spaced and set a trifle obliquely. The expression is keen, but friendly; interested and even mischievous. Eyes may be brown or blue in color; one of each or parti-colored are acceptable. *Faults*—Eyes set too obliquely; set too close together. *Nose*—Black in gray, tan or black dogs; liver in copper dogs; may be flesh-colored in pure white dogs. The pink-streaked "snow nose" is acceptable.

BODY: *Neck*—Medium in length, arched and carried proudly erect when dog is standing. When moving at a trot, the neck is extended so that the head is carried slightly forward. *Faults*—Neck too short and thick; neck too long. *Shoulders*—The shoulder blade is well laid back at an approximate angle of 45° to the ground. The upper arm angles slightly backward from point of shoulder to elbow, and is never perpendicular to the ground. The muscles and ligaments holding the shoulder to the rib cage are firm and well-developed. *Faults*—Straight shoulders; loose shoulders. *Chest*—Deep and strong, but not too broad, with the deepest point being just behind the level with the elbows. The ribs are well-sprung from the spine but flattened on the sides to allow for freedom of action. *Faults*—Chest too broad; "barrel ribs"; ribs too flat or weak. *Back*—The back is straight and strong, with a level topline from withers to croup. It is of medium length, neither cobby nor slack from excessive length. The loin is taut and lean, narrower than the rib cage, and with a slight tuck-up. The croup slopes away from the spine at an angle, but never so steeply as to restrict the rearward thrust of the hind legs. In profile, the length of the body from the point of the shoulder to the rear point of the croup is slightly longer than the height of the body from the ground to the top of the withers. *Faults*—Weak or slack back; roached back; sloping topline.

LEGS AND FEET: *Forelegs*—When standing and viewed from the front, the legs are moderately spaced, parallel and straight, with elbows close to the body and turned neither in nor out. Viewed from the side, pasterns and slightly slanted, with pastern joint strong, but flexible. Bone is substantial but never heavy. Length of the leg from elbow to ground is slightly more than the distance from the elbow to the top of withers. Dew-claws on forelegs may be removed. *Faults*—Weak pasterns; too heavy bone; too narrow or too wide in the front; out at the elbows. *Hindquarters*—When standing and viewed from the rear, the hind legs are moderately spaced and parallel. The upper thighs are well-muscled and powerful, the stifles well-bent, the hock joint well-defined and set low to the ground. Dew-claws, if any, are to be removed. *Faults*—Straight stifles, cowhocks, too narrow or too wide in the rear. *Feet*—Oval in shape, but not

UNDERSHOT

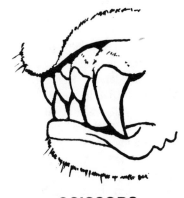

SCISSORS

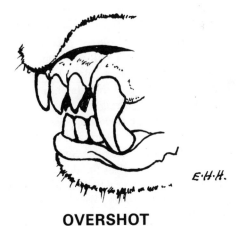

E·H·H·

OVERSHOT

Examples of jaw and teeth conformations resulting in various bites. Drawings by Ernest H. Hart.

long. The paws are medium in size, compact and well-furred between the toes and pads. The pads are tough and thickly cushioned. The paws neither turn in nor out when dog is in natural stance. *Faults*—Soft or splayed toes; paws too large and clumsy; paws too small and delicate; toeing in or out.

TAIL: The well-furred tail of fox-brush shape is set on just below the level of the topline, and is usually carried over the back in a graceful sickle curve when the dog is at attention. When carried up, the tail does not curl to either side of the body, nor does it snap flat against the back. A trailing tail is normal for the dog when working or in repose. Hair on the tail is of medium length and approximately the same length on top, sides and bottom, giving the appearance of a round brush. *Faults*—A snapped or tightly curled tail; highly plumed tail; tail set too low or too high.

GAIT: The Siberian Husky's characteristic gait is smooth and seemingly effortless. He is quick and light on his feet, and when in the show ring should be gaited on a loose lead at a moderately fast trot, exhibiting good reach in the forequarters and good drive in the hindquarters. When viewed from the front to rear while moving at a walk, the Siberian Husky does not single-track, but as the speed increases the legs gradually angle inward until the pads are falling on a line directly under the longitudinal center of the body. As the pad marks converge, the forelegs and hing legs are carried straight forward, with neither elbows nor stifles turned in or out. Each hind leg moves in the path of the foreleg on the same side. While the dog is gaiting, the topline remains firm and level. *Faults*—Short, prancing or choppy gait, lumbering or rolling gait; crossing; crabbing.

COAT: The coat of the Siberian Husky is double and medium in length, giving a well-furred appearance, but is never so long as to obscure the clean-cut outline of the dog. The undercoat is soft and dense and of sufficient length to support the outer coat. The guard hairs of the outer coat are straight and somewhat smooth-lying, never harsh nor standing straight off from the body. It should be noted that the absence of the undercoat during the shedding season is normal. Trimming of the whiskers and fur between the toes and around the feet to present a neater appearance is permissible. Trimming of the fur on any other part of the dog is not to be condoned and should be severely penalized. *Faults*—Long, rough, or shaggy coat; textured too harsh or too silky; trimming of the coat, except as permitted above.

The famous Eva "Short" Seeley captured on film during a "love-in" at her Chinook Kennels in Wonalancet, New Hampshire, photographed by Judy Rosemarin.

This lovely head study showing the true expression of the Siberian is of Setting Sun's Anthem, owned by Catherine A. Halcomb, Setting Sun Kennels, Portola, California.

COLOR: All colors from black to pure white are allowed. A variety of markings on the head is common, including many striking patterns not found in other breeds.

TEMPERAMENT: The characteristic temperament of the Siberian Husky is friendly and gentle, but also alert and outgoing. He does not display the possessive qualities of the guard dog, nor is he overly suspicious of stranger or aggressive with other dogs. Some measure of reserve and dignity may be expected in the mature dog. His intelligence, tractability, and eager disposition make him an agreeable companion and willing worker.

SIZE: *Height*—Dogs, 21 to 23½ inches at the withers. Bitches, 20 to 22 inches at the withers. *Weight*—Dogs, 45 to 60 pounds. Bitches, 35 to 50 pounds. Weight is in proportion to height. The measurements mentioned above represent the extreme height and weight limits, with no preference given to either extreme. *Disqualification*—Dogs over 23½ inches and bitches over 22 inches.

SUMMARY: The most important breed characteristics of the Siberian Husky are medium size, moderate bone, well balanced proportions, ease and freedom of movement, proper coat, pleasing head and ears, correct tail, and good disposition. Any appearance of excessive bone or weight, constricted or clumsy gait, or long, rough coat should be penalized. The Siberian Husky never appears so heavy or coarse as to suggest a freighting animal; nor is he so light and fragile as to suggest a sprint-racing animal. In both sexes the Siberian Husky gives the appearance of being capable of great endurance. In addition to the faults already noted, obvious structural faults common to all breeds are as undesirable in the Siberian Husky as in any other breed, even though they are not specifically mentioned herein.

CHAPTER 12
SIBERIAN HUSKY COLOR, COAT AND MARKINGS

One of the keenest delights with the Siberian Husky breed is that any and all colors and markings are acceptable. Their very colors and markings make them so unique and exotic! Each dog seems to have its very own individual patterns that sets it apart from every other.

Many admirers prefer the Siberian Husky when it is marked mostly in the pattern and color of the wolf! Most Husky enthusiasts love them in any color or with any pattern, and every litter is a complete and wonderful surprise. The black markings around the eyes, up the forehead and around the nose and ears are intriguing and lean toward an expression which can best be compared with saying the dog seems to be looking far off across endless miles of snow to the North Pole.

EYE COLOR

The same unique markings accent their beautiful eyes. The blue eyes which are most frequently associated with this breed are truly magnificent. And, of course, the deeper the blue the better! While brown eyes are also acceptable, they never seem to draw the excited comments that the lovely blue eyes evoke from the crowds and from those seeing the breed for the first time.

Many Siberian Huskies possess one blue eye and one brown eye, and this odd-eyed combination is also completely acceptable. The eye rims should have black pigmentation, the exception being flesh-colored rims on the all white Siberian Husky, though, here again, the black pigmentation on a pure white dog is highly desirable. Red Siberian Huskies also have flesh-colored pigmentation around the eyes and nose; such coloration is within the Standard for the breed.

Since both color eyes and a combination of both are permissible in the breed, eye color should never be more than a final consideration in your selection of a dog for the show ring, the obedience ring or for racing. The true devotee of the breed would consider the whole dog rather than any one individual characteristic, no matter how beautiful the shade of blue eyes, which are almost guaranteed to make your dog a crowd-pleaser!

The Fireside Kennels' new ring hopeful, Fireside's Patent Pending. Note the eyes of different colors. Patent is owned by Mr. and Mrs. A. Rossetto of Walled Lake, Michigan.

CHANGING COAT COLORS

One occurrence for which you must be prepared is the gradual change in your dog's coat color. Not every Husky changes color, but not only do many of them change color from dark to light, or light to dark, but a few may change from dark to red or copper! Another fascinating idiosyncrasy of the breed!

Most puppies in any breed are usually born black, or with a blackish cast to them (unless they will always be pure white!) so it is not at all unlikely that the majority of your puppies will be born almost black, and it is also unlikely that most of them will remain black as they mature.

THE SIBERIAN HUSKY COAT

There are two major types of coat in the Husky breed, the medium-to-long coat and the short coat. Some long coats are allowed—and even get by in the show ring! —but the wooly or ''brillo-y'' or harsher textured coat is not to be desired, especially in

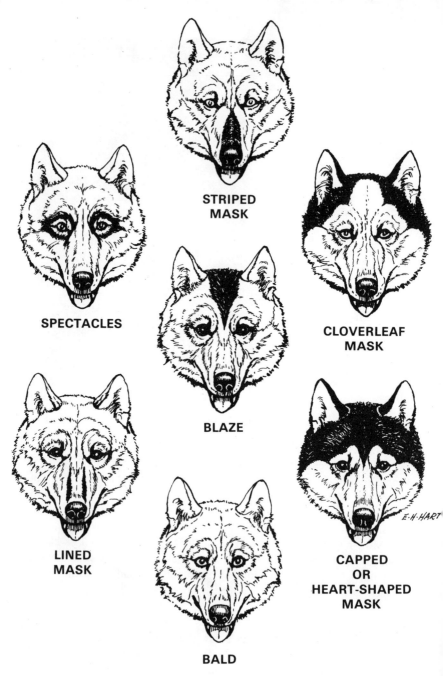

STRIPED
MASK

SPECTACLES

CLOVERLEAF
MASK

BLAZE

LINED
MASK

CAPPED
OR
HEART-SHAPED
MASK

E·H·HART

BALD

Masks, or facial markings. Drawings by Ernest H. Hart.

Sierra Kimookteeka pictured at ten weeks of age, in June, 1971. Teeka is owned by Michael Burnside of Saugus, California and exhibits a perfect example of the unusual facial markings which endear this breed to dog lovers.

Florence Clark of North Woodstock, New Hampshire, with a team of dogs in which black heads predominate.

Ch. Oomik's Quista, a blue-eyed silver white and buff Husky owned by the Woodside Kennels in Elizabethtown, Pa. Quista was #5 Siberian Husky in 1970, according to *Popular Dogs* magazine's Phillips System awards. A Stephen Klein photograph.

the show ring. While the under coat is soft, it should very definitely be in contrast to the outer thick coat.

When the dog is in its natural state the coat should present a definite clear, smooth, outline of the body structure. The diet is also important to maintaining a good coat. A dog which is properly fed will usually have a good coat with a high gloss to it without having to apply the commercial sprays, etc., to achieve it. Also heredity plays a major part. Good breeding stock will produce good coat, and the Siberian Husky is easy to care for when it is in proper coat.

SHEDDING

All dogs shed. . .yet the question of just how much is always asked by anyone thinking seriously about buying a dog, especially if it is a new breed to them.

The Siberian Husky generally sheds twice a year, and it is usually exactly when he feels like it! There has been no positive proof that a full shedding has to do with whether or not they race, little to do with extreme heat or cold weather conditions, little or nothing to do with diet, or the part of the world in which they live! Generally speaking, they shed twice a year—spring and fall.

Shedding season! The results of a single brushing during shedding time for the Siberian Husky. Alice Angel, Norstarr Kennels, Rockford, Illinois.

Some Huskies shed completely and all at once. One day they are magnificent in the show ring, the next day they are naked! Others shed in clumps, and still others just lose varying amounts of the loose hair. Many Siberians go through no more than a sort of thinning process and merely lose hair evenly all over.

For those who exhibit their Huskies in the show ring, this uncertainty can be frustrating. But if you see the shedding coming on, you can help speed the process along by helping to remove the dead hair with extra brushing or combing, or with the use of a stripper. A bath can also aid in the removal of this dead hair.

John and Martha Hankowsky's Olivet, better known as Ollie, beautiful white Husky with black pigmentation. Ollie and the Hankowskys' Ch. Dichoda's Tokusak, C.D., had their names combined to form the Tokol Kennels, now in Poway, California.

The beautiful brown-eyed white American and Canadian Champion Little Sepp's Stormy of Sno Dak, C.D.X. Whelped in 1955 (died in 1968), Stormy was the first Siberian Husky owned by Mrs. Lillian Peitzman of Mapleton, North Dakota.

Once a dog "blows his coat" or sheds unevenly or to any great degree, you can count on a good two or three months' lapse of time before you make any more show entries! It will probably take that much time before the dog comes into full bloom once again. Some exhibitors add a coat conditioner to their dogs' diet to help encourage the growth of the new hair. But there are just as many exhibitors who will tell you after years of experience that the new coat comes in no faster than the general good health of the dog will allow!

Between shedding periods you can count on your Siberian Husky's coat causing you little concern. The coat's texture being what it is, it does not mat, and regular daily brushings are not necessary. An occasional going-over with a rubber-based wire brush will be sufficient to keep your dog in well groomed condition and will present him in his natural beauty.

SHOWING DURING THE SHEDDING PERIOD

If you have a few important shows coming up and you have already sent in your entries, there are a few things to remember that might help your chances of winning in spite of the loss of hair. One is *not* to give a hot bath if shedding has started. There are dry shampoos to use on legs and face and tail or other places where dirt has gathered so that a regular brushing dry will not take out most of the coat. There are also sprays that can be used to give a little extra gloss to the coat without having to wet down the dog or submerge it entirely in water.

Lack of undercoat during the shedding season is normal, and most judges will allow for it. But trimming the dog to make it look more even is not allowable! Trimming toes and whiskers is one thing. . .scissoring a dog to even it out, or trimming guard hairs to level off a body line, is not permissible. And if you use chalk or cornstarch or powder of any kind on the white areas, we caution once again to be sure to get it all out before entering the show ring!

PIE-BALD SIBERIAN HUSKIES

Occasionally spotted puppies appear in a litter. These spotted puppies are sometimes referred to as pintos, but more correctly they should be called pie-balds. More often than not breeders are inclined to put them down at birth, considering them as mis-marks or as "unsaleable." A rare few breeders will sell them as pets; starting in 1972 we have had one shown in the show ring, and it is winning.

Her name is Marlytuk's Caspera The Ghost, and she is co-owned by Jean Fournier and Debra Ensminger. She is largely white with

A rare piebald Siberian Husky. This is Marlytuk's Casper the Ghost, showing winning Winners Bitch and Best of Winners at the 1973 Harford County Kennel Club show under judge Mrs. C. Seaver Smith. Bred by Marguerite Grant and P. McDermott, Casper was whelped December 6, 1971, and is owned by Jean Fournier (handling) and Debra Ensminger.

black markings and is typically Siberian Husky in every other way. In 13 AKC point shows during the 1972-1973 show reason she placed in 13 and had a three-point major to her credit. She is an excellent sled dog, steady, strong and reliable. She is the first pie-bald in the Eastern Seaboard area to win points toward championship.

She was whelped December 6, 1971 and was bred by Marguerite Grant and Patrick McDermott. Her eye color is amber. The sire was Ch. Doonauk's Jeuahnee of Keemah *ex* Malinka's Pride.

CHAPTER 13
SIBERIAN HUSKY TEMPERAMENT
AND CHARACTERISTICS

You've decided you like the exotic appearance of the Siberian Husky and you want to know a lot more about what the dog is really like. You have also decided that you probably won't want to race your Husky or exhibit it as a show dog. . . you just want to enjoy your dog at home as a companion and member of your family. Now you want to know what you can expect in the way of temperament.

The Siberian Husky makes a great house dog! He adores the companionship of people of all ages, he has an alert and charming personality, and except for the semiannual shedding, the rest of the year he loses very little hair. He is a stable, even-tempered dog, but one which you must realize can display a stubborn streak now and then. With certain dogs, you sometimes get the feeling — and rightly so — that they are never quite giving you their "all." Siberian Huskies are exceptionally smart in their own particular way and this fact, combined with their exceptional good looks and desirable medium body size, wins you over to the point where you honestly believe you have chosen the most wonderful breed in the world! And this is probably quite true. . . .

In over 500 questionnaires sent out in the course of researching this book I received 100% agreement on the answer to my question as to what was the breed's strongest selling point, its outstanding desirable characteristic. It was unanimously agreed that their marvelous disposition and the way they take to family living in any climate, under any circumstances, and still excel in the outdoor activities for which they were created and bred, is the major desirable characteristic.

THE SIBERIAN HUSKY AND ITS
RELATIONSHIPS WITH OTHER ANIMALS

The legends of the hunting instincts and keen nose of the Siberian Husky are many! Drivers from the earliest times could recall countless stories of lead dogs finding the way home when the driver became hopelessly lost, and of teams suddenly veering off course when they caught the scent of bear, moose or reindeer, leaving the driver hanging on desperately until he could manage to stop them and get back on course again. Huskies were hunting with their owners long before they were pulling sleds.

Their hunting instinct, however, caused one of the major problems in trying to get Huskies used to domestic animals. With this strong, inherent hunting instinct they could not discern which animals belonged to the family and which they were meant to pursue and bring down. Everything from chickens to calves and foals were within their territory, with cats favorite victims. All were chased, caught by the throat, and with a swiftness that almost could not be observed, finished off! Waldemar Jochelson wrote in 1908 that on occasions when he had tried to domesticate dogs he had brought back from the wilds he found that they never lost this instinct to hunt, and did all sorts of damage to local game and domestic animals while showing no hostility to strangers or their owners.

But Huskies are no longer the aggressive hunters they were during the days they were first kept as pets as opposed to strictly work animals. Perhaps it is because they are no longer half-starved and always hungry. And it has been a long time since they lived in the wilds where game was plentiful and they were expected to make a kill. Domestication has made stalking prey an exception rather than a rule of life. Also, it depends on the owner, and on the individual dog. The instinct to capture anything that moves is inherent in many animals — especially in the cat family. It is up to the owner to prevent "the law of the jungle" from causing a tragedy within the household if you are to harbor animals in addition to the Siberian Husky.

THE CALL OF THE WILD!

All of us who love dogs and remember Clark Gable in the movie *Call of the Wild,* whether you saw it when it was first produced or one of the countless times it has been re-run on television, will remember the distant howl of the Arctic wolves!

Siberian Huskies are also given more to howling than to barking. In the dead of night they are likely to lift their voices in "song," and there it remains at fever pitch for long periods of time and carrying over great distances. Just like in the movies!

The voices of these dogs have been described in earlier written records by men in the North as "long, melancholy howls of a wolf-

Call of the wild! Phyllis and Vincent Buoniello's Ch. Bushka of Hauppauge listens as Ch. Fort Salonga's Kemo of Baltic reaches for a high note.

like dog,'' and early commentators have remarked to the effect that you never hear these dogs bark — they are like wolves and only howl. Any dog, except perhaps the Basenji, can learn to bark, simply by observing other dogs. Anyone who has owned a Siberian Husky will also attest that they seldom make noise unnecessarily, but when they do it *is* similar to the cry of the wolf.

Down through the centuries as man needed his dog to serve also as a guard for him it was trained to give voice and bark on certain occasions. However, Huskies' inclination not to bark is one reason why they do not make superior watch dogs. . .the other reason is that they *love everybody!*

STAKING OUT

One of the best ways to keep a Siberian Husky that you intend to use as a working or racing dog is to stake it outside rather than allow it to live indoors. Here again, the workings of the Husky mind can

It's been a long hard night! Barrel kenneling is a feature at the Synordik Kennels of Drs. Richard and Cynthia Nist of Snohomish, Washington.

Kennel facilities at Norstarr Kennels in Rockford, Illinois. Norstarr is owned by Dave and Alice Angel, advocates of "barrel" housing for the dogs.

better tolerate the thoughts and conditions of a stake, because Huskies generally find the confinement of four fence walls, no matter how large the enclosure, much less tolerable.

A soft, secure harness with a chain not more than ten feet long will give the dog a sufficiently large area to move in, (six feet would also be adequate,) with the only obstacle being the attachment to the harness. Shelter should be provided in some form, perhaps a simply constructed dog house made from plywood half an inch thick, with a flat though slightly tilted roof to allow the rain to run off, and for the dog to lie on if the ground is not to his liking.

It is a good idea to feed the dog on this roof also. The food is away from contact with the ground and the insect problem is therefore somewhat lessened; the roof also provides some protection against wandering animals which might stray onto the scene.

However, if you stake your dog outside and wish to campaign the dog in the show ring, shade must be provided, since constant exposure to the sun can sunburn the coat, changing both the color and the texture.

Sled dog huts made from barrels that have the open end framed and attached to lateral rails for stability can be considered as adequate quarters, but in many cases the dogs stay outside in the snow anyway.

LIVING OUT

You must determine at the beginning whether your Siberian Husky is to be an indoor or outdoor dog. Depending on the severity of the climate in the region where you live, your dog may be more comfortable living outdoors all year round. In the great snows which occur in the North, the Husky is able to take care of itself under most any conditions. He sleeps in a hole he digs for himself in the snow, curled in a semi-circle with his furry tail as a cover for his face; this helps to prevent the frigid air from blasting into his face.

It is not to the dog's best interests to suddenly take pity on him during a blizzard and bring him inside to warm up. Once the ice and snow melt and wet the coat, it must be *completely* dry before the dog is put outside again, or the wet hair will freeze to it and either give the dog pneumonia or cause it to freeze to death.

A dog which lives outdoors must be given enough chain to be able to walk about and keep its circulation going or it will freeze. The chain must be long enough for it to move out of the way of the drifting snow so that it does not get buried and suffocate beneath the snow. The dog must be able to move about and shake off the snow periodically.

LIVING IN

Aside from the shedding problem, the Husky makes an ideal indoor dog. He is not clumsy in the house, nor is he particularly given to jumping on the furniture, being content to remain on the floor.

It is almost useless, however, to try to designate a special bed for the dog. You will find that he will much prefer to sleep near a favorite member of the family. Siberian Huskies also are unusually clean eaters. They eat their food promptly and all at once and aren't known to play in their water dishes the way certain other breeds do, at least not after they have grown up!

The Siberian Husky is a particularly clean dog in other respects, too. At times they lick themselves clean in somewhat the same manner as a cat. This cleanliness most likely goes back to the North where they could always keep themselves clean by rolling in the snow. They have no typical "doggy odor" the way some of the other breeds have, except occasionally when they are soaking wet or have been exposed to special circumstances that might cause odors to cling to their coats. Occasional brushings will keep them clean and odor-free under normal circumstances.

The best kind of baby-sitter! Ch. Karnovanda's Zenda, C.D., looks after Natalie Russell, aged 4½ months. Owner is Judith M. Russell, Karnovanda Kennels, Davisburg, Michigan.

All aboard! Jimmy, Eddie and Laura Rutan and their "skipper," Yeti's Tin-Taiga, set to sail! The children and dog belong to Mr. and Mrs. Thomas Rutan, of Indian Lake, Denville, New Jersey.

For the dog that will be living in and will get its exercise in the form of walks each day, make sure that the dog is handled by a capable person. It is not considered "cute" to see a tiny child being pulled along by a dog that has just caught scent of a bitch in heat down the street, or suddenly gets the urge to chase some children flashing by on bicycles. If the dog has to defend itself in a fight, the child could end up in the middle of a canine scrap. Also, since the exotic appearance of the Siberian Husky sometimes inspires fear in those who don't understand its docile temperament, such persons often doubt the ability of the child to handle it when it is in their vicinity.

A dog that lives in must be exercised several times a day, and it should be done by an adult with sufficient strength to restrain the dog under any circumstances and sufficient walking speed to let the dog exercise at its normal gait. More and more people are seen on the roads and in the parks jogging with their dogs. Signs of the times!

CHAPTER 14
BUYING YOUR SIBERIAN HUSKY PUPPY

There are several paths that will lead you to a litter of puppies where you can find the puppy of your choice. Write to the parent club and ask for the names and addresses of members who have puppies for sale. The addresses of Siberian Husky clubs can be obtained by writing the American Kennel Club, 51 Madison Avenue, New York, N.Y. 10010. They keep an accurate, up-to-date list of reputable breeders from whom you can seek information on obtaining a good, healthy puppy. You might also check listings in the classified ads of major newspapers. The various dog magazines also carry listings and usually a column each month which features information and news on the breed.

If is to your advantage to attend a few dog shows in the area where purebred dogs of just about every breed are being exhibited in the show ring. Even if you do not wish to buy a show dog, you should be familiar with what the better specimens look like so that you may at least get a decent looking representative of the breed for your money. You will learn a lot by observing the dogs in action in the show ring, or in a public place where their personalities come to the fore. The dog show catalogue will list the dogs and their owners with local kennel names and breeders whom you can visit to see the types and colors they are breeding and winning with at the shows. Exhibitors at these shows are usually delighted to talk to people about their dogs and the specific characteristics of their particular breed.

Once you have chosen the Siberian Husky above all others because you admire its exceptional beauty, intelligence and personality, and because you feel the breed will fit in with your family's way of life, it is wise to do a little research on it. The American Kennel Club library, your local library, bookshops, and the breed clubs can usually supply you with a list of reading matter or written material on the breed, past and present. Then, once you have drenched yourself in the breed's illustrious history and have definitely decided that this is the breed for you, it is time to start writing letters and making phone calls to set up appointments to see litters of puppies.

A word of caution here: don't let your choice of a kennel be determined by its nearness to your home, and then buy the first cute puppy that races up to you or licks the end of your nose. All puppies are cute, and naturally you will have a preference among those you see. But don't let preferences sway you into buying the wrong puppy.

If you are buying your dog as a family pet, a preference might not be a serious offense. But if you have had, say, a color preference since you first considered this breed, you would be wise to stick to it. If you are buying a show dog, all physical features must meet with the Standard for the breed. In considering your purchase you must think clearly, choose carefully, and make the very best possible choice. You will, of course, learn to love whichever puppy you finally decide upon, but a case of "love at first sight" can be disappointing and expensive later on if a show career was your primary objective.

To get the broadest possible concept of what is for sale and the current market prices, it is recommended that you visit as many kennels and private breeders as you can. With today's reasonably safe, inexpensive and rapid non-stop flights on the major airlines, it is possible to secure dogs from far-off places at nominal additional charges, allowing you to buy the valuable bloodlines of your choice if you have a thought toward a breeding program in the future.

While it is always safest to actually *see* the dog you are buying, there are enough reputable breeders and kennels to be found for you to buy a dog with a minimum of risk once you have made up your mind what you want, and when you have decided whether you will buy in your own country or import to satisfy your concept of the breed Standard. If you are going to breed dogs, breeding Standard type can be a moral obligation, and your concern should be with buying the very best bloodlines and individual animals obtainable, in spite of cost or distance.

It is customary for the purchaser to pay the shipping charges, and the airlines are most willing to supply flight information and prices upon request. Rental on the shipping crate, if the owner does not provide one for the dog, is nominal. While unfortunate incidents have occurred on the airlines in the transporting of animals by air, the major airlines are making improvements in safety measures and have reached the point of reasonable safety and cost. Barring unforeseen circumstances, the safe arrival of a dog you might buy can pretty much be assured if both seller and purchaser adhere to and follow up on even the most minute details from both ends.

Grooming time at Norstarr Kennels. Dave Angel gets one of their Siberians ready for the show ring. Norstarr Kennels are in Rockford, Illinois.

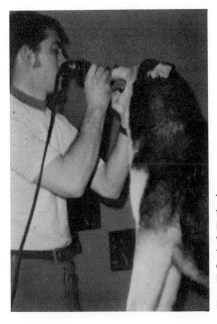

Taskan's Timikito getting final finishing touches before going into the show ring. This photo was taken on the day she took a four-point major win over specials from Bred By Exhibitor bitch class. Owned by Mr. and Mrs. Thomas Hacker of Milwaukee, Wisconsin.

THE PUPPY YOU BUY

Let us assume you want to enjoy all the cute antics of a young puppy and decide to buy a six-to-eight-week-old puppy. This is about the age when a puppy is weaned, wormed and ready to go out into the world with a responsible new owner. It is better not to buy a puppy under six weeks of age; it simply is not yet ready to leave the mother or the security of the other puppies. At eight to twelve weeks of age you will be able to notice much about the appearance and the behavior. Puppies, as they are recalled in our fondest childhood memories, are gay and active and bouncy, as well they should be! The normal puppy should be interested, alert, and curious, especially about a stranger. If a puppy acts a little reserved or distant, however, such act need not be misconstrued as shyness or fear. It merely indicates he hasn't made up his mind whether he likes you as yet! By the same token, he should not be fearful or terrified by a stranger — and especially should not show any fear of his owner!

In direct contrast, the puppy should not be ridiculously over-active either. The puppy that frantically bounds around the room and is

Two young 'uns! An unbeatable combination owned by Lillian M. Russell, Karnovanda Kennels, Davisburg, Michigan.

The lineup! Four Karnovanda puppies, Yukon Twilite, Kenen, Illya and Cheka, owned and bred by Lillian M. Russell, Karnovanda Kennels, Davisburg, Michigan.

Morning outing at the Goldberg Kennels in Cream Ridge, New Jersey.

Best in Show winning Siberian Husky pictured at five months of age with Kathleen Kanzler's daughter Trish. This photo was taken on the day Clipper was purchased from the Innisfree Kennels by Clarence and Gladys Dudley of North. Syracuse, New York.

never still is not especially desirable. And beware of the "spinners"! Spinners are the puppies or dogs that have become neurotic from being kept in cramped quarters or in crates and behave in an emotionally unstable manner when loosed in adequate space. When let out they run in circles and seemingly "go wild." Puppies with this kind of traumatic background seldom ever regain full composure or adjust to the big outside world. The puppy which has had the proper exercise and appropriate living quarters will have a normal, though spirited, outlook on life and will do his utmost to win you over without having to go into a tailspin.

If the general behavior and appearance of the dog thus far appeal to you, it is time for you to observe him more closely for additional physical requirements. First of all, you cannot expect to find in the puppy all the coat he will bear upon maturity. That will come with time and good food, and will be additionally enhanced by the many wonderful grooming aids which can be found on the market today. Needless to say, the healthy puppy's coat should have a nice shine to it, and the more dense at this age, the better the coat will be when the dog reaches adulthood.

Look for clear, dark, sparkling eyes, free of discharge. Dark eye rims and lids are indications of good pigmentation, which is important in a breeding program, and even for generally pleasing good looks. . .unless, of course, the dog is a red.

When the time comes to select your puppy, take an experienced breeder along with you if this is possible. If it is not possible, take the Standard for the breed with you. Try to interpret the Standard as best you can by making comparisons between the puppies you see.

Check the bite completely and carefully. While the first set of teeth can be misleading, even the placement of teeth at this young age can be a fairly accurate indication of what the bite will be in the grown dog. The gums should be a good healthy pink in color, and the teeth should be clear, clean and white. Any brown cast to them could mean a past case of distemper and would assuredly count against the dog in the show ring and against the dog's general appearance at maturity.

Puppies take anything and everything into their mouths to chew on while they are teething, and a lot of infectious diseases are transmit-

They don't quite see eye to eye! Two litter sisters who grew up to be champions and brood bitches at Dichoda Kennels in Escalon, California: Ch. Dichoda's Chiota of Berik and Dichoda's Chiota Saskylakh.

ted this way. The aforementioned distemper is one, and the brown teeth as a result of this disease never clear. The puppy's breath should not be sour or even unpleasant or strong. Any acrid odor could indicate a poor mixture of food, or low quality of meat, especially if it is being fed raw. Many breeders have compared the breath of a healthy puppy to that of fresh toast, or as being vaguely like garlic. At any rate, a puppy should never be fed just table scraps, but should have a well-balanced diet containing a good dry puppy chow and a good grade of fresh meat. Poor meat and too much cereal or fillers tend to make the puppy too fat. We like puppies to be in good flesh, but not fat from the wrong kind of food.

It goes without saying that we want to find clean puppies. The breeder or owner who shows you a dirty puppy is one from whom to steer away! Look closely at the skin. Rub the fur the wrong way or against the grain; make sure it is not spotted with insect bites or red, blotchy sores or dry scales. The vent area around the tail should not show evidences of diarrhea or inflammation. By the same token, the puppy's fur should not be matted with dry excrement or smell of urine.

True enough, you can wipe dirty eyes, clean dirty ears and give the puppy a bath when you get it home, but these things are all indications of how the puppy has been cared for during the important formative first months of its life, and can vitally influence its future health and development. There are many reputable breeders raising healthy puppies that have been reared in proper places and under the proper conditions in clean housing, so why take a chance on a series of veterinary bills and a questionable constitution?

MALE OR FEMALE?

The choice of sex in your puppy is also something that must be given serious thought before you buy. For the pet owner, the sex that would best suit the family life you enjoy would be the paramount choice to consider. For the breeder or exhibitor, there are other vital considerations. If you are looking for a stud to establish a kennel, it is essential that you select a dog with both testicles evident, even at a tender age, and verified by a veterinarian before the sale is finalized if there is any doubt.

The visibility of only one testicle, known as monorchidism, automatically disqualifies the dog from the show ring or from a breeding program, though monorchids are capable of siring. Additionally, it must be noted that monorchids frequently sire dogs with the same deficiency, and to introduce this into a bloodline knowingly is an

Hi there! Love and kisses with Ch. Zapodna, owned by John Baxter, and a small friend. The other dog is Ch. Darbo.

unwritten sin in the dog fancy. Also, a monorchid can sire dogs that are completely sterile. These are referred to as cryptorchids and have no testicles.

If you want the dog to be a member of the family, the best selection would probably be a female. You can always go out for stud service if you should decide to breed. You can choose the bloodlines doing the most winning because they should be bred true to type, and you will not have to foot the bill for the financing of a show career. You can always keep a male from your first litter that will bear your own "kennel name" if you have decided to proceed in the kennel "business."

An additional consideration in the male versus female decision for the private owner is that with males there might be the problem of leg-lifting and with females there is the inconvenience while they are in season. However, this need not be the problem it used to be — pet shops sell "pants" for both sexes, which help to control the situation.

THE PLANNED PARENTHOOD BEHIND YOUR PUPPY

Never be afraid to ask pertinent questions about the puppy, as well as questions about the sire and dam. Feel free to ask the breeder if you might see the dam, the purpose of your visit to determine her general health and her appearance as a representative of the breed. Ask also to see the sire if the breeder is the owner. Ask what the puppy has been fed and should be fed after weaning. Ask to see the pedigree, and inquire if the litter or the individual puppies have been registered with the American Kennel Club, how many of the temporary and/or permanent inoculations the puppy has had, when and if the puppy has been wormed, and whether it has had any illness, disease or infection.

You need not ask if the puppy is housebroken. . .it won't mean much. He may have gotten the idea as to where "the place" is where he lives now, but he will need new training to learn where "the place" is in his new home! And you can't really expect too much from puppies at this age anyway. Housebreaking is entirely up to the new owner. We know puppies always eliminate when they first awaken and sometimes dribble when they get excited. If friends and relatives are coming over to see the new puppy, make sure he is walked just before he greets them at the front door. This will help.

The normal time period for puppies around three months of age to eliminate is about every two or three hours. As the time draws near, either take the puppy out or indicate the newspapers for the same purpose. Housebreaking is never easy, but anticipation is about 90 per cent of solving the problem. The schools that offer to housebreak your dog are virtually useless. Here again the puppy will learn the "place" at the schoolhouse, but coming home he will need special training for the new location.

A reputable breeder will welcome any and all questions you might ask and will voluntarily offer additional information, if only to brag about the tedious and loving care he has given the litter. He will also sell a puppy on a 24-hour veterinary approval. This means you have a full day to get the puppy to a veterinarian of your choice to get his opinion on the general health of the puppy before you make a final decision. There should also be veterinary certificates and full particulars on the dates and types of inoculations the puppy has been given up to that time.

PUPPIES AND WORMS

Let us give further attention to the unhappy and very unpleasant subject of worms. Generally speaking, most all puppies — even those raised in clean quarters — come into contact with worms early in life. The worms can be passed down from the mother before birth or picked up during the puppies' first encounters with the earth or their kennel facilities. To say that you must not buy a puppy because of an infestation of worms is nonsensical. You might be passing up a fine animal that can be freed of worms in one short treatment, although a heavy infestation of worms of any kind in a young dog is dangerous and debilitating.

The extent of the infection can be readily determined by a veterinarian, and you might take his word as to whether the future health and conformation of the dog has been damaged. He can prescribe the dosage and supply the medication at the time and you will already have one of your problems solved. The kinds and varieties of worms and how to detect them is described in detail elsewhere in this book and we advise you to check the matter out further if there is any doubt in your mind as to the problems of worms in dogs.

VETERINARY INSPECTION

While your veterinarian is going over the puppy you have selected to purchase, you might just as well ask him for his opinion of it as a breed as well as the facts about its general health. While few veterinarians can claim to be breed conformation experts, they usually have a good eye for a worthy specimen and can advise you where to go for further information. Perhaps your veterinarian could also recommend other breeders if you should want another opinion. The veterinarian can point out structural faults or organic problems that affect all breeds and can usually judge whether an animal has been abused or mishandled and whether it is oversized or undersized.

I would like to emphasize here that it is only through this type of close cooperation between owners and veterinarians that we can expect to reap the harvest of modern research in the veterinary field. Most reliable veterinarians are more than eager to learn about various breeds of purebred dogs, and we in turn must acknowledge and apply what they have proved through experience and research in their field. We can buy and breed the best dog in the world, but when disease strikes we are only as safe as our veterinarian is capable — so let's keep them informed breed by breed, and dog by dog. The veterinarian represents the difference between life and death!

THE CONDITIONS OF SALE

While it is customary to pay for the puppy before you take it away with you, you should be able to give the breeder a deposit if there is any doubt about the puppy's health. You might also (depending on local laws) postdate a check to cover the 24-hour veterinary approval. If you decide to take the puppy, the breeder is required to supply you with a pedigree, along with the puppy's registration paper. He is also obliged to supply you with complete information about the inoculations and American Kennel Club instructions on how to transfer ownership of the puppy into your name.

Dudley's Vodki of Koryak pictured at just six months of age. Better known as "Tanker," he is owned by Clarence and Gladys Dudley of North Syracuse, New York.

A litter of puppies whelped at Racecrest Kennels in January, 1971. Sire was Ch. Troika's De Mischka; dam was Ch. Racecrest's Marika's Katrine. Racecrest, established in 1958, is owned by Mrs. J.W. Anderson of Ontario, Canada.

Some breeders will offer buyers time payment plans for convenience if the price on a show dog is very high or if deferred payments are the only way you can purchase the dog. However, any such terms must be worked out between buyer and breeder and should be put in writing to avoid later complications.

You will find most breeders cooperative if they believe you are sincere in your love for the puppy and that you will give it the proper home and the show ring career it deserves (if it is sold as a show quality specimen of the breed). Remember, when buying a show dog, it is impossible to guarantee nature. A breeder can only tell you what he *believes* will develop into a show dog. . .so be sure your breeder is an honest one.

Also, if you purchase a show prospect and promise to show the dog, you definitely should show it! It is a waste to have a beautiful dog that deserves recognition in the show ring sitting at home as a family pet, and it is unfair to the breeder. This is especially true if the breeder offered you a reduced price because of the advertising his kennel and bloodlines would receive by your showing the dog in the ring. If you want a pet, buy a pet. Be honest about it, and let the breeder decide on this basis which is the best dog for you. Your conscience will be clear and you'll both be doing a real service to the breed.

BUYING A SHOW PUPPY

If you are positive about breeding and showing your dog, make it clear that you intend to do so so that the breeder will sell you the best possible puppy. If you are dealing with an established kennel, you will have to rely partially if not entirely on their choice, since they know their bloodlines and what they can expect from the breeding. They know how their stock develops, and it would be foolish of them to sell you a puppy that could not stand up as a show specimen representing their stock in the ring.

However, you must also realize that the breeder may be keeping the best puppy in the litter to show and breed himself. If this is the case, you might be wise to select the best puppy of the opposite sex so that the dogs will not be competing against one another in the show rings for their championship title.

THE PURCHASE PRICE

Prices vary on all puppies, of course, but a good show prospect at six weeks to six months of age will sell for several hundred dollars. If the puppy is really outstanding, and the pedigree and parentage is also outstanding, the price will be even higher. Honest breeders, however, will all be around the same figure, so price should not be a deciding factor in your choice. If there is any question as to the current price range, a few telephone calls to different kennels will give you a good average. Breeders will usually stand behind their puppies; should something drastically wrong develop, such as hip dysplasia, etc., their obligation to make an adjustment is usually honored. Therefore, your cost is covered.

THE COST OF BUYING ADULT STOCK

Prices for adult dogs fluctuate greatly. Some grown dogs are offered free of charge to good homes; others are put out with owners on breeders' terms. But don't count on getting a "bargain" if it doesn't cost you anything! Good dogs are always in demand, and worthy studs or brood bitches are expensive. Prices for them can easily go up into the four-figure range. Take an expert with you if you

Kaylee Kitkit Kayikay pictured at ten months of age. Kitkit was sired by Savdajaure's Cognac *ex* Kaylee Keenu and is owned by the Kaylee Kennels, Baltimore, Maryland.

intend to make this sort of investment. Just make sure the ''expert'' is free of professional jealousy and will offer unprejudiced opinion. If you are reasonably familiar with the Standard, and get the expert's opinion, between the two you can usually come up with a proper decision.

Buying grown stock does remove some of the risk if you are planning a kennel. You will know exactly what you are getting for your foundation stock and will also save time on getting your kennel started.

CHAPTER 15
BREEDING YOUR SIBERIAN HUSKY

Let us assume the time has come for your dog to be bred, and you have decided you are in a position to enjoy producing a litter of puppies that you hope will make a contribution to the breed. The bitch you purchased is sound, her temperament is excellent and she is a most worthy representative of the breed.

You have taken a calendar and counted off the ten days since the first day of red staining and have determined the tenth to fourteenth day, which will more than likely be the best days for the actual mating. You have additionally counted off 65 to 63 days before the puppies are likely to be born to make sure everything necessary for their arrival will be in good order by that time.

From the moment the idea of having a litter occurred to you, your thoughts should have been given to the correct selection of a proper stud. Here again the novice would do well to seek advice on analyzing pedigrees and tracing bloodlines for your best breedings. As soon as the bitch is in season and you see color (or staining) and a swelling of the vulva, it is time to notify the owner of the stud you selected and make appointments for the breedings. There are several pertinent questions you will want to ask the stud owners after having decided upon the pedigree. The owners, naturally, will also have a few questions they wish to ask you. These questions will concern your bitch's bloodlines, health, age, how many previous litters if any, etc.

THE HEALTH OF THE BREEDING STOCK

Some of your first questions should concern whether or not the stud has already proved himself by siring a normal healthy litter. Also inquire as to whether or not the owners have had a sperm count made to determine just exactly how fertile or potent the stud is. Also ask whether he has been X-rayed for hip dysplasia and found to be clear. Determine for yourself whether the dog has two normal testicles.

When considering your bitch for this mating, you must take into consideration a few important points that lead to a successful breeding. You and the owner of the stud will want to recall whether she has had normal heat cycles, whether there too many runts in the litter, and whether Caesarean section was ever necessary. Has she ever had a vaginal infection? Could she take care of her puppies by herself, or was there a milk shortage? How many surviving puppies were there from the litter, and what did they grow up to be in comparison to the requirements of the breed Standard?

Don't buy a bitch that has problem heats and has never had a litter. But don't be afraid to buy a healthy maiden bitch, since chances are, if she is healthy and from good stock, she will be a healthy producer. Don't buy a monorchid male, and certainly not a cryptorchid. If there is any doubt in your mind about his potency, get a sperm count from the veterinarian. Older dogs that have been good producers and are for sale are usually not too hard to find at good established kennels. If they are not too old and have sired quality show puppies, they can give you some excellent show stock from which to establish your own breeding lines.

THE DAY OF THE MATING

Now that you have decided upon the proper male and female combination to produce what you hope will be — according to the pedigrees — a fine litter of puppies, it is time to set the date. You have selected the two days (with a one day lapse in between) that you feel are best for the breeding, and you call the owner of the stud. The bitch always goes to the stud, unless, of course, there are extenuating circumstances. You set the date and the time and arrive with the bitch *and* the money.

Standard procedure is payment of a stud fee at the time of the first breeding, if there is a tie. For the stud fee, you are entitled to two breedings with ties. Contracts may be written up with specific conditions on breeding terms, of course, but this is general procedure. Often a breeder will take the pick of a litter to protect and maintain his bloodlines. This can be especially desirable if he needs an outcross for his breeding program or if he wishes to continue his own bloodlines if he sold you the bitch to start with, and this mating will continue his line-breeding program. This should all be worked out ahead of time and written and signed before the two dogs are bred. Remember that the payment of the stud fee is for the services of the stud — not for a guarantee of a litter of puppies. This is why it is so important to make sure you are using a proven stud. Bear in mind also that the American Kennel Club will not register a litter of puppies sired by a male that is under eight months of age. In the case of an older dog, they will not register a litter sired by a dog over 12 years of age, unless there is a witness to the breeding in the form of a veterinarian or other responsible person.

Many studs over 12 years of age are still fertile and capable of producing puppies, but if you do not witness the breeding there is always the danger of a "substitute" stud being used to produce a litter. This brings up the subject of sending your bitch away to be bred if you cannot accompany her.

The disadvantages of sending a bitch away to be bred are numerous. First of all, she will not be herself in a strange place, so she'll

Debbie Ensminger and an ardent admirer captured on film by Judy Rosemarin.

Ch. Doonauk's Gidget shown going Best of Breed at the Rhode Island Kennel Club show in April, 1971; the judge was Theodore Wurmser. Gidget is one of the stud dogs at Charlotte and Judith Anderson's Panuck-Denali Kennels In Laconia, New Hampshire. Photo by Ashbey.

be difficult to handle. Transportation if she goes by air, while reasonably safe, is still a traumatic experience, and there is the danger of her being put off at the wrong airport, not being fed or watered properly, etc. Some bitches get so upset that they go out of season and the trip, which may prove expensive, especially on top of a substantial stud fee, will have been for nothing.

If at all possible, accompany your bitch so that the experience is as comfortable for her as it can be. In other words, make sure before setting this kind of schedule for a breeding that there is no stud in the area that might be as good for her as the one that is far away. Don't sacrifice the proper breeding for convenience, since bloodlines are so important, but put the safety of the bitch above all else. There is always a risk in traveling, since dogs are considered cargo on a plane.

HOW MUCH DOES THE STUD FEE COST?

The stud fee will vary considerably — the better the bloodlines, the more winning the dog does at shows, the higher the fee. Stud service from a top winning dog could run up to $500.00. Here again, there may be exceptions. Some breeders will take part cash and then, say, third pick of the litter. The fee can be arranged by a private contract rather than the traditional procedure we have described.

Here again, it is wise to get the details of the payment of the stud fee in writing to avoid trouble.

THE ACTUAL MATING

It is always advisable to muzzle the bitch. A terrified bitch may fear-bite the stud, or even one of the people involved, and the wild bitch may snap or attack the stud, to the point where he may become discouraged and lose interest in the breeding. Muzzling can be done with a lady's stocking tied around the muzzle with a half knot, crossed under the chin and knotted at the back of the neck. There is enough "give" in the stocking for her to breathe or salivate freely and yet not open her jaws far enough to bite. Place her in front of her owner, who holds onto her collar and talks to her and calms her as much as possible.

If the male will not mount on his own initiative, it may be necessary for the owner to assist in lifting him onto the bitch, perhaps even in guiding him to the proper place. But usually, the tie is accomplished once the male gets the idea. The owner should remain

Ch. Arahaz' Ebony Beauty, foundation bitch of the Edward Fischers' Arahaz Kennels in Cannonsburg, Pennsylvania. She is a dam of champions and is handled to this win by Jack Kent under judge Charles Hamilton. A Norton of Kent photograph.

Head study of the Fireside Kennels' top stud dog, Ch. Fireside Ladies Man. He is a son of their Am. and Can. Ch. Lostland's Leadying Lady.

Ch. Kodiak's Kamiak, owned by Peggy and Ed Samerson of Woodland Park, Colorado. Kamiak is pictured winning in the show ring and is one of the stud forces at the Samersons' Domeyko Kennels.

close at hand, however, to make sure the tie is not broken before an adequate breeding has been completed. After a while the stud may get bored and try to break away. This could prove injurious. It may be necessary to hold him in place until the tie is broken.

We must stress at this point that while some bitches carry on physically, and vocally, during the tie, there is no way the bitch can be hurt. However, a stud can be seriously or even permanently damaged by a bad breeding. Therefore the owner of the bitch must be reminded that she must not be alarmed by any commotion. All concentration should be devoted to the stud and a successful and properly executed service.

Many people believe that breeding dogs is simply a matter of placing two dogs, a male and a female, in close proximity, and letting nature take its course. While often this is true, you cannot count on it. Sometimes it is hard work, and in the case of valuable stock it is essential to supervise to be sure of the safety factor, especially if one or both of the dogs are inexperienced. If the owners are also inexperienced it may not take place at all!

ARTIFICIAL INSEMINATION

Breeding by means of artificial insemination is usually unsuccessful, unless under a veterinarian's supervision, and can lead to an infection for the bitch and discomfort for the dog. The American Kennel Club requires a veterinarian's certificate to register puppies from such a breeding. Although the practice has been used for over two decades, it now offers new promise, since research has been conducted to make it a more feasible procedure for the future.

Great dogs may eventually look forward to reproducing themselves years after they have left this earth. There now exists a frozen semen concept that has been tested and found successful. The study, headed by Dr. Stephen W. J. Seager, M.V.B., an instructor at the University of Oregon Medical School, has the financial support of the American Kennel Club, indicating that organization's interest in the work. The study is being monitored by the Morris Animal Foundation of Denver, Colorado.

Dr. Seager announced in 1970 that he had been able to preserve dog semen and to produce litters with the stored semen. The possibilities of selective, world-wide breedings by this method are exciting. Imagine simply mailing a vial of semen to the bitch! The perfection of line-breeding by storing semen without the threat of death interrupting the breeding program is exciting, also.

Ch. Joli Badga
with Lila Weir,
handler, win-
ning at a show
in 1969. Badga
is owned by Karl
and Pat Hahn,
Jr., Anchorage,
Alaska and was
top brood bitch
at their Keachi
Kennels.

A bevy of beauties!
These three Siberians
are the bulwark of the
Kaylee Kennels of
Carolyn Windsor in Bal-
timore, Maryland. From
left to right: Kaylee Kitkit Kulik, Kaylee Kitkit
Kayikay, and Kaylee
Kittee Katek. This litter
of three photographed
for Mrs. Windsor by
Photography by U.S.

As it stands today, the technique for artificial insemination requires the depositing of semen (taken directly from the dog) into the bitch's vagina, past the cervix and into the uterus by syringe. The correct temperature of the semen is vital, and there is no guarantee of success. The storage method, if successfully adopted, will present a new era in the field of purebred dogs.

THE GESTATION PERIOD

Once the breeding has taken place successfully, the seemingly endless waiting period of about 63 days begins. For the first ten days after the breeding, you do absolutely nothing for the bitch — just spin dreams about the delights you will share with the family when the puppies arrive.

Around the tenth day it is time to begin supplementing the diet of the bitch with vitamins and calcium. We strongly recommend that you take her to your veterinarian for a list of the proper or perhaps necessary supplements and the correct amounts of each for your particular bitch. Guesses, which may lead to excesses or insufficiencies, can ruin a litter. For the price of a visit to your veterinarian, you will be confident that you are feeding properly.

The bitch should be free of worms, or course, and if there is any doubt in your mind, she should be wormed now, before the third week of pregnancy. Your veterinarian will advise you on the necessity of this and proper doságe as well.

PROBING FOR PUPPIES

Far too many breeders are overanxious about whether the breeding "took" and are inclined to feel for puppies or persuade a veterinarian to radiograph or X-ray their bitches to confirm it. Unless there is reason to doubt the normalcy of a pregnancy, this is risky. Certainly 63 days are not too long to wait, and why risk endangering the litter by probing with your inexperienced hands? Few bitches give no evidence of being in whelp, and there is no need to prove it for yourself by trying to count puppies.

ALERTING YOUR VETERINARIAN

At least a week before the puppies are due, you should telephone your veterinarian and notify him that you expect the litter and give him the date. This way he can make sure that there will be someone available to help, should there by any problems during the whelping.

Most veterinarians today have answering services and alternate vets on call when they are not available themselves. Some veterinarians suggest that you call them when the bitch starts labor so that they may further plan their time, should they be needed. Discuss this matter with your veterinarian when you first take the bitch to him for her diet instructions, etc., and establish the method which will best fit in with his schedule.

Ch. Arctic's Badger of Kolyma, one of the leading stud dogs at Charlotte and Earl Reynolds' Arctic Kennels in Dryden, Michigan. Badger is pictured winning at one of the shows.

DO YOU NEED A VETERINARIAN IN ATTENDANCE?

Even if this is your first litter, I would advise that you go through the experience of whelping without panicking and calling desperately for the veterinarian. Most animal births are accomplished without complications, and you should call for assistance only if you run into trouble.

When having her puppies, your bitch will appreciate as little interference and as few strangers around as possible. A quiet place, with her nest, a single familiar face and her own instincts are all that is necessary for nature to take its course. An audience of curious children squealing and questioning, other family pets nosing around, or strange adults should be avoided. Many a bitch which has been distracted in this way has been known to devour her young. This can be the horrible result of intrusion into the bitch's privacy. There are other ways of teaching children the miracle of birth, and there will be plenty of time later for the whole family to enjoy the puppies. Let them be born under proper and considerate circumstances.

LABOR

Some litters — many first litters — do not run the full term of 63 days. So, at least a week before the puppies are actually due, and at the time you alert your veterinarian as to their arrival, start observing the bitch for signs of the commencement of labor. This will manifest itself in the form of ripples running down the sides of her body, which will come as a revelation to her as well. It is most noticeable when she is lying on her side — and she will be sleeping a great deal as the arrival date comes closer. If she is sitting or walking about, she will perhaps sit down quickly or squat peculiarly. As the ripples become more frequent, birth time is drawing near; you will be wise not to leave her. Usually within 24 hours before whelping, she will stop eating, and as much as a week before she will begin digging a nest. The bitch should be given something resembling a

Mother Siberian Husky and her one-hour-old puppies, captured on film by Judy Rosemarin, Roslyn, New York.

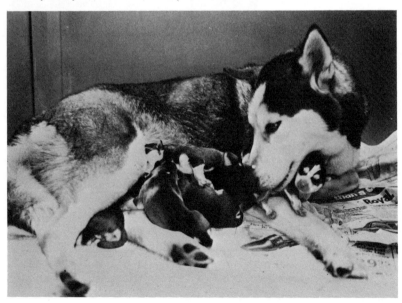

whelping box with layers of newspaper (black and white only) to make her nest. She will dig more and more as birth approaches, and this is the time to begin making your promise to stop interfering unless your help is specifically required. Some bitches whimper and others are silent, but whimpering does not necessarily indicate trouble.

THE ARRIVAL OF THE PUPPIES

The sudden gush of green fluid from the bitch indicates that the water or fluid surrounding the puppies has "broken" and they are about to start down the canal and come into the world. When the water breaks, birth of the first puppy is imminent. The first puppies are usually born within minutes to a half hour of each other, but a couple of hours between the later ones is not uncommon. If you notice the bitch straining constantly without producing a puppy, or if a puppy remains partially in and partially out for too long, it is cause for concern. Breech births (puppies born feet first instead of head first) can often cause delay or hold things up, and this is often a problem which requires veterinarian assistance.

FEEDING THE BITCH BETWEEN BIRTHS

Usually the bitch will not be interested in food for about 24 hours before the arrival of the puppies, and perhaps as long as two or three days after their arrival. The placenta which she cleans up after each puppy is high in food value and will be more than ample to sustain her. This is nature's way of allowing the mother to feed herself and her babies without having to leave the nest and hunt for food during the first crucial days. The mother always cleans up all traces of birth in the wilds so as not to attract other animals to her newborn babies.

However, there are those of us who believe in making food available should the mother feel the need to restore her strength during or after delivery — especially if she whelps a large litter. Raw chopmeat, beef boullion, and milk are all acceptable and may be placed near the whelping box during the first two or three days. After that, the mother will begin to put the babies on a sort of schedule. She will leave the whelping box at frequent intervals, take longer exercise periods, and begin to take interest in other things. This is where the fun begins for you. Now the babies are no longer soggy little pinkish blobs. They begin to crawl around and squeal and hum and grow before your very eyes!

It is at this time, if all has gone normally, that the family can be introduced gradually and great praise and affection given to the mother.

BREECH BIRTHS

Puppies normally are delivered head first. However, some are presented feet first, or in other abnormal positions, and this is referred to as a ''breech birth.'' Assistance is often necessary to get the puppy out of the canal, and great care must be taken not to injure the puppy or the dam.

Aid can be given by grasping the puppy with a piece of turkish toweling and pulling gently during the dam's contractions. Be careful not to squeeze the puppy too hard; merely try to ease it out by mov-

Future champion at the age of three months: Sy and Ann Goldberg's Tokco of Bolshoi.

ing it gently back and forth. Because even this much delay in delivery may mean the puppy is drowning, do not wait for the bitch to remove the sac. Do it yourself by tearing the sac open to expose the face and head. Then cut the cord anywhere from one-half to three-quarters of an inch away from the navel. If the cord bleeds excessively, pinch the end of it with your fingers and count five. Repeat if necessary. Then pry open the mouth with your finger and hold the puppy upside-down for a moment to drain any fluids from the lungs. Next, rub the puppy briskly with turkish or paper toweling. You should get it wriggling and whimpering by this time.

What one would call a uniform litter. . . a seven-day-old litter from the Blackwatch Kennels, Arlington, Virginia.

Before and after! Obviously it's nap time at Blackwatch Kennels. This week-old puppy couldn't care less about having its picture taken. Bred by Arlene and Mac-Knight Black in Arlington, Virginia.

An eight-week-old Akalan puppy whelped in April, 1972. This puppy was sired by Ch. Innisfree's Royal Purple *ex* Ch. Dichoda's Arora Chena, C.D.

The same Akalan puppy photographed at nine weeks of age.

The same Akalan puppy, this time shown at fifteen weeks of age. Dean and Dolores Warner are the breeders, Livermore, California.

If the litter is large, this assistance will help conserve the strength of the bitch and will probably be welcomed by her. However, it is best to allow her to take care of at least the first few herself to preserve the natural instinct and to provide the nutritive values obtained by her consumption of the afterbirths.

DRY BIRTHS

Occasionally the sac will break before the delivery of a puppy and will be expelled while the puppy remains inside, thereby depriving the dam of the necessary lubrication to expel the puppy normally. Inserting vaseline or mineral oil via your finger will help the puppy pass down the birth canal. This is why it is essential that you be present during the whelping so that you can count puppies and afterbirths and determine when and if assistance is needed.

THE TWENTY-FOUR-HOUR CHECKUP

It is smart to have a veterinarian check the mother and her puppies within 24 hours after the last puppy is born. The vet can check for cleft palates or umbilical hernia and may wish to give the dam — particularly if she is a show dog — an injection of Pituitin to make sure of the expulsion of all afterbirths and to tighten up the uterus. This can prevent a sagging belly after the puppies are weaned and the bitch is being readied for the show ring.

FALSE PREGNANCY

The disappointment of a false pregnancy is almost as bad for the owner as it is for the bitch. She goes through the gestation period with all the symptoms — swollen stomach, increased appetite, swollen nipples — even makes a nest when the time comes. You may even take an oath that you noticed the ripples on her body from the labor pains. Then, just as suddenly as you made up your mind that she was definitely going to have puppies, you will know that she definitely is not! She may walk around carrying a toy as if it were a puppy for a few days, but she will soon be back to normal and acting just as if nothing happened — and nothing did!

CAESAREAN SECTION

Should the whelping reach the point where there is a complication, such as the bitch's not being capable of whelping the puppies herself, the "moment of truth" is upon you and a Caesarean section may be necessary. The bitch may be too small or too immature to expel the puppies herself; or her cervix may fail to dilate enough to allow the young to come down the birth canal; or there may be torsion of the uterus, a dead or monster puppy, a sideways puppy blocking the canal, or perhaps toxemia. A Caesarean section will be the only solution. No matter what the cause, get the bitch to the veterinarian immediately to insure your chances of saving the mother and/or puppies.

The Caesarean section operation (the name derived from the idea that Julius Caesar was delivered by this method) involves the removal of the unborn young from the uterus of the dam by surgical incision into the walls through the abdomen. The operation is performed when it has been determined that for some reason the puppies cannot be delivered normally. While modern surgical methods have made the operation itself reasonably safe, with the dam being perfectly capable of nursing the puppies shortly after the completion of the surgery, the chief danger lies in the ability to spark life into the puppies immediately upon their removal from the womb. If the mother dies, the time element is even more important in saving the young, since the oxygen supply ceases upon the death of the dam, and the difference between life and death is measured in seconds.

After surgery, when the bitch is home in her whelping box with the babies, she will probably nurse the young without distress. You must be sure that the sutures are kept clean and that no redness or swelling or ooze appears in the wound. Healing will take place naturally, and no salves or ointments should be applied unless prescribed by the veterinarian, for fear the puppies will get it into their systems. If there is any doubt, check the bitch for fever, restlessness (other than the natural concern for her young) or a lack of appetite, but do not anticipate trouble.

EPISIOTOMY

Even though large dogs are generally easy whelpers, any number of reasons might occur to cause the bitch to have a difficult birth. Before automatically resorting to Caesarean section, many veterinarians are now trying the technique known as episiotomy.

Used rather frequently in human deliveries, episiotomy (pronounced A-PEASE-E-**OTT**-O-ME) is the cutting of the membrane between the rear opening of the vagina back almost to the opening of the anus. After delivery it is stitched together, and barring complications, heals easily, presenting no problem in future births.

SOCIALIZING YOUR PUPPY

The need for puppies to get out among other animals and people cannot be stressed enough. Kennel-reared dogs are subject to all sorts of idiosyncrasies and seldom make good house dogs or normal members of the world around them when they grow up.

The crucial age, which determines the personality and general behavior patterns which will predominate during the rest of the dog's life, are formed between the ages of three and ten weeks. This is particularly true during the 21st to 28th day. It is essential that the puppy be socialized during this time by bringing him into family life as much as possible. Floor surfaces, indoor and outdoor, should be experienced; handling by all members of the family and visitors is important; preliminary grooming gets him used to a lifelong necessity; light training, such as setting him up on tables and cleaning teeth and ears and cutting nails, etc., has to be started early if he is to become a show dog. The puppy should be exposed to car riding,

Happy trio consisting of Ch. Karnovanda's Ivan Groznyi and Andrea, aged 3½ and Natalie, aged 1½ at the Karnovanda Kennels in Davisburg, Michigan.

shopping tours, a leash around its neck, children — your own and others — and in all possible ways develop relationships with humans.

It is up to the breeder, of course, to protect the puppy from harm or injury during this initiation into the outside world. The benefits reaped from proper attention will pay off in the long run with a well-behaved, well-adjusted grown dog capable of becoming an integral part of a happy family.

CHAPTER 16
GENETICS

No one can guarantee the workings of nature. But, with facts and theories as guides, you can plan, at least on paper, a litter of puppies that should fulfill your fondest expectations. Since the ultimate purpose of breeding is to try to improve the breed, or maintain it at the highest possible standard, such planning should be earnestly done, no matter how uncertain particular elements may be.

There are a few terms with which you should become familiar to help you understand the breeding procedure and the workings of genetics. The first thing that comes to mind is a set of formulae known as Mendelian Laws. Gregor Mendel was an Austrian cleric and botanist born 22 July 1822 in what is now named Hyncice and is in Czechoslovakia. He developed his theories on heredity by working for several years with garden peas. A paper on his work was published in a scientific journal in 1866, but for many years it went unnoticed. Today the laws derived from these experiments are basic to all studies of genetics and are employed by horticulturists and animal breeders.

To use these laws as applicable to the breeding of dogs, it is necessary to understand the physical aspects of reproduction. First, dogs possess reproductive glands called gonads. The male gonads are the testicles and there are produced the sperms (spermatozoa) that impregnate the female. Eggs (ova) are produced in the female gonads (ovaries). When whelped, the bitch possesses in rudimentary form all the eggs that will develop throughout her life, whereas spermatozoa are in continual production within the male gonads. When a bitch is mature enough to reproduce, she periodically comes in heat (estrus). Then a number of eggs descend from the ovaries via the fallopian tubes and enter the two horns of the uterus. There they are fertilized by male sperm deposited in semen while mating, or they pass out if not fertilized.

In the mating of dogs, there is what is referred to as a tie, a period during which anatomical features bind the male and female together and about 600 million spermatozoa are ejected into the female to fertilize the ripened eggs. When sperm and ripe eggs meet, zygotes are

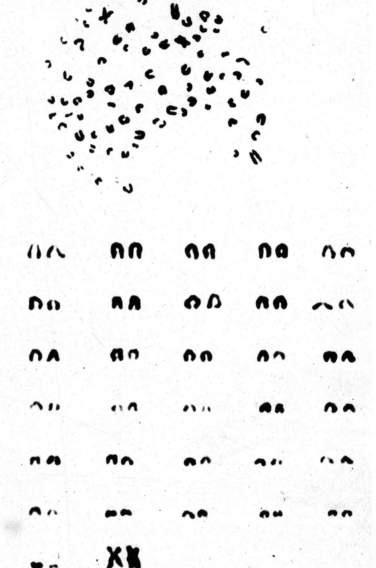

The dog has 78 chromosomes while man has 46 and the cat has 38. The two members of each pair of chromosomes look alike except for the sex chromosomes. A female has two large X chromosomes (see lower right in the illustration). The male has one X chromosome and a small Y chromosome which is the determinant for maleness. The preparation pictured above was made from a white blood cell of a female Keeshond. The chromosomes have been paired according to size.

created and these one-celled future puppies descend from the fallopian tubes, attach themselves to the walls of the uterus, and begin
the developmental process of cell production known as mitosis. With
all inherited characteristics determined as the zygote was formed, the
dam then assumes her role as an incubator for the developing organisms. She has been bred and is in whelp; in these circumstances
she also serves in the exchange of gases and in furnishing nourish-
ment for the puppies forming within.

Let us take a closer look at what is happening during the breeding
process. We know that the male deposits millions of sperms within
the female and that the number of ripe eggs released by the female
will determine the number of puppies in the litter. Therefore, those
breeders who advertise a stud as a "producer of large litters" do not
know the facts or are not sticking to them. The bitch determines the
size of the litter; the male sperm determines the sex of the puppies.
Half of the millions of sperm involved in a mating carry the characteristic that determines development of a male and the other half
carry the factor which triggers development of a female, and distribution of sex is thus decided according to random pairings of sperms
and eggs.

Each dog and bitch possesses 39 pairs of chromosomes in each
body cell; these pairs are split up in the formation of germ cells so
that each one carries half of the hereditary complement. The chromosomes carry the genes, approximately 150,000 like peas in a pod in
each chromosome, and these are the actual factors that determine inherited characteristics. As the chromosomes are split apart and rear-
ranged as to genic pairings in the production of ova and spermatozoa, every zygote formed by the joining of an egg and a sperm
receives 39 chromosomes from each to form the pattern of 78
chromosomes inherited from dam and sire which will be reproduced
in every cell of the developing individual and determine what sort of
animal it will be.

To understand the procedure more clearly, we must know that
there are two kinds of genes — dominant and recessive. A dominant
gene is one of a pair whose influence is expressed to the exclusion of
the effects of the other. A recessive gene is one of a pair whose influence is subdued by the effects of the other, and characteristics determined by recessive genes become manifest only when both genes
of a pairing are recessive. Most of the important qualities we wish to
perpetuate in our breeding programs are carried by the dominant
genes. It is the successful breeder who becomes expert at eliminating
recessive or undesirable genes and building up the dominant or desirable gene patterns.

Ch. Arctic's Colorado Sleet and Ch. Arctic's Pretti, owned by Charlotte Reynolds.

There are many excellent books available which take you deeper into the fascinating subject of canine genetics. You can learn about your chances of getting so many black, so many white, or so many black-and-white puppies proportionally in a litter, and the ratio of other such expectations. Avail yourself of such information to put purpose into your breeding program.

We have merely touched upon genetics here to point out the importance of planned mating. Any librarian can help you find further information, or books may be purchased offering the very latest findings on canine genetics. It is a fascinating and rewarding program toward creating better dogs.

CHAPTER 17
THE POWER OF PEDIGREES

An old dog philosopher once remarked that the definition of a show prospect puppy is one third the pedigree, one third what you see, and one third what you *hope* it *will* be! Well, no matter how you break down your qualifying percentages, we all quite agree that good breeding is essential if you have any plans at all for a show career for your dog! Many breeders will buy on pedigree alone, counting largely on what they can do with the puppy themselves by way of feeding, conditioning and training. Needless to say, that very important piece of paper commonly referred to as "the pedigree" is mighty reassuring to a breeder or buyer new at the game or to one who has a breeding program in mind and is trying to establish his own bloodline.

One of the most fascinating aspects of tracing pedigrees is the way the names of the really great dogs of the past keep appearing in the pedigrees of the great dogs of today. . .proof positive of the strong influence of heredity, and witness to a great deal of truth in the statement that great dogs frequently reproduce themselves, though not necessarily in appearance only. A pedigree represents something of value when one is dedicated to breeding better dogs.

To the novice buyer, or one who is perhaps merely switching to another breed, and see only a frolicking, leggy, squirming bundle of energy in a fur coat, a pedigree can mean *everything!* To those of us who believe in heredity, a pedigree is more like an insurance policy.

I have gathered in this chapter several pedigrees of prominent dogs in the twentieth century which have had strong influence on this breed. I hope you find the lineage of these Siberian Huskies interesting to follow and an aid in extending the pedigrees you have on your own dogs.

CH. NORTHERN LIGHT KOBUCK
WHELPED NOV. 20, 1928

NORTHERN LIGHT KOLYMA
- JACK FROST
  - SCOTTY
    - BOSCO
    - DOLLY
  - VASTA
    - SUGGEN
    - NELLIE
- NORTHERN LIGHT SNOWFLAKE
  - UNKNOWN
    - UNKNOWN
    - UNKNOWN
  - SOFIA
    - UNKNOWN
    - UNKNOWN

NORTHERN LIGHT PATSY
- NORTHERN LIGHT TOGO
  - JACK FROST
    - SCOTTY
    - VASTA
  - NORTHERN LIGHT SNOWFLAKE
    - UNKNOWN
    - SOFIA
- PATSY
  - ACE
    - ICI
    - MARY
  - MAGGIE (MARGARET)
    - ICI
    - WANDA

N'YA N'YA OF SEPPALA
WHELPED NOV. 21, 1939

- **KINGEAK OF SEPPALA II**
  - KREE VANKA
    - UNKNOWN
    - UNKNOWN
  - TOSCA
    - HARRY
      - FRITZ
      - SHIKA
    - KOLYMA
      - PUTZA
      - DUSKA
- **PEARL OF SEPPALA II**
  - SMOKEY OF SEPPALA
    - KINGEAK
      - TOGO
      - ROSIE
    - PEARL
      - NUTOK
      - CZARINA
  - NANNA
    - WOLF
      - UNKNOWN
      - UNKNOWN
    - NAN
      - UNKNOWN
      - UNKNOWN

CH. KIRA OF MONADNOCK
WHELPED JULY 14, 1940

VANKA OF SEPPALA (I)	KREE VANKA	UNKNOWN	UNKNOWN
			UNKNOWN
		UNKNOWN	UNKNOWN
			UNKNOWN
	TOSCA	HARRY	FRITZ
			SHIKA
		KOLYMA	PUTZA
			DUSKA
TOSCA OF ALYESKA	DUKE	ICI	THOR
			UNKNOWN
		WANDA	UNKNOWN
			UNKNOWN
	TANTA OF ALYESKA	TUCK	UNKNOWN
			UNKNOWN
		TOTO	TOGO
			NOME

KOLMA OF KOMATIC
WHELPED JAN. 28, 1941

- **VANYA OF MONADNOCK (I)**
  - SAPSUK OF SEPPALA
    - TSERKO
      - UNKNOWN
      - UNKNOWN
    - DUSHKA
      - BONZO
      - NANUK
  - TOSCA OF ALYESKA
    - DUKE
      - ICI
      - WANDA
    - TANTA OF ALYESKA
      - TUCK
      - TOTO
- **SILVI GIRL OF KOMATIC**
  - WHITE FANG
    - TOGO II
      - TOGO
      - SUGUDIN
    - EASTER
      - BIG BOY
      - LADY LU
  - SATAN III
    - TOGO II
      - TOGO
      - SUGUDIN
    - SATAN II
      - SATAN
      - DARKA

BAYOU OF FOXSTAND
WHELPED 1943

```
BAYOU OF FOXSTAND
WHELPED 1943
│
├── SURGUT OF SEPPALA
│   ├── KREE VANKA
│   │   ├── UNKNOWN
│   │   └── UNKNOWN
│   └── TOSCA
│       ├── HARRY
│       │   ├── UNKNOWN
│       │   └── UNKNOWN
│       └── KOLYMA
│           ├── FRITZ
│           ├── SHIKA
│           ├── PUTZA
│           └── DUSKA
│
└── DUCHESS OF HUSKYLAND
    ├── SAPSUK OF SEPPALA
    │   ├── TSERKO
    │   │   ├── UNKNOWN
    │   │   └── UNKNOWN
    │   └── DUSHKA
    │       ├── BONZO
    │       └── NANUK
    └── ROLLINSFORD NINA OF
        MARILYN
        ├── KOTLIK
        │   ├── YUKON
        │   └── RIGA
        └── NERA OF MARILYN
            ├── CH. NORTHERN LIGHT KOBUCK
            └── TILLIE
```

NANUK OF ALYESKA
CHINOOK'S ALLADIN OF ALYESKA
WHELPED MAY 9, 1944

CZAR OF ALYESKA
- WOLFE OF SEPPALA
  - SMOKEY OF SEPPALA
    - KINGEAK
    - PEARL
  - SIGRID OF SEPPALA
    - TSERKO
    - DUSHKA
- CH. CHEENAH OF ALYESKA
  - SEPP III
    - TOGO
    - UNKNOWN
  - TOSCA OF ALYESKA
    - DUKE
    - TANTA OF ALYESKA

TCHEEAKIO OF ALYESKA
- BELFORD'S WOLF
  - SMOKY
    - UNKNOWN
    - UNKNOWN
  - TOSCA
    - HARRY
    - KOLYMA
- CHEEAK OF ALYESKA
  - DUKE
    - ICI
    - WANDA
  - TANTA OF ALYESKA
    - TUCK
    - TOTO

CH. VANYA OF MONADNOCK III
WHELPED DEC. 15, 1944

VALUIKI OF COLD RIVER

- BURKA OF SEPPALA
  - KREE VANKA
    - UNKNOWN
    - UNKNOWN
  - TOSCA
    - HARRY
    - KOLYMA
- DELZEUE OF COLD RIVER
  - SAPSUK OF SEPPALA
    - TSERKO
    - DUSHKA
  - CHUCHI OF SEPPALA (CUCHI)
    - TSERKO
    - BILKA OF SEPPALA

CH. PANDA

- BELFORD'S WOLF
  - SMOKY
    - UNKNOWN
    - UNKNOWN
  - TOSCA
    - HARRY
    - KOLYMA
- TOSCA OF ALYESKA
  - DUKE
    - ICI
    - WANDA
  - TANTA OF ALYESKA
    - TUCK
    - TOTO

CH. IGLOO PAK'S ANVIC
WHELPED OCT. 3, 1945

BLUIE OF CHINOOK

CH. TURU OF ALYESKA

CH. WONALANCET'S BALDY OF ALYESKA

TOSCA OF WONALANCET

TCHEEAKIO OF ALYESKA

BELFORD'S WOLF

CHEEAK OF ALYESKA

BELFORD'S WOLF

CHEEAK OF ALYESKA

SAPSUK OF SEPPALA

TOSCA OF ALYESKA

SMOKY

TOSCA

DUKE

TANTA OF ALYESKA

UNKNOWN

UNKNOWN

CH. SITKA'S WONA OF ALYESKA

BELFORD'S WOLF

SMOKY

TOSCA

SITKA OF FOXSTAND

DUKE

TANTA OF ALYESKA

HARRY

KOLYMA

ICI

WANDA

TUCK

TOTO

349

DICHODA'S AKIMO KIO
WHELPED 1950

GOUDA OF KABKOL

- CH. KOLYA OF MONADNOCK
  - VANKA OF SEPPALA (I)
    - KREE VANKA
    - TOSCA
  - TOSCA OF ALYESKA
    - DUKE
    - TANTA OF ALYESKA
- KABLOONA
  - UNKNOWN
    - UNKNOWN
    - UNKNOWN
  - UNKNOWN
    - UNKNOWN
    - UNKNOWN

ECHO OF KABKOL

- CH. KOLYA OF MONADNOCK
  (CH. KIRA'S BROTHER)
  - VANKA OF SEPPALA (I)
    - KREE VANKA
    - TOSCA
  - TOSCA OF ALYESKA
    - DUKE
    - TANTA OF ALYESKA
- NANUK OF ALYESKA
  (ALLADIN'S SISTER)
  - CZAR OF ALYESKA
    - WOLFE OF SEPPALA
    - CH. CHEENAH OF ALYESKA
  - TCHEEAKIO OF ALYESKA
    - BELFORD'S WOLF
    - CHEEAK OF ALYESKA

FOXSTAND'S PONTIAC
WHELPED JULY 10, 1951

- **FOXSTAND'S LIPPY**
  - POLARIS OF SAPAWE
    - CHARNEY OF SEPPALA
      - UNKNOWN
      - UNKNOWN
    - DINA OF SEPPALA
      - UNKNOWN
      - UNKNOWN
  - FOXSTAND'S SUKEY
    - CH. VANKA OF SEPPALA II
      - KREE VANKA
      - TOSCA
    - SIGRID III OF FOXSTAND
      - CHENUK
      - MOLINKA

- **FOXSTAND'S CLEO**
  - FOXSTAND'S RUDOLF
    - FOXSTAND'S ROMBO
      - CH. VANKA OF SEPPALA II
      - SIGRID III OF FOXSTAND
    - FOXSTAND'S SHERRY
      - JEVAHNEE OF COLD RIVER
      - FOXSTAND'S SUKEY
  - FOXSTAND'S FATIMA
    - FOXSTAND'S SHANGO
      - CH. VANKA OF SEPPALA II
      - SIGRID III OF FOXSTAND
    - FOXSTAND'S GEORGIA
      - FOXSTAND'S SUGGEN
      - FOXSTAND'S COLLEEN

MONADNOCK'S NADYA
WHELPED JUNE 6, 1953

- **NICHOLAS OF MONADNOCK**
  - SASHA OF MONADNOCK
    - CH. TOGO OF ALYESKA
      - DUKE
      - TANTA OF ALYESKA
    - CH. KIRA OF MONADNOCK
      - VANKA OF SEPPALA (I)
      - TOSCA OF ALYESKA
  - CH. PANDA
    - BELFORD'S WOLF
      - SMOKY
      - TOSCA
    - TOSCA OF ALYESKA
      - DUKE
      - TANTA OF ALYESKA
- **AKIAK OF ANADYR**
  - CHINOOK'S ALLADIN OF ALYESKA
    - CZAR OF ALYESKA
      - WOLFE OF SEPPALA
      - CH. CHEENAH OF ALYESKA
    - TCHEEAKIO OF ALYESKA
      - BELFORD'S WOLF
      - CHEEAK OF ALYESKA
  - DIRKA OF ANADYR
    - CHINOOK'S ALLADIN OF ALYESKA
      - CZAR OF ALYESKA
      - TCHEEAKIO OF ALYESKA
    - CANDIA
      - BUGS
      - FOXSTAND'S SUKEY

CH. ARAHAZ' TENGRI KHAN
WHELPED JUNE 26, 1967

- **CH. TOKI OF ROCKRIMMON**
  - CH. SAVDAJAURE'S COGNAC
    - CH. MONADNOCK'S SAVDA BAKKO
      - CH. MONADNOCK'S PANDO
      - CH. SINTALUTA
    - MONADNOCK'S SAVDA PANDI
      - CH. MONADNOCK'S RED TANGO OF MUREX
      - MONADNOCK'S EB'NY LASS OF MUREX
  - ALYESKA CHENA OF CHINOOK
    - ALYESKA TWINKLE OF CHINOOK
      - CH. ALYESKA'S SUGGEN OF CHINOOK
      - MONADNOCK'S FLASH
    - TCHEEAKIO OF CHINOOK
      - MUREX'S SNOW SPOOK
      - GRAY WOLF

- **CH. ARAHAZ EBONY BEAUTY**
  - CH. TOCKA OF MONADNOCK
    - MULPUS BROOK'S THE ROADMASTER
      - IZOK OF GAP MOUNTAIN
      - CH. ALEKA'S CZARINA
    - MONADNOCK'S VOLNA
      - CH. MONADNOCK'S PANDO
      - MONADNOCK'S CZARINA
  - LYEESA OF BOLSHOI
    - CH. FROSTY AIRE'S BEAU-TUK BALTO
      - CH. FROSTY AIRE'S BEAUCHIEN C.D.
      - CH. KLUTUK'S CARRIE
    - CH. FROSTY AIRE'S STARINA
      - CH. MONADNOCK'S SERGE
      - CH. FROSTY AIRE'S CHENA

LITTLE SEPP OF BOW LAKE
WHELPED FEB. 18, 1949

TORR OF SEPPALA

- ZEPHYR DECARE OF SAINT JOVITE
  - ZEPHYR BISSON OF SEPPALA
    - KINGEAK OF SEPPALA II
    - SIGRID OF SEPPALA
  - FIDELAINE DECARE OF ST. JOVITE
    - ZEPHYR BISSON OF SEPPALA
    - GUINA OF SEPPALA
- IRINA OF CALEDONIA
  - WOLFE OF SEPPALA
    - SMOKEY OF SEPPALA
    - SIGRID OF SEPPALA
  - NEENAH OF ALYESKA
    - BELFORD'S WOLF
    - CHEEAK OF ALYESKA

LEDA OF BOW LAKE

- NICKO OF GATINEAU
  - FOXSTAND'S SKIVAR II
    - FOXSTAND'S SHANGO
    - N'YA N'YA OF SEPPALA
  - VICKA OF GATINEAU
    - FOXSTAND'S SAINT
    - BAYOU OF FOXSTAND
- TINA OF GATINEAU
  - FOXSTAND'S SAINT
    - TONY OF FOXSTAND
    - TYKA OF FOXSTAND
  - ILONA OF SEPPALA
    - KINGEAK OF SEPPALA
    - PEARL OF SEPPALA II

CARKA OF ANADYR
NATASHA OF ANADYR
WHELPED AUG. 2, 1949

YADDAM OF HUSKIE HAVEN

- CHARNEY OF SEPPALA
  - UNKNOWN
    - UNKNOWN
    - UNKNOWN
  - UNKNOWN
    - UNKNOWN
    - UNKNOWN
- NONY OF WHITE
  - UNKNOWN
    - UNKNOWN
    - UNKNOWN
  - UNKNOWN
    - UNKNOWN
    - UNKNOWN

DIRKA OF ANADYR

- CHINOOK'S ALLADIN OF ALYESKA
  - CZAR OF ALYESKA
    - WOLFE OF SEPPALA
    - CH. CHEENAH OF ALYESKA
  - TCHEEAKIO OF ALYESKA
    - BELFORD'S WOLF
    - CHEEAK OF ALYESKA
- CANDIA
  - BUGS
    - BURKA OF SEPPALA
    - DELZEUE OF COLD RIVER
  - FOXSTAND'S SUKEY
    - CH. VANKA OF SEPPALA II
    - SIGRID III OF FOXSTAND

CH. KENAI KITTEE OF BEAUCHIEN CDX

- **CH. TYNDRUM'S OSLO, CDX**
  - PANDO OF MONADNOCK
    - CH. VANYA OF MONADNOCK III
      - VALUIKI OF COLD RIVER
      - CH. PANDA
    - CH. PANDA
      - BELFORD'S WOLF
      - TOSCA OF ALYESKA
  - CH. U-CHEE OF ANADYR
    - CHINOOK'S ALLADIN OF ALYESKA
      - CZAR OF ALYESKA
      - TCHEEAKIO OF ALYESKA
    - BAYOU OF FOXSTAND
      - SURGUT OF SEPPALA
      - DUCHESS OF HUSKYLAND
- **TYNDRUM'S SHIVA**
  - MISHA OF BREEZYMERE
    - SNOW STORM
      - CH. IGLOO PAK'S ANVIC
      - NADEJDA
    - SIKHA
      - DICHODA'S AKIMO KIO
      - DOONAH OF MONADNOCK
  - TYNDRUM'S COMANCHEE
    - PANDO OF MONADNOCK
      - CH. VANYA OF MONADNOCK III
      - CH. PANDA
    - GRETEL OF TYNDRUM
      - KEETNA OF MONADNOCK
      - CH. U-CHEE OF ANADYR

Josie Weinstein with her "natural" stole, photographed by Judy Rosemarin of Roslyn, New York.

CHAPTER 18
TRAINING YOUR SIBERIAN HUSKY

There are few things in the world a dog would rather do than please his master. Therefore, obedience training, or even the initial basic training, will be a pleasure for your dog, if taught correctly, and will make him a much nicer animal to live with for the rest of his life.

WHEN TO START TRAINING

The most frequently asked question by those who consider training their dog is, naturally, "What is the best age to begin training?" The answer is, "not before six months." A dog simply cannot be sufficiently or permanently trained before this age and be expected to retain all he has been taught. If too much is expected of him, he can become frustrated and it may ruin him completely for any serious training later on, or even jeopardize his disposition. Most things a puppy learns and repeats before he is six months of age should be considered habit rather than training.

THE REWARD METHOD

The only proper and acceptable kind of training is the kindness and reward method which will build a strong bond between dog and owner. A dog must have confidence in and respect for his teacher. The most important thing to remember in training any dog is that the quickest way to teach, especially the young dog, is through repetition. Praise him when he does well, and scold him when he does wrong. This will suffice. There is no need or excuse for swinging at a dog with rolled up newspapers, or flailing hands which will only tend to make the dog hand shy the rest of his life. Also, make every word count. Do not give a command unless you intend to see it through. Pronounce distinctly with the fewest possible words, and use the same words for the same command every time.

Include the dog's name every time to make sure you have his undivided attention at the beginning of each command. Do not go on to another command until he has successfully completed the previous

Ch. Tohamm II of Cheanah, an unforgettable companion to his master Frank Brayton. Eager to please, he would respond to both verbal and hand signals or even just a nod of the head. He also pulled their Austin chassis alone once it got rolling. Owned by the Braytons, Dichoda Kennels, Escalon, California.

Akalan's Ebony Frost, one year-old Siberian owned by E. Lipke of Livermore, California. Frost was bred by the Akalan Kennels, owned by Dean and Dolores Warner. Frost was born January 9, 1971 and was sired by Ch. Akalan's Yuri, C.D.X., *ex* Ch. Akalan's Sonia, C.D.

one and is praised for it. Of course, you should not mix play with the serious training time. Make sure the dog knows the difference between the two.

In the beginning, it is best to train without any distractions whatsoever. After he has learned to concentrate and is older and more proficient, he should perform the exercises with interference, so that the dog learns absolute obedience in the face of all distractions. Needless to say, whatever the distractions, you never lose control. You must be in command at all times to earn the respect and attention of your dog.

HOW LONG SHOULD THE LESSONS BE?

The lessons should be brief with a young dog, starting at five minutes, and as the dog ages and becomes adept in the first lessons, increase the time all the way up to one-half hour. Public training classes are usually set for one hour, and this is acceptable since the full hour of concentration is not placed on your dog alone. Working under these conditions with other dogs, you will find that he will not be as intent as he would be with a private lesson where the commands are directed to him alone for the entire thirty minutes.

If you should notice that your dog is not doing well, or not keeping up with the class, consider putting off training for awhile. Animals, like children, are not always ready for schooling at exactly the same age. It would be a shame to ruin a good obedience dog because you insist on starting his training at six months rather than at, say, nine months, when he would be more apt to be receptive both physically and mentally. If he has particular difficulty in learning one exercise, you might do well to skip to a different one and come back to it again at another session. There are no set rules in this basic training, except, "don't push"!

WHAT YOU NEED TO START TRAINING

From three to six months of age, use the soft nylon show leads, which are the best and safest. When you get ready for the basic training at six months of age, you will require one of the special metal-link choke chains sold for exactly this purpose. Do not let the word "choke" scare you. It is a soft, smooth chain and should be held slack whenever you are not actually using it to correct the dog. This chain should be put over the dog's head so that the lead can be attached over the dog's neck rather than underneath against his throat. It is wise when you buy your choke collar to ask the sales person to show you how it is put on. Those of you who will be taking your dog to a training class will have an instructor who can show you.

To avoid undue stress on the dog, use both hands on the lead. The dog will be taught to obey commands at your left side, and therefore, your left hand will guide the dog close to his collar on a six-foot training lead. The balance of the lead will be held in your right hand. Learn at the very beginning to handle your choke collar and lead correctly. It is as important in training a dog as is the proper equipment for riding a horse.

WHAT TO TEACH FIRST

The first training actually should be to teach the dog to know his name. This, of course, he can learn at an earlier age than six months, just as he can learn to walk nicely on a leash or lead. Many puppies will at first probably want to walk around with the leash in their mouths. There is no objection to this if the dog will walk while doing it. Rather than cultivating this as a habit, you will find that if you don't make an issue of it, the dog will soon realize that carrying the lead in his mouth is not rewarding and he'll let it fall to his side where it belongs.

We also let the puppy walk around by himself for a while with the lead around his neck. If he wishes to chew on it a little, that's all right too. In other words, let it be something he recognizes and associates with at first. Do not let the lead start out being a harness.

If the dog is at all bright, chances are he has learned to come on command when you call him by name. This is relatively simple with sweet talk and a reward. On lead, without a reward, and on command without a lead is something else again. If there has been, or is now, a problem, the best way to correct it is to put on the choke collar and the six-foot lead. Then walk away from the dog, and call him, "Pirate, come!" and gently start reeling him in until the dog is in front of you. Give him a pat on the head and/or a reward.

Walking, or heeling, next to you is also one of the first and most important things for him to learn. With the soft lead training starting very early, he should soon take up your pace at your left side. At the command to "heel" he should start off with you and continue alongside until you stop. Give the command, "Pirate, sit!" This is taught by leaning over and pushing down on his hindquarters until he sits next to you, while pulling up gently on the collar. When you have this down pat on the straight away, then start practicing it in circles, with turns and figure eights. When he is an advanced student, you can look forward to the heels and sits being done neatly, spontaneously, and off lead as well.

Ch. Scandia's Turukhan Tyger, high-scoring dog in trials at the Imperial Valley Kennel Club trials in December, 1972. Judge for this event was Carl Spitz. Owner Vivienne Lundquist of Marina Del Rey, California. Schley photo.

THE "DOWN" COMMAND

One of the most valuable lessons or commands you can teach your dog is to lie down on command. Some day it may save his life, and is invaluable when traveling with a dog or visiting, if behavior and manners are required even beyond obedience. While repeating the words, "Pirate, down!" lower the dog from a sitting position in front of you by gently pulling his front legs out in front of him. Place your full hand on him while repeating the command, "Pirate, down!" and hold him down to let him know you want him to *stay* down. After he gets the general idea, this can be done from a short distance away on a lead along with the command, by pulling the lead down to the floor. Or perhaps you can slip the lead under your shoe (between the heel and sole) and pull it directly to the floor. As the dog progresses in training, a hand signal with or without verbal command, or with or without lead, can be given from a considerable distance by raising your arm and extending the hand palm down.

THE "STAY" COMMAND

The stay command eventually can be taught from both a sit and a down position. Start with the sit. With your dog on your left side in the sitting position give the command, "Pirate, stay!" Reach down with the left hand open and palm side to the dog and sweep it in close to his nose. Then walk a short distance away and face him. He will at first, having learned to heel immediately as you start off, more than likely start off with you. The trick in teaching this is to make sure he hears "stay" before you start off. It will take practice. If he breaks, sit him down again, stand next to him, and give the command all over again. As he masters the command, let the distance between you and your dog increase while the dog remains seated. Once the command is learned, advance to the stay command from the down position.

THE STAND FOR EXAMINATION

If you have any intention of going on to advanced training in obedience with your dog, or if you have a show dog which you feel you will enjoy showing yourself, a most important command which should be mastered at six months of age is the stand command. This is essential for a show dog since it is the position used when the show judge goes over your dog. This is taught in the same manner as the stay command, but this time with the dog remaining up on all four feet. He should learn to stand still, without moving his feet and

Heel on lead is performed by the Garden State Siberian Husky Club obedience team. Photographed by Judy Rosemarin.

without flinching or breaking when approached by either you or strangers. The hand with palm open wide and facing him should be firmly placed in front of his nose with the command, "Pirate, stand!" After he learns the basic rules and knows the difference between stand and stay, ask friends, relatives, and strangers to assist you with this exercise by walking up to the dog and going over him. He should not react physically to their touch. A dog posing in this stance should show all the beauty and pride of being a sterling example of his breed.

FORMAL SCHOOL TRAINING

We mentioned previously about the various training schools and classes given for dogs. Your local kennel club, newspaper, or the yellow pages of the telephone book will put you in touch with organizations in your area where this service is performed. You and your dog will learn a great deal from these classes. Not only do they offer formal training, but the experience for you and your dog in public, with other dogs of approximately the same age and with the same purpose in mind is invaluable. If you intend to show your dog, this training is valuable ring experience for later on. If you are having difficulty with the training, remember, it is either too soon to start — or YOU are doing something wrong!

ADVANCED TRAINING AND OBEDIENCE TRI-ALS

The A.K.C. obedience trials are divided into three classes: Novice, Open and Utility.

In the Novice Class, the dog will be judged on the following basis:

TEST	MAXIMUM SCORE
Heel on lead	35
Stand for examination	30
Heel free—on lead	45
Recall (come on command)	30
One-minute sit (handler in ring)	30
Three-minute down (handler in ring)	30
Maximum total score	200

If the dog "qualifies" in three shows by earning at least 50% of the points for each test, with a total of at least 170 for the trial, he has earned the Companion Dog degree and the letters C.D. (Companion Dog) are entered after his name in the A.K.C. records.

After the dog has qualified as a C.D., he is eligible to enter the Open Class competition, where he will be judged on this basis:

TEST	MAXIMUM SCORE
Heel free	40
Drop on Recall	30
Retrieve (wooden dumbbell) on flat	25
Retrieve over obstacle (hurdle)	35
Broad jump	20
Three-minute sit (handler out of ring)	25
Five-minute down (handler out of ring)	25
Maximum total score	200

Again he must qualify in three shows for the C.D.X. (Companion Dog Excellent) title and then is eligible for the Utility Class, where he can earn the Utility Dog (U.D.) degree in these rugged tests:

This official United States Marine Corps photo taken on the front lines during the fighting for Guam in World War II shows a Siberian Husky among the sniper hunters. These dogs played a major part in tracking down Japanese snipers during World War II.

TEST	MAXIMUM SCORE
Scent discrimination (picking up article handled by master from group) Article 1	20
Scent discrimination Article 2	20
Scent discrimination Article 3	20
Seek back (picking up an article dropped by handler)	30
Signal exercise (heeling, etc., on hand signal	35
Directed jumping (over hurdle and bar jump)	40
Group examination	35
Maximum total score	200

For more complete information about these obedience trials, write for the American Kennel Club's *Regulations and Standards for Obedience Trials.* Dogs that are disqualified from breed shows because of alteration or physical defects are eligible to compete in these trials.

CHAPTER 19
SHOWING YOUR SIBERIAN HUSKY

Let us assume that after a few months of tender loving care, you realize your dog is developing beyond your wildest expectations and that the dog you selected is very definitely a show dog! Of course, every owner is prejudiced. But if you are sincerely interested in going to dog shows with your dog and making a champion of him, now is the time to start casting a critical eye on him from a judge's point of view.

There is no such thing as a perfect dog. Every dog has some faults, perhaps even a few serious ones. The best way to appraise your dog's degree of perfection is to compare him with the Standard for the breed, or before a judge in a show ring.

MATCH SHOWS

For the beginner there are "mock" dog shows, called Match Shows, where you and your dog go through many of the procedures of a regular dog show, but do not gain points toward championship. These shows are usually held by kennel clubs, annually or semiannually, and much ring poise and experience can be gained there. The age limit is reduced to two months at match shows to give puppies four months of training before they compete at the regular shows when they reach six months of age. Classes range from two to four months; four to six months; six to nine months; and nine to twelve months. Puppies compete with others of their own age for comparative purposes. Many breeders evaluate their litters in this manner, choosing which is the most outgoing, which is the most poised, the best showman, etc.

For those seriously interested in showing their dog to full championship, these match shows provide important experience for both the dog and the owner. Class categories may vary slightly, according to number of entries, but basically include all the classes that are included at a regular point show. There is a nominal entry fee and, of course, ribbons and usually trophies are given for your efforts as well. Unlike the point shows, entries can be made on the day of the show right on the show grounds. They are unbenched and provide an

True Siberian Husky beauty! Ch. Kiska of Kantua, silver and white bitch owned by Frank and Marie King of the Kantua Kennels in Coalinga, California. Kiska was a family pet for five years and then was shown to her championship. Kiska runs with a wheeled cart or sled and is undisputed "boss" at Kantua.

informal, usually congenial atmosphere for the amateur, which helps to make the ordeal of one's first adventures in the show ring a little less nerve-wracking.

THE POINT SHOWS

It is not possible to show a puppy at an American Kennel Club sanctioned point show before the age of six months. When your dog reaches this eligible age, your local kennel club can provide you with the names and addresses of the show-giving superintendents in your area who will be staging the club's dog show for them, and where you must write for an entry form.

The forms are mailed in a pamphlet called a premium list. This also includes the names of the judges for each breed, a list of the prizes and trophies, the name and address of the show-giving club and where the show will be held, as well as rules and regulations set up by the American Kennel Club which must be abided by if you are to enter.

A booklet containing the complete set of show rules and regulations may be obtained by writing to the American Kennel Club, Inc., 51 Madison Avenue, New York, N.Y., 10010.

When you write to the Dog Show Superintendent, request not only your premium list for this particular show, but ask that your name be added to their mailing list so that you will automatically receive all premium lists in the future. List your breed or breeds and they will see to it that you receive premium lists for Specialty shows as well.

Unlike the match shows where your dog will be judged on ring behavior, at the point shows he will be judged on conformation to the breed Standard. In addition to being at least six months of age (on the day of the show) he must be a thoroughbred for a point show. This means both of his parents and he are registered with the American Kennel Club. There must be no alterations or falsifications regarding his appearance. Females cannot have been spayed and males must have both testicles in evidence. No dyes or powders may be used to enhance the appearance, and any lameness or deformity or major deviation form the Standard for the breed constitutes a disqualification.

With all these things in mind, groom your dog to the best of your ability in the specified area for this purpose in the show hall and walk into the show ring with great pride of ownership and ready for an appraisal of your dog by the judge.

The presiding judge on that day will allow each and every dog a certain amount of time and consideration before making his deci-

Ch. Czar Nicholas, Best of Breed winner at the Siberian Husky Club of America national specialty held at Santa Barbara, July, 1966. Owned by Frank and Phyllis Brayton, Dichoda Kennels, Escalon, California. Joan Ludwig photograph.

sions. It is never permissible to consult the judge regarding either your dog or his decision while you are in the ring. An exhibitor never speaks unless spoken to, and then only to answer such questions as the judge may ask — the age of the dog, the dog's bite, or to ask you to move your dog around the ring once again.

However, before you reach the point where you are actually in the ring awaiting the final decisions of the judge, you will have had to decide in which of the five classes in each sex your dog should compete.

Point Show Classes

The regular classes of the AKC are: Puppy, Novice, Bred-by-Exhibitor, American-Bred, Open; if your dog is undefeated in any of the regular classes (divided by sex) in which it is entered, he or she is **required** to enter the Winners Class. If your dog is placed second in the class to the dog which won Winners Dog or Winners Bitch, hold the dog or bitch in readiness as the judge must consider it for Reserve Winners.

Puppy Classes shall be for dogs which are six months of age and over but under twelve months, which were whelped in the U.S.A. or Canada, and which are not champions. Classes are often divided 6 and (under) 9, and 9 and (under) 12 months. The age of a dog shall be calculated up to and inclusive of the first day of a show. For example, a dog whelped on Jan. 1st is eligible to compete in a puppy class on July 1st, and may continue to compete up to and including Dec. 31st of the same year, but is not eligible to compete Jan. 1st of the following year.

The Novice Class shall be for dogs six months of age or over, whelped in the U.S.A. or Canada which have not, prior to the closing of entries, won three first prizes in the Novice Class, a first prize in Bred-by-Exhibitor, American-Bred or Open Class, nor one or more points toward a championship title.

The Bred-by-Exhibitor Class shall be for dogs whelped in the U.S.A. which are six months of age and over, which are not champions, and which are owned wholly or in part by the person or by the spouse of the person who was the breeder or one of the breeders of record. Dogs entered in the BBE Class must be handled by an owner or by a member of the immediate family of an owner, i.e., the husband, wife, father, mother, son, daughter, brother or sister.

The American-Bred Class shall be for all dogs (except champions) six months of age or over, whelped in the U.S.A. by reason of a mating that took place in the U.S.A.

The Open Class is for any dog six months of age or over, except in a member specialty club show held for only American-Bred dogs, in which case the class is for American-Bred dogs only.

Winners Dogs and **Winners Bitches:** After the above male classes have been judged, the first-place winners are then **required** to compete in the ring. The dog judged "Winners Dog" is awarded the points toward his championship title.

Reserve Winners are selected immediately after the Winners Dog. In case of a disqualification of a win by the AKC, the Reserve Dog moves up to "Winners" and receives the points. After all male classes are judged, the bitch classes are called.

Best of Breed or Best of Variety Competition is limited to Champions of Record or dogs (with newly acquired points, for a 90-day period prior to AKC confirmation) which have completed championship requirements, and Winners Dog and Winners Bitch (or the dog awarded Winners if only one Winners prize has been awarded), together with any undefeated dogs which have been shown only in non-regular classes; all compete for Best of Breed or Best of Variety (if the breed is divided by size, color, texture or length of coat hair, etc.).

Best of Winners: If the WD or WB earns BOB or BOV, it automatically becomes BOW; otherwise they will be judged together for BOW (following BOB or BOV judging).

Best of Opposite Sex is selected from the remaining dogs of the opposite sex to Best of Breed or Best of Variety.

Other Classes may be approved by the AKC: **Stud Dogs, Brood Bitches, Brace Class, Team Class;** classes consisting of local dogs and bitches may also be included in a show if approved by the AKC (special rules are included in the AKC Rule Book).

The **Miscellaneous Class** shall be for purebred dogs of such breeds as may be designated by the AKC. No dog shall be eligible for entry in this class unless the owner has been granted an Indefinite Listing Privilege (ILP) and unless the ILP number is given on the entry form. Application for an ILP shall be made on a form provided by the AKC and when submitted must be accompanied by a fee set by the Board of Directors.

All Miscellaneous Breeds shall be shown together in a single class except that the class may be divided by sex if so specified in the premium list. There shall be **no** further competition for dogs entered in this class. Ribbons for 1st, 2nd, 3rd and 4th shall be Rose, Brown, Light Green and Gray, respectively. This class is open to the following Miscellaneous Breeds: Akitas, Australian Cattle Dogs, Australian Kelpies, Border Collies, Cavalier King Charles Spaniels, Ibizan Hounds, Miniature Bull Terriers, and Spinoni Italiani.

If Your Dog Wins a Class. . .

Study the classes to make certain your dog is entered in a proper class for his or her qualifications. If your dog wins his class, the rule states: *You are required* to enter classes for Winners, Best of Breed and Best of Winners (no additional entry fees). The rule states, "No eligible dog may be withheld from competition." It is not mandatory that you stay for group judging. If *your dog wins a group,* however, *you must stay for Best-in-Show competition.*

THE PRIZE RIBBONS AND WHAT THEY STAND FOR

No matter how many entries there are in each class at a dog show, if you place first through fourth position you will receive a ribbon. These ribbons commemorate your win and can be impressive when collected and displayed to prospective buyers when and if you have puppies for sale, or if you intend to use your dog at public stud.

All ribbons from the American Kennel Club licensed dog shows will bear the American Kennel Club seal, the name of the show, the date and the placement. In the classes the colors are blue for first, red for second, yellow for third, and white for fourth. Winners Dog or Winners Bitch ribbons are purple, while Reserve Dog and Reserve Bitch ribbons are purple and white. Best of Winners ribbons are blue and white; Best of Breed, purple and gold; and Best of Opposite Sex ribbons are red and white.

In the six groups, first prize is a blue rosette or ribbon, second placement is red, third yellow, and fourth white. The Best In Show rosette is either red, white and blue, or incorporates the colors used in the show-giving club's emblem.

QUALIFYING FOR CHAMPIONSHIP

Championship points are given for Winners Dog and Winners Bitch in accordance with a scale of points established by the American Kennel Club based on the popularity of the breed in entries, and the number of dogs competing in the classes. This scale of points varies in different sections of the country, but the scale is published

Ch. Winsum's Salacious Sergei finishing for his championship at eleven months of age under the famous Short Seely. "Sarge" is handled by Warren Keefer, co-owner with his wife Winnie of the Winsum Kennels, Rocky Ridge, Maryland.

A lovely snow scene for photographing American and Canadian Ch. Arctic's Storm Frost, owned by the Arctic Kennels, Dryden, Michigan.

in the front of each dog show catalog. These points may differ between the dogs and the bitches at the same show. You may, however, win additional points by winning Best of Winners, if there are fewer dogs than bitches entered, or vice versa. Points never exceed five at any one show, and a total of fifteen points must be won to constitute a championship. These fifteen points must be won under at least three different judges, and you must acquire at least two major wins. Anything from a three to five point win is a major, while one and two point wins are minor wins. Two major wins must be won under two different judges to meet championship requirements.

OBEDIENCE TRIALS

Some shows also offer Obedience Trials which are considered as separate events. They give the dogs a chance to compete and score on performing a prescribed set of exercises intended to display their training in doing useful work.

There are three obedience titles for which they may compete. First, the Companion Dog or CD title; second, the Companion Dog Excellent or CDX; and third, the Utility Dog or UD. Detailed information on these degrees is contained in a booklet entitled Official Obedience Regulations and may be obtained by writing to the American Kennel Club.

JUNIOR SHOWMANSHIP COMPETITION

Junior Showmanship Competition is for boys and girls in different age groups handling their own dogs or one owned by their immediate family. There are four divisions: Novice A, for the ten to 12 year olds; Novice B, for those 13 to 16 years of age, with no previous

Miss Lori Dauer showing her Ch. Karnovanda's Miss Vodka is pictured receiving Top Junior Handler Trophy from Rosemary Fischer, then president of the Siberian Husky Club of Greater Pittsburgh. Lori's parents, Richard and Joanne Dauer, own the Cherwenlo's Kennel in Glenshaw, Pennsylvania.

junior showmanship wins; Open C, for ten to 12 year olds; and Open D, for 13 to 16 year olds who have earned one or more JS awards.

As Junior Showmanship at the dog shows increased in popularity, certain changes and improvements had to be made. As of April 1, 1971, the American Kennel Club issued a new booklet containing the Regulations for Junior Showmanship which may be obtained by writing to the A.K.C. at 51 Madison Avenue, New York, N.Y. 10010.

Ch. Kodii Kuska De Sforza, C.D.X., is pictured winning in the show ring with owner Tony Zarlenga of Denver, Colorado.

Mrs. Lou Richardson and her Siberian Huskies win Best Brace at one of the major California shows several years ago. Photo by Joan Ludwig.

Specialty Show of the Siberian Husky Club of America held at Framingham Centre, Massachusetts, in June, 1952 found judge Louis Hall awarding Best of Breed to Ch. Otchi of Monadnock, C.D., owned and handled by Mrs. Lorna Demidoff, and Best of Opposite Sex to Mrs. W.H. Lane's Aleka's Czarina. Photograph by Evelyn Shafer.

DOG SHOW PHOTOGRAPHERS

Every show has at least one official photographer who will be more than happy to take a photograph of your dog with the judge, ribbons and trophies, along with you or your handler. These make marvelous remembrances of your top show wins and are frequently framed along with the ribbons for display purposes. Photographers can be paged at the show over the public address system, if you wish to obtain this service. Prices vary, but you will probably find it costs little to capture these happy moments, and the photos can always be used in the various dog magazines to advertise your dog's wins.

TWO TYPES OF DOG SHOWS

There are two types of dog shows licensed by the American Kennel Club. One is the all-breed show which includes classes for all the recognized breeds, and groups of breeds; i.e., all terriers, all toys, etc. Then there are the specialty shows for one particular breed which also offer championship points.

Dudley's Vodki of Koryak pictured going Best of Winners on the way to his championship. Tanker won this 5-point major under judge Harold F. Hardin. Shown by his owner Clarence Dudley of North Syracuse, New York.

Beautiful brace-mates! Winners under under William Kendrick are Ch. Karnovanda's Zenzarya and Ch. Baron of Karnovanda, C.D. Handled by owner Judith M. Russell, Karnovanda Kennels, Davisburg, Michigan. Norton of Kent photo.

BENCHED OR UNBENCHED DOG SHOWS

The show-giving clubs determine, usually on the basis of what facilities are offered by their chosen show site, whether their show will be benched or unbenched. A benched show is one where the dog show superintendent supplies benches (cages for toy dogs). Each bench is numbered and its corresponding number appears on your entry identification slip which is sent to you prior to the show date. The number also appears in the show catalog. Upon entering the show you should take your dog to the bench where he should remain until it is time to groom him before entering the ring to be judged. After judging, he must be returned to the bench until the official time of dismissal from the show. At an unbenched show the club makes no provision whatsoever for your dog other than an enormous tent (if an outdoor show) or an area in a show hall where all crates and grooming equipment must be kept.

Ch. Snow Ridge Rina, owned by Robert E. Anderson and handled by Dick Cooper, poses after a recent show win. Photo by Bart Harris.

Benched or unbenched, the moment you enter the show grounds you are expected to look after your dog and have it under complete control at all times. This means short leads in crowded aisles or getting out of cars. In the case of a benched show, a "bench chain" is needed. It should allow the dog to move around, but not get down off the bench. It is also not considered "cute" to have small tots leading enormous dogs around a dog show where the child might be dragged into the middle of a dog fight.

PROFESSIONAL HANDLERS

If you are new in the fancy and do not know how to handle your dog to his best advantage, or if you are too nervous or physically unable to show your dog, you can hire a licensed professional handler who will do it for you for a specified fee. The more successful or well-known handlers charge slightly higher rates, but generally speaking there is a pretty uniform charge for this service. As the dog progresses with his wins in the show ring, the fee increases proportionately. Included in this service is professional advice on when and where to show your dog, grooming, a statement of your wins at each show, and all trophies and ribbons that the dog accumulates. Any cash award is kept by the handler as a sort of "bonus."

When engaging a handler, it is advisable to select one that does not take more dogs to a show than he can properly and comfortably

Judge Henry Stoecker bestows a win on the Hermes' Ch. Silver Coins Juneau. Photo by Graham.

handle. You want your dog to receive his individual attention and not be rushed into the ring at the last moment, because the handler has been busy with too many other dogs in other rings. Some handlers require that you deliver the dog to their establishment a few days ahead of the show so they have ample time to groom and train him. Others will accept well-behaved and previously trained and groomed dogs at ringside, if they are familiar with the dog and the owner. This should be determined well in advance of the show date. NEVER expect a handler to accept a dog at ringside that is not groomed to perfection!

There are several sources for locating a professional handler. Dog magazines carry their classified advertising; a note or telephone call to the American Kennel Club will put you in touch with several in your area. Usually, you will be billed after the day of the show.

DO YOU REALLY NEED A HANDLER?

The answer to the above question is sometimes yes! However, the answer most exhibitors give is, "But I can't *afford* a professional handler!" or, "I want to show my dog myself. Does that mean my dog will never do any big winning?"

Do you *really* need a handler to win? If you are mishandling a good dog that should be winning and isn't, because it is made to look simply terrible in the ring by its owner, the answer is yes. If you don't know how to handle a dog properly, why make your dog look bad when a handler could show it to its best advantage?

Some owners simply cannot handle a dog well and still wonder why their dogs aren't winning in the ring, no matter how hard they try. Others are nervous and this nervousness travels down the leash to the dog and the dog behaves accordingly. Some people are extroverts by nature, and these are the people who usually make excellent handlers. Of course, the biggest winning dogs at the shows usually have a lot of "show off" in their nature, too, and this helps a great deal.

THE COST OF CAMPAIGNING A DOG WITH A HANDLER

Many Husky champions are shown an average of 25 times before completing a championship. In entry fees at today's prices, that adds up to about $200. This does not include motel bills, traveling expenses, or food. There have been dog champions finished in fewer shows, say five to ten shows, but this is the exception rather than the

The 1962 Siberian Husky Club of America Specialty Show saw judge John W. Cross, Jr., award Best of Breed to Mrs. Andrzej Korbonski's Foxhaunt's Tovarisch, CD. The dog was owner-handled for this coveted win. Evelyn Shafer photo.

rule. When and where to show should be thought out carefully so that you can perhaps save money on entries. Here is one of the services a professional handler provides that can mean a considerable saving. Hiring a handler can save money in the long run if you just wish to make a champion. If your dog has been winning reserves and not taking the points and a handler can finish him in five to ten shows, you would be ahead financially. If your dog is not really top quality, the length of time it takes even a handler to finish it (depending upon competition in the area) could add up to a large amount of money.

Campaigning a show specimen that not only captures the wins in his breed but wins group and Best in Show awards gets up into the big money. To cover the nation's major shows and rack up a record as one of the top dogs in the nation usually costs an owner between ten and fifteen thousand dollars a year. This includes not only the professional handler's fees for taking the dog into the ring, but the cost of conditioning and grooming, board, advertising in the dog magazines, photographs, etc.

There is great satisfaction in winning with your own dog, especially if you have trained and cared for it yourself. With today's enormous entries at the dog shows and so many worthy dogs competing for top wins, many owners who said "I'd rather do it myself!" and meant it became discouraged and eventually hired a handler anyway.

However, if you really are in it just for the sport, you can and should handle your own dog if you want to. You can learn the tricks by attending training classes, and you can learn a lot by carefully observing the more successful professional handlers as they perform in the ring. Model yourself after the ones that command respect as being the leaders in their profession. But, if you find you'd really rather be at ringside looking on, then do get a handler so that your worthy dog gets his deserved recognition in the ring. To own a good dog and win with it is a thrill, so good luck, no matter how you do it.

CHAPTER 20
FEEDING AND NUTRITION

FEEDING PUPPIES

There are many diets today for young puppies, including all sorts of products on the market for feeding the newborn, for supplementing the feeding of the young and for adding this or that to diets, depending on what is lacking in the way of a complete diet.

When weaning puppies, it is necessary to put them on four meals a day, even while you are tapering off with the mother's milk. Feeding at six in the morning, noontime, six in the evening and midnight is about the best schedule, since it fits in with most human eating plans. Meals for the puppies can be prepared immediately before or after your own meals, without too much of a change in your own schedule.

6 A.M.

Two meat and two milk meals serve best and should be served alternately, of course. Assuming the 6 A.M. feeding is a milk meal, the contents should be as follows: Goat's milk is the very best milk to feed puppies but is expensive and usually available only at drug stores, unless you live in farm country where it could be readily available fresh and still less expensive. If goat's milk is not available, use evaporated milk (which can be changed to powdered milk later on) diluted two parts evaporated milk and one part water, along with raw egg yoke, honey or Karo syrup, sprinkled with a high-protein baby cereal and some wheat germ. As the puppies mature, cottage cheese may be added or, at one of the two milk meals, it can be substituted for the cereal.

NOONTIME

A puppy chow which has been soaked in warm water or beef broth according to the time specified on the wrapper should be mixed with raw or simmered chopped meat in equal proportions with a vitamin powder added.

6 P.M.

Repeat the milk meal — perhaps varying the type of cereal from wheat to oats, or corn or rice.

MIDNIGHT

Repeat the meat meal. If raw meat was fed at noon, the evening meal might be simmered.

Please note that specific proportions on this suggested diet are not given. However, it is safe to say that the most important ingredients are the milk and cereal, and the meat and puppy chow which forms the basis of the diet. Your veterinarian can advise on the portion sizes if there is any doubt in your mind as to how much to use.

If you notice that the puppies are cleaning their plates you are perhaps not feeding enough to keep up with their rate of growth. Increase the amount at the next feeding. Observe them closely; puppies

Ch. Fra-Mar's Karo Mia Diavol, pictured in this lovely head study and owned by Marie Wamser, Fra-Mar Kennels, Cleveland, Ohio.

should each "have their fill," because growth is very rapid at this age. If they have not satisfied themselves, increase the amount so that they do not have to fight for the last morsel. They will not over-eat if they know there is enough food available. Instinct will usually let them eat to suit their normal capacity.

If there is any doubt in your mind as to any ingredient you are feeding, ask yourself, "Would I give it to my own baby?" If the answer is no, then don't give it to your puppies. At this age, the comparison between puppies and human babies can be a good guide.

If there is any doubt in your mind, I repeat: ask your veterinarian to be sure.

Many puppies will regurgitate their food, perhaps a couple of times, before they manage to retain it. If they do bring up their food, allow them to eat it again, rather than clean it away. Sometimes additional saliva is necessary for them to digest it, and you do not want them to skip a meal just because it is an unpleasant sight for you to observe.

This same regurgitation process holds true sometimes with the bitch, who will bring up her own food for her puppies every now and then. This is a natural instinct on her part which stems from the days when dogs were giving birth in the wilds. The only food the mother could provide at weaning time was too rough and indigestible for her puppies. Therefore, she took it upon herself to pre-digest the food until it could be taken and retained by her young. Bitches today will sometimes resort to this, especially bitches which love having litters and have a strong maternal instinct. Some dams will help you wean their litters and even give up feeding entirely once they see you are taking over.

WEANING THE PUPPIES

When weaning the puppies the mother is kept away from the little ones for longer and longer periods of time. This is done over a period of several days. At first she is separated from the puppies for several hours, then all day, leaving her with them only at night for comfort and warmth. This gradual separation aids in helping the mother's milk to dry up gradually, and she suffers less distress after feeding a litter.

If the mother continues to carry a great deal of milk with no signs of its tapering off, consult your veterinarian before she gets too un-comfortable. She may cut the puppies off from her supply of milk too abruptly if she is uncomfortable, before they should be com-pletely on their own.

There are many opinions on the proper age to start weaning puppies. If you plan to start selling them between six and eight weeks, weaning should begin between two and three weeks of age. Here again, each bitch will pose a different situation. The size and weight of the litter should help determine the time, and your veterinarian will have an opinion, as he determines the burden the bitch is carrying by the size of the litter and her general condition. If she is being pulled down by feeding a large litter, he may suggest that you start at two weeks. If she is glorying in her motherhood without any apparent taxing of her strength, he may suggest three to four weeks. You and he will be the best judges. But remember, there is no substitute that is as perfect as mother's milk — and the longer the puppies benefit from it, the better. Other food yes, but mother's milk first and foremost for the healthiest puppies!

FEEDING THE ADULT DOG

The puppies' schedule of four meals a day should drop to three by six months and then to two by nine months; by the time the dog reaches one year of age, it is eating one meal a day.

The time when you feed the dog each day can be a matter of the dog's preference or your convenience, so long as once in every 24 hours the dog receives a meal that provides him with a complete, balanced diet. In addition, of course, fresh clean water should be available at all times.

There are many brands of dry food, kibbles and biscuits on the market which are all of good quality. There are also many varieties of canned dog food which are of good quality and provide a balanced diet for your dog. But, for those breeders and exhibitors who show their dogs, additional care is given to providing a few "extras" which enhance the good health and good appearance of show dogs.

A good meal or kibble mixed with water or beef broth and raw meat is perhaps the best ration to provide. In cold weather many breeders add suet or corn oil (or even olive or cooking oil) to the mixture and others make use of the bacon fat after breakfast by pouring it over the dog's food.

Salting a dog's food in the summer helps replace the salt he "pants away" in the heat. Many breeders sprinkle the food with garlic powder to sweeten the dog's breath and prevent gas, especially in breeds that gulp or wolf their food and swallow a lot of air. I prefer garlic powder; the salt is too weak and the clove is too strong.

There are those, of course, who cook very elaborately for their dogs, which is not necessary if a good meal and meat mixture is

Ch. Dean's Snow Czar, owned by Jacqueline Van Dusen and Nina A. Fischer of Seven Hills, Ohio.

Teenah of Martha Lake, an example of the pure Bow Lake breeding. Dam was Ch. Susha of Martha Lake and the sire Ike of Bow Lake. Owned by Don and Anne Hanson of the Windwillow Kennels, Leavenworth, Washington.

provided. Many prefer to add vegetables, rice, tomatoes, etc., in with everything else they feed. As long as the extras do not throw the nutritional balance off, there is little harm, but no one thing should be fed to excess. Occasionally liver is given as a treat at home. Fish, which most veterinarians no longer recommend even for cats, is fed to puppies, but should not be given in excess of once a week. Always remember that no one thing should be given as a total diet. Balance is most important; a 100 per cent meat diet can kill a dog.

THE ALL MEAT DIET CONTROVERSY

In March of 1971, the National Research Council investigated a great stir in the dog fancy about the all-meat dog-feeding controversy. It was established that meat and meat by-products constitute a complete balanced diet for dogs only when it is further fortified with vitamins and minerals.

Therefore, a good dog chow or meal mixed with meat provides the perfect combination for a dog's diet. While the dry food is a complete diet in itself, the fresh meat additionally satisfies the dog's anatomically and physiologically meat-oriented appetite. While dogs are actually carnivores, it must be remembered that when they were feeding themselves in the wild they ate almost the entire animal they captured, including its stomach contents. This provided some of the vitamins and minerals we must now add to the diet.

In the United States, the standards for diets which claim to be "complete and balanced" are set by the Subcommittee on Canine Nutrition of the National Research Council (NRC) of the National Academy of Sciences. This is the official agency for establishing the nutritional requirements of dog foods. Most foods sold for dogs and cats meet these requirements, and manufacturers are proud to say so on their labels, so look for this when you buy. Pet food labels must be approved by the Associaition of American Feed Control Officials, Pet Foods Committee. Both the Food and Drug Administration and the Federal Trade Commission of the AAFCO define the word "balanced" when referring to dog food as:

"Balanced is a term which may be applied to pet food having all known required nutrients in a proper amount and proportion based upon the recommendations of a recognized authority (The National Research Council is one) in the field of animal nutrition, for a given set of physiological animal requirements."

With this much care given to your dog's diet, there can be little reason for not having happy well-fed dogs in proper weight and proportions for the show ring.

OBESITY

As we mentioned above, there are many "perfect" diets for your dogs on the market today. When fed in proper proportions, they should keep your dogs in "full bloom." However, there are those owners who, more often than not, indulge their own appetites and are inclined to overfeed their dogs as well. A study in Great Britain in the early 1970's found that a major percentage of obese people also had obese dogs. The entire family was overfed and all suffered from the same condition.

Obesity in dogs is a direct result of the animal's being fed more food than he can properly "burn up" over a period of time, so it is stored as fat or fatty tissue in the body. Pet dogs are more inclined to become obese than show dogs or working dogs, but obesity also is a factor to be considered with the older dog, since his exercise is curtailed.

A lack of "tuck up" on a dog, or not being able to feel the ribs, or great folds of fat which hang from the underside of the dog can all be considered as obesity. Genetic factors may enter into the picture, but usually the owner is at fault.

The life span of the obese dog is decreased on several counts. Excess weight puts undue stress on the heart as well as the joints. The dog becomes a poor anesthetic risk and has less resistance to viral or bacterial infections. Treatment is seldom easy or completely effective, so emphasis should be placed on not letting your dog get FAT in the first place!

ORPHANED PUPPIES

The ideal solution to feeding orphaned puppies is to be able to put them with another nursing dam who will take them on as her own. If this is not possible within your own kennel, or a kennel that you know of, it is up to you to care for and feed the puppies. Survival is possible but requires a great deal of time and effort on your part.

Your substitute formula must be precisely prepared, always served heated to body temperature and refrigerated when not being fed. Esbilac, a vacuum-packed powder, with complete feeding instructions on the can, is excellent and about as close to mother's milk as you can get. If you can't get Esbilac, or until you do get Esbilac, there are two alternative formulas that you might use.

Mix one part boiled water with five parts of evaporated milk and add one teaspoonful of di-calcium phosphate per quart of formula. Di-calcium phosphate can be secured at any drug store. If they have it in tablet form only, you can powder the tablets with the back part of a tablespoon. The other formula for newborn puppies is a combination of eight ounces of homogenized milk mixed well with two egg yolks.

You will need baby bottles with three-hole nipples. Sometimes doll bottles can be used for the newborn puppies, which should be fed at six-hour intervals. If they are consuming sufficient amounts, their stomachs should look full, or slightly enlarged, though never distended. The amount of formula to be fed is proportionate to size and age and growth and weight of puppy, and is indicated on the can of Esbilac or on the advice of your veterinarian. Many breeders like to keep a baby scale nearby to check the weight of the puppies to be sure they are thriving on the formula.

At two to three weeks you can start adding Pablum or some other high protein baby cereal to the formula. Also, baby beef can be licked from your finger at this age, or added to the formula. At four weeks the surviving puppies should be taken off the diet of Esbilac and put on a more substantial diet, such as wet puppy meal or chopped beef. However, Esbilac powder can still be mixed in with the food for additional nutrition. The jarred baby foods of puréed meats make for a smooth changeover also, and can be blended into the diet.

HOW TO FEED THE NEWBORN PUPPIES

When the puppy is a newborn, remember that it is vitally important to keep the feeding procedure as close to the natural mother's routine as possible. The newborn puppy should be held in your lap in your hand in an almost upright position with the bottle at an angle to allow the entire nipple area to be full of the formula. Do not hold the bottle upright so the puppy's head has to reach straight up toward the ceiling. Do not let the puppy nurse too quickly or take in too much air and possibly get the colic. Once in a while, take the bottle away and let it rest for a moment and swallow several times. Before feeding, always test the nipple to see that the fluid does not come out too quickly, or by the same token, too slowly so that the puppy gets tired of feeding before he has had enough to eat.

When the puppy is a little older, you can place him on his stomach on a towel to eat, and even allow him to hold on to the bottle or to "come and get it" on his own. Most puppies enjoy eating and this will be a good indication of how strong an appetite he has and his ability to consume the contents of the bottle.

It will be necessary to "burp" the puppy. Place a towel on your

Ch. Doonauk Ivanova's Tzarina at two years of age. Owned by Mrs. Mae Vetterlein of Gladwyne, Pennsylvania. Photo by Gilbert.

shoulder and hold the puppy on your shoulder as if it were a human baby, patting and rubbing it gently. This will also encourage the puppy to defecate. At this time, you should observe for diarrhea or other intestinal disorders. The puppy should eliminate after each feeding with occasional eliminations between times as well. If the puppies do not eliminate on their own after each meal, massage their stomachs and under their tails gently until they do.

You must keep the puppies clean. If there is diarrhea or if they bring up a little formula, they should be washed and dried off. Under no circumstances should fecal matter be allowed to collect on their skin or fur.

All this — plus your determination and perseverance — might save an entire litter of puppies that would otherwise have died without their real mother.

Ch. Natashia's Tatayna of Ussuri, owned by Kenneth W. Fowler of Missouri. Mr. Fowler is active in local sled dog club activities. Interested in Siberians since 1963, Mr. Fowler chose Ussuri as his kennel prefix.

GASTRIC TORSION

Gastric torsion, or bloat, sometimes referred to simply as "twisted stomach," has become more and more prevalent. Many dogs that in the past had been thought to die of blockage of the stomach or intestines because they had swallowed toys or other foreign objects are now suspected of having been the victims of gastric torsion and the bloat that followed.

Though life can be saved by immediate surgery to untwist the organ, the rate of fatality is high. Symptoms of gastric torsion are unusual restlessness, excessive salivation, attempts to vomit, rapid respiration, pain and the eventual bloating of the abdominal region.

The cause of gastric torsion can be attributed to overeating, excess gas formation in the stomach, poor function of the stomach or intestine, blockage to entrances or exits of the stomach or intestine, or general lack of exercise. As the food ferments in the stomach, gases form which may twist the stomach in a clockwise direction so that the gas is unable to escape. Surgery, where the stomach is untwisted counter-clockwise, is the safest and most successful way to correct the situation.

To avoid the threat of gastric torsion, it is wise to keep your dog well exercised to be sure the body is functioning normally. Make sure that food and water are available for the dog at all times, thereby reducing the tendency to overeat. With self-service dry feeding, where the dog is able to eat intermittenly during the day, there is not the urge to "stuff" at one time.

If you notice any of the symptoms of gastric torsion, call your veterinarian immediately! Death can result within a matter of hours!

FEEDING THE RACING SIBERIAN HUSKY

While the Husky is known to be capable of extreme drive over long distances, a relatively simple diet is required.

Owners who race their dogs — including the real professionals who have been in the racing game for a long time — will tell you that the basic diet is a good dog meal and that the average amount of food for a racing dog of average size is approximately a one-pound coffee can full. Most Siberian Huskies have voracious appetites and will overeat if permitted to do so, so try to establish the correct amount for keeping each of your racing dogs in proper flesh, and then stick to it.

Ch. Ty-Cheko of Baltic, owned by Mr. Ronald Smithson of Denver, Colorado.

Norstarr's Mokee Sa, owned by the Norstarr Kennels, Rockford, Illinois. Sire was Ch. Frosty Aire's Banner Boy, C.D.; dam was Monadnock's Elsa.

This ration of a good dog meal, plus drinking water, are all that is really required for a proper and balanced diet, even if your dog races. However, there are those who choose to supplement a racing dog's diet in the belief that the "extras" add to the all-around good health of the animal.

Alaskans, for instance, might add moose meat or other wild game meat to the diet. But in the Alaskan region mainly fish is used as an added ingredient. And when we mention fish, we mean to say the *entire* fish — inside and out, head and tail included!

Rear Admiral and Mrs. Robert J. Foley's lovely Siberian wins at the Catonsville, Maryland show in October 1958. The Foleys are from Washington, D.C. William Brown photo.

Lovely head study of Ch. Arctic's Timber, owned by the Earl Reynolds in Dryden, Michigan.

Some owners of racing teams will supplement with liver, or keep their dogs on vitamins mixed in with the meal or feed. They might even use the vitamin tablets as treats or as a reward. Still others just feed the added vitamins a few days before a racing schedule begins. On the day of the race some drivers feed lumps of sugar or add Karo syrup to the ration. But those "in the know" will tell you that while it will not harm the dog, sugar and Karo syrup are instant energy and are burned up so quickly it will in no way sustain a dog throughout the entire distance of the race. Therefore, the proper basic diet is still the best way to condition a dog fully for racing without your having to reply on last-minute superficial extras.

This same principle applies to the vitamin B shots which some owners of racing dogs believe to be of help. A dog that has been properly and substantially fed will not need any additional vitamin or energy supplements. There is always the risk of diarrhea when a diet is suddenly supplemented to any marked degree. Those that do add meat — or anything else for that matter — to the diet before racing their dogs do so for several days ahead of time so that the dog has time to adjust to it.

It is possible to buy huge frozen blocks of beef for the team and add it to the ration on a regular basis so it will not shock the dog's system. It is an unpleasant experience to have a racing dog with diarrhea, and diarrhea can certainly throw a dog off his performance and thereby hold back an entire team.

The correct procedure is to feed the dog his customary diet, to have him in the peak of condition, and use a suppository about an hour before the race if the dog has not emptied himself entirely without prompting.

DRINKING WATER

Just as it is not wise to feed before a race, it is not wise to let a racing dog drink too much water before a race. Watch the water intake carefully. If the dog is still thirsty as race time approaches, he usually will lick snow, but it is not wise to offer any water immediately before or immediately after a heat.

CHAPTER 21
GENERAL CARE AND MANAGEMENT
OF YOUR SIBERIAN HUSKY

TATTOOING

Ninety per cent success has been reported on the return of stolen or lost dogs that have been tattooed. More and more this simple, painless, inexpensive method of positive identification for dogs is being reported all over the United States. Long popular in Canada, along with nose prints, the idea gained interest in this country when dognapping started to soar as unscrupulous people began stealing dogs for resale to research laboratories. Pet dogs that wander off and lost hunting dogs have always been a problem. The success of tattooing has been significant.

Tattooing can be done by the veterinarian for a minor fee. There are several dog "registries" that will record your dog's number and help you locate it should it be lost or stolen. The number of the dog's American Kennel Club registration is most often used on thoroughbred dogs, or the owner's Social Security number in the case of mixed breeds. The best place for the tattoo is the groin. Some prefer the inside of an ear, and the American Kennel Club has ruled that the judges officiating at the AKC dog shows not penalize the dog for the tattoo mark.

The tattoo mark serves not only to identify your dog should it be lost or stolen, but offers positive identification in large kennels where several litters of the same approximate age are on the premises. It is a safety measure against unscrupulous breeders "switching" puppies. Any age is a proper age to tattoo, but for safety's sake, the sooner the better.

The buzz of the needle might cause your dog to be apprehensive, but the pricking of the needle is virtually painless. The risk of infection is negligible when done properly, and the return of your beloved pet may be the reward for taking the time to insure positive identification for your dog. Your local kennel club will know of a dog registry in your area.

OUTDOOR HOUSEBREAKING

If you are particular about your dog's behavior in the house, where you expect him to be clean and respectful of the carpets and furniture, you should also want him to have proper manners outdoors. Just because the property belongs to you doesn't necessarily mean he should be allowed to empty himself any place he chooses. Before long the entire yard will be fouled and odorous and the dog will be completely irresponsible on other people's property as well. Dogs seldom recognize property lines.

If your dog does not have his own yard fenced in, he should be walked on leash before being allowed to run free and before being penned up in his own yard. He will appreciate his own run being kept clean. You will find that if he has learned his manners outside, his manners inside will be better. Good manners in "toilet training" are especially important with big dogs!

OTHER IMPORTANT OUTDOOR MANNERS

Excessive barking is perhaps the most objectionable habit a dog indulges in out of doors. It annoys neighbors and makes for a noisy dog in the house as well. A sharp jerk on the leash will stop a dog from excessive barking while walking; trees and shrubs around a dog run will cut down on barking if a dog is in his own run. However, it is unfair to block off his view entirely. Give him some view — preferably of his own home — to keep his interest. Needless to say, do not leave a dog that barks excessively out all night.

You will want your dog to bark at strangers, so allow him this privilege. Then after a few "alerting" barks tell the dog to be quiet (with the same word command each time). If he doesn't get the idea, put him on leash and let him greet callers with you at the door until he does get the idea.

Do not let your dog jump on visitors either. Leash training may be necessary to break this habit as well. As the dog jumps in the air, pull back on the lead so that the dog is returned to the floor abruptly. If he attempts to jump up on you, carefully raise your knee and push him away by leaning against his chest.

Do not let your dog roam free in the neighborhood no matter how well he knows his way home. Especially do not let your dog roam free to empty himself on the neighbors' property or gardens!

A positive invitation to danger is to allow your dog to chase cars or bicycles. Throwing tin cans or chains out of car windows at them has been suggested as a cure, but can also be dangerous if they hit

Ch. Arctic's Nyte, outstanding sled and show dog owned by the Arctic Kennels. Nyte's sire is American and Canadian Ch. Arctic's Storm Frost; his sire is Arctic's Frost. Norton of Kent photograph.

the dog instead of the street. Streams of water from a garden hose or water pistol are the least dangerous, but leash control is still the most scientific and most effective.

If neighbors report that your dog barks or howls or runs from window to window while you are away, crate training or room training for short periods of time may be indicated. If you expect to be away for longer periods of time, put the dog in the basement or a single room where he can do the least damage. The best solution of all is to buy him another dog or cat for companionship. Let them enjoy each other while you are away and have them both welcome you home!

Ch. Mount Holly's Noble Nikki, owned by Leo Scarzello, Jr., and handled by Tom Scarzellow. Nikki's sire is Ch. Frosty Aire's Banner Boy, C.D., and his dam is Alakazan's Crown Princess. Photo by Ashbey.

GERIATRICS

If you originally purchased good healthy stock and cared for your dog throughout his life, there is no reason why you cannot expect your dog to live to a ripe old age. With research and the remarkable foods produced for dogs, especially this past decade or so, his chances of longevity have increased considerably. If you have cared for him well, your dog will be a sheer delight in his old age, just as he was while in his prime.

We can assume you have fed him properly if he is not too fat. Have you ever noticed how fat people usually have fat dogs because they indulge their dogs' appetite as they do their own? If there has been no great illness, then you will find that very little additional care and attention are needed to keep him well. Exercise is still essential, as is proper food, booster shots, and tender loving care.

Even if a heart condition develops, there is still no reason to believe your dog cannot live to an old age. A diet may be necessary, along with medication and limited exercise, to keep the condition under control. In the case of deafness, or partial blindness, additional care must be taken to protect the dog, but neither infirmity will in any way shorten his life. Prolonged exposure to temperature variances, overeating, excessive exercise, lack of sleep, or being housed with younger, more active dogs may take an unnecessary toll on the

Ch. Fournier's Zachariah of Toko (on the left) and Ch. Dovercrest Awsinee Pesna are caught by the camera of Judy Rosemarin to preserve this impressive study. The dogs are owned by Jean and Rift Fournier of Atlantic Highlands, New Jersey.

dog's energies and introduce serious trouble. Good judgment, periodic veterinary checkups and individual attention will keep your dog with you for many added years.

When discussing geriatrics, the question of when a dog becomes old or aged usually is asked. We have all heard the old saying that one year of a dog's life is equal to seven years in a human. This theory is strictly a matter of opinion, and must remain so, since so many outside factors enter into how quickly each individual dog "ages." Recently, a new chart was devised which is more realistically equivalent:

DOG	MAN
6 months	10 years
1 year	15 years
2 years	24 years
3 years	28 years
4 years	32 years
5 years	36 years
6 years	40 years
7 years	44 years
8 years	48 years
9 years	52 years
10 years	56 years
15 years	76 years
21 years	100 years

It must be remembered that such things as serious illnesses, poor food and housing, general neglect and poor beginnings as puppies will all take their toll on a dog's general health and age him more quickly than a dog that has led a normal, healthy life. Let your veterinarian help you determine an age bracket for your dog in his later years.

While good care should prolong your dog's life, there are several "old age" disorders to be on the lookout for no matter how well he may be doing. The tendency toward obesity is the most common, but constipation is another. Aging teeth and a slowing down of the digestive processes may hinder digestion and cause constipation, just as any major change in diet can bring on diarrhea. There is also the possibility of loss or impairment of hearing or eyesight which will also tend to make the dog wary and distrustful. Other behavioral changes may result as well, such as crankiness, loss of patience and lack of interest; these are the most obvious changes. Other ailments

Exotic head study of Ch. Fournier's Zachariah of Toko, owned and bred by Jean Fournier, Atlantic Highlands, New Jersey.

A classic outdoor shot of Ch. Arctic's Isar Tygre, owned by Charlotte and Earl Reynolds, Arctic Kennels, Dryden, Michigan.

may manifest themselves in the form of rheumatism, arthritis, tumors and warts, heart disease, kidney infections, male prostatism and female disorders. Of course, all of these require a veterinarian's checking the degree of seriousness and proper treatment.

Take care to avoid infectious diseases. When these hit the older dog, they can debilitate him to an alarming degree, leaving them open to more serious complications and a shorter life.

DOG INSURANCE

Much has been said for and against canine insurance, and much more will be said before this kind of protection for a dog becomes universal and/or practical. There has been talk of establishing a Blue Cross-type plan similar to that now existing for humans. However, the best insurance for your dog is You! Nothing compensates for tender, loving care. Like the insurance policies for humans, there will be a lot of fine print in the contracts revealing that the dog is not covered after all. These limited conditions usually make the acquisition of dog insurance expensive and virtually worthless.

Ch. Alakazan's Banner Blue, owned and bred by Alakazan Kennels, Gill, Massachusetts. He was sired by Ch. Frosty Aire's Banner Boy, C.D., *ex* Kameo of Kazan. He is handled for his owners by Robert Cullinane. William P. Gilbert photo.

Blanket coverage policies for kennels or establishments which board or groom dogs can be an advantage, especially in transporting dogs to and from their premises. For the one-dog owner, however, whose dog is a constant companion, the cost for limited coverage is not necessary.

THE HIGH COST OF BURIAL

Pet cemeteries are mushrooming across the nation. Here, as with humans, the sky can be the limit for those who wish to bury their pets ceremoniously. The costs of satin-lined caskets, grave stones, flowers, etc. run the gamut of prices to match the emotions and means of the owner. This is strictly a matter of what the bereaved owner wishes to do.

IN THE EVENT OF YOUR DEATH. . .

This is a morbid thought perhaps, but ask yourself the question, "If death were to strike at this moment, what would become of my beloved dogs?"

Perhaps you are fortunate enough to have a relative, friend or spouse who could take over immediately, if only on a temporary basis. Perhaps you have already left instructions in your last will and testament for your pet's dispensation, as well as a stipend for their perpetual care.

Provide definite instructions before a disaster occurs and your dogs are carted off to the pound, or stolen by commercially minded neighbors with "resale" in mind. It is a simple thing to instruct your lawyer about your wishes in the event of sickness or death. Leave instructions as to feeding, etc., posted on your kennel room or kitchen bulletin board, or wherever your kennel records are kept. Also, tell several people what you are doing and why. If you prefer to keep such instructions private, merely place them in sealed envelopes in a known place with directions that they are to be opened only in the event of your demise. Eliminate the danger of your animals suffering in the event of an emergency that prevents your personal care of them.

KEEPING RECORDS

Whether or not you have one dog, or a kennel full of them, it is wise to keep written records. It takes only a few moments to record dates of inoculations, trips to the vet, tests for worms, etc. It can

Ch. Nikoluk of Chu-Nik, one of the magnificent Huskies at Harry and Velma Wades' Kennels in Amboy, Washington, which excels in the show ring and at the races.

A lovely sylvan scene featuring two Domeyko Kennel Siberian Huskies, owned by Peggy and Ed Samerson of Colorado. On the left is Ch. Darbo Domeyko of Long's Peak, and on the right is Ch. Domeyko's Zadar.

avoid confusion or mistakes, or having your dog not covered with immunization if too much time elapses between shots because you have to guess at the last shot.

Make the effort to keep all dates in writing rather than trying to commit them to memory. A rabies injection date can be a problem if you have to recall that "Fido had the shot the day Aunt Mary got back from her trip abroad, and, let's see, I guess that was around the end of June."

In an emergency, these records may prove their value if your veterinarian cannot be reached and you have to use another, or if you move and have no case history on your dog for the new veterinarian. In emergencies, you do not always think clearly or accurately, and if dates, and types of serums used, etc., are a matter of record, the veterinarian can act more quickly and with more confidence.

CHAPTER 22
YOUR DOG, YOUR VETERINARIAN, AND YOU!

The purpose of this chapter is to explain why you should never attempt to be your own veterinarian. Quite the contrary, we urge emphatically that you establish good liaison with a reputable veterinarian who will help you maintain happy, healthy dogs. Our purpose is to bring you up to date on the discoveries made in modern canine medicine and to help you work with your veterinarian by applying these new developments to your own animals.

We have provided here "thumbnail" histories of many of the most common types of diseases your dog is apt to come in contact with during his lifetime. We feel that if you know a little something about the diseases and how to recognize their symptoms, your chances of catching them in the preliminary stages will help you and your veterinarian effect a cure before a serious condition develops.

Today's dog owner is a realistic, intelligent person who learns more and more about his dog — inside and out — so that he can care for and enjoy the animal to the fullest. He uses technical terms for parts of the anatomy, has a fleeting knowledge of the miracles of surgery and is fully prepared to administer clinical care for his animals at home. This chapter is designed for study and/or reference and we hope you will use it to full advantage.

We repeat, we do *not* advocate your playing "doctor." This includes administering medication without veterinary supervision, or even doing your own inoculations. General knowledge of diseases, their symptoms and side effects will assist you in diagnosing diseases for your veterinarian. He does not expect you to be an expert, but will appreciate your efforts in getting a sick dog to him before it is too late and he cannot save its life.

ASPIRIN: A DANGER

There is a common joke about doctors telling their patients, when they telephone with a complaint, to take an aspirin, go to bed and let him know how things are in the morning! Unfortunately, that is exactly the way it turns out with a lot of dog owners who think aspirins are cfrom cureats and give them to their dogs indiscriminately. Then they call the veterinarian when the dog has an unfavorable reaction.

Aspirins are not panaceas for everything — certainly not for every dog. In an experiment, fatalities in cats treated with aspirin in one laboratory alone numbered ten out of 13 within a two-week period. Dogs' tolerance was somewhat better, as far as actual fatalities, but there was considerable evidence of ulceration in varying degrees on the stomach linings when necropsy was performed.

Aspirin has been held in the past to be almost as effective for dogs as for people when given for many of the everyday aches and pains. The fact remains, however, that medication of any kind should be administered only after veterinary consultation and a specific dosage suitable to the condition is recommended.

While aspirin is chiefly effective in reducing fever, relieving minor pains and cutting down on inflammation, the acid has been proven harmful to the stomach when given in strong doses. Only your veterinarian is qualified to determine what that dosage is, or whether it should be administered to your particular dog at all.

WHAT THE THERMOMETER CAN TELL YOU

You will notice in reading this chapter dealing with the diseases of dogs that practically everything a dog might contract in the way of sickness has basically the same set of symptoms. Loss of appetite, diarrhea, dull eyes, dull coat, warm and/or runny nose, and FEVER!

Therefore, it is most advisable to have a thermometer on hand for checking temperature. There are several inexpensive metal rectal-type thermometers that are accurate and safer than the glass variety which can be broken. This may happen either by dropping, or perhaps even breaking off in the dog because of improper insertion or an aggravated condition with the dog that makes him violently resist the injection of the thermometer. Either kind should be lubricated with Vaseline to make the insertion as easy as possible, after it has been sterilized with alcohol.

The normal temperature for a dog is 101.5° Fahrenheit, as compared to the human 98.6°. Excitement as well as illness can cause this to vary a degree or two, but any sudden or extensive rise in body temperature must be considered as cause for alarm. Your first indication will be that your dog feels unduly "warm" and this is the time to take the temperature, not when the dog becomes very ill or manifests additional serious symptoms. With a thermometer on hand,

Zakarov of the Midnight Sun, photographed in 1968. Owned by Catherine A. Halcomb of Setting Sun Kennels in Portola, California.

you can check temperatures quickly and perhaps prevent some illness from becoming serious.

COPROPHAGY

Perhaps the most unpleasant of all phases of dog breeding is to come up with a dog that takes to eating stool. This practice, which is referred to politely as coprophagy, is one of the unsolved mysteries in the dog world. There simply is no explanation to why some dogs do it.

However, there are several logical theories, all or any of which may be the cause. Some say nutritional deficiencies; another says that dogs inclined to gulp their food (which passes through them not entirely digested) find it still partially palatable. There is another theory that the preservatives used in some meat are responsible for an appealing odor that remains through the digestive process. Then again poor quality meat can be so tough and unchewable that dogs

415

Ch. Alakazan's Saanki, owned by Dave and Alice Angel, Norstarr Kennels, Rockford, Illinois.

swallow it whole and it passes through them in large undigested chunks.

There are others who believe the habit is strictly psychological, the result of a nervous condition or insecurity. Others believe the dog cleans up after itself because it is afraid of being punished as it was when it made a mistake on the carpet as a puppy. Others claim boredom is the reason, or even spite. Others will tell you a dog does not want its personal odor on the premises for fear of attracting other hostile animals to itself or its home.

The most logical of all explanations and the one most veterinarians are inclined to accept is that it is a deficiency of dietary enzymes. Too much dry food can be bad and many veterinarians suggest trying meat tenderizers, monosodium glutamate, or garlic powder which gives the stool a bad odor and discourages the dog. Yeast or certain vitamins or a complete change of diet are even more often suggested. By the time you try each of the above you will probably discover that the dog has outgrown the habit anyway. However, the condition cannot be ignored if you are to enjoy your dog to the fullest.

There is no set length of time that the problem persists, and the only real cure is to walk the dog on leash, morning and night and after every meal. In other words, set up a definite eating and exercising schedule before coprophagy is an established pattern.

MASTURBATION

A source of embarrassment to many dog owners, masturbation can be eliminated with a minimum of training.

The dog which is constantly breeding anything and everything, including the leg of the piano or perhaps the leg of your favorite guest, can be broken of the habit by stopping its cause.

The over-sexed dog — if truly that is what he is — which will never be used for breeding can be castrated. The kennel stud dog can be broken of the habit by removing any furniture from his quarters or keeping him on leash and on verbal command when he is around people, or in the house where he might be tempted to breed pillows, people, etc.

Hormone imbalance may be another cause and your veterinarian may advise injections. Exercise can be of tremendous help. Keeping the dog's mind occupied by physical play when he is around people will also help relieve the situation.

Females might indulge in sexual abnormalities like masturbation during their heat cycle, or again, because of a hormone imbalance. But if they behave this way because of a more serious problem, a hysterectomy may be indicated.

A sharp "no!" command when you can anticipate the act, or a sharp "no!" when caught in the act will deter most dogs if you are consistent in your correction. Hitting or other physical abuse will only confuse a dog.

RABIES

The greatest fear in the dog fancy today is still the great fear it has always been — rabies!

What has always held true about this dreadful disease still holds true today. The only way rabies can be contracted is through the saliva of a rabid dog entering the bloodstream of another animal or person. There is, of course, the Pasteur treatment for rabies which is very effective. There was of late the incident of a little boy bitten by a rabid bat having survived the disease. However, the Pasteur treatment is administered immediately if there is any question of exposure. Even more than dogs being found to be rabid, we now know that the biggest carriers are bats, skunks, foxes, rabbits and other warm-blooded animals, which pass it from one to another, since they do not have the benefit of inoculation. Dogs that run free should be inoculated for protection against these animals. For city or house dogs that never leave their owner's side, it may not be as necessary.

For many years, Great Britain, because it is an island and because of the country's strictly enforced six-month quarantine, was entirely free of rabies. But in 1969, a British officer brought back his dog from foreign duty and the dog was found to have the disease soon after being released from quarantine. There was a great uproar about it, with Britain killing off wild and domestic animals in a great scare campaign, but the quarantine is once again down to six months and things seem to have returned to a normal, sensible attitude.

Health departments in rural towns usually provide rabies inoculations free of charge. If your dog is outdoors a great deal, or exposed to other animals that are, you might wish to call the town hall and get information on the program in your area. One cannot be too cautious about this dread disease. While the number of cases diminishes each year, there are still thousands being reported and there is still the constant threat of an outbreak where animals roam free. And never forget, there is no cure.

Rabies is caused by a neurotropic virus which can be found in the saliva, brain and sometimes the blood of the warm-blooded animal afflicted. The incubation period is usually two weeks or as long as six months, which means you can be exposed to it without any visible symptoms. As we have said, while there is still no known cure, it can be controlled. It is up to every individual to help effect this control by reporting animal bites, educating the public to the dangers and symptoms and prevention of it, so that we may reduce the fatalities.

There are two kinds of rabies; one form is called "furious," and the other is referred to as "dumb." The mad dog goes through several stages of the disease. His disposition and behavior change radically and suddenly; he becomes irritable and vicious; the eating habits alter, and he rejects food for things like stones and sticks; he becomes exhausted and drools saliva out of his mouth almost constantly. He may hide in corners, look glassy eyed and suspicious, bite at the air as he races around snarling and attacking with his tongue hanging out. At this point paralysis sets in, starting at the throat so that he can no longer drink water though he desires it desperately; hence, the term hydrophobia is given. He begins to stagger and eventually convulse and death is imminent.

Respected judge Alva Rosenberg awards Best Working Group Brace at the International Kennel Club Show in Chicago in 1956 to the Siberian Huskies of Carol J. and Andrew J. Maxfield, Jr. Frasie Studio photo.

That's what I want for Christmas!. . . Fireside's Mini-Ha-Ha visits Santa Claus at the local department store toy department in Walled Lake, Michigan, site of the Fireside Kennels, owned by Mr. and Mrs. Andrew Rossetto.

In "dumb" rabies paralysis is swift; the dog seeks dark, sheltered places and is abnormally quiet. Paralysis starts with the jaws, spreads down the body and death is quick. Contact by humans or other animals with the drool from either of these types of rabies on open skin can produce the fatal disease, so extreme haste and proper diagnosis is essential. In other words, you do not have to be bitten by a rabid dog to have the virus enter your system. An open wound or cut that comes in touch with the saliva is all that is needed.

The incubation and degree of infection can vary. You usually contract the disease faster if the wound is near the head, since the virus travels to the brain through the spinal cord. The deeper the wound, the more saliva is injected into the body, the more serious the infection. So, if bitten by a dog under any circumstances — or any warm-blooded animal for that matter — immediately wash out the wound with soap and water, bleed it profusely, and see your doctor as soon as possible.

Also, be sure to keep track of the animal that bit, if at all possible. When rabies is suspected the public health officer will need to send the animal's head away to be analyzed. If it is found to be rabies free, you will not need to undergo treatment. Otherwise, your doctor may advise that you have the Pasteur treatment, which is extremely painful. It is rather simple, however, to have the veterinarian examine a dog for rabies without having the dog sent away for positive diagnosis of the disease. A ten-day quarantine is usually all that is necessary for everyone's peace of mind.

Rabies is no respecter of age, sex or geographical location. It is found all over the world from North Pole to South Pole, and has nothing to do with the old wives' tale of dogs going mad in the hot summer months. True, there is an increase in reported cases during summer, but only because that is the time of the year for animals to roam free in good weather and during the mating season when the battle of the sexes is taking place. Inoculation and a keen eye for symptoms and bites on our dogs and other pets will help control the disease until the cure is found.

VACCINATIONS

If you are to raise a puppy, or a litter of puppies, successfully, you must adhere to a realistic and strict schedule of vaccination. Many puppyhood diseases can be fatal — all of them are debilitating. According to the latest statistics, 98 per cent of all puppies are being inoculated after 12 weeks of age against the dread distemper, hepatitis, and leptospirosis and manage to escape these horrible infections. Orphaned puppies should be vaccinated every two weeks until the age of 12 weeks. Distemper and hepatitis live-virus vaccine should be used, since they are not protected with the colostrum normally supplied to them through the mother's milk. Puppies weaned at six to seven weeks should also be inoculated repeatedly because they will no longer be receiving mother's milk. While not all will receive protection from the serum at this early age, it should be given and they should be vaccinated once again at both nine and 12 weeks of age.

Leptospirosis vaccination should be given at four months of age with thought given to booster shots if the disease is known in the area, or in the case of show dogs which are exposed on a regular basis to many dogs from far and wide. While annual boosters are in order for distemper and hepatitis, every two or three years is sufficient for leptospirosis, unless there is an outbreak in your immediate area. The one exception should be the pregnant bitch since there is reason to believe that inoculation might cause damage to the fetus.

Strict observance of such a vaccination schedule will not only keep your dog free of these debilitating diseases, but will prevent an epidemic in your kennel, or in your locality, or to the dogs which are competing at the shows.

SNAKEBITE

As field trials and hunts and the like become more and more popular with dog enthusiasts, the incident of snakebite becomes more of a likelihood. Dogs that are kept outdoors in runs or dogs that work the fields and roam on large estates are also likely victims.

Most veterinarians carry snakebite serum, and snakebite kits are sold to dog owners for just such purpose. To catch a snakebite in time might mean the difference between life and death, and whether your area is populated with snakes or not, it behooves you to know what to do in case it happens to your or your dog.

Your primary concern should be to get to a doctor or veterinarian immediately. The victim should be kept as quiet as possible (excitement or activity spreads the venom through the body more quickly) and if possible the wound should be bled enough to clean it out before applying a tourniquet, if the bite is severe.

First of all, it must be determined if the bite is from a poisonous or non-poisonous snake. If the bite carries two horseshoe shaped pinpoints of a double row of teeth, the bite can be assumed to be non-poisonous. If the bite leaves two punctures or holes — the result of the two fangs carrying venom — the bite is very definitely poisonous and time is of the essence.

Recently, physicians have come up with an added help in the case of snakebite. A first aid treatment referred to as hypothermia, which is the application of ice to the wound to lower body temperature to a point where the venom spreads less quickly, minimizes swelling, helps prevent infection and has some influence on numbing the pain. If ice is not readily available, the bite may be soaked in ice-cold water. But even more urgent is the need to get the victim to a hospital or a veterinarian for additional treatment.

Anezeka of the Setting Sun is shown here winning at the Salinas Valley Kennel Club show on the way to her championship. The judge was Melbourne Downing, and she was handled by her owner, Catherine A. Halcomb of Portola, California. Bennett Associates photo.

Ch. Keachi's Eltigre Torvo pictured winning under judge Ken Mc-Donald. Lila Weir, handler, owned and bred by Karl and Pat Hahn, Jr., at Keachi Kennels, Anchorage, Alaska.

EMERGENCIES

No matter how well you run your kennel or keep an eye on an individual dog, there will almost invariably be some emergency at some time that will require quick treatment until you get the animal to the veterinarian. The first and most important thing to remember is to keep calm! You will think more clearly and your animal will need to know he can depend on you to take care of him. However, he will be frightened and you must beware of fear biting. Therefore, do not shower him with kisses and endearments at this time, no matter how sympathetic you feel. Comfort him reassuringly, but keep your wits about you. Before getting him to the veterinarian try to alleviate the pain and shock.

If you can take even a minor step in this direction it will be a help toward the final cure. Listed here are a few of the emergencies which might occur and what you can do AFTER you have called the vet and told him you are coming.

Burns

If you have been so foolish as not to turn your pot handles toward the back of the stove — for your children's sake as well as your dog's — and the dog is burned, apply ice or ice cold water and treat for shock. Electrical or chemical burns are treated the same; but with an acid or alkali burn, use, respectively, a bicarbonate of soda or vinegar solution. Check the advisability of covering the burn when you call the veterinarian.

Drowning

Most animals love the water, but sometimes get in "over their heads." Should your dog take in too much water, hold him upside down and open his mouth so that water can empty from the lungs, then apply artificial respiration, or mouth-to-mouth resuscitation. Then treat for shock by covering him with a blanket, administering a stimulant such as coffee with sugar, and soothing him with voice and hand.

Fits and Convulsions

Prevent the dog from thrashing about and injuring himself, cover with a blanket and hold down until you can get him to the veterinarian.

Frostbite

There is no excuse for an animal getting frostbite if you are on your toes and care for the animal. However, should frostbite set in, thaw out the affected area slowly with a circulatory motion and stimulation. Use vaseline to help keep the skin from peeling off and/or drying out.

Heart Attack

Be sure the animal keeps breathing by applying artificial respiration. A mild stimulant may be used and give him plenty of air. Treat for shock as well, and get to the veterinarian quickly.

Suffocation

Artificial respiration and treat for shock with plenty of air.

Sun Stroke

Cooling the dog off immediately is essential. Ice packs, submersion in ice water, and plenty of cool air are needed.

Wounds

Open wounds or cuts which produce bleeding must be treated with hydrogen peroxide and tourniquets should be used if bleeding is excessive. Also, shock treatment must be given, and the animal must be kept warm.

THE FIRST AID KIT

It would be sheer folly to try to operate a kennel or to keep a dog without providing for certain emergencies that are bound to crop up when there are active dogs around. Just as you would provide a first aid kit for people you should also provide a first aid kit for the animals on the premises.

The first aid kit should contain the following items:

BFI or other medicated powder
jar of Vaseline
Q-tips
bandage—1 inch gauze
adhesive tape
Band-Aids
cotton
boric acid powder

A trip to your veterinarian is always safest, but there are certain preliminaries for cuts and bruises of a minor nature that you can care for yourself.

Cuts, for instance, should be washed out and medicated powder or Vaseline applied with a bandage. The lighter the bandage the better so that the most air possible can reach the wound. Q-tips can be used for removing debris from the eyes after which a mild solution of boric acid wash can be applied. As for sores, use dry powder on wet sores, and Vaseline on dry sores. Use cotton for washing out wounds and drying them.

A particular caution must be given here on bandaging. Make sure that the bandage is not too tight to hamper the dog's circulation. Also, make sure the bandage is made correctly so that the dog does not bite at it trying to get it off. A great deal of damage can be done to a wound by a dog tearing at a bandage to get it off. If you notice the dog is starting to bite at it, do it over or put something on the bandage that smells and tastes bad to him. Make sure, however, that the solution does not soak through the bandage and enter the wound. Sometimes, if it is a leg wound, a sock or stocking slipped on the dog's leg will cover the bandage edges and will also keep it clean.

HOW NOT TO POISON YOUR DOG

Ever since the appearance of Rachel Carson's book *Silent Spring,*

Dwi Kars Kuger, outstanding sled dog owned by Don and Anne Hanson of the Windwillow Kennels, Leavenworth, Washington.

Windwillow's Vixen, sired by Ch. Bandit of Windwillow, C.D., *ex* Windwillow's Dark Secret. Owners Don and Anne Hanson of Windwillow Kennels, Leavenworth, Washington.

people have been asking, "Just how dangerous are chemicals?" In the animal world where disinfectants, room deodorants, parasitic sprays, solutions and aerosols are so widely used, the question has taken on even more meaning. Veterinarians are beginning to ask, "What kind of disinfectant do you use?" or "Have you any fruit trees that have been sprayed recently?" When animals are brought in to their offices in a toxic condition, or for unexplained death, or when entire litters of puppies die mysteriously, there is good reason to ask such questions.

The popular practice of protecting animals against parasites has given way to their being exposed to an alarming number of commercial products, some of which are dangerous to their very lives. Even flea collars can be dangerous, especially if they get wet or somehow touch the genital regions or eyes. While some products are a great deal more poisonous than others, great care must be taken that they be applied in proportion to the size of the dog and the area to be covered. Many a dog has been taken to the vet with an unusual skin problem that was a direct result of having been bathed with a detergent rather than a proper shampoo. Certain products that are safe for dogs can be fatal for cats. Extreme care must be taken to read all ingredients and instructions carefully before use on any animal.

The same caution must be given to outdoor chemicals. Dog owners must question the use of fertilizers on their lawns. Lime, for instance, can be harmful to a dog's feet. The unleashed dog that covers the neighborhood on his daily rounds is open to all sorts of tree and lawn sprays and insecticides that may prove harmful to him, if not as a poison, as a producer of an allergy. Many puppy fatalities are reported when they consume mothballs.

There are various products found around the house which can be lethal, such as rat poison, boric acid, hand soap, detergents, and insecticides. The garage too may provide dangers: Antifreeze for the car, lawn, garden and tree sprays, paints, etc., are all available for tipping over and consuming. All poisons should be placed on high shelves for the sake of your children as well as your animals.

Perhaps the most readily available of all household poisons are plants. Household plants are almost all poisonous, even if taken in small quantities. Some of the most dangerous are the elephant ear, the narcissus bulb, any kind of ivy leaves, burning bush leaves, the jimson weed, the dumb cane weed, mock orange fruit, castor beans, Scotch broom seeds, the root or seed of the plant called four o'clock, cyclamen, pimpernel, lily of the valley, the stem of the sweet pea, rhododendrons of any kind, spider lily bulbs, bayonet root, foxglove leaves, tulip bulbs, monkshood roots, azalea, wisteria, poinsettia

Ch. Frosty Aire's Masked Bandit, owned by Dorothy Page of the Chotovotka Kennels, Chatham, Illinois.

Ch. Arahaz' Tengri Khan sits in back of the wagon that takes the Kaylee dogs to the dog shows. The license plate is suggestive of the sled dog connotation by which the breed is known. Khan is owned by Carolyn Windsor of Baltimore, Maryland.

leaves, mistletoe, hemlock, locoweed and arrowglove. In all, there are over 500 poisonous plants in the United States. Peach, elderberry and cherry trees can cause cyanide poisoning if the bark is consumed. Rhubarb leaves either raw or cooked can cause death or violent convulsions. Check out your closets, fields and grounds around your home to see what might be of danger to your pets.

SYMPTOMS OF POISONING

Be on the lookout for vomiting, hard or labored breathing, whimpering, stomach cramps, and trembling as a prelude to the convulsions. Any delay in a visit to your veterinarian can mean death. Take along the bottle or package or a sample of the plant you suspect to be the cause to help the veterinarian determine the correct antidote.

The most common type of poisoning, which accounts for nearly one-fourth of all animal victims, is staphylococcic-infected food. Salmonella ranks third. These can be avoided by serving fresh food and not letting it lie around in hot weather.

There are also many insect poisonings caused by animals eating cockroaches, spiders, flies, butterflies, etc. Toads and some frogs give off a fluid which can make a dog foam at the mouth — and even kill him — if he bites just a little too hard!

Some misguided dog owners think it is "cute" to let their dogs enjoy a cocktail with them before dinner. There can be serious effects resulting from encouraging a dog to drink — sneezing fits, injuries as a result of intoxication, and heart stoppage are just a few. Whiskey for medicinal purposes, or beer for brood bitches should be administered only on the advice of your veterinarian.

There have been cases of severe damage and death when dogs emptied ash trays and consumed cigarettes, resulting in nicotine poisoning. Leaving a dog alone all day in a house where there are cigarettes available on a coffee table is asking for trouble. Needless to say, the same applies to marijuana. The narcotic addict who takes his dog along with him on "a trip" does not deserve to have a dog. All the ghastly side effects are as possible for the dog as for the addict, and for a person to submit an animal to this indignity is indeed despicable. Don't think it doesn't happen. Ask the veterinarians that practice near some of your major hippie havens! Unfortunately, in all our major cities the practice is becoming more and more a problem for the veterinarian.

Be on the alert and remember that in the case of any type of poisoning, the best treatment is prevention.

THE CURSE OF ALLERGY

The heartbreak of a child being forced to give up a beloved pet because he is suddenly found to be allergic to it is a sad but true story. Many families claim to be unable to have dogs at all; others seem to be able only to enjoy them on a restricted basis. Many children know animals only through occasional visits to a friend's house or the zoo.

While modern veterinary science has produced some brilliant allergists, such as Dr. Edward Baker of New Jersey, the field is still working on a solution for those who suffer from exposure to their pets. There is no permanent cure as yet.

Over the last quarter of a century there have been many attempts at a permanent cure, but none has proven successful, because the treatment was needed too frequently, or was too expensive to maintain over extended periods of time.

However, we find that most people who are allergic to their animals are also allergic to a variety of other things as well. By eliminating the other irritants, and by taking medication given for the control of allergies in general, many are able to keep pets on a restricted basis. This may necessitate the dog's living outside the house, being groomed at a professional grooming parlor instead of by the owner, or merely being kept out of the bedroom at night. A discussion of this "balance" factor with your medical and veterinary doctors may give new hope to those willing to try.

A paper presented by Mathilde M. Gould, M.D., a New York allergist, before the American Academy of Allergists in the 1960's, and reported in the September-October 1964 issue of the *National Humane Review* magazine, offered new hope to those who are allergic by a method referred to as hyposensitization. You may wish to write to the magazine and request the article for discussion with your medical and veterinary doctors on your individual problem.

DO ALL DOGS CHEW?

All young dogs chew! Chewing is the best possible method of cutting teeth and exercising gums. Every puppy goes through this teething process. True, it can be destructive if not watched carefully, and it is really the responsibility of every owner to prevent the damage before it occurs.

When you see a puppy pick up an object to chew, immediately remove it from his mouth with a sharp "No!" and replace the object with a Nylon or rawhide bone which should be provided for him to do his serious chewing. Puppies take anything and everything into their mouths so they should be provided with proper toys which they cannot chew up and swallow.

BONES

There are many opinions on the kind of bones a dog should have. Anyone who has lost a puppy or dog because of a bone chip puncturing the stomach or intestinal wall will say "no bones" except for the

Nylon or rawhide kind you buy in pet shops. There are those who say shank or knuckle bones are permissible. Use your own judgment, but when there are adequate processed bones which you know to be safe, why risk a valuable animal? Cooked bones, soft enough to be pulverized and put in the food can be fed if they are reduced almost to a powder. If you have the patience for this sort of thing, okay. Otherwise, stick to the commercial products.

As for dogs and puppies chewing furniture, shoes, etc., replace the object with something allowable and safe and put yourself on record as remembering to close closet doors. Keep the puppy in the same room with you so you can stand guard over the furniture.

Electrical cords and sockets, or wires of any kind, present a dangerous threat to chewers. Glass dishes which can be broken are hazardous if not picked up right after feeding.

Little Russell Sasso, six years old, with his best pal, Rebecca of Sunnybrook. Marylou and Russell Sasso own the Sunnybrook Kennels in Putnam Valley, New York.

Chewing can also be a form of frustration or nervousness. Dogs sometimes chew for spite, if owners leave them alone too long or too often. Bitches will sometimes chew if their puppies are taken away from them too soon; insecure puppies often chew thinking they're nursing. Puppies which chew wool or blankets or carpet corners or certain types of materials may have a nutritional deficiency or something lacking in their diet, such as craving the starch that might be left in material after washing. Perhaps the articles have been near something that tastes good and they retain the odor.

The act of chewing has no connection with particular breeds or ages, any more than there is a logical reason for dogs to dig holes outdoors or dig on wooden floors indoors.

So we repeat, it is up to you to be on guard at all times until the need — or habit — passes.

HIP DYSPLASIA

Hip dysplasia, or HD, is one of the most widely discussed of all animal afflictions, since it has appeared in varying degrees in just about every breed of dog. True, the larger breeds seem most susceptible, but it has hit the small breeds and is beginning to be recognized in cats as well.

While HD in man has been recorded as far back as 370 B.C., HD in dogs was more than likely referred to as rheumatism until veterinary research came into the picture. In 1935, Dr. Otto Schales, at Angell Memorial Hospital in Boston, wrote a paper on hip dysplasia and classified the four degrees of dysplasia of the hip joint as follows:

Grade 1—slight (poor fit between ball and socket)

Grade 2—moderate (moderate but obvious shallowness of the socket)

Grade 3—severe (socket quite flat)

Grade 4—very severe (complete displacement of head of femur at early age)

HD is an incurable, hereditary, though not congenital disease of the hip sockets. It is transmitted as a dominant trait with irregular manifestations. Puppies appear normal at birth but the constant wearing away of the socket means the animal moves more and more on muscle, thereby presenting a lameness, a difficulty in getting up and severe pain in advanced cases.

The degree of severity can be determined around six months of age, but its presence can be noticed from two months of age. The

Ch. Marlytuks Red Sun of Kiska, the second highest ranking Siberian Husky in the Phillips System ratings for 1971. This lovely dog, handled here by Debbie Ensminger, is owned by the Marlytuks Kennels of Carlisle, Massachusetts and is pictured here taking a recent win under judge Virginia Hampton. William Gilbert photo.

problem is determined by X-ray, and if pain is present it can be relieved temporarily by medication. Exercise should be avoided since motion encourages the wearing away of the bone surfaces.

Dogs with HD should not be shown or bred, if quality in the breed is to be maintained. It is essential to check a pedigree for dogs known to be dysplastic before breeding, since this disease can be dormant for many generations.

ELBOW DYSPLASIA

The same condition can also affect the elbow joints and is known as elbow dysplasia. This also causes lameness, and dogs so affected should not be used for breeding.

PATELLAR DYSPLASIA

Some of the smaller breeds of dogs also suffer from patella dysplasia, or dislocation of the knee. This can be treated surgically, but the surgery by no means abolishes the hereditary factor. Therefore, these dogs should not be used for breeding.

All dogs — in any breed — should be X-rayed before being used for breeding. The X-ray should be read by a competent veterinarian, and the dog declared free and clear.

HD PROGRAM IN GREAT BRITAIN

The British Veterinary Association (BVA) has made an attempt to control the spread of HD by appointing a panel of members of their profession who have made a special study of the disease to read X-rays. Dogs over one year of age may be X-rayed and certified as free. Forms are completed in triplicate to verify the tests. One copy remains with the panel, one copy is for the owner's veterinarian, and one for the owner. A record is also sent to the British Kennel Club for those wishing to check on a particular dog for breeding purposes.

THE UNITED STATES REGISTRY

In the United States we have a central Hip Dysplasia Foundation, known as the OFA (Orthopedic Foundation for Animals). This HD control registry was formed in 1966. X-rays are sent for expert evaluation by qualified radiologists.

All you need do for complete information on getting an X-ray for your dog is to write to the Orthopedic Foundation for Animals at 817

Virginia Ave., Columbia, Mo., 65201, and request their dysplasia packet. There is no charge for this kit. It contains an envelope large enough to hold your X-ray film (which you will have taken by your own veterinarian), and a drawing showing how to position the dog properly for X-ray. There is also an application card for proper identification of the dog. Then, hopefully, your dog will be certified "normal." You will be given a registry number which you can put on his pedigree, use in your advertising, and rest assured your breeding program is in good order.

All X-rays should be sent to the address above. Any other information you might wish to have may be requested from Mrs. Robert Bower, OFA, Route 1, Constantine, Mo., 49042.

We cannot urge strongly enough the importance of doing this. While it involves time and effort, the reward in the long run will more than pay for your trouble. To see the heartbreak of parents and children when their beloved dog has to be put to sleep because of severe hip dysplasia as the result of bad breeding is a sad experience. Don't let this happen to you or to those who will purchase your puppies!

Additionally, we should mention that there is a method of palpation to determine the extent of affliction. This can be painful if the animal is not properly prepared for the examination. There have also been attempts to replace the animal's femur and socket. This is not only expensive, but the percentage of success is small.

For those who refuse to put their dog down, there is a new surgical technique which can relieve pain, but in no way constitutes a cure. This technique involves the severing of the pectinius muscle which for some unknown reason brings relief from pain over a period of many months — even up to two years. Two veterinary colleges in the United States are performing this operation at the present time. However, the owner must also give permission to "de-sex" the dogs at the time of the muscle severance. This is a safety measure to help stamp out hip dysplasia, since obviously the condition itself remains and can be passed on.

Ch. Joli Badga, pictured winning at a show. Badga was sired by Ch. Chuchi of Anadyr *ex* American and Canadian Ch. Joli Tchike of Martha Lake. Keachi Kennels, Anchorage, Alaska.

CHAPTER 23
THE BLIGHT OF PARASITES

Anyone who has ever spent countless hours peering down intently at his dog's warm, pink stomach waiting for a flea to appear will readily understand why we call this chapter the "blight of parasites." For it is that dreaded onslaught of the pesky flea that heralds the subsequent arrival of worms.

If you have seen even one flea scoot across that vulnerable expanse of skin you can be sure there are more fleas lurking on other favorite areas of your dog. They seldom travel alone. So it is now an established fact that *la puce,* as the French would say when referring to the flea, has set up housekeeping on your dog and it is going to demand a great deal of your time before you manage to evict them completely, and probably just temporarily, no matter which species your dog is harboring.

Fleas are not always choosy about their host, but chances are your dog has what is commonly known as *Ctenocephalides canis,* the dog flea. If you are a lover of cats also, your dog might even be playing host to a few *Ctenocephalides felis,* the cat flea, or vice versa! The only thing you can be really sure of is that your dog is supporting an entire community of them, all hungry and all sexually oriented, and you are going to have to be persistent in your campaign to get rid of them.

One of the chief reasons they are so difficult to catch is that what they lack in beauty and eyesight (they are blind at birth, throughout infancy and see very poorly or are blind during adulthood,) they make up for in their fantastic ability to jump and scurry about.

While this remarkable ability to jump — some say 150 times the length of their bodies — stands them in good stead with circus entrepeneurs and has given them claim to fame as chariot pullers and acrobats in side show attractions, the dog owner can be reduced to tears at the very thought of the onset of fleas.

Modern research has provided a remedy in the form of flea sprays, dips, collars and tags which can be successful in varying degrees. But there are those who swear by the good old-fashioned methods of removing them by hand, which can be a challenge to your sanity as well as your dexterity.

Since the fleas' conformation (they are built like envelopes, long and flat) with their spiny skeletal system on the outside of their bodies, is specifically provided for slithering through hair forests, they are given a distinct advantage to start with. Two antennae on the head select the best spot for digging and then two mandibles penetrate the skin and hit a blood vessel. It is also at this moment that the flea brings into play his spiny contours to prop himself against a few surrounding hairs which prevent him from being scratched off as he puts the bite on your dog. A small tubular tongue is then lowered into the hole to draw out blood and another tube is injected into the hole to pump the saliva of the flea into the wound which prevents the blood from clotting. This allows the flea to drink freely. Simultaneously your dog jumps into the air and gets one of those back legs into action scratching endlessly and in vain.

Now while you may catch an itinerant flea as he mistakenly shortcuts across your dog's stomach, the best hunting grounds are usually in the deep fur down along the dog's back from neck to the base of the tail. However, the flea, like every other creature on earth must have water, so several times during its residency it will make its way to the moister areas of your dog, such as the corners of the mouth, the eyes or the genital areas. This is when the flea collars and tags are useful. The fumes from them prevent the fleas from passing the neck to get to the head of your dog.

Your dog can usually support several generations of fleas if he doesn't scratch himself to death or go out of his mind with the itching in the interim. The population of the flea is insured by the strong mating instinct and the wise personal decision of the female flea as to the best time to deposit her eggs. She has the useful capacity to store semen until the time is right to lay the eggs after some previous brief encounter with a passing member of the opposite sex.

When that time comes for her to lay the eggs, she does so without so much as a backward glance and moves on. The dog, during a normal day's wandering, shakes the eggs off along his way, and there the eggs remain until hatched and the baby fleas are ready to jump back on a dog. If any of the eggs remain on the dog, chances are your dog will help them emerge from their shells with his scratching when some adult flea passes in the vicinity.

Larval fleas look like very small and slender maggots; they begin their lives feasting off their own egg shells until your dog comes along and offers the return to the world of adult fleas, whose excrement provides the predigested blood pellets they must have to thrive. They cannot survive on fresh blood, nor are they capable at this tender age of digging for it themselves. We are certain that the expression "two can eat as cheaply as one" originated after some curious scientist made a detailed study of the life cycle of the flea.

After a couple of weeks of this free loading, the baby flea makes his own cocoon and becomes a pupa. This stage lasts long enough for the larval flea to grow legs, mandibles, and sharp spines and to flatten out and in general get to be identifiable as the commonly known and obnoxious *Ctenocephalides canis*. The process can take several weeks or several months, depending on weather conditions, heat, moisture, etc., but generally three weeks is all that is required to enable it to start chomping on your dog in its own right.

And so the life of the flea is renewed and begun again, and if you don't have plans to stem the tide, you will certainly see a population explosion that will make the human one resemble an endangered species. Getting rid of fleas can be accomplished by the aforementioned spraying of the dog, or the flea collars and tags, but air, sunshine and a good shaking out of beds, bedding, carpets, cushions, etc., certainly must be undertaken to get rid of the eggs or larvae lying around the premises.

However, if you love the thrill of the chase, and have the stomach for it, you can still try to catch them on safari across your dog's stomach. Your dog will love the attention, that is, if you don't keep pinching a bit of skin instead of that little blackish critter. Chances are great you will come up with skin rather than the flea and your dog will lose interest and patience.

Should you be lucky enough to get hold of one, you must either squeeze it to death (which isn't likely) or break it in two with a sharp, strong fingernail (which also isn't likely) or you must release it *underwater* in the toilet bowl and flush immediately. This prospect is only slightly more likely. We strongly suggest that you shape up, clean up, shake out and spray — on a regular basis.

There are those people, however, who are much more philosophical about the flea, since, like the cockroach, it has been around since the beginning of the world. For instance, that old-time philosopher, David Harum, who has been much quoted with his remark, "A reasonable amount of fleas is good for a dog. They keep him from broodin' on bein' a dog." We would rather agree with John Donne who in his *Devotions* reveals that, "The flea, though he kill none, he does all the harm he can." This is especially true if your dog is a show dog! If the scratching doesn't ruin the coat, the inevitable infestations of the parasites the fleas will leave with your dog will!

So we readily see that dogs can be afflicted by both internal and external parasites. The external parasites are known as the aforementioned fleas, plus ticks and lice; while all of these are bothersome, they can be treated. However, the internal parasites, or worms of various kinds, are usually well-infested before discovery and require more substantial means of ridding the dog of them completely.

INTERNAL PARASITES

The most common worms are the round worms. These, like many other worms, are carried and spread by the flea and go through a cycle within the dog host. They are excreted in egg or larval form and passed on to other dogs in this manner.

Worm medicine should be prescribed by a veterinarian, and dogs should be checked for worms at least twice a year, or every three months if there is a known epidemic in your area, and during the summer months when fleas are plentiful.

Major types of worms are hookworms, whipworms, tapeworms (the only non-round worms in this list), ascarids (the "typical" round worms), heartworms, kidney and lung worms. Each can be peculiar to a part of the country or may be carried by a dog from one area to another. Kidney and lung worms are quite rare, fortunately. The others are not. Symptoms for worms might be vomiting intermittently, eating grass, lack of pep, bloated stomach, rubbing their tail along the ground, loss of weight, dull coat, anemia and pale gums, eye discharge, or unexplained nervousness and irritability. A dog with worms will usually eat twice as much as he normally would also.

Never worm a sick dog, or a pregnant bitch after the first two weeks she has been bred, and never worm a constipated dog. . .it will retain the strong medicine within the body for too long a time. The best, safest way to determine the presence of worms is to test for them before they do excessive damage.

HOW TO TEST FOR WORMS

Worms can kill your dog if the infestation is severe enough. Even light infestations of worms can debilitate a dog to the point where he is more susceptible to other serious diseases that can kill, if the worms do not.

Today's medication for worming is relatively safe and mild, and worming is no longer the traumatic experience for either dog or owner that it used to be. Great care must be given, however, to the proper administration of the drugs. Correct dosage is a "must" and clean quarters are essential to rid your kennel of these parasites. It is almost impossible to find an animal that is completely free of para-

Arctura's Thurus of Sundana, pictured winning Winners Dog at the Golden Gate Kennel Club in San Francisco, California in January, 1972. Thurus is bred and owned by Tom and Sylvia Palmer, Arctura's Kennels, Napa, California.

Ch. Dokemic's Nukenak, exotic Siberian Husky owned by Peggy and Ed Samerson, Domeyko Kennels, Woodland Park, Colorado.

sites, so we must consider worming as a necessary evil.

However mild today's medicines may be, it is inadvisable to worm a dog unnecessarily. There are simple tests to determine the presence of worms and this chapter is designed to help you learn how to make these tests yourself. Veterinarians charge a nominal fee for this service, if it is not part of their regular office visit examination. It is a simple matter to prepare fecal slides that you can read yourself on a periodic basis. Over the years it will save you much time and money, especially if you have more than one dog or a large kennel.

All that is needed by way of equipment is a microscope with 100x power. These can be purchased in the toy department in a department or regular toy store for a few dollars, depending on what else you want to get with it, but the basic, least expensive sets come with the necessary glass slides and attachments.

After the dog has defecated, take an applicator stick, or a toothpick with a flat end, or even an old-fashioned wooden matchstick, and gouge off a piece of the stool about the size of a small pea. Have one of the glass slides ready with a large drop of water on it. Mix the two together until you have a cloudy film over a large area of the slide. This smear should be covered with another slide, or a cover slip — though it is possible to obtain readings with just the one open slide. Place your slide under the microscope and prepare to focus in on it. To read the slide you will find that your eye should follow a certain pattern. Start at the top and read from left to right, then right back to the left side and then left over to the right side once again until you have looked at every portion of the slide from the top left to the bottom right side, as illustrated here:

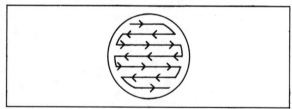

Make sure that your smear is not too thick or watery or the reading will be too dark and confused to make proper identification. Included in this chapter are drawings which will show you what to look for when reading the slides to identify the four most common varieties of worms. If you decide you would rather not make your own fecal examinations, but would prefer to have the veterinarian do it, the proper way to present a segment of the stool for him to examine is as follows:

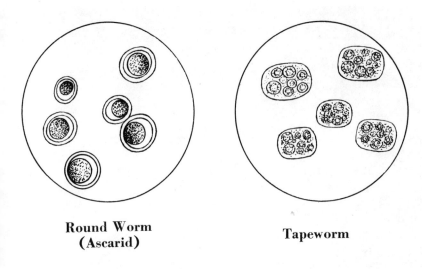

**Round Worm
(Ascarid)**

Tapeworm

Hookworm

Whipworm

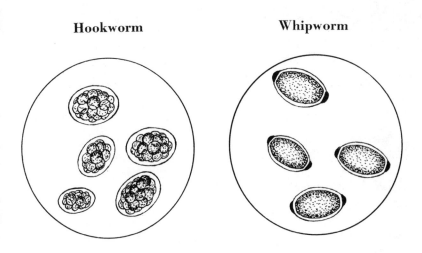

Eggs of certain parasites commonly seen in dogs.

Akalan's Konya, bred by the Akalan Kennels and owned by Mrs. Lynn Arroyo of Campbell, California. Whelped in 1971, Konya was sired by Dichoda's Helios Apollo *ex* Ch. Dichoda's Arora Chena, C.D.

After the dog has defecated, a portion of the stool, say a square inch from different sections of it, should be placed in a glass jar or plastic container, and labeled with the dog's name and address of the owner. If the sample cannot be examined within three to four hours after passage, it should be refrigerated. Your opinion as to what variety of worms you suspect is sometimes helpful to the veterinarian and may be noted on the label of the jar you submit to him for the examination.

Checking for worms on a regular basis is advisable not only for the welfare of the dog but for the protection of your family, since most worms are transmissible, under certain circumstances, to humans.

CHAPTER 24

DICTIONARY OF DOG DISEASES

AN AID TO DIAGNOSIS
— A —

ABORTION—The premature expulsion of embryos from the uterus. If part of a fetus is left in the uterus, serious infection may occur. The first indication of this will be high fever, dry nose and lethargy. The immediate services of a veterinarian are necessary.

ABSCESS—A skin eruption characterized by a localized collection of pus formed as a result of disintegrating tissues of the body. Abscesses may be acute or chronic. An acute abscess forms rapidly and will more than likely burst within a week. It is accompanied by pain, redness, heat and swelling, and may cause a rise in temperature. An abscess is usually the result of infection of a bacterial nature. Treatment consists of medication in the form of antibiotics and salves, ointments, powders or a poultice designed to bring it to a head. A chronic abscess is a slow-developing headless lump surrounded by gathering tissue. This infection is usually of internal origin, and painless unless found in a sensitive area of the body. The same antibiotics and medications are used. Because abscesses of this nature are slow in developing, they are generally slow in dissolving.

ACARUS—One of the parasitic mites which cause mange.

ACHONDROPLASIA—A disease which results in the stunting of growth, or dwarfing of the limbs before birth.

ADENOMA—A non-inflammatory growth or benign tumor found in a prominent gland; most commonly found in the mammary gland of the bitch.

AGALACTIA—A contagious, viral disease resulting in lowered or no production of milk by a nursing bitch. It usually occurs in warm weather, and is accompanied by fever and loss of appetite. Abscesses may also form. In chronic cases the mammary gland itself may atrophy.

ALARIASIS—An infection caused by flukes *(Alaria arisaemoides)*, which are ingested by the dog. They pass on to the bronchial tract and into the small intestine where they grow to maturity and feed on intestinal contents.

ALLERGY—Dogs can be allergic as well as people to outdoor or indoor surroundings, such as carpet fuzz, pillow stuffings, food, pollen, etc. Recent experiments in hyposensitization have proved effective in many cases when injections are given with follow-up "boosters." Sneezing, coughing, nasal discharges, runny, watery eyes, etc., are all symptomatic.

ALOPECIA—A bare spot, or lack of full growth of hair on a portion of the body; another name for baldness and can be the end result of a skin condition.

AMAUROSIS—Sometimes called "glass eye." A condition that may occur during a case of distemper if the nervous system has been affected, or head injuries sustained. It is characterized by the animal bumping into things or by a lack of coordination. The condition is incurable and sooner or later the optic nerve becomes completely paralyzed.

ANALGESIA—Loss of ability to feel pain with the loss of consciousness or the power to move a part of the body. The condition may be induced by drugs which act on the brain or central nervous system.

ANAL SAC OBSTRUCTION—The sacs on either side of the rectum, just inside the anus, at times may become clogged. If the condition persists, it is necessary for the animal to be assisted in their opening, so that they do not become infected and/or abscess. Pressure is applied by the veterinarian and the glands release a thick, horrible-smelling excretion. Antibiotics or a "flushing" of the glands if infected is the usual treatment, but at the first sign of discomfort in the dog's eliminating, or a "sliding along" the floor, it is wise to check for clogged anal glands.

ANASARCA—Dropsy of the connective tissues of the skin. It is occasionally encountered in fetuses and makes whelping difficult.

ANEMIA—A decrease of red blood cells which are the cells that carry oxygen to the body tissues. Causes are usually severe infestation of parasites, bad diet, or blood disease. Transfusions and medications can be given to replace red blood cells, but the disease is sometimes fatal.

ANEURYSM—A rupture or dilation of a major blood vessel, causing a bulge or swelling of the affected part. Blood gathers in the tissues forming a swelling. It may be caused by strain, in-

Two of the exotic and very beautiful champions at the Arctic Kennels of Earl and Charlotte Reynolds in Dryden, Michigan: Ch. Arctic's Snow Buck and Ch. Arctic's Starfire.

jury, or when arteries are weakened by debilitating disease or old age. Surgery is needed to remove the clot.

ANESTROUS—When a female does not come into heat.

ANTIPERISTALSIS—A term given to the reverse action of the normal procedures of the stomach or intestine, which brings their contents closer to the mouth.

ANTIPYRETICS—Drugs or methods used to reduce temperature during fevers. These may take the form of cold baths, purgatives, etc.

ANTISPASMODICS— Medications which reduce spasms of the muscular tissues and soothe the nerves and muscles involved.

449

ANTISIALICS—Term applied to substances used to reduce excessive salivation.

ARSENIC POISONING—Dogs are particularly susceptible to this type of poisoning. There is nausea, vomiting, stomach pains and convulsions, even death in severe cases. An emetic may save the animal in some cases. Salt or dry mustard (1 tablespoon mixed with 1 teaspoonful of water) can be effective in causing vomiting until the veterinarian is reached.

ARTHRITIS—A painful condition of the joints which results in irritation and inflammation. A disease that pretty much confines itself to older dogs, especially in the larger breeds. Limping, irritability and pain are symptomatic. Anti-inflammatory drugs are effective after X-ray determines the severity. Heat and rest are helpful.

ASCITES—A collection of serous fluid in the abdominal cavity, causing swelling. It may be a result of heavy parasitic infestation or a symptom of liver, kidney, tuberculosis or heart diseases.

ASPERGILLOSIS—A disease contracted from poultry and often mistaken for tuberculosis since symptoms are quite similar. It attacks the nervous system and sometimes has disastrous effects on the respiratory system. This fungus growth in the body tissue spreads quickly and is accompanied by convulsions. The dog rubs his nose and there is a bloody discharge.

ASTHMA—Acute distress in breathing. Attacks may occur suddenly at irregular intervals and last as long as half an hour. The condition may be hereditary or due to allergy or heart condition. Antihistamines are effective in minor attacks.

ATAXIA—Muscular incoordination or lack of movement causing an inhibited gait, although the necessary organs and muscle power are coherent. The dog may have a tendency to stagger.

ATOPY—Manifestations of atopy in the dog are a persistent scratching of the eyes and nose. Onsets are usually seasonal—the dog allergic to, say, ragweed will develop the condition when ragweed is in season, or say, house dust all year round. Most dogs afflicted with atopy are multi-sensitive and are affected by something several months out of the year. Treatment is by antihistamines or systemic corticosteroids, or both.

— B —

BABESIA GIBSONI (or Babesiosis)—A parasitic disease of the tropics, reasonably rare in the U.S.A. to date. Blood tests can

Babichee of Hoonah, well-known lead dog of Hank Buege and one of the foundation sires of Windwillow and Snowbrier Kennels.

reveal its presence and like other parasitic infections the symptoms are loss of appetite, no pep, anemia and elevations in temperature as the disease advances, and enlarged spleen and liver are sometimes evident.

BALANITIS—The medical term for a constant discharge of pus from the penis which causes spotting of clothing or quarters or causes the dog to clean himself constantly. When bacteria gather at the end of the sheath, it causes irritations in the tissue and pus. If the condition becomes serious, the dog may be cauterized or ointment applied.

BLASTOMYCOSIS—A rare infectious disease involving the kidneys and liver. The animal loses its appetite and vomits. Laboratory examination is necessary to determine presence.

BRADYCARDIA—Abnormal slowness of the heartbeat and pulse.

BRONCHITIS—Inflammation of the mucus lining in the respiratory tract, the windpipe or trachea, and lungs. Dampness and cold are usually responsible and the symptoms usually follow a

The Siberian Husky Club of America Specialty Show held in conjunction with the South Shore Kennel Club in 1957 saw Best of Breed win go to Mrs. Nicholas Demidoff's Ch. Monadnock's Pando. Pictured at the left is Mrs. Betram D. Hulen with her Best of Opposite Sex winner, Monadnock's Belka. A William Brown photo.

chill, or may be present with cases of pneumonia or distemper. Symptoms are a nagging dry cough, fever, quickened pulse rate, runny nose, perhaps vomiting, and congested nasal passages which must be kept open. Old dogs are particularly affected. It is a highly transmissible disease and isolation from other animals is important. Antibiotics are given.

BRUCELLA CANIS—An infectious disease associated with abortion in bitches in the last quarter of gestation, sterility or stillbirths. A comparable is testicle trouble in male dogs. It is highly contagious and can be diagnosed through blood tests and animals having the infection should be isolated.

— C —

CANCER (tumors, neoplasia, etc.)—A growth of cells which serve no purpose is referred to as a cancer. The growth may be

Ch. Little Joe of North Wind, owned by Doris A. Knorr's North Wind Kennels, wins the Working Group at the Sheboygan Kennel Club show in 1962 under judge Frank Foster Davis. A Frasie Studio photo.

malignant or benign. Malignancy is the spreading type growth and may invade the entire body. Treatment, if the condition is diagnosed and caught in time, may be successful by surgical methods, drugs, or radioactive therapy. Haste in consulting your veterinarian cannot be urged too strongly.

CANKER (Otitis)—A bacterial infection of the ear where the ear may drain, have a dreadful odor, and ooze a dark brown substance all the way out to the ear flap. Cause of canker can be from mites, dirt, excessive hair growth in the ear canal, wax, etc. A daily cleaning and administering of antifungal ointment or powder are in order until the condition is cured. Symptoms are the dog shaking his head, scratching his ear and holding the head to the side.

CARIES—A pathologic change causing destruction of the enamel on teeth and subsequent invasion of the dentine; in other words, a cavity in a tooth. This may result in bad breath, toothache, digestive disorders, etc., depending upon the severity. Cavities in dogs are rare, though we hear more and more of false teeth being made for dogs and occasionally even root canal work for show dogs.

CASTRATION—Surgical removal of the male gonads or sex organs. An anesthesia is necessary and the animal must be watched for at least a week to see that hemorrhage does not occur. It is best performed at an early age — anywhere from three to nine months. Older dogs suffering from a hormonal imbalance or cancer of the gonads are castrated.

CATARACT—An opaque growth covering the lens of the eye. Surgical removal is the only treatment. Cataract may be a result of an injury to the eye or in some cases may be an inherited trait.

CELLULITIS—Inflammation of the loose subcutaneous tissue of the body. A condition which can be symptomatic of several other diseases.

CHEILITIS—Inflammation of the lips.

CHOLECYSTITIS—A condition affecting the gall bladder. The onset is usually during the time an animal is suffering from infectious canine hepatitis. Removal of the gall bladder, which thickens and becomes highly vascular, can effect a complete cure.

CHOREA—Brain damage as a result of distemper which has been severe is characterized by convulsive movements of the legs. It is progressive and if it affects the facial muscles, salivating or difficulty in eating or moving the jaws may be evident. Sedatives may bring relief, but this disease is incurable.

Ch. Arctic's Pretti, one of the brood bitches and show and sled dogs at Charlotte and Earl Reynolds Arctic Kennels in Dryden, Michigan.

Ch. Karnovanda's Ivan Groznyi, owned by the Karnovanda Kennels, Davisburg, Michigan.

One of the more recent homebreds at the Edward Fischers' Arahaz' Kennels pictured winning a three-point major on the way to the championship. This dark red and white dog later became Ch. Arahaz Red Rocket. Photo by Norton of Kent.

CHOROIDITIS—Inflammation of the choroid coat of the eye which is to be regarded as serious. Immediate veterinary inspection is required.

COCCIDIOSIS—An intestinal disease of parasitic nature and origin. Microscopic organisms reproduce on the walls of the intestinal tract and destroy tissue. Bloody diarrhea, loss of weight and appetite and general lethargy result. Presence of parasites is determined by fecal examination. Sulfur drugs are administered and a complete clean up of the premises is in order since the parasite is passed from one dog to another through floor surfaces or eating utensils.

COLOSTRUM—A secretion of the mammary glands for the first day or so after the bitch gives birth. It acts as a purgative for the young, and contains antibodies against distemper, hepatitis and other bacteria.

CONJUNCTIVITIS—Inflammation of the conjunctiva of the eye.

CONVULSIONS—A fit, or violent involuntary contractions of groups of muscles, accompanied by unconsciousness. They are in themselves a symptom of another disease, especially traceable to one affecting the brain; i.e., rabies, or an attack of encephalitis or distemper. It may also be the result of a heavy infestation of parasites or toxic poisonings. Care must be taken that the animal does not injure itself and a veterinarian must be consulted to determine and eliminate the cause.

CRYPTORCHID—A male animal in which neither testicle is present or descended. This condition automatically bars a dog from the show ring.

CYANOSIS—A definite blueness seen in and around the mucous membranes of the face; i.e. tongue, lips and eyes. It is usually synonymous with a circulatory obstruction or heart condition.

CYSTITIS—A disease of the urinary tract which is characterized by inflammation and/or infection in the bladder. Symptoms are straining, frequent urination with little results or with traces of blood, and perhaps a fever. Antibiotics, usually in the sulfur category, as well as antiseptics are administered. This is a condition which is of great discomfort to the animal and is of lengthy duration. Relief must be given by a veterinarian, who will empty bladder by means of catheter or medication to relax the bladder so that the urine may be passed.

— D —

DEMODECTIC MANGE—A skin condition caused by a parasitic mite, *Demodex,* living in hair follicles. This is a difficult condi-

Akalan's Kodiak Red, owned by Dean H. Warner and Michelle Yeoman, and bred by Dean and Dolores Warner at their Akalan Kennels in Livermore, California.

tion to get rid of and is treated internally as well as externally. It requires diligent care to free the animal of it entirely.

DERMATITIS—There are many forms of skin irritations and eruptions but perhaps the most common is "contact dermatitis." Redness and itching are present. The irritation is due to something the animal has been exposed to and to which it is allergic. The irritant must be identified and removed. Antihistamines and anti-inflammatory drugs are administered, and in severe cases sedatives or tranquilizers are prescribed to lessen the dog's scratching.

DIABETES (Insipidus)—A deficiency of antidiuretic hormone produced by the posterior pituitary gland. It occurs in older animals and is characterized by the animal's drinking excessive amounts of water and voiding frequently. Treatment is by periodic injection of antidiuretic drug for the rest of the animal's life.

DIABETES (Mellitus)—Sometimes referred to as sugar diabetes, this is a disorder of the metabolism of carbohydrates caused by lack of insulin production by the cells of the pancreas. Symptoms are the same as in the insipidus type, and in severe cases loss of weight, vomiting or coma may occur. Blood and urine analysis confirm its presence. It is treated by low carbohydrate diet, oral medication and/or insulin injections.

DIGITOXIN—A medication given to a dog with congestive heart failure. Dosage is, of course, adjusted to severeness of condition and size of the individual animal.

DISC ABNORMALITIES (Intervertebral)—Between each bone in the spine is a connecting structure called an intervertebral disc. When the disc between two vertebrae becomes irritated and protrudes into the spinal canal it forms lesions and is painful. (This is a disease which particularly affects the Dachshund because of its long back in comparison to length of legs.) Paralysis of the legs, reluctance to move, and loss of control of body functions may be symptoms. X-ray and physical examination will determine extent of the condition. Massage helps circulation and pain relievers may be prescribed. Surgery is sometimes successful and portable two-wheel carts which support the hindquarters help.

DISTEMPER—Highly transmissible disease of viral origin which spreads through secretions of nose, eyes or direct oral contact. May be fatal in puppies under 12 weeks. Symptoms of this disease are alternately high and low fevers, runny eyes and nose, loss of appetite and general lassitude, diarrhea and loss of

Inquisitive puppy at Synordik Kennels, owned by Drs. Richard and Cynthia Nist of Snohomish, Washington.

Running free! Kaylee Kittee Katek and Kaylee Kitkit Kulik have fun in their backyard. Owner Carolyn Windsor, Kaylee Kennels, Baltimore, Maryland.

weight. This disease sometimes goes into pneumonia or convulsions if the virus reaches the brain. Chorea may remain if infection has been severe or neglected. Antibiotics are administered and fluids and sedation may be advised by your veterinarian. If the dog has been inoculated, the disease may remain a light case, BUT it is not to be treated lightly. Warmth and rest are also indicated.

DROPSY—Abnormal accumulation of fluid in the tissues or body cavities. Also referred to as edema when accumulations manifest themselves below the skin. In the stomach region it is called ascites. Lack of exercise or poor circulation, particularly in older dogs, may be the cause. While the swellings are painless, excess accumulations in the stomach can cause digestive distress or heart disturbances, and may be associated with diabetes. Occasional diarrhea, lack of appetite, loss of wieght, exhaustion, emaciation and death may occur if the condition is not treated.

DYSGERMINOMA—A malignant ovarian tumor. Symptoms are fever, vaginal discharge, vomiting and diarrhea. Tumors vary in size, though more commonly are of the large size and from reports to date, the right ovary is more commonly affected. Radiotherapy may be successful; if not, surgery is required.

— E —

EAR MANGE—Otodectic mange, or parasitic otitis externa. Ear mites suck lymph fluids through the walls of the ear canal. Infections are high where mites are present and a brownish, horrible smelling ooze is present deep down in the canal all the way out to the flap where the secretion has a granular texture. The dog shakes his head, rubs and scrapes. In extreme cases convulsions or brain damage may result. The ear must be cleaned daily and drugs of an antibiotic and anti-inflammatory nature must be given.

ECLAMPSIA—A toxemia of pregnancy. Shortly before the time a bitch whelps her puppies, her milk may go bad. She will pant as a result of high fever, and go into convulsions. The puppies must be taken away from the mother immediately. This is usually the result of an extreme lack of calcium during pregnancy. Also known as milk fever.

ECTROPION—All breeders of dogs with drooping eyelids or exaggerated haws will be familiar with this condition, where the lower eyelid turns out. It can be a result of an injury, as well as hereditary in some breeds, but can be corrected surgically.

At rest is the very beautiful Ch. Alyeska's Chena of Chinook, owned by Mrs. Milton Seeley and captured on film by Judy Rosemarin.

Nina and Charles Schaefer with sons Paul and George pose with Windy Hills Piva for the charming photograph which adorned their Christmas card in 1972.

Donna Rosemarin with Ch. Chilka's Treska of Weldon, photographed by Donna's mother, Judy Rosemarin of Roslyn, New York.

Mrs. Lula Brattis and her Kheta of Casper. Mrs. Brattis' Kaspar Kennel is in Casper, Wyoming.

ECZEMA—Eczema is another form of skin irritation which may confine itself to redness and itching, or go all the way to a scaly skin surface or open wet sores. This is sometimes referred to as "hot spots." A hormone imbalance or actual diet deficiency may prevail. Find the cause and remove it. Medicinal baths and ointments usually provide a cure, but cure is a lengthy process and the condition frequently recurs.

EDEMA—Abnormal collection of fluids in the tissues of the body.

ELBOW DYSPLASIA—Term applies to a developmental abnormality of the elbow joints. It is hereditary.

EMPHYSEMA—Labored breathing caused by distended or ruptured lungs. May be acute or chronic and is not uncommon.

EMPYEMA—Accumulation of pus or purulent fluid, in a body cavity, resembling an abscess. Another term for pleurisy.

ENCEPHALITIS—Brain fever associated with meningitis. An inflammation of the brain caused by a virus, rabies or perhaps tuberculosis. It may also be caused by poisonous plants, bad food or lead poisoning. Dogs go "wild," running in circles, falling over, etc. Paralysis and death frequently result. Cure depends on extent of infection and speed with which it is diagnosed and treated.

ENDOCARDITIS—Inflammation and bacterial infection of the smooth membrane that lines the inside of the heart.

ENTERITIS—Intestinal inflammation of serious import. It can be massive or confine itself to one spot. Symptoms are diarrhea, bloody at times, vomiting, and general discomfort. Antibiotics are prescribed and fluids, if the diarrhea and vomiting have been excessive. Causes are varied; may follow distemper or other infections or bacterial infection through intestinal worms.

ENTROPION—A turning in of the margin of the eyelids. As a result, the eyelashes rub on the eyeball and cause irritation resulting in a discharge from the eye. Here again it is a condition peculiar to certain breeds — particularly Chow Chows — or may be the result of an injury which failed to heal properly. Infection may result as the dog will rub his eyes and cause a swelling. It is painful, but can be cured surgically.

ENTEROTOXEMIA—A result of toxins and gases in the intestine. As bacteria increase in the intestine, intermittent diarrhea and/or constipation results from maldigestion. If the infection reaches the kidney through the circulatory system, nephritis results. The digestive system must be cleaned out by use of castor oil or colonic irrigation, and outwardly by antibiotics.

EOSINOPHILIC MYOSITIS—Inflammation of the muscles dogs use for chewing. Persistent attacks usually lasting one or more weeks. They come and go over long periods of time, coming closer and closer together. Difficulty in swallowing, swelling of the face, or even the dog holding his mouth open will indicate the onset of an attack. Anti-inflammatory drugs are the only known treatment. Cause unknown, outlook grave.

EPILEPSY—The brain is the area affected and fits and/or convulsions may occur early or late in life. It cannot be cured; however, it can be controlled with medication. Said to be hereditary. Convulsions may be of short duration or the dog may just appear to be dazed. It is rarely fatal. Care must be taken to see that the dog does not injure itself during an attack.

EPIPHORA—A constant tearing which stains the face and fur of dogs. It is a bothersome condition which is not easily remedied either with outside medication or by surgical tear duct removal. There has been some success in certain cases reported from a liquid medication given with the food and prescribed by veterinarians. This condition may be caused by any one or more of a number of corneal irritations, such as nasal malfunction or the presence of foreign matter in the superficial gland of the third eyelid. After complete examination as to the specific cause, a veterinarian can decide whether surgery is indicated.

ESOPHAGEAL DIVERTICULUM—Inflammation or sac-like protrusions on the walls of the esophagus resembling small hernias. It is uncommon in dogs, but operable, and characterized by gagging, listlessness, temperature and vomiting in some cases.

— F —

FALSE PREGNANCY (or pseudopregnancy)—All the signs of the real thing are present in this heart-breaking and frustrating condition. The bitch may even go into false labor near the end of the 63-day cycle and build a nest for her hoped-for puppies. It may be confirmed by X-ray or a gentle feeling for them through the stomach area. Hormones can be injected to relieve the symptoms.

FROSTBITE—Dead tissue as a result of extreme cold. The tissues become red, swollen and painful, and may peel away later, causing open lesions. Ointments and protective coverings should be administered until irritation is alleviated.

FUSOSPIROCHETAL DISEASE—Bad breath is the first and most formidable symptom of this disease of the mouth affecting the gums. Bloody saliva and gingivitis or ulcers in the mouth may

Peekaboo! Ch. Arahaz' Tengri Khan takes a look around the corner at the Kaylee Kennels in Baltimore, Maryland. Photography by US.

The lovely Ch. Arahaz' Tengri Khan, five years old, sired by Ch. Toki of Rockrimmon *ex* Ch. Arahaz' Ebony Beauty. He is owned by Carolyn and Sue Windsor, Kaylee Kennels, Baltimore. Photography by US.

465

also be present, and the dog may be listless due to lack of desire to eat. Cleaning the teeth and gums daily with hydrogen peroxide in prescribed dosage by the veterinarian is required. Further diagnosis of the disease can be confirmed by microscopic examination of smears, though these fusiform bacteria might be present in the mouth of a dog which never becomes infected. Attempts to culture these anaerobes have been unsuccessful.

— G —

GASTRIC DILATION—This is an abnormal swelling of the abdomen due to gas or overeating. Consumption of large amounts of food especially if dry foods are eaten, and then large quantities of water make the dog "swell." The stomach twists so that both ends are locked off. Vomiting is impossible, breathing is hampered and the dog suffers pain until the food is expelled. Dogs that gulp their food and swallow air with it are most susceptible. Immediate surgery may be required to prevent the stomach from bursting. Commonly known as bloat.

GASTRITIS—Inflammation of the stomach caused by many things — spoiled food which tends to turn to gas, overeating, eating foreign bodies, chemicals or even worms. Vomiting is usually the first symptom though the animal will usually drink great quantities of water which more often than not it throws back up. A 24-hour fast which eliminates the cause is the first step toward cure. If vomiting persists chunks of ice cubes put down the throat may help. Hopefully the dog will lick them himself. Keep the dog on a liquid diet for another 24 hours before resuming his regular meals.

GASTRO-ENTERITIS—Inflammation of the stomach and intestines. There is bleeding and ulceration in the stomach and this serious condition calls for immediate veterinary help.

GASTRODUODENITIS—Inflammation of the stomach and duodenum.

GINGIVITIS or gum infection—Badly tartared teeth are usually the cause of this gum infection characterized by swelling, redness at the gum line, bleeding and bloody saliva. Bad breath also. Improper diet may be a cause of it. Feeding of only soft foods as a steady diet allows the tartar to form and to irritate the gums. To effect a cure, clean the teeth and perhaps the veterinarian will also recommend antibiotics.

GLAUCOMA—Pressure inside the eyeball builds up, the eyeball becomes hard and bulgy and a cloudiness of the entire corneal area occurs. The pupil is dilated and the eye is extremely sensi-

American and Canadian Ch. Chuchi of Anadyr, pictured winning in the show ring. Harry and Velma Wade, Chu-Nik Kennels, Amboy, Washington.

A family portrait: Sy Goldberg and his children David, Gerri Lynn and Steven. The grown dogs are Ch. Koryaks Black Charger, American and Canadian Ch. Tanya of Cinnaminson and Ch. Tokco of Bolshoi. Sy and his wife Ann own the Cinnaminson Kennels in Cream Ridge, New Jersey.

tive. Blindness is inevitable unless treatment is prompt at the onset of the disease. Cold applications as well as medical prescriptions are required with also the possibility of surgery, though with no guarantee of success.

GLOSSITIS—Inflammation of the tongue.

GOITER—Enlargement of the thyroid gland, sometimes requiring surgery. In minor cases, medication — usually containing iodine — is administered.

— H —

HARELIP—A malformation of the upper lip characterized by a cleft palate. Difficulty in nursing in exaggerated cases can result in starvation or puny development. Operations can be performed late in life.

HEART DISEASE—Heart failure is rare in young dogs, but older dogs which show an unusual heavy breathing after exercise or are easily tired may be victims of heart trouble, and an examination is in order. As it grows worse, wheezing, coughing or gasping may be noticed. Other symptoms indicating faulty circulation may manifest themselves as the animal retains more body fluids as the circulation slows down. Rest, less exercise, and non-fattening diets are advised and medication to remove excess fluids from the body are prescribed. In many cases, doses of digitalis may be recommended.

HEARTWORM *(Dirofilaria immitis)*—This condition does not necessarily debilitate a working dog or a dog that is extremely active. It is diagnosed by a blood test and a microscopic examination to determine the extent of the microfilariae. If positive, further differentials are made for comparison with other microfilariae. Treatment consists of considerable attention to the state of nutrition, and liver and kidney functions are watched closely in older dogs. Medication is usually treatment other than surgery and consists of dithiazine iodine therapy over a period of two weeks. Anorexia and/or fever may occur and supplemental vitamins and minerals may be indicated. Dogs with heavy infestations are observed for possible foreign protein reaction from dying and decomposing worms, and are watched for at least three months.

HEATSTROKE—Rapid breathing, dazed condition, vomiting, temperature, and collapse in hot weather indicate heatstroke. It seems to strike older dogs especially if they are overweight or have indulged in excessive activity. Reduce body temperature immediately by submerging dog in cold water, apply ice packs, cold enemas, etc. Keep dog cool and quiet for at least 24 hours.

Ch. Fra-Mar's Aja-Tu Diavol, beautiful bitch owned by Marie Wamser, Fra-Mar's Kennels in Cleveland, Ohio, pictured winning under judge Phil Marsh on the way to her championship. Handler is George Heitzman. Frank photograph. Aja-Tu had champions in three of her litters and finished for her championship in five shows in six weeks and at nine months of age.

Two magnificent Siberian Huskies, Blueie of Chinook and Mina of Monadnock. Photo by Percy T. Jones.

HEMATOMA—A pocket of blood that may collect in the ear as a result of an injury or the dog's scratching. Surgery is required to remove the fluid and return skin to cartilage by stitching.

HEMOPHILIA—Excessive bleeding on the slightest provocation. Only male subjects are susceptible and it is a hereditary disease passed on by females. Blood coagulants are now successfully used in certain cases.

HEPATITIS, Infectious canine—This disease of viral nature enters the body through the mouth and attacks primarily the liver. Puppies are the most susceptible to this disease and run a fever and drink excessive amounts of water. Runny eyes, nose, vomiting, and general discomfort are symptoms. In some cases blood builders or even blood transfusions are administered since the virus has a tendency to thin the blood. This depletion of the blood often leaves the dog open to other types of infection and complete recovery is a lengthy process. Antibiotics are usually given and supplemental diet and blood builders are a help. Vaccination for young puppies is essential.

HERNIA (diaphragmatic)—An injury is usually responsible for this

Ch. Arctic's Starfire finishing for his title at the Toledo Kennel Club Show in 1972. He was sired by Ch. Arctic's Star Tygre, *ex* Innisfree's Miska and is owned by Charlotte and Earl Reynolds of the Artic Kennels in Dryden, Michigan. Photo by Ritter.

separation or break in the wall of diaphragm. Symptoms depend on severity; breathing may become difficult, there is some general discomfort or vomiting. X-rays can determine the extent of damage and the only cure is surgery.

HERNIA (umbilical)—Caused by a portion of the abdominal viscera protruding through a weak spot near the navel. Tendency toward hernia is said to be largely hereditary.

HIP DYSPLASIA or HD is a wearing away of the ball and socket of the hip joint. It is a hereditary disease. The symptoms of this bone abnormality are a limp and an awkwardness in raising or lowering the body. X-ray will establish severity and it is wise in buying or selling a dog of any breed to insist on a radiograph to prove the animal is HD clear. The condition can be detected as early as three months and if proven the dog should have as little exercise as possible. There is no cure for this condition. Only pain relievers can be given for the more severe cases. No animal with HD should be used for breeding.

HOOKWORM—Hookworms lodge in the small intestines and suck blood from the intestinal wall. Anemia results from loss of blood. Loss of weight, pale gums, and general weakness are symptoms. Microscopic examination of the feces will determine presence. Emphasis on diet improvement and supplements to build up the blood is necessary and, of course, medication for the eradication of the hookworms. This can be either oral or by veterinary injection.

HYDROCEPHALUS—A condition also known as "water head" since a large amount of fluid collects in the brain cavity, usually before birth. This may result in a difficult birth and the young are usually born dead or die shortly thereafter. Euthanasia is recommended on those that do survive since intelligence is absent and violence to themselves or to others is liable to occur.

HYDRONEPHROSIS—Due to a cystic obstruction the kidney collects urine which cannot be passed through the ureter into the bladder, causing the kidney to swell (sometimes to five times its normal size) and giving pain in the lumbar region. The kidney may atrophy, if the condition goes untreated.

— I —

ICHTHYOSIS—A skin condition over elbows and hocks. Scaliness and cracked skin cover the area particularly that which comes in contact with hard surfaces. Lubricating oils well rubbed into the skin and keeping the animal on soft surfaces are solutions.

IMPETIGO—Skin disease seen in puppies infested by worms, distemper, or teething problems. Little soft pimples cover the surface of the skin. Sulfur ointments and ridding the puppy of the worms are usually sufficient cure as well.

INTERDIGITAL CYSTS—Growths usually found in the legs. They are painful and cause the dog to favor the paw or not walk on it at all. Surgery is the only cure and antibiotic ointments to keep dirt and infection out are necessary.

INTESTINAL OBSTRUCTIONS—When a foreign object becomes lodged in the intestines and prevents passage of stool constipation results from the blockage. Hernia is another cause of obstruction or stoppage. Pain, vomiting, loss of appetite are

Must be a full moon! This Siberian Husky puppy, owned by dog photographer Thomas McLaughlin of Morrison, Colorado, lets the world know it in no uncertain terms!

symptoms. Fluids, laxatives or enemas should be given to remove blockage. Surgery may be necessary after X-ray determines cause. Action must be taken since death may result from long delay or stoppage.

IRITIS—Inflammation of the iris or colored part of the eye. May be caused by the invasion of foreign bodies or other irritants.

— J —

JAUNDICE—A yellow discoloration of the skin. Liver malfunction causes damage by bile seeping into the circulatory system and being dispensed into the body tissue, causing discoloration of the skin. It may be caused by round worms, liver flukes or gall stones. It may be either acute or chronic and the animal loses ambition, convulses or vomits, sometimes to excess. It may be cured once the cause has been eliminated. Neglect can lead to death.

— K —

KERATITIS—Infection of the cornea of the eye. Distemper or hepatitis may be a cause. Sensitivity to light, watery discharge and pain are symptomatic. Treatment depends on whether the lesion is surface irritation or a puncture of the cornea. Warm compresses may help until the veterinarian prescribes the final treatment. Sedatives or tranquilizers may be prescribed to aid in preventing the dog from rubbing the eye.

KIDNEY WORM—The giant worm that attacks the kidney and kidney tissue. It can reach a yard in length. The eggs of this rare species of worm are passed in the dog's urine rather than the feces. These worms are found in raw fish. It is almost impossible to detect them until at least one of the kidneys is completely destroyed or an autopsy reveals its presence. There is no known cure at this point and, therefore, the only alternative is not to feed raw fish.

— L —

LEAD POISONING—Ingestion of lead-based paints or products such as linoleum containing lead is serious. Symptoms are vomiting, behavior changes and/or hysteria or even convulsions in severe cases. It can be cured by medication if caught early enough. Serious damage can be done to the central nervous system. Blood samples are usually taken to determine amount in the blood. Emetics may be required if heavy intake is determined.

LEPTOSPIROSIS—This viral infection is dangerous and bothersome because if affects many organs of the body before lodging itself in the kidneys. Incubation is about two weeks after exposure to the urine of another affected dog. Temperature, or subtemperature, pain and stiffness in the hindquarters are not uncommon, nor is vomiting. Booster shots after proper vaccination at a young age are usually preventative, but once afflicted, antibiotics are essential to cure.

LOCKJAW (tetanus)—Death rate is very high in this bacterial disease. Puncture wounds may frequently develop into lockjaw. Symptoms are severe. As the disease progresses high fever and stiffness in the limbs become serious though the dog does not lose consciousness. Sedatives must be given to help relax the muscles and dispel the spasms. When the stiffness affects the muscles of the face, intravenous feeding must be provided. If a cure is effected, it is a long drawn out affair. Lockjaw bacteria are found in soil and in the feces of animals and humans.

Ch. Arahaz Astrakhan pictured at ten months of age. Astrakhan is owned by the Edward Fischers, Arahaz Kennels, Canonsburg, Pennsylvania.

LYMPHOMA (Hodgkins disease)—Malignant lymphoma most frequently is found in dogs under four years of age, affects the lymph glands, liver and spleen. Anorexia and noticeable loss of weight are apparent as well as diarrhea. Depending on area and organ, discharge may be present. The actual neoplasm or tumorous growth may be surrounded by nodules or neoplastic tissue which should be surgically removed under anesthesia.

— M —

MAMMARY NEOPLASMS—25 per cent of all canine tumors are of mammary origin. About half of all reported cases are benign. They are highly recurrent and, when cancerous, fatalities are high. Age or number of litters has nothing to do with the condition itself or the seriousness.

MANGE—The loss of a patch of hair usually signals the onset of mange, which is caused by any number of types of microscopic mites. The veterinarian will usually take scrapings to determine which of the types it is. Medicated baths and dips plus internal and external medication is essential as it spreads rapidly and with care can be confined to one part of the body. Antibiotics are prescribed.

MASTITIS (mammary gland infection)—After the birth of her young, a bitch may be beset by an infection causing inflammation of the mammary glands which produce milk for the puppies. Soreness and swelling make it painful for her when the puppies nurse. Abscess may form and she will usually run a fever. Hot compresses and antibiotics are necessary and in some instances hormone therapy.

MENINGITIS—Inflammation affecting the membranes covering the brain and/or spinal cord. It is a serious complication which may result from a serious case of distemper, tuberculosis, hardpad, head injury, etc. Symptoms are delirium, restlessness, high temperature, and dilated pupils in the eyes. Paralysis and death are almost certain.

METRITIS—This infection, or inflammation of the uterus, causes the dog to exude a bloody discharge. Vomiting and a general lassitude are symptoms. Metritis can occur during the time the bitch is in season or right after giving birth. Antibiotics are used, or in severe cases hysterectomy.

MONORCHIDISM—Having only one testicle.

MOTION SICKNESS—On land, on sea, or in the air, your dog may be susceptible to motion sickness. Yawning, or excessive salivation, may signal the onset, and there is eventual vomiting.

Ch. Dovercrest Alehta Pesna, owned by Mrs. Rift Fournier of Atlantic Highlands, New Jersey. E.H. Frank photo.

Ch. Cinnaminson's Soaya Fournier, co-owned by Sy and Ann Goldberg and Jean Fournier, is pictured here winning first in the Working Group at the Kennel Club of Northern New Jersey in March, 1972 under judge Virginia Hampton. William P. Gilbert photo.

One or all of the symptoms may be present and recovery is miraculously fast once the motion ceases. Antinauseant drugs are available for animals which do not outgrow this condition.

MYELOMA—Tumor of the bone marrow. Lameness and evidence of pain are symptoms as well as weight loss, depression and palpable tumor masses. Anemia or unnatural tendency to bleed in severe cases may be observed. The tumors may be detected radiographically, but no treatment has yet been reported for the condition.

— N —

NEONATAL K-9 HERPESVIRUS INFECTION—Though K-9 herpesvirus infection, or CHV, has been thought to be a disease of the respiratory system in adult dogs, the acute necrotizing and hemorraghic disease occurs only in infant puppies. The virus multiplies in the respiratory system and female genital tracts of older dogs. Puppies may be affected in the vaginal canal. Unfortunately the symptoms resemble other neonatal infections, even hepatitis, and only after autopsy can it be detected.

NEPHROTIC SYNDROME—Symptoms may be moist or suppurative dermatitis, edema or hypercholesteremia. It is a disease of the liver and may be the result of another disease. Laboratory data and biopsies may be necessary to determine the actual cause if it is other than renal disease. This is a relatively uncommon thing in dogs, and liver and urinal function tests are made to determine its presence.

NEURITIS—Painful inflammation of a nerve.

NOSEBLEED (epistaxis)—A blow or other injury which causes injury to the nasal tissues is usually the cause. Tumors, parasites, foreign bodies, such as thorns or burs or quills, may also be responsible. Ice packs will help stem the tide of blood, though coagulants may also be necessary. Transfusions in severe cases may be indicated.

— O —

ORCHITIS—Inflammation of the testes.

OSTEOGENESIS IMPERFECTA—or "brittle bones" is a condition that can be said to be both hereditary and dietary. It may be due to lack of calcium or phosphorus or both. Radiographs show "thin" bones with deformities throughout the skeleton. Treatment depends on cause.

OSTEOMYELITIS (enostosis)—Bone infection may develop after a bacterial contamination of the bone, such as from a compound fracture. Pain and swelling denote the infection and wet sores

Fireside's Miss Scandia pictured "sitting pretty" at just five weeks of age. Owners, Mr. and Mrs. Andrew Rossetto, Fireside Kennels, Walled Lake, Michigan.

American and Canadian Ch. Lostland's Leading Lady pictured winning under judge Dr. W. Shute at a recent show. Lady is handled by Miss Diane Rossetto, whose parents own the Fireside Kennels in Walled Lake, Michigan. Norton of Kent photo.

may accompany it. Lack of appetite, fever and general inactivity can be expected. Antibiotics are advised after X-ray determines severity. Surgery eliminates dead tissue or bone splinters to hasten healing.

OTITIS—Inflammation of the ear.

— P —

PANCREATITIS—It is difficult to palpate for the pancreas unless it is enlarged, which it usually is if this disease is present. Symptoms to note are as in other gastronomic complaints such as vomiting, loss of appetite, anorexia, stomach pains and general listlessness. This is a disease of older dogs though it has been diagnosed in young dogs as well. Blood, urine and stool examination and observation of the endocrine functions of the dog are in order. Clinical diseases that may result from a serious case of pancreatitis are acute pancreatitis which involves a complete degeneration of the pancreas, atrophy, fibrous and/or neoplasia, cholecystitis. Diabetes mellitus is also a possibility.

PATELLAR LUXATION—"Trick knees" are frequent in breeds that have been "bred down" from Standard to Toy size, and is a condition where the knee bone slips out of position. It is an off again, on again condition that can happen as a result of a jump or excessive exercise. If it is persistent, anti-inflammatory drugs may be given or in some cases surgery can correct it.

PERITONITIS—Severe pain accompanies this infection or inflammation of the lining of the abdominal cavity. Extreme sensitivity to touch, loss of appetite and vomiting occur. Dehydration and weight loss is rapid and anemia is a possibility. Antibiotics should kill the infection and a liquid diet for several days is advised. Painkillers may be necessary or drainage tubes in severe cases.

PHLEBITIS—Inflammation of a vein.

PLACENTA—The afterbirth which accompanies and has been used to nourish the fetus. It is composed of three parts; the chorion, amnion, and allantois.

POLYCYTHEMIA VERA—A disease of the blood causing an elevation of hemoglobin concentration. Blood-letting has been effective. The convulsions that typify the presence can be likened to epileptic fits and last for several minutes. The limbs are stiff and the body feels hot. Mucous membranes are congested, the dog may shiver, and the skin has a ruddy discoloration. Blood samples must be taken and analyzed periodically. If medication to reduce the production of red blood cells is given, it usually means the dog will survive.

The exotic Ch. Karnovanda's Wolfgang, owned by Judith M. Russell, Karnovanda Kennels, Davisburg, Michigan.

PROCTITIS—Inflammation of the rectum.

PROSTATITIS—Inflammation of the prosate gland.

PSITTACOSIS—This disease which affects birds and people has been diagnosed in rare instances in dogs. A soft, persistent cough indicates the dog has been exposed, and a radiograph will show a cloudy portion on the affected areas of the lung. Antibiotics such as aureomycin have been successful in the known cases and cure has been effected in two to three weeks' time. This is a highly contagious disease, to the point where it can be contracted during a post mortem.

PYOMETRA—This uterine infection presents a discharge of pus from the uterus. High fever may turn to below normal as the infection persists. Lack of appetite with a desire for fluids and frequent urination are evidenced. Antibiotics and hormones are known cures. In severe cases, hysterectomy is done.

— R —

RABIES (hydrophobia)—The most deadly of all dog diseases. The Pasteur treatment is the only known cure for humans. One of the viral diseases that affects the nervous system and damages the brain. It is contracted by the intake, through a bite or cut, of saliva from an infected animal. It takes days or even months for the symptoms to appear, so it is sometimes difficult to locate, or isolate, the source. There are two reactions in a dog to this disease. In the paralytic rabies the dog can't swallow and salivates from a drooping jaw, and progressive paralysis eventually overcomes the entire body. The animal goes into coma and eventually dies. In the furious type of rabies the dog turns vicious, eats strange objects, in spite of a difficulty in swallowing, foams at the mouth, and searches out animals or people to attack—hence the expression "mad dog." Vaccination is available for dogs that run loose. Examination of the brain is necessary to determine actual diagnosis.

RECTAL PROLAPSE—Diarrhea, straining from constipation or heavy infestations of parasites are the most common cause of prolapse which is the expulsion of a part of the rectum through the anal opening. It is cylindrical in shape, and must be replaced within the body as soon as possible to prevent damage. Change in diet, medication to eliminate the cause, etc. will effect a cure.

RETINAL ATROPHY—A disease of the eye that is highly hereditary and may be revealed under ophthalmoscopic examination. Eventual blindness inevitably results. Dogs with retinal atrophy should not be used for breeding. Particularly prominent in certain breeds 'where current breeding trends have tended to change the shape of the head.

RHINITIS—Acute or chronic inflammation of the mucous membranes of the nasal passages. It is quite common in both dogs and cats. It is seldom fatal, but requires endless "nursing" on the part of the owner for survival, since the nose passages must be kept open so the animal will eat. Dry leather on the nose though there is excessive discharge, high fever, sneezing, etc., are symptoms. Nose discharge may be bloody and the animal will refuse to eat, making it listless. The attacks may be recurrent and medication must be administered.

Beautiful Siberian Husky expression on the face of Arahaz' Kaylee Konkon, 2½-year-old dog owned by Mrs. Carolyn McDonough Windsor of Baltimore, Maryland. Konkon was sired by Ch. Arahaz' Tengri Khan *ex* Arahaz' Ilka and was captured on film by "Photography by US."

RICKETS—The technical name for rickets is osteomalacia and is due to not enough calcium in the body. The bones soften and the legs become bowed or deformed. Rickets can be cured if caught in early stages by improvement in diet.

RINGWORM—The dread of the dog and cat world! This is a fungus disease where the hair falls out in circular patches. It spreads rapidly and is most difficult to get rid of entirely. Drugs must be administered "inside and out!" The cure takes many weeks and much patience. Ultraviolet lights will show hairs green in color so it is wise to have your animal, or new puppy, checked out by the veterinarian for this disease before introducing him to the household. It is contracted by humans.

ROOT CANAL THERAPY—Injury to a tooth may be treated by prompt dental root canal therapy which involves removal of damaged or necrotic pulp and placing of opaque filling material in the root canal and pulp chamber.

— S —

SALIVARY CYST—Surgery is necessary when the salivary gland becomes clogged or non-functional, causing constant salivation. A swelling becomes evident under the ear or tongue. Surgery will release the accumulation of saliva in the duct of the salivary gland, though it is at times necessary to remove the salivary gland in its entirety. Zygomatic salivary cysts are usually a result of obstructions in the four main pairs of salivary glands in the mouth. Infection is more prevalent in the parotid of the zygomatic glands located at the rear of the mouth, lateral to the last upper molars. Visual symptoms may be protruding eyeballs, pain when moving the jaw, or a swelling in the roof of the mouth. If surgery is necessary, it is done under general anesthesia and the obstruction removed by dissection. Occasionally, the zygomatic salivary gland is removed as well. Stitches or drainage tubes may be necessary or dilation of the affected salivary gland. Oral or internal antibiotics may be administered.

SCABIES—Infection from a skin disease caused by a sarcoptic mange mite.

SCURF (dandruff)—A scaly condition of the body in areas covered with hair. Dead cells combined with dried sweat and sebaceous oil gland materials.

SEBORRHEA—A skin condition also referred to as "stud tail," though studding has nothing to do with the condition. The sebaceous or oil-forming glands are responsible. Accumulation of dry skin, or scurf, is formed by excessive oily deposits while the hair becomes dry or falls out altogether.

SEPTICEMIA—When septic organisms invade the bloodstream, it is called septicemia. Severe cases are fatal as the organisms in the blood infiltrate the tissues of the body and all the body organs are affected. Septicemia is the result of serious wounds, especially joints and bones. Abscess may form. High temperature and/or shivering may herald the onset, and death occurs shortly thereafter since the organisms reproduce and spread rapidly Close watch on all wounds, antibiotics and sulfur drugs are usually prescribed.

SHOCK (circulatory collapse)—The symptoms and severity of shock vary with the cause and nervous system of the individual dog. Severe accident, loss of blood, and heart failure are the most common cause. Keep the dog warm, quiet and get him to a veterinarian right away. Symptoms are vomiting, rapid pulse, thirst, diarrhea, "cold, clammy feeling" and then eventually physical collapse. The veterinarian might prescribe plasma transfusion, fluids, perhaps oxygen, if pulse continues to be too rapid. Tranquilizers and sedatives are sometimes used as well as antibiotics and steroids. Relapse is not uncommon, so the animal must be observed carefully for several days after initial shock.

SINUSITIS—Inflammation of a sinus gland that inhibits breathing.

SNAKEBITE—The fact must be established as to whether the bite was poisonous or non-poisonous. A horse-shoe shaped double row of toothmarks is a non-poisonous bite. A double, or two-hole puncture, is a poisonous snake bite. Many veterinarians now carry anti-venom serum and this must be injected intramuscularly almost immediately. The veterinarian will probably inject a tranquilizer and other antibiotics as well. It is usually a four-day wait before the dog is normal once again, and the swelling completely gone. During this time the dog should be kept on medication.

SPIROCHETOSIS—Diarrhea which cannot be checked through normal anti-diarrhea medication within a few days may indicate spirochetosis. While spirochete are believed by some authorities to be present and normal to gastrointestinal tracts, unexplainable diarrhea may indicate its presence in great numbers. Large quantities could precipitate diarrhea by upsetting the normal balance of the organ, though it is possible for some dogs which are infected to have no diarrhea at all.

SPONDYLITIS—Inflammation and loosening of the vertebrae.

STOMATITIS—Mouth infection. Bleeding or swollen gums or excessive salivation may indicate this infection. Dirty teeth are usually the cause. Antibiotics and vitamin therapy are indicated; and, of course, scraping the teeth to eliminate the original cause. See also GINGIVITIS.

STRONGYLIDOSIS—Disease caused by strongle worms that enter the body through the skin and lodge in the wall of the small

At the Specialty Show of the Siberian Husky Club of America in Wellesley, Massachusetts in May, 1958, judge Mrs. Milton Seeley gave Best of Breed to Ch. Monadnock's Pando, handled by William Trainer. This was a repeat win for Pando, who also captured this top award at the 1957 show. Best of Opposite Sex win was also a repeat of last year, Ch. Monadnock's Belka, owned by Mrs. Bertram D. Hulen.

intestine. Bloody diarrhea, stunted growth, and thinness are general symptoms, as well as shallow breathing. Heavy infestation or neglect leads to death. Isolation of an affected animal and medication will help eliminate the problem, but the premises must also be cleaned thoroughly since the eggs are passed through the feces.

SUPPOSITORY—A capsule comprised of fat or glycerine introduced into the rectum to encourage defecation. A paper match with the ignitible sulfur end torn off may also be used. Medicated suppositories are also used to treat inflammation of the intestine.

TACHYCARDIA—An abnormal acceleration of the heartbeat. A rapid pulse signaling a disruption in the heart action. Contact a veterinarian at once.

TAPEWORM—There are many types of tapeworms, the most common being the variety passed along by the flea. It is a white, segmented worm which lives off the wall of the dog's intestine and keeps growing by segments. Some of these are passed and can be seen in the stool or adhering to the hairs on the rear areas of the dog or even in his bedding. It is a difficult worm to get rid of since, even if medication eliminates segments, the head may remain in the intestinal wall to grow again. Symptoms are virtually the same as for other worms: Debilitation, loss of weight, occasional diarrhea, and general listlessness. Medication and treatment should be under the supervision of a veterinarian.

TETANUS (lockjaw)—A telarius bacillus enters the body through an open wound and spreads where the air does not touch the wound. A toxin is produced and affects the nervous system, particularly the brain or spine. The animal exhibits a stiffness, slows down considerably and the legs may be extended out beyond the body even when the animal is in a standing position. The lips have a twisted appearance. Recovery is rare. Tetanus is not common in dogs, but it can result from a bad job of tail docking or ear cropping, as well as from wounds received by stepping on rusty nails.

THALLOTOXICOSIS or thallium poisoning—Thallium sulfate is a cellular-toxic metal used as a pesticide or rodenticide and a ready cause of poisoning in dogs. Thallium can be detected in the urine by a thallium spot test or by spectrographic analysis by the veterinarian. Gastrointestinal disturbances signal the onset with vomiting, diarrhea, anorexia, stomach cramps. Sometimes a cough or difficulty in breathing occurs. Other intestinal disorders may also manifest themselves as well as convulsions. In mild cases the disease may be simply a skin eruption, depending upon the damage to the kidneys. Enlarged spleens edema or nephrosis can develop. Antibiotics and a medication called dimercaprol are helpful, but the mortality rate is over 50 per cent.

THROMBUS—A clot in the blood vessel or the heart.

TICK PARALYSIS—Seasonal attacks of ticks or heavy infestations of ticks can result in a dangerous paralysis. Death is a distinct reality at this point and immediate steps must be taken to pre-

Marlytuk's Red Kawik of Kiska, owned by Vincent Buoniello, Jr. of Long Island, New York. Photograph by Judy Rosemarin.

vent total paralysis. The onset is observed usually in the hindquarters. Lack of coordination, a reluctance to walk, and difficulty in getting up can be observed. Complete paralysis kills when infection reaches the respiratory system. The paralysis is the result of the saliva of the tick excreted as it feeds.

TOAD POISONING—Some species of toads secrete a potent toxin. If while chasing a toad your dog takes it in his mouth, more than likely the toad will release this toxin from its parotid glands which will coat the mucous membranes of the dog's throat. The dog will salivate excessively, suffer prostration, cardiac arrhythmia. Some tropical and highly toxic species cause convulsions that result in death. Caught in time, there are certain drugs that can be used to counteract the dire effects. Try washing the dog's mouth with large amounts of water and get him to a veterinarian quickly.

TONSILLECTOMY—Removal of the tonsils. A solution called epinephrine, injected at the time of surgery, makes excessive bleeding almost a thing of the past in this otherwise routine operation.

TOXEMIA—The presence of toxins in the bloodstream, which normally should be eliminated by the excretory organs.

TRICHIASIS—A diseased condition of the eyelids, the result of neglect of earlier infection or inflammation.

Say "Ah-h-h-h!" Mother and puppy belonging to Dr. Richard and Dr. Cynthia Nist of Snohomish, Washington.

Ch. Arahaz' Tengri Khan, owned by Mrs. Carolyn Windsor, Kaylee Kennels, Baltimore, Maryland. Photo by Earl Graham.

A magnificent head study of Ch. Cinnaminson's Soaya Fournier, owned by Sy and Ann Goldberg, Cream Ridge, New Jersey.

A jubilant winner, Sy Goldberg, and his six-month-old Soaya after winning Best Puppy in Match.

Eu Mor quadruplets sired by Ch. Eu Mor's Kiev, C.D., *ex* Ch. Eu Mor's Taiga, and owned by Eunice Moreno and Lynne Witkinq of Central Islip, New York.

— U —

UREMIA—When poisonous materials remain in the body, because they are not eliminated through the kidneys, and are recirculated in the bloodstream. A nearly always fatal disease — sometimes within hours — preceded by convulsions and unconsciousness. Veterinary care and treatment are urgent and imperative.

URINARY BLADDER RUPTURE—Injury or pelvic fractures are the most common causes of a rupture in this area. Anuria usually occurs in a few days when urine backs up into the stomach area. Stomach pains are characteristic and a radiograph will determine the seriousness. Bladder is flushed with saline solution and surgery is usually required. Quiet and little exercise is recommended during recovery.

— V —

VENTRICULOCORDECTOMY—Devocalization of dogs, also known as aphonia. In diseases of the larynx this operation may be used. Portions of the vocal cords are removed by manual means or by electrocautery. Food is wittheld for a day prior to surgery and premedication is administered. Food is again provided 24 hours after the operation. At the end of three or four

Fireside's Little Big Man, owned by the A. Rosettos, Fireside Kennels, Walled Lake, Michigan.

Ch. Baron of Karnovanda, C.D., pictured winning at a recent show. Baron is owned by the Karnovanda Kennels in Davisburg, Michigan. E.H. Frank photo.

Wamser's Cara Mia pictured at three months of age. This beautiful and exotic little bitch grew up to be a champion owned by the Weydigs and bred by the Alakazan Kennels.

months, scar tissue develops and the dog is able to bark in a subdued manner. Complications from surgery are few, but the psychological effects on the animal are to be reckoned with. Suppression of the barking varies from complete to merely muted, depending on the veterinarian's ability and each individual dog's anatomy.

— W —

WHIPWORMS—Parasites that inhabit the large intestine and the cecum. Two to three inches in length, they appear "whip-like" and symptoms are diarrhea, loss of weight, anemia, restlessness or even pain, if the infestation is heavy enough. Medication is best prescribed by a veterinarian. Cleaning of the kennel is essential, since infestation takes place through the mouth. Whipworms reach maturity within thirty days after intake.

CHAPTER 25

GLOSSARY OF DOG TERMS

ACHILLES HEEL—The major tendon attaching the muscle of the calf from the thigh to the hock

AKC—The American Kennel Club. Address; 51 Madison Avenue, N.Y., N.Y. 10010

ALBINO—Pigment deficiency, usually a congenital fault, which renders skin, hair and eyes pink

AMERICAN KENNEL CLUB—Registering body for canine world in the United States. Headquarters for the stud book, dog registrations, and federation of kennel clubs. They also create and enforce the rules and regulations governing dog shows in the U.S.A.

ALMOND EYE—The shape of the eye opening, rather than the eye itself, which slants upwards at the outer edge, hence giving it an almond shape

ANUS—Anterior opening found under the tail for purposes of alimentary canal elimination

ANGULATION—The angles formed by the meeting of the bones

APPLE-HEAD—An irregular roundedness of topskull. A domed skull

APRON—On long-coated dogs, the longer hair that frills outward from the neck and chest

BABBLER—Hunting dog that barks or howls while out on scent

BALANCED—A symmetrical, correctly proportioned animal; one with correct balance with one part in regard to another

BARREL—Rounded rib section; thorax; chest

BAT EAR—An erect ear, broad at base, rounded or semicircular at top, with opening directly in front

BAY—The howl or bark of the hunting dog

BEARD—Profuse whisker growth

BEAUTY SPOT—Usually roundish colored hair on a blaze of another color. Found mostly between the ears

BEEFY—Overdevelopment or overweight in a dog, particularly hindquarters

BELTON—A color designation particularly familiar to Setters. An intermingling of colored and white hairs

BITCH—The female dog

BLAZE—A type of marking. White strip running up the center of the face between the eyes

BLOCKY—Square head

BLOOM—Dogs in top condition are said to be "in full bloom"

BLUE MERLE—A color designation. Blue and gray mixed with black. Marbled-like appearance

BOSSY—Overdevelopment of the shoulder muscles

BRACE—Two dogs which move as a pair in unison

BREECHING—Tan-colored hair on inside of the thighs

BRINDLE—Even mixture of black hairs with brown, tan or gray

BRISKET—The forepart of the body below the chest

BROKEN COLOR—A color broken by white or another color

BROKEN-HAIRED—A wiry coat

BROKEN-UP FACE—Receding nose together with deep stop, wrinkle, and undershot jaw

Ch. Satan of Big Trail winning under judge Howard Tyler. Satan is handled by his owner, Herbert Hitchcock of the Big Trail Kennels, Holly, Michigan.

American and Canadian Ch. Arctic's Storm Frost, pictured winning at a show in 1969 under judge Melbourne Downing. Storm is owned by Charlotte and Earl Reynolds, Arctic Kennels, Dryden, Michigan. Mrs. Reynolds is shown handling.

BROOD BITCH—A female used for breeding

BRUSH—A bushy tail

BURR—Inside part of the ear which is visible to the eye

BUTTERFLY NOSE—Parti-colored nose or entirely flesh color

BUTTON EAR—The edge of the ear which folds to cover the opening of the ear

CANINE—Animals of the Canidae family which includes not only dogs but foxes, wolves, and jackals

CANINES—The four large teeth in the front of the mouth often referred to as fangs

CASTRATE—The surgical removal of the testicles on the male dog

CAT-FOOT—Round, tight, high-arched feet said to resemble those of a cat

CHARACTER—The general appearance or expression said to be typical of the breed

CHEEKY—Fat cheeks or protruding cheeks

CHEST—Forepart of the body between the shoulder blades and above the brisket

CHINA EYE—A clear blue wall eye

CHISELED—A clean cut head, especially when chiseled out below the eye

CHOPS—Jowls or pendulous lips

CLIP—Method of trimming coats according to individual breed standards

CLODDY—Thick set or plodding dog

Ch. Monadnock Pando and Ch. Monadnock King win Best Brace in Show at the Eastern Dog Club in 1971. Owner-bred and handled by Lorna B. Demidoff of the Monadnock Kennels, Fitzwilliam, New Hampshire. The judge was Virgil Johnson. Brown photograph.

Sy Goldberg wins another Best of Breed with one of his Cinnaminson Siberians, this time under judge Vincent Perry.

CLOSE-COUPLED—A dog short in loins; comparatively short from withers to hipbones

COBBY—Short-bodied; compact

COLLAR—Usually a white marking, resembling a collar, around the neck

CONDITION—General appearance of a dog showing good health, grooming and care

CONFORMATION—The form and structure of the bone or framework of the dog in comparison with requirements of the Standard for the breed

CORKY—Active and alert dog

COUPLE—Two dogs

COUPLING—Leash or collar-ring for a brace of dogs

COUPLINGS—Body between withers and the hipbones indicating either short or long coupling

COW HOCKED—When the hocks turn toward each other and sometimes touch

CRANK TAIL—Tail carried down

CREST—Arched portion of the back of the neck

CROPPING—Cutting or trimming of the ear leather to get ears to stand erect

Arahaz' Kaylee Keenu, owned by Carolyn and Sue Windsor of the Kaylee Kennels in Baltimore. This charming photograph taken for Kaylee by Photography by US.

Norstarr's Ykshu, owned by Dave and Alice Angel of Norstarr Kennels in Rockford, Illinois. Ykshu was sired by Ch. Alakazan's Saanki *ex* Monadnock's Elsa.

CROSSBRED—A dog whose sire and dam are of two different breeds

CROUP—The back part of the back above the hind legs. Area from hips to tail

CROWN—The highest part of the head; the topskull

CRYPTORCHID—Male dog with neither testicle visible

CULOTTE—The long hair on the back of the thighs

CUSHION—Fullness of upper lips

DAPPLED—Mottled marking of different colors with none predominating

DEADGRASS—Dull tan color

DENTITION—Arrangement of the teeth

DEWCLAWS—Extra claws, or functionless digits on the inside of the four legs; usually removed at about three days of age

DEWLAP—Loose, pendulous skin under the throat

DISH-FACED—When nasal bone is so formed that nose is higher at the end that in the middle or at the stop

DISQUALIFICATION—A dog which has a fault making it ineligible to compete in dog show competition

DISTEMPER TEETH—Discolored or pitted teeth as a result of having had distemper

DOCK—To shorten the tail by cutting

DOG—A male dog, though used freely to indicate either sex

DOMED—Evenly rounded in topskull; not flat but curved upward

DOWN-FACED—When nasal bone inclines toward the tip of the nose

DOWN IN PASTERN—Weak or faulty pastern joints; a let-down foot

DROP EAR—The leather pendant which is longer than the leather of the button ear

DRY NECK—Taut skin

DUDLEY NOSE—Flesh-colored or light brown pigmentation in the nose

ELBOW—The joint between the upper arm and the forearm

ELBOWS OUT—Turning out or off the body and not held close to the sides

EWE NECK—Curvature of the top of neck

EXPRESSION—Color, size and placement of the eyes which give the dog the typical expression associated with his breed

FAKING—Changing the appearance of a dog by artificial means to make it more closely resemble the Standard. White chalk to whiten fur, etc.

FALL—Hair which hangs over the face

FEATHERING—Longer hair fringe on ears, legs, tail, or body

FEET EAST AND WEST—Toes turned out

FEMUR—The large heavy bone of the thigh

FIDDLE FRONT—Forelegs out at elbows, pasterns close, and feet turned out

FLAG—A long-haired tail

FLANK—The side of the body between the last rib and the hip

FLARE—A blaze that widens as it approaches the topskull

FLAT BONE—When girth of the leg bones is correctly elliptical rather than round

FLAT-SIDED—Ribs insufficiently rounded as they meet the breastbone

FLEWS—Upper lips, particularly at inner corners

FOREARM—Bone of the foreleg between the elbow and the pastern

FOREFACE—Front part of the head; before the eyes; muzzle

FROGFACE—Usually overshot jaw where nose is extended by the receding jaw

FRINGES—Same as feathering

FRONT—Forepart of the body as viewed head-on

FURROW—Slight indentation or median line down center of the skull to the top

GAY TAIL—Tail carried above the top line

Anezeka of the Setting Sun is pictured winning on the way to her championship at the Contra Costa Kennel Club Show in 1972 under judge Nicholas Kay. Anezeka is handled by her owner, Catherine Halcomb of the Setting Sun Kennels in Portola, California. Bennett Associates photo.

GESTATION—The period during which bitch carries her young; 63 days in the dog

GOOSE RUMP—Too steep or sloping a croup

GRIZZLE—Blueish-gray color

GUN-SHY—When a dog fears gun shots

GUARD HAIRS—The longer stiffer hairs which protrude through the undercoat

HARD-MOUTHED—The dog that bites or leaves tooth marks on the game he retrieves

HARE-FOOT—A narrow foot

HARLEQUIN—A color pattern, patched or pied coloration, predominantly black and white

HAW—A third eyelid or membrane at the inside corner of the eye

HEEL—The same as the hock

HEIGHT—Vertical measurement from the withers to the ground, or shoulder to the ground

HOCK—The tarsus bones of the hind leg which form the joint between the second thigh and the metatarsals.

HOCKS WELL LET DOWN—When distance from hock to the ground is close to the ground

HOUND—Dogs commonly used for hunting by scent

HOUND-MARKED—Three-color dogs; white, tan and black, predominating color mentioned first

HUCKLEBONES—The top of the hipbones

HUMERUS—The bone of the upper arm

INBREEDING—The mating of closely related dogs of the same standard, usually brother to sister

INCISORS—The cutting teeth found between the fangs in the front of the mouth

ISABELLA—Fawn or light bay color

KINK TAIL—A tail which is abruptly bent appearing to be broken

KNUCKLING-OVER—An insecurely knit pastern joint often causes irregular motion while dog is standing still

LAYBACK—Well placed shoulders

LAYBACK—Receding nose accompanied by an undershot jaw

LEATHER—The flap of the ear

LEVEL BITE—The front or incisor teeth of the upper and low jaws meet exactly

LINE BREEDING—The mating of related dogs of the same breed to a common ancestor. Controlled inbreeding. Usually grandmother to grandson, or grandfather to granddaughter.

LIPPY—Lips that do not meet perfectly

LOADED SHOULDERS—When shoulder blades are out of alignment due to overweight or overdevelopment on this particular part of the body

LOIN—The region of the body on either side of the vertebral column between the last ribs and the hindquarters

LOWER THIGH—Same as second thigh

LUMBER—Excess fat on a dog

LUMBERING—Awkward gait on a dog

MANE—Profuse hair on the upper portion of neck

MANTLE—Dark-shaded portion of the coat or shoulders, back and sides

MASK—Shading on the foreface

MEDIAN LINE—Same as furrow

MOLERA—Abnormal ossification of the skull

MONGREL—Puppy or dog whose parents are of two different breeds

MONORCHID—A male dog with only one testicle apparent

Norstarr's Chad Nova, sired by Norstarr's Ykahn *ex* Norstarr's Mystic Wind. Norstarr owners are Dave and Alice Angel, Rockford, Illinois.

MUZZLE—The head in front of the eyes—this includes nose, nostrils and jaws as well as the foreface

MUZZLE-BAND—White markings on the muzzle

MOLAR—Rear teeth used for actual chewing

NICTITATING EYELID—The thin membrane at the inside corner of the eye which is drawn across the eyeball. Sometimes referred to as the third eyelid

NOSE—Scenting ability

OCCIPUT—The upper crest or point at the top of the skull

OCCIPITAL PROTUBERANCE—The raised occiput itself

OCCLUSION—The meeting or bringing together of the upper and lower teeth.

OLFACTORY—Pertaining to the sense of smell

OTTER TAIL—A tail that is thick at the base, with hair parted on under side

OUT AT SHOULDER—The shoulder blades are set in such a manner that the joints are too wide, hence jut out from the body

OUTCROSSING—The mating of unrelated individuals of the same breed

Canadian Ch. Dudley's Tava of Innisfree enjoying the snow in the back yard. "Star" finished her Canadian championship at 13 months of age with three Best of Opposite Sex awards and had a major toward her American championship as of the beginning of 1973. Star is owned by Gladys and Clarence Dudley of North Syracuse, New York.

OVERHANG—a very pronounced eyebrow

OVERSHOT—The front incisor teeth on top overlap the front teeth of the lower jaw. Also called pig jaw.

PACK—Several hounds kept together in one kennel

PADDLING—Moving with the forefeet wide, to encourage a body roll motion

PADS—The underside, or soles, of the feet

PARTI-COLORED—Variegated in patches of two or more colors

PASTERN—The collection of bones forming the joint between the radius and ulna, and the metacarpals

PEAK—Same as occiput

PENCILING—Black lines dividing the tan colored hair on the toes

PIED—Comparatively large patches of two or more colors. Also called parti-colored or piebald

PIGEON-BREAST—A protruding breastbone

PIG JAW—Jaw with overshot bite

PILE—The soft hair in the undercoat

PINCER BITE—A bite where the incisor teeth meet exactly

PLUME—A feathered tail which is carried over the back

POINTS—Color on face, ears, legs and tail in contrast to the rest of the body color

POMPON—Rounded tuft of hair left on the end of the tail after clipping

PRICK EAR—Carried erect and pointed at tip

PUPPY—Dog under one year of age

QUALITY—Refinement, fineness

QUARTERS—Hind legs as a pair

RACY—Tall, of comparatively slight build

RAT TAIL—The root thick and covered with soft curls—tip devoid of hair or having the appearance of having been clipped

RINGER—A substitute for close resemblance

RING TAIL—Carried up and around and almost in a circle

ROACH BACK—Convex curvature of back

ROAN—A mixture of colored hairs with white hairs. Blue roan, orange roan, etc.

ROMAN NOSE—A nose whose bridge has a convex line from forehead to nose tip. Ram's nose

ROSE EAR—Drop ear which folds over and back revealing the burr

ROUNDING—Cutting or trimming the ends of the ear leather

RUFF—The longer hair growth around the neck

SABLE—A lacing of black hair in or over a lighter ground color

SADDLE—A marking over the back, like a saddle

SCAPULA—The shoulder blade

SCREW TAIL—Naturally short tail twisted in spiral formation

SCISSORS BITE—A bite in which the upper teeth just barely overlap the lower teeth

SELF COLOR—One color with lighter shadings

SEMIPRICK EARS—Carried erect with just the tips folding forward

SEPTUM—The line extending vertically between the nostrils

SHELLY—A narrow body which lacks the necessary size required by the Breed Standard

SICKLE TAIL—Carried out and up in a semicircle

SLAB SIDES—Insufficient spring of ribs

SLOPING SHOULDER—The shoulder blade which is set obliquely or "laid back"

SNIPEY—A pointed nose

SNOWSHOE FOOT—Slightly webbed between the toes

SOUNDNESS—The general good health and appearance of a dog in its entirety

SPAYED—A female whose ovaries have been removed surgically

SPECIALTY CLUB—An organization to sponsor and promote an individual breed

SPECIALTY SHOW—A dog show devoted to the promotion of a single breed

SPECTACLES—Shading or dark markings around the eyes or from eyes to ears

SPLASHED—Irregularly patched, color on white or vice versa

SPLAY FOOT—A flat or open-toed foot

SPREAD—The width between the front legs

SPRING OF RIBS—The degree of rib roundness

SQUIRREL TAIL—Carried up and curving slightly forward

STANCE—Manner of standing

STARING COAT—Dry harsh hair; sometimes curling at the tips

STATION—Comparative height of a dog from the ground—either high or low

STERN—Tail of a sporting dog or hound

STERNUM—Breastbone

STIFLE—Joint of hind leg between thigh and second thigh. Sometimes called the ham

STILTED—Choppy, up-and-down gait of straight-hocked dog

STOP—The step-up from nose to skull between the eyes

STRAIGHT-HOCKED—Without angulation; straight behind

SUBSTANCE—Good bone. Or in good weight, or well muscled dog

SUPERCILIARY ARCHES—The prominence of the frontal bone of the skull over the eye

SWAYBACK—Concave curvature of the back between the withers and the hipbones

TEAM—Four dogs usually working in unison

THIGH—The hindquarter from hip joint to stifle

THROATINESS—Excessive loose skin under the throat

THUMB-MARKS—Black spots in the tan markings on the pasterns

TICKED—Small isolated areas of black or colored hairs on a white background

TIMBER—Bone, especially of the legs

TOPKNOT—Tuft of hair on the top of head

TRIANGULAR EYE—The eye set in surrounding tissue of triangular shape. A three-cornered eye

TRI-COLOR—Three colors on a dog, white, black and tan

TRUMPET—Depression or hollow on either side of the skull just behind the eye socket; comparable to the temple area in man

Ch. Monadnock's Kiana of Keachi, pictured winning under judge Phil Marsh in 1971 with Lila Weir handling for owners Karl and Pat Hahn, Keachi Kennels, Anchorage, Alaska.

Ch. Arctic's Blizzard, owned by Charlotte and Earl Reynolds, Arctic Kennels, Dryden, Michigan. A Frank photograph.

Seven-month-old Sierra's Silver Shadow, owned by Michael E. Burnside, Sierra Kennels, Saugus, California.

TUCK-UP—Body depth at the loin

TULIP EAR—Ear carried erect with slight forward curvature along the sides

TURN-UP—Uptilted jaw

TYPE—The distinguishing characteristics of a dog to measure its worth against the Standard for the breed

UNDERSHOT—The front teeth of the lower jaw overlapping or projecting beyond the front teeth of the upper jaw

UPPER-ARM—The humerus bone of the foreleg between the shoulder blade and forearm

VENT—Tan-colored hair under the tail

WALLEYE—A blue eye also referred to as a fish or pearl eye

WEAVING—When the dog is in motion, the forefeet or hind feet cross

WEEDY—A dog too light of bone

WHEATEN—Pale yellow or fawn color

WHEEL-BACK—Back line arched over the loin; roach back

WHELPS—Unweaned puppies

WHIP TAIL—Carried out stiffly straight and pointed

WIRE-HAIRED—A hard wiry coat

WITHERS—The peak of the first dorsal vertebra; highest part of the body just behind the neck

WRINKLE—Loose, folding skin on forehead and/or foreface

CHAPTER 26
PURSUING A CAREER IN DOGS

One of the biggest joys for those of us who love dogs is to see someone we know or someone in our family grow up in the fancy and go on to enjoy the sport of dogs in later life. Many dog lovers, in addition to leaving codicils in their wills, are providing in other ways for veterinary scholarships for deserving youngsters who wish to make their association with dogs their profession.

Unfortunately, many children who have this earnest desire are not always able to afford the expense of an education that will take them through veterinary school, and they are not eligible for scholarships. In recent years, however, we have had a great innovation in this field — a college course for those interested in earning an Animal Science degree, which costs less than half of what it costs to complete veterinary courses. These students have been a boon to the veterinarians, and a number of colleges are now offering the program.

With each passing year, the waiting rooms of veterinarians have become more crowded, and the demands on the doctors' time for research, consultation, surgery and treatment have consumed more and more of the working hours over and above his regular office hours. The tremendous increase in the number of dogs and cats and other domestic animals, both in cities and in the suburbs, has resulted in an almost overwhelming consumption of veterinarians' time.

Until recently most veterinary help consisted of kennel men or women who were restricted to services more properly classified as office maintenance rather than actual veterinary assistance. Needless to say, their part in the operation of a veterinary office is both essential and appreciated, as are the endless details and volumes of paperwork capably handled by office secretaries and receptionists. However, still more of a veterinarian's duties could be handled by properly trained semiprofessionals.

With exactly this additional service in mind, many colleges are now conducting two-year courses in animal science for the training of such semiprofessionals, thereby opening a new field for animal technologists. The time saved by the assistance of these trained semiprofessionals will relieve veterinarians of the more mechanical chores and will allow them more time for diagnosing and general servicing of their clients.

"Delhi Tech," the State University Agricultural and Technical College at Delhi, New York, has recently graduated several classes of these technologists, and many other institutions of learning are offering comparable two-year courses at the college level. Entry requirements are usually that each applicant must be a graduate of an approved high school or have taken the State University admissions examination. In addition, each applicant for the Animal Science Technology program must have some previous credits in mathematics and science, with chemistry an important part of the science background.

The program at Delhi was a new educational venture dedicated to the training of competent technicians for employment in the biochemical field and has been generously supported by a five-year grant, designated as a "Pilot Development Program in Animal Science." This grant provided both personal and scientific equipment with such obvious good results when it was done originally pursuant to a contract with the United States Department of Health, Education, and Welfare. Delhi is a unit of the State University of New York and is accredited by the Middle States Association of Colleges and Secondary Schools. The campus provides offices, laboratories and animal quarters and is equipped with modern instruments to train technicians in laboratory animal care, physiology, pathology, microbiology, anesthesia, X-ray and germ-free techniques. Sizable animal colonies are maintained in air-conditioned quarters: animals housed include mice, rats, hamsters, guinea-pigs, gerbils and rabbits, as well as dogs and cats.

First-year students are given such courses as livestock production, dairy food science, general, organic and biological chemistry, mammalian anatomy, histology and physiology, pathogenic microbiology and quantitative and instrumental analysis, to name a few. Second year students matriculate in general pathology, animal parasitology, animal care and anesthesia, introductory psychology, animal breeding, animal nutrition, hematology and urinalysis, radiology, genetics, food sanitation and meat inspection, histological techniques, animal laboratory practices and axenic techniques. These, of course, may be supplemented by electives that prepare the student for contact with the public in the administration of these duties. Such recommended electives include public speaking, botany, animal reproduction and other related subjects.

In addition to Delhi and the colleges which got in early on the pre-

Sue Windsor poses Kaylee Kitkit Kulik in the living room of Kaylee Kennels. Kulik is by Ch. Savdajaure's Cognac *ex* Arahaz' Kaylee Keenu and is pictured here at ten months of age. Photography by US.

sentation of these courses, more and more universities are offering training for animal technologists. Students at the State University of Maine, for instance, receive part of their practical training at the Animal Medical Center in New York City, and after this actual experience can perform professionally immediately upon entering a veterinarian's employ.

Under direct veterinary supervision they are able to perform all of the following procedures as a semi-professional:

* Recording of vital information relative to a case. This would include such information as the client's name, address, telephone number and other facts pertinent to the visit. The case history

would include the breed, age of the animal, its sex, temperature, etc.

* Preparation of the animal for surgery
* Preparation of equipment and medicaments to be used in surgery.
* Preparation of medicaments for dispensing to clients on prescription of the attending veterinarian.
* Administration and application of certain medicines.
* Administration of colonic irrigations.
* Application or changing of wound dressings.
* Cleaning of kennels, exercise runs and kitchen utensils
* Preparation of food and the feeding of patients
* Explanation to clients on the handling and restraint of their pets, including needs for exercise, house training and elementary obedience training.
* First-aid treatment for hemorrhage, including the proper use of tourniquets
* Preservation of blood, urine and pathologic material for the purpose of laboratory examination
* General care and supervision of the hospital or clinic patients to insure their comfort.
* Nail trimming and grooming of patients.

High school graduates with a sincere affection and regard for animals and a desire to work with veterinarians and perform such clinical duties as mentioned above will find they fit in especially well. Women particularly will be useful since, over and beyond the strong maternal instinct that goes so far in the care and the recovery phase when dealing with animals, women will find the majority of their duties well within their physical capabilities. Since a majority of the positions will be in the small animal field, their dexterity will also fit in well. Students having financial restrictions that preclude their education and licensing as full-fledged veterinarians can in this way pursue careers in an area close to their actual desire. Their assistance in the pharmaceutical field, where drug concerns deal with laboratory animals, covers another wide area for trained assistance. The career opportunities are varied and reach into job opportunities in medical centers, research institutions and government health agencies; at present, the demand for graduates far exceeds the current supply of trained personnel.

As far as the financial remunerations, yearly salaries are estimated at an average of $5,000.00 for a starting point. As for the estimate of basic college education expenses, they range from $1800.00 to $2200.00 per year for out-of-state residents, and include tuition,

Poetry in motion! Ch. Karnovanda's Wolfgang moves out. Owner: Lillian M. Russell, Karnovanda Kennels, Reg., Davisburg, Michigan. Action photograph by Booth.

room and board, college fees, essential textbooks and limited personal expenses. These personal expenses, of course, will vary with individual students, as well as the other expenses, but we present an average. It is obvious that the costs are about half of the costs involved in becoming a full-fledged veterinarian, however.

PART TIME KENNEL WORK

Youngsters who do not wish to go on to become veterinarians or animal technicians can get valuable experience and extra money by working part-time after school and weekends, or full-time during summer vacations, in a veterinarian's office. The exposure to animals and office procedure will be time well spent.

Another great help to veterinarians has been the housewife who loves animals and wishes to put in some time at a job away from the house, especially if her children are grown or away at college. If she can clean up in her own kennel she can certainly clean up in a veterinarian's office, and she will learn much about handling and caring for her own animals while she is making money.

Kennel help is also an area that is wide open for retired men. They are able to help out in many areas where they can learn and stay active, and most of the work allows them to set their own pace. The gentility that age and experience brings is also beneficial to the animals they will deal with; for their part, the men find great reward in their contribution to animals and will be keeping their hand in the business world as well.

PROFESSIONAL HANDLERS

For those who wish to participate in the sport of dogs and whose interests or abilities do not center around the clinical aspects of the fancy, there is yet another avenue of involvement.

For those who excel in the show ring, who enjoy being in the limelight and putting their dogs through their paces, a career in pro-

Monadnock's Elsa, owned by Dave and Alice Angel, Norstarr Kennel, Rockford, Illinois.

fessional handling may be the answer. Handling may include a weekend of showing a few dogs for special clients, or it may be a full-time career which can also include boarding, training, conditioning, breeding and showing of dogs for several clients.

Depending on how deeply your interest runs, the issue can be solved by a lot of preliminary consideration before it becomes necessary to make a decision. The first move would be to have a long, serious talk with a successful professional handler to learn the pros and cons of such a profession. Watching handlers in action from ringside as they perform their duties can be revealing. A visit to their kennels for an on-the-spot revelation of the behind-the-scenes responsibilities is essential! And working for them full or part time would be the best way of all to resolve any doubt you might have!

Professional handling is not all glamour in the show ring. There is plenty of "dirty work" behind the scenes 24 hours of every day. You must have the necessary ability and patience for this work, as well as the ability and patience to deal with the CLIENTS — the dog owners who value their animals above almost anything else and would expect a great deal from you in the way of care and handling. The big question you must ask yourself first of all is: do you *really* love dogs enough to handle it. . . .

DOG TRAINING

Like the professional handler, the professional dog trainer has a most responsible job! You not only need to be thoroughly familiar with the correct and successful methods of training a dog but also must have the ability to communicate with dogs. True, it is very rewarding work, but training for the show ring, obedience, or guard dog work must be done exactly right for successful results to maintain a business reputation.

Training schools are quite the vogue nowadays, with all of them claiming success. But careful investigation should be made before enrolling a dog. . .and even more careful investigation should be made of their methods and of their actual successes before becoming associated with them.

GROOMING PARLORS

If you do not wish the 24-hour a day job which is required by a professional handler or professional trainer, but still love working with and caring for dogs, there is always the very profitable grooming business. Poodles started the ball rolling for the swanky, plush grooming establishments which sprang up like mushrooms all over the major cities, many of which seem to be doing very well. Here again, handling dogs and the public is necessary for a successful operation, as well as skill in the actual grooming of the dogs, and of all breeds.

While shops flourish in the cities, some of the suburban areas are now featuring mobile units which by appointment will visit your home with a completely equipped shop on wheels and will groom your dog right in your own driveway!

THE PET SHOP

Part-time or full-time work in a pet shop can help you make up your mind rather quickly as to whether or not you would like to have a shop of your own. For those who love animals and are concerned with their care and feeding, the pet shop can be a profitable and satisfying association. Supplies which are available for sale in these shops are almost limitless, and a nice living can be garnered from pet supplies if the location and population of the city you choose warrant it.

DOG JUDGING

There are also those whose professions or age or health prevent them from owning or breeding or showing dogs, and who turn to judging at dog shows after their active years in the show ring are no longer possible. Breeder-judges make a valuable contribution to the fancy by judging in accordance with their years of experience in the fancy, and the assignments are enjoyable. Judging requires experience, a good eye for dogs and an appreciation of a good animal.

MISCELLANEOUS

If you find all of the aforementioned too demanding or not within your abilities, there are still other aspects of the sport for you to enjoy and participate in at will. Writing for the various dog magazines, books or club newsletters, dog photography, portrait painting, club activities, making dog coats, or needlework featuring dogs, typing pedigrees or perhaps dog walking. All, in their own way, contribute to the sport of dogs and give great satisfaction. Perhaps, where Huskies are concerned, you may wish to learn to train for racing, or sled hauling, or you might even wish to learn the making of the sleds!

CHAPTER 27
SIBERIAN SHORT STORIES

THE L'IL ABNER DOG TEAM

This story comes from Leonhard Seppala via Irving Reed, so it not only bears repeating but also must be regarded as true. Irving Reed says that Seppala told him of an incident which occurred during a dogteam race in New England. The course ran along a road by which stood a house in which a woman was frying pork chops. The doors to the house were open, and when the dogs picked up the scent of the cooking meat there simply was no stopping them. The woman fled the house screaming at what she believed to be a pack of wolves coming in her front door. The team hardly broke stride, but went through the house and on out the back door, picking up the pork chops on the way. Seppala was just along for the ride, and holding on for dear life!

KODII AND THE RESCUE

A. J. Tony Zarlenga owes his life to his dog. On a fall night in 1966, his Siberian Husky, Ch. Kodii Kuska de Sforza, C.D.X., smelled gas escaping in the house. Kodii usually slept on the terrace just outside the Zarlengas' bedroom, and Tony became aware of the deadly fumes only because Kodii kept barking and chewing at his feet.

Tony tells that he could hardly open his eyes; he simply could not seem to wake up, but he managed to crawl out of the house on Kodii's insistence. He had fallen down after finally dragging himself out of bed, but Kodii roused him. The pilot light had gone out on the furnace and the house had filled with the deadly gas.

As mentioned elsewhere in this book, Kodii is a willing-worker in obedience and reached his twelfth birthday on March 17, 1973. Unfortunately, Tony Zarlenga died on January 13, 1973, while compiling illustrative material for inclusion in this book; fortunately, Colleen Zarlenga devotedly finished the task.

Magnificent head study of Tony Zarlenga's Ch. Kodii Kuska de Sforza, C.D.X., from Denver, Colorado.

Both Tony and Kodii had for some time delighted in the performance of a clown act they staged for the entertainment of children.

HAI KARATE FOR HUSKIES

In 1971 three Siberian Huskies took part in a Hai Karate television commercial.

It started out simply enough. . .Ch. Eu-Mors Zhulek of Siber, owned by Lynne Witkin and Eunice Moreno; Ch. Nomad's Shane, owned by Lynne, and Ch. Eu-Mor's Kiev, C.D., owned by Eunice were asked to appear in a film commercial. The commercial featured a scientist in an Arctic laboratory, who after dousing himself with the potent aftershave lotion suddenly and violently attracts three Huskies dragging their Eskimo maidens behind them. . .on snowshoes!

Originally the script called for use of a sled, but when Lynne and Eunice arrived at the television studio the sled would not fit through the door of the studio, so the script was re-written to say that the Huskies would drag the girls along on snowshoes. This decided, the cameras rolled and the three smitten maidens "attacked" the scientist, with him fighting them off. The ardent display of affection drove the "fierce" Husky sled dogs into a frenzy, with the result that Shulek and Kiev dashed out the door of the studio, and Shane took a dive under the scientist's bench.

If you watch the commercial closely you can catch a glimpse of him hiding under the table. End of commercial. . .end of television careers!

A PHOTOGRAPHIC GALLERY OF SIBERIAN HUS-KIES AT HOME AROUND THE WORLD.

Identical twins! Two puppies at 7 days of age from a litter bred by MacKnight and Arlene Black, Blackwatch Kennels, Arlington, Virginia.

A Karnovanda puppy finds plenty to chew on at his Karnóvanda Kennels in Davisburg, Michigan. Wotan is pictured at five weeks of age and is one of the show and obedience trained Siberian Hus-kies bred by Judith M. Russell, owner of Karnovanda, Reg.

A team of the future and their driver! All have a lot of growing up to do first, but there is no harm in making friends now. Photo by Judy Rosemarin.

Lumimaan Igor at eight weeks of age. Owners is Mrs. Laila Leppanen, Finland. Photo by Kerttu Alm.

Guess it would be safe to say this is a Christmas litter. . . this one is from Catherine A. Halcomb's Setting Sun Kennels in Portola, California.

Cinnaminson's Babba and a few Doberman Pinscher puppies on a visit. Babba is owned by Sy and Ann Goldberg, Cinnaminson Kennels, Cream Ridge, New Jersey.

Norstarr's Tara in a lovely woodland setting. Tara is owned by Dave and Alice Angel of the Norstarr Kennels, Rockford, Illinois.

An informal shot of Clarence and Gladys Dudley with their American and Canadian champion Dudley's Tavar of Innisfree, Best in Show winning Siberian Husky.

A 12-week-old Vales-kamo puppy bred by Eleanor Grahn, Vales-kamo Kennels, Florissant, Missouri.

Felix A. Leser of Saranac Lake, New York, photographed in 1935. Mr. Leser has judged Siberian Huskies at Morris and Essex. Photo by E.L. Gockeler.

Finnish and Norwegian Champion Lumimaan Raisuli, owned by Mrs. Raija Renholm, Finland. In the picture Raisuli is six months old and is photographed with Hanne Renholm, by photographer J. Renholm.

Time for a walk! Top kennel maid at the Karnovanda Kennels in Davisburg, Michigan, takes one of her charges for a walk.

Three Siberians owned by Stina Blomquist of Nickby, Finland. Left to right, Sera, Pikoo and Angara.

Lumimaan Valka, pictured at three months of age, running free in Finland. Owner M. Hakala.

On Lonesome Lake in the White Mountains, with the Franconia Range in the background, Edward P. Clark runs his team across the snow. The Appalachian Mountain Club camp is pictured in the background.

The striking Ch. Cinnaminson's Soaya Fournier owned by the Goldbergs of Cream Ridge, New Jersey. Photo by Judy Rosemarin.

Love is. . . a Siberian Husky of your very own! Donna Rosemarin and her Ch. Chilka's Treska of Weldon, photographed on the lawn of their home in Roslyn, New York by her mother, Judy Rosemarin.

INDEX